# 1 MONTH OF
# FREE
# READING

at

## www.ForgottenBooks.com

By purchasing this book you are eligible for one month membership to ForgottenBooks.com, giving you unlimited access to our entire collection of over 1,000,000 titles via our web site and mobile apps.

To claim your free month visit:

www.forgottenbooks.com/free876750

ISBN 978-0-265-65944-1
PIBN 10876750

'EN SALUSBURY BRERETON Efq

F. R. & A.S.

*te Vice President of the Society for*

*the Encouragement of*

*Arts, Manufactures & Commerce*

*Engraved by W. Evans from an original miniature*

*furnished by the late [...] W. Seward Esq*

# TRANSACTIONS

## OF THE

# SOCIETY

### INSTITUTED AT LONDON,

#### FOR THE

# ENCOURAGEMENT

#### OF

# ARTS, MANUFACTURES, and COMMERCE;

#### WITH THE

### PREMIUMS offered in the YEAR 1801.

## VOL. XIX.

---

Printed by W and C. SPILSBURY, Snowhill.

Sold by the REGISTER, at the SOCIETY's HOUSE, in the ADELPHI; and by Meffrs. ROBSON, J. WHITE, BECKET, JOHNSON, CADELL and DAVIES, ELMSLEY and BREMNER, WALTER, RICHARDSON, SEWELL, and TAYLOR.

[ Price TEN SHILLINGS and SIX-PENCE. ]

M.DCCCI.

T
1
S 6 42

mU

# PREFACE.

THE views of the Society instituted at London, for the Encouragement of Arts, Manufactures, and Commerce, extend, independent of their domestic regulations, to general improvements in Agriculture, Chemistry, Polite and Liberal Arts, Manufactures, Mechanicks, and the products of our Colonies. On examining the Communications which compose the present Volume, it will be found that the Society have been occupied, during the last Session, in each of the above-mentioned Departments; and it is hoped the Public will derive useful information from each distinct Class.

Before a regular detail is entered into of the numerous Articles of which this

Volume

Volume is composed, it may not be
deemed improper to pay a tribute to
the memory of the late Owen Salusbury
Brereton, Esq. by inserting the following particulars of his life, communicated
by the late John Holliday, Esq. F. R. S.
O. S. Brereton, Esq. whose portrait is
annexed to the Frontispiece, long took
a lively and active part in the concerns
of the Society, as one of their Vice-
Presidents.  He was the son of Thomas
Brereton, Esq. of the County Palatine
of Chester, and was born in the year
1715: he received his education partly
at Westminster School on the foundation, partly at Trinity College, Cambridge; and, on the death of his father,
inherited the ancient family-estates, in
the above-mentioned county, and in
Flintshire.

In 1738 Mr. Brereton was called to
the Bar, and in 1746 became Recorder
of the great and flourishing town of
Liverpool; which office he filled with

great

# PREFACE.

great impartiality and dignity during fifty-two years. In 1796, on his proposing to resign, the Corporation requested him to retain his situation, and appointed a person to discharge its active duties.

Mr. Brereton became a Member of the Society of Arts so early as 1762; and by his assiduity, zeal, and order, filled the distinguished office of Vice-President with great credit to himself and advantage to the Society, from March 1765 till his last illness in 1798. He was also an early Member of the Royal and Antiquarian Societies. The Archæologia of the latter, contains his Observations on Peter Collinson's Account of the Round Towers in Ireland;[*] his Tour through South Wales;[†] his Extracts from the Household Book of Henry VIII;[‡] his Account of a painted window in Brereton Church, Cheshire;[§]

and

---

[*] Archæol. ii. 80.   [†] Id. iii. 3.   [‡] Id. iii. 154.
[§] Id. ix. 368.

and that of a non-descript Coin, supposed to be Philip VI of France. *
Mr. Pennant has also, in his Welsh Tour, described and given an engraving of several Roman Antiquities, found by his horse accidentally disturbing them, at a Roman station called Croes Atti, on his estate in Flintshire. †

Mr. Brereton was a Bencher of the Honourable Society of Lincoln's-Inn, filled the office of Treasurer, and was Keeper of the Black-Book. He also represented the borough of Ilchester in Parliament. He took the name of Salusbury with an estate, and became Constable of the Castle of Flint, a valuable privilege to his adjacent possessions. His domestic happiness was manifest to his numerous and respectable acquaintance, among whom were some of the most learned men of the age.

Mr.

---

* Archæol. x. 463.

† Pennant's Tour, Vol. i. p. 52, 54, 67, 73.

Mr. Brereton died on the 8th of September, 1798, in the eighty-fourth year of his age, and was interred in St. George's Chapel, Windsor. His wife was sister of Sir Thomas Whitmore, K. B. Mr. Brereton lived happily with her more than fifty years. They had five children, who all died young; he bequeathed the rents of his estates to her during her life, and after her decease (which happened in 1799), to his relations; the only son of the late General Trelawney, of Soho-Square, and the second son of the Rev. Sir Harry Trelawney, Baronet, of Trelawne, in Cornwall.

The Premiums usually proposed by the Society have, during this Session, undergone a minute investigation: several are discontinued; and many, relative to objects in Planting, Husbandry, &c. offered, for some succeeding years, in the last Volume of Transactions, still remain open to Claimants, until the

times

times there noted are expired, though not particularised in the present Volume.

Modifications of them, or other Premiums expected to answer the purpose better, will probably succeed them, as occasion may require.

New Premiums will be found introduced, under the Articles *Comparative Tillage; Rotation of Crops; Preserving of Turnips, Cabbages, Carrots, Parsnips, Beets, and Potatoes; inventing Thrashing-Machines; manufacturing Tallow-Candles; Preparation of Tan; Preparations of Red and Green Colours for printing on Cotton-Cloth; artificial Ultramarine; Stroke Engravings; Chintz and Copper-Plate Designs for Calico-Printers; Engravings on Wood; Bronzes; improved Ventilation; Cultivation of Hemp in Canada, and curing Herrings in the Dutch method.*

The Society will attend to any informations respecting such matters, as may be proper objects for further Premiums;

and

and invite the Public to furnish them with such Communications, addressed to the Secretary.

On perusal of the present Volume, it will be seen that a long detail of Certificates, which formed a considerable part of the former Volumes, has been contracted, in order to admit a greater number of subjects; by which means the present Volume contains twelve more articles of intelligence than any preceding one, all of which it is hoped will be found interesting to the Public.

The Papers and Communications are disposed in the order heretofore observed; a few remarks are here made, in addition to the Accounts introduced, as they follow in rotation.

In the Class of Agriculture it will be found that Henry Vernon, Esq. of Hilton Park, amongst a variety of other Trees, disposed with much taste and judgment, has planted a great number of English Elms, which are likely to

form

form good timber. From subsequent
accounts we have been informed, that
the whole of his plantations are flourishing and picturesque.

The variety of uses to which Osiers
are applied, renders their culture desirable. Mr. Thomas Selby, of Otford
Castle, in Kent, has made very considerable plantations of them, and much
improved Land which was naturally wet
and barren.

The very extensive plantations of
Timber-Trees, by Thomas Johnes, Esq.
of Hafod, in Cardiganshire, demand
particular attention. This Gentleman,
by his excellent discrimination, and by
exertions perhaps unparalleled, has converted a Desert to a Paradise; and in a
wild uncultivated part of Wales, has
raised such enchanting scenes, as afford
inexpressible pleasure to every spectator.
Mr. George Cumberland, whose taste
and judgment have been displayed in
several publications, made the following
                           observations

observations on seeing Hafod, in the year
1796. " So many are the delights af-
" forded by the scenery of this place
" and its vicinity, to a mind imbued
" with any taste, that the impression on
" mine was increased after an interval
" of ten years from the first visit, em-
" ployed chiefly in travelling among the
" Alps, the Appennines, the Sabine-
" Hills, the Tyrolese, along the shores
" of the Adriatic, over the Glaciers of
" Switzerland, and up the Rhine, where,
" though in search of beauty, I never saw
" any thing so fine; never so many
" pictures collected in one point of
" view."

Every person will feel a pleasure on
being informed that, since the above
description, very considerable improvements have been made there, particularly very lately, in the farms; that
the additions in this line, and fertilising
Waste Ground, take place every year;
that the number of Trees planted on
Hafod

Hafod estate, between October 1795 and
April 1801, amount to 2,065,000, of
which 1,200,000 are Larches; that, besides the above Trees, fifty-five acres of
land have been sown with Acorns, or
planted with Oaks; that Mr. Johnes is
still extending his plantations, and
greatly improving the scenery of his
estate. We are told, that the Cheese
sold by him the last season, amounted
to four tons, and his Butter 1200 lbs.
He expects his Dairy will furnish him,
during the next year, ten tons of Cheese
for sale. Mr. Johnes has been indefatigable in his pursuits in Agriculture;
and has not only shown, by practice,
what may be done, but in a late ingenious Publication, presented to this Society, entitled " A Cardiganshire Landlord's Advice to his Tenants," pointed
out to others the means of doing it.

In a climate so variable as that of
Great-Britain, it is of importance to
know how to counteract the disadvantages

tages arising from unfavourable autumnal seasons.    The Account given by Mr. Brown, of Markle, in Scotland, of the Wheat sown by him in the spring of 1800, and the valuable crop housed the same year, is well deserving attention.

As similar disadvantages of climate attend the housing of Crops when ripe, the method of making Clover-Hay in Courland, communicated by Mr. John Taylor, opens to this country a new line of management for this purpose, which bids fair to be of great utility.    The process of vegetable fermentation, in the preparation of Hay, has been hitherto little attended to or understood: the consequence of neglect in this point, has occasioned many stacks of Hay to take fire and be destroyed; which loss the method here recommended may probably prevent.

Mr. Palmer's method of Housing Corn in Wet Weather, as mentioned in the present Volume, appears to be scarcely known

known in England, but has been successfully practised in Fifeshire, and other
parts of Scotland. . The more general
introduction of Thrashing-Machines, has
been the means of preventing the loss of
many crops of Corn in Great-Britain,
by affording quick dispatch to the separation of the Corn from the wet sheaf
in bad seasons, and (as is proved by
Mr. Palmer's experiments) without injuring the quality of the grain.

Immense tracts of Land lie uncultivated in different parts of Great-Britain.
As such Land, when once improved,
seldom recurs to its orignal barren state,
it shows that every improvement of this
kind is a source of permanent wealth
to the Nation. In few parts of England
is the land naturally worse than in the
County of Lancaster, or more valuable when improved. In that county,
Mr. Fogg, of Bolton in the Moors, has un-
dertaken, with great spirit and judgment,
the improvement of a part of a large tract
of

of Waste Land lately inclosed, and has succeeded in the trial with honour and advantage. There is great probability of his example exciting a noble spirit of emulation, for similar agricultural exertions in that neighbourhood. He has also furnished some hints on the propagation of Potatoes, and on the means of preventing a wasteful expenditure of that useful food.

The long continuance of water upon land during the winter season, is perhaps one of the greatest mischiefs that can befall it, and ought most carefully to be guarded against; this has occasioned the adoption of a variety of modes for its removal :—viz. open or covered Drains, made by the spade; Pipe or Tube Drains, made under the surface by Mr. Scott's Mole-Plough; the triangular Indent, ingeniously contrived by Mr. Middleton, as noticed in the Commercial and Agricultural Magazine, and performed by a cart-wheel, prepared,

prepared for the purpose, which presses down the grass sod, and, without destroying the grass, furnishes, by the indent which it makes, a passage for the stagnant water. Each of the above methods may have advantages in particular situations, but probably none of them is more generally useful than the Drain-Plough, of which a Model was this Session presented to the Society by his Grace the Duke of Bridgewater: it performs the operation of Surface-Draining with neatness, ease, and celerity; destroys but little herbage, and furnishes, at a trifling expence, in the following spring, an excellent compost for a top-dressing.

The Drill Husbandry continues to gain advocates; and repeated experiments confirm its advantages.

The Public are under great obligations to Thomas Andrew Knight, Esq. of Ludlow, for a Drill Machine for sowing Turnips and other seeds, presented by
him

him to the Society. This very ingenious and useful implement possesses the
powers of making an indent or furrow
for the seed; of depositing the seed
within that channel, and covering it
instantaneously in a more effectual manner than can be done by the harrow
or rake. Its construction is simple and
cheap; and it can be expeditiously worked, on any soil, by a man or boy.

The Society are much indebted to the
same Gentleman for some very accurate
Observations upon the Nature of Blight,
the destructive effects of the Aphis, and
the means of obviating the sudden
changes to which our climate is subjected, and by which Vegetation is im-
peded.

Mr. Lester, of Northampton, has introduced an implement, named a Cultivator, which, from its powers of contraction and expansion, may probably
be very useful in working rough fallows
after ploughed crops, and reducing the
b soil

soil to a greater degree of pulverization than can be effected by repeated
ploughings and harrowings in the common method.

. The advantages of the Drill over the
Broad-cast husbandry, in the culture of
Turnips, is further elucidated by the
Rev. T. C. Munnings, whose paper upon
that subject points out a number of
minutiæ apparently necessary to the
success of the crop; amongst which it
is particularly recommended to cover
the seed with earth instantly when sown.
The method which he suggests for the
preservation of Turnips on the land,
by means of ploughed ridges, as food
for cattle during the winter season,
claims public attention. Mr. Munnings
has presented the Society with his Drill-
Machine for sowing Seed.

.. Mr. Eccleston, of Scarisbrick, who
has for many years been very attentive
to Agricultural pursuits, has obliged the
Society this Session by his Observations

on

on a method of Draining Boggy Land; and presented an implement which forms an outlet for water when retained in peat-earth, by the spongy texture of the vegetable surface growing within the ditches.

It was an observation of the celebrated Swift, that " whoever could make two ears of corn, or two blades of grass, to grow, where only one had grown before, would deserve better of mankind than the whole race of politicians." The same remark may be extended, with propriety, to other vegetable products; and the merit acknowledged of Mr. Ashton, of Woolton Hall, who has lately converted one hundred and thirty-three acres of waste sandy land, unproductive of herbage, to a valuable plantation of Timber-trees, the flourishing state of which affords great encouragement for thus employing land apparently barren.

Mr.

Mr. Edward Jones's Paper on the
Destruction of the Grub of the Cockchaffer, contains curious observations
on the habits of Moles; and points out
the necessity of a cool and candid consideration upon the alternative choice
of permitting the increase of Moles, or
of suffering from the ravages of the
Cockchaffer, worms, and other noxious
insects.

The preparation and application of
Composts for Manure are of very essential
consequence in husbandry; and a knowledge of the modes adapted for such
purpose in different parts of Great Britain, is of the utmost importance.
Great exertions are necessary to eradi-
cate the topical prejudices on this head
which are known to prevail throughout
the kingdom, and to encourage methods
more efficient for the purpose. In the
isle of Thanet, for instance, we observe,
that sea-weeds, and even sea-sand, are
diligently collected, and attended with
great

great advantage to the clay-land on
which they are applied; whilst on the
coast of Lancashire, and in other parts
of England, the same advantages are
wholly neglected, where similar opportunities offer for their use. The application of peat-earth and powdered lime,
prepared as a compost, were thought
improper in the populous district of
Bolton in the Moors, for the production
of Potatoes, though this vegetable furnishes a principal part of the food of
its inhabitants: but the active exertions
of Mr. Horridge, of Raikes, have brought
this Manure into estimation, and will
probably be the means of increasing
highly in value large tracts of land in
that neighbourhood, at present barren
and uncultivated.

Mr. Kirwan, in a valuable pamphlet
published in 1796, upon the Manures
most advantageously applicable to various sorts of Soils, and the causes of
their beneficial effects, grounds his

theory

theory on this simple proposition, " that Manures are applied to supply either the defective ingredients of a soil, improve its texture, or correct its vices."

It is certainly of the first consequence to every person concerned in agricultural improvements, to examine well the different soils, minerals, and natural products, furnished by the adjoining lands in his possession; he will generally find that he may make from them judicious mixtures, and form such Composts as will fertilize the whole.

Under the class of Chemistry, the experiment made by order of General Bentham, shows that the principal reason of Spring-Water becoming putrid at Sea, is owing to its being stowed in wood-vessels, and that this putridity may be prevented by using vessels not likely to be acted upon by water; he has successfully employed, for this purpose, copper tanks well tinned.

The.

The Rev. Mr. Cartwright, who hath on many occasions applied his ingenuity and extensive abilities to the public good, has this session favoured the Society with a communication on the subject of the Inspissated Juice of Lettuces, and of the analogy of its effects with the Opium prepared from Poppies.

Under the class of Polite Arts, Mr. Sheldrake has taken much pains to elucidate the composition of the Colours used in painting by the Ancients, and to improve the permanency and brilliancy of those employed by modern artists.

A reference to the Premiums bestowed in the Polite Arts (see page 374) will show the attention paid by the Society to different branches of them. It may be noted with great justice, that some performances were exhibited, which would have done honour to persons of high professional reputation.

The scarcity of the usual materials for making Paper has been a consider-

able

able impediment to the progress of literature, and called for every possible remedy.

The Paper prepared by Mr. Willmott, from the Paut-Plant, is of good quality, as may be seen by the specimen annexed to the communication.

The manufacture of Chicoree Root, as a substitute for Coffee, has lately extended rapidly over the Continent; and as this article furnishes a considerable part of the nutriment of many thousand persons in Germany, Mr. John Taylor, from personal observation and minute inquiries, has furnished an accurate Account of its culture, preparation, and use, which it is hoped will contribute to the comforts of great numbers of the inhabitants of this country.

In the line of Mechanicks, the Society have been very assiduously engaged, during the whole of their last Session. It must, however, be remembered, that the acting powers in Mechanicks are not

numerous,

numerous, and that it is difficult to make such application of these powers as to produce novelty and advantage. Many Machines laid before the Society have been rejected, owing to their want of simplicity, their not being new, or not adequate to the purposes intended. Great differences will also arise in public opinion, upon the proportion of reward due to the several Claimants, which is frequently rated too much by one person, or too little by another.

The Society have, however, earnestly endeavoured to discriminate with propriety, to do justice to merit, and to encourage every spark of genius, which may lead to real improvement. Wherever they have discovered that the machine produced, though not fully adequate to the object proposed, was likely to lead to beneficial consequences, they have inclined to give encouragement. In the Machines noted in the present Volume, each will be found entitled to

merit

merit in this point of view, and the whole, it is hoped, may lead to improvements in practice.

The Machine recommended by Mr. Sarjeant for raising Water, is of a cheap and simple construction, and answers well the purpose to which it is applied.

The advantage of the Gun-Harpoon is further confirmed, by the distance from whence the three Whales were shot by Robert Hays, which probably would not have admitted a boat to approach so near as to allow the harpooner to strike them by the hand.

. From many experiments made before the Committee, with the model of the Water-Wheel from the late Mr. Besant, it appears to possess advantages sufficient to recommend its trial in places subject to Back-Water.

Very strong recommendations of Mr. Phillips's method of driving Copper-Bolts into ships, have been given, independent of the Certificates annexed to

his

his Account, and afford great reason to hope it will be of material benefit to our Naval Architecture. The principal difficulty to encounter seems to arise from the prejudice which workmen have in general for old modes of practice, however ineffectual and absurd.

Mr. Arkwright's Machine for raising Ore from Mines, possesses the advantages of supplying itself with the articles to be raised; of lifting them above the surface of the earth, and delivering them into carts attending for them : its motion is simple and regular, and the different parts of the machine are easily kept in order.

The importance of procuring from Quarries in Great Britain, Mill-Stones equal to those imported from France, is obvious. In the last Volume, an Account was given of a Quarry of Burr-Stone, discovered at Conway by the late Mr. Bowes, and one hundred pounds awarded. The present Volume contains

Mr.

Mr. Field Evans's Communication of
another Quarry now worked in Montgomeryshire; it is probable that the detached Burr-Stones, found promiscuously in the soil near to this Quarry, will
be equal to the French in every respect,
as their best Burr-Stones are collected
from similar situations.

Mr. Garnet Terry's Mill for Grinding
Hard Substances, is free from the friction
of the screw, which presses on the
grinding cylinder in the common hand-
mills, and is more easily regulated.

Mr. William Bullock's improvement
of the Drawback House-Lock possesses
every advantage of simplicity and effect,
and deserves to be introduced into general use, as it prevents the unpleasant
noise arising from the common locks,
and furnishes additional security to the
house.

Where only a small space of ground
can be allotted for the use of a Crane,
Mr. Gent's Crane may be employed: it

has

has the powers of raising a considerable weight, and projecting that weight to a distance proper for loading it.

Sir George Onesiphorus Paul, Baronet, who has taken infinite pains for a long time in the cause of humanity, and in the alleviation of distress, has strongly pointed out the necessity of the admission of Fresh Air into Hospitals and crowded Rooms, and furnished a very satisfactory Account of the mechanical modes of Ventilation, which he has put in practice with success.

Mr. De Lafon's Watch-Escapement displays an ingenious combination of mechanism, which it is hoped will furnish useful hints to persons occupied in that line.

It has long been the earnest wish of the Society that Great Britain should procure, from the produce of her Colonies, such articles as cannot be grown in England, and have therefore been hitherto obtained from foreign Governments.

ments. In the article of Indigo, this point has been for some time accomplished, as upwards of half a million sterling in value has been annually imported from our East-India settlements, for several years past, and this nation rendered independent of Spain for this valuable product.

The Paper furnished in the present Volume, upon the subject of Myrabolans from Bengal, tends to prove, that a valuable substitute for Aleppo Galls may be procured from thence.

Mr. Stephens's Communication on the Lake prepared by him from *fresh* Stick-Lack, yielding a scarlet dye resembling that from Cochineal, notices that upwards of 18,000 lbs. weight of this Lake have been received in England. The experiments made by Dr. Bancroft and others, show that it is at least equal in effect to one fourth its weight of Cochineal. The Society are informed, that great pains are taking in India to produce

duce the best Cochineal; and there is reason to hope that ultimately resources may
be found in our Colonies, to supply
our wants and increase our manufactures.

The public-spirited and disinterested
manner in which this Society, in their
last Session, extended their Premiums to
Ireland, will doubtless meet with universal approbation, and tend greatly to
encourage the patriotic endeavours of
this and the Dublin Society, to promote
the benefit of the united kingdom.

The very handsome manner in which
the Dublin Society have expressed themselves on this occasion, evinces great
probability of advantage from these
united exertions. A letter from one
of their Vice-Presidents, addressed to
this Society, contains the following observation:—" It is with no small degree of satisfaction we behold the Premiums of the London Society opened
to this country, and we hope that by
joint

joint efforts hereafter, our Premiums
may produce what individually each
might fail in."

The Society take the present opportunity of acknowledging their obligations for the sundry Presents they have
received from different public Societies
and Individuals, the particulars of which
are inserted in the 380th page of the
present volume.

It is a pleasure to notice, that the
Society flourishes greatly under the
public auspices; that nearly two hundred
additional Members were elected during
the last Session; and that many Candidates are now making application for
admission.

It is necessary, particularly, to notice,
that the grand Series of Moral and Historical Paintings, in the Great Room of
the Society, have been lately greatly
improved: through the whole of the
last recess of the Society, Mr. Barry
has been zealously engaged in bringing

to

to mature perfection those matchless fruits of his talents; nor has his active genius been alone confined to the finishing what was before conceived: he has also created new objects for the *contemplation* of the Philosopher, and *admiration* of the Artist.

A valuable detail of part of these improvements will follow the present Preface; and a further account will probably be furnished to the Public at a future period.

In the last Volume of Transactions it was mentioned, that the Gold Medal of the Society had been presented to Mr. Alexander Mackenzie, for the Discovery of a Passage, over Land, from Upper Canada to the South Sea.

Agreeably to the intimation given in that Volume, his arduous and interesting journey has since been published, with Maps illustrative of his Route.

The Society have commenced the October Session with vigour and spirit; the

ingenious

ingenious of both sexes, and of every description, are invited to lay before them such objects as are new and important, addressed to their Secretary, Mr. Charles Taylor, at the Society's house in the Adelphi, London. Due attention will be paid to merit in every department of Arts, Manufactures, and Commerce, and it will be amply rewarded by honorary or pecuniary compensations. It is particularly requested, however, that the information sent on the several subjects, where Premiums or Bounties are expected, be full, clear, and explicit. Any gratuitous hints or communications, likely to promote the objects of the Society, will be esteemed a favour, and be properly noticed.

The Society desire it to be clearly understood, that, as a body, they are not responsible for any opinion or representation of facts, contained in the following Papers; and it is necessary to state, that they have admitted the Accounts

counts to pass, in the language and manner of the several persons concerned. They have allowed every man to tell his tale in his own way, and have preferred such plain statements in the language sent, to alterations by the Society in a more embellished style.

The Dublin Society have lately annexed the Premiums of this Society to their publications. Though the funds and government of the two Societies are entirely distinct, yet both being actuated by that noble principle *the public good,* there is a pleasing prospect of mutual success. The efforts of both, as has been before observed, are united for the general welfare; and there is every reason to hope that such powers of exertion will produce a copious source of information and happiness to the world.

The Society have been favoured by
JAMES BARRY, Esq. with the following Account of the late additional
Improvements made by him in the
PICTURES in their Great Room,
which were begun in the year 1777
by that eminent Artist.

No. 36, Castle-Street, Oxford-Street,
November 26, 1801.

MR. BARRY presents his respectful
compliments to the most noble
the President, the Vice-President, and
the rest of the Society for the Encouragement of Arts, &c. and having in
a letter, dated October 25, 1801, communicated to them his reasons at large
for the several matters of recent introduction into the Pictures he has executed in their Great Room, he now,
in compliance with the request of their
Committee of Correspondence and Papers, offers to them such explanatory

c 3      extracts

extracts therefrom, as he conceives may be of some use to the Members of the Society, and the Public at large.

Mr. Barry has exemplified his idea for the improvement of Medals and Coins, originally suggested in a letter to His Majesty's Most Honourable Privy Council, dated July 31, 1798 (see Letter to the Dilletanti Society, p. 218, 8vo. edit.) by introducing into the Picture of the Society two models for Medals or Coins; the one, a more than profile female head, with the imperial shield of Great Britain and Ireland suspended from her shoulder; the other, a head of Alfred, the great improver and founder: the latter of which he adopted from necessity, not from choice, as he had no portrait of his present Majesty with which he was satisfied. He was particularly desirous to shelter this improvement under the wings of the Society, as he thought it probable that the noble relievo, and the security of that

relievo

relievo exemplified in those heads, would be imitated in our coinage; and, from its obvious utility and dignity, be adopted all over Europe: and, in an object of such importance as the conservation of the portraiture and inscription, two points of the highest *desiderata*, the lead would be taken by a Society which has given rise to so many others, and has been so long remarkable for its exemplary, patriotic, and philanthropic conduct.

As the suggestions in the former letter to the Privy Council were delivered generally, without the specification of those minute particulars necessary for the execution of Mr. Barry's ideas, the person who executed the new Halfpenny and Farthing, issued shortly after, entirely misconceived Mr. Barry's idea of the proper convexity, or of the cavo bed in which it should have been raised; the spirit had evaporated in his ill-managed experiment, and there was nothing remaining but a *residuum*, a mere *caput*

*mortuum*

*mortuum* of little value, by which one important part was unnecessarily sacri-ficed to the other, and consequently nothing desirable obtained, but rather the contrary ; as the head, which ought to be most important and principal, is flat, and without relievo, and triflingly buried in the centre of the coin, like a mite in a cheese, in order to allow space for an unnecessarily mischievous circle of large letters, which might have been so well disposed of in another manner, according to the usage of the Greeks. Nay, even in the halfpenny and farthing of George II. the head, as it should always do, importantly fills the coin, and the circular inscription is even so contrived as to be subservient to that end.

If the contrivance visible on the slightest glance at those models had been adopted, the fine heads on the Grecian and Roman coins, those of the Hamerani's on the Papal medals, or

those

those admirable ones executed by Hed-
linger for Sweden, though now so liable
to injury from their bold and noble relievo, as to be exposed to speedy ruin
from time and usage, might preserve
their most essential parts from being injured until those parts, which were least
essential, had been entirely worn away.
Thus, too, one of our current half-crowns
of King William, or Queen Anne, had
they been executed in this way, would
have gone through many centuries, and
from the wearing would be hardly worth
a shilling, by the time the likeness and
inscription, the two most essential parts,
came to be injured. It is worth remarking, that those of the Grecian and Roman
coins which are preserved in the collec-
tions of the curious, are not those which
were in constant use, but those which,
from the superstitious notions of the
time, were buried while fresh with their
dead, in order to satisfy the demands of
a certain grisly Ferryman, or any other
that

might occur in their long and gloomy journey, or from some other accidents or calamities; all the rest which were subject to the vicissitudes of current usage being obliterated ages ago.

The better to elucidate these two models, Mr. Barry introduced an aged figure stooping over them, looking very intently on a medal, and holding in his other hand a letter or paper on which is written, " On the gousto of Medals and Coins, and the best mode of preserving them from injuries by friction," the identical wish expressed by the Privy Council to the Royal Academy, and which produced Mr. Barry's letter before referred to. On the same paper is also introduced the necessary section of such a coin.

These ideas Mr. Barry had the honour of submitting, immediately after their introduction into the Picture, to the Right Honourable the Earl of Liverpool, in a letter dated July 3, 1801.

It

It may be well, before closing these remarks on Medals and Coins, to take notice here of a very curious and extraordinary particular, which occurs in those coins that are supposed to be the most ancient, and are placed amongst the *incognita*, as they are without mark or inscription of any kind, which might denote time or place, and are no less remarkable for the transcendant excellence of their style of highly-cultivated design and execution than for their extraordinary and perfect preservation, which is owing to their great relievo, and to the rising of the metal round the sides of the square coffers in which they are bedded, like the roses in the architectonic soffita's, and the hieroglyphics on the Egyptian obelisks. A few of those most extraordinary and unaccountable of all numismatic remains may be found in Dr. Hunter's truly noble collection; and, as far as they go, for a female head and its kerchief or accompaniment, they are

but

but rarely (if at all) equalled even by the Greeks themselves, either Asiatic or European, or their Sicilian or Italian colonies. These Coins have all the simplicity of the Egyptian bas-relief, but. without its bald uniformity, or the petite, wirey, husky, dry, cutting manner of either the Persian, Hetruscan, or Punic Coins. They exhibit a venustas and unrestrained easy, urbane, graceful deportment, which appears equally to have resulted from the high cultivation and amenity of the state of society where the artist found his models, as of the delicacy and ability with which those models were imitated. Herodotus (in Clio) says, " that the Lydians were the first of all the nations we know, who introduced the art of coining gold and silver to facilitate trade, and first practised the way of retailing merchandize." This perhaps is the reason why these Coins are supposed to be Lydian, as they are evidently prior to the Greeks;

and

and appear to have been imitated in the Grecian settlements of Ionia; and yet the Greeks seem to have had no Coins in Homer's time, as he does not any where allude to them: and it is difficult to bring one's self to believe that the remarkable perfection of these coins could have been effected by the Heraclidæ, who were settled in Sardis, admitting these Heraclidæ to have been the descendants of that Grecian Hercules, the friend of Philoctetes, so memorable in the Trojan war; and that the Greeks before and in Homer's time could have been such strangers to coinage. It is difficult also to reconcile with the sum of things, the names of Belus, and his grandson Ninus, which occur in the list of these Heraclidæ: so many difficulties start up on every side, as would induce one to look for a higher origin of these Heraclidæ, the supposed inventors of Coinage; and instead of Hercules the friend of Philoctetes, to substitute the Titannic Hercules,

cules, the friend and relation of Atlas, who flourished many ages before. This would comport better with the highly-cultivated gusto of those Coins, so completely estranged as they are from all the different modes and degrees of barbarism of the surrounding nations. They stand insulated like that mundane system of Pythagoras's importation, and cannot be ascribed to any known people, except perhaps to these Titans or Atlantides, whence so many other knowledges seem to have been derived as from a common source. But Coinage is not traceable farther back than in this supposed Lydian money, which we find in a state of complete perfection, without any of those previous stages of progressive growth which must incontrovertibly have preceded that perfection.

In order to finish entirely this part of the subject, Mr. Barry begs leave to add, from a letter read by him to the Society, October 25, 1801, that in consequence

sequence of the application for designs
for a new die for their Medal, he stated
his intention of introducing a modifi-
cation of their former design, which he
thought would fully answer their intended
purpose. The more the subject matter
of that design is considered, the more
one must admire and respect the sterling good sense and weighty consideration of the original Founders of the
Society. Nothing can be more happily
imagined than the idea consisting of
Britannia aided by Minerva and Mercury, the classical tutelary deities of
Arts, Manufactures, and Commerce;
and this old device, like many other
good old usages, cannot be amended by
any change in the substratum. It requires nothing more in its essence, and
will most happily coalesce and accom-
modate with all the acquisitions and improvements of the most enlarged and
refined culture. For this purpose, a little
more of *goût* and character in the
figures,

figures, is all that is necessary; en‑
larging them so as to fill the space with
more dignity, and taking away from
their individual scattered appearance by
the little graces and arts of a more im‑
proved composition. And as there is
always a considerable dignity and con‑
sequence attached to magnitude, which
is one of the constituents of sublimity,
his suggested alterations would amount
simply to this—to substitute, instead of
the little entire figures of Minerva and
Mercury, only two large heads of those
deities; and he would omit the head of
Britannia altogether; and by a wreath
of the shamrock, rose, and thistle, boldly
rising round the edge of the Medal,
playing in and out in a graceful gustoso
manner, he would represent the present
happily united Kingdom of Great Britain
and Ireland, with a felicity at least equal
to the owl, the horse's head, or the dol‑
phins, on the Athenian, Punic, or Sici‑
lian coins. It may be observed by the
way,

way, that this mode of rim, with an enlarged noble head of His Majesty, with
the relieved and incused parts gracefully
and happily diversified, and the inscription well secured within, would not be
unworthy of the Royal Mint.

Another matter which Mr. Barry is
happy in offering to the attention of the
Society, is a Naval Pillar which he has
introduced in the picture of the Thames,
or Triumph of Navigation. This design
occurred to his mind at the time when
his Royal Highness the Duke of Clarence,
and other Noblemen and Gentlemen, as-
sociated for the purpose, advertised
their idea of obtaining designs for a
Naval Pillar, or other trophy, which
might serve for the commemoration of
great national achievements. In consequence, however, of the dark and
mysterious opposition which had so long
followed him, and of which he has had
such frequent reason to complain, Mr.
Barry laid aside the design till its con-

nexion,

nexion with the subject of this picture of the Thames, pressed upon him with accumulated and irresistible force ; and finding nothing had been done, which would answer the intended purpose, to his satisfaction, he rolled the scaffold to the picture, and began such a trophy of a mausoleum, observatory, or light-house, as is no where else in existence, and he believes never had existence before. Nothing can have more simplicity and *naïveté* than the idea of it as a totality; the British Tars so well and obviously typified by the naval Gods, the Tritons, upon sea-horses, dashing up the sides of a rock, upon the top of which they erect this trophy to the first Naval Power.

Mr. Barry cannot help pausing to notice the dark designs of interested individuals against his honour, his interest, and his peace ; and especially as they have been so managed as to influence the mind of his Sovereign. Amongst

other

other reports equally unfounded, it has been generally said that His Majesty had been induced to believe that Mr. Barry had written the Supplement to Pilkington's Dictionary of Painters, where, page 825, the King is grossly abused. This, had he been allowed the opportunity, he could then, as he does now, have flatly contradicted; and have then affirmed, as he does now, that he had never any part or concern in the writing or devising that Supplement; and that, though his name was impudently and fraudulently affixed to it, yet that he had no knowledge whatever of any such matter, until, in common with the rest of his Majesty's subjects, he saw it, after its publication, with a garbled portion of his Letter to the Dilettanti bound up along with it.— This justification he offered in a Letter addressed to His Majesty, and afterwards inserted in the Morning Post of December 3, 1799. Whether it ever

was

was laid before His Majesty or not, Mr.
Barry is uncertain; but a matter so
flagitiously fraudulent he cannot resist
every opportunity of denying.

In the year 1792, it appeared that
Mr. Barry had occasion to offer another
(though much more limited) scheme for
a national Mausoleum (see page 28,
Letter to the Dilettanti), where the
subjects sculptured in the round and in
basso-relievo, being all near the eye,
afforded to the spectator every opportunity of considering them with convenience, pleasure, and utility, the want
of which was so deeply regretted by all
who had seen the fine column at Rome,
erected to commemorate the victories
of Trajan; the greatest part of these
fine sculptures being to every purpose
of desirable inspection, as much lost
and buried in the air, as if they had
been so many feet under ground; and
the beautiful labour bestowed upon them
could never be appreciated but in the

plaster

plaster casts, moulded from them at two different times, and from the prints of Pietro Sancto Bartoli, executed from these casts. No doubt the statue of the Emperor, placed on the top of this column, might, from its magnitude, be less liable to suffer by the distance as a totality, and might be seen all over Rome, which was the grand motive that induced to the undertaking, and would in every respect have been worthy the great artist and most excellent Emperor, had another form of shaft been adopted, which would have admitted of an exterior ascent, like this in the picture of the Thames: then nothing would have been lost in the appreciation of such admirable workmanship, as the bas-relief all the way up. But this had not occurred hitherto in any instance, ancient or modern, except in such where there was nothing of sculptural record to inform as to the subject matter, and to give delight by the dignified, impressive

d 3                              manner

manner of conveying that information. The column of Antoninus is liable to the same objections as this of Trajan, and still further aggravated by the clumpy, too much detached way of rendering the sculptured groups, which is not less injurious to the general effect, than perplexing and disgusting when considered singly. Of the same nature with these of Trajan and Antoninus is the great column at Constantinople, though, no doubt, from the intervening decline of the arts, greatly inferior in gusto of every kind: and as to Pompey's Pillar at Alexandria, it commemorates nothing, except perhaps by something on the pedestal.

As the Pyramids of Egypt have been contrived, their immense mass seems thrown away, without use, as nothing is recorded on them, either in the universal language of forms, or in those more confined and precarious hieroglyphic or alphabetical characters; and all succeeding ages have

have been utterly unable to divine the utility adequate to such expensive constructions. It may be disputed, whether the Chaldaic Temple of Belus and the tower within it, was of equal antiquity with the Pyramids in Egypt; but, according to the account in Herodotus, this Chaldaic tower was by much a more artistlike performance, and from what will appear below, more appositely convertible to various purposes of the most interesting utility. This Babylonian tower consisted of square bodies placed one on the other. The first body or platform was (to use the words of Herodotus) of one stadium in height, and in length and breadth of the same measure. On this tower another is built, and a third upon that, till they make up the number of eight. The ascent to these is by a circular way carried round the outside of the building to the highest part. We are enabled to form a clear conception of the circular ascent round the several

square

square stories of this building in Chaldea, by adverting to the account published by the Rev. Father Clavigero, of the ancient pyramidal temples in Mexico and the country about it, which appear to have been constructed with more genius than those of Egypt, and to the great surprise of all who have concerned themselves in matters of antiquity, are found to be constructed after identically the same mode with this of Chaldea, consisting of a certain number of stories, round each of which their processions marched, ascending by a separate flight of steps at the same angle of each.

One of these Mexican temples consisted of nine stories or platforms; others were of a single body, in the form of a pyramid, with a stair-case. The height of the Pyramid of Cholula was, by Clavigero's account, upwards of 500 feet. " One may ascend (says he) to the top by a path made in a spiral direction round the pyramid, and I went

up

up on horsebask in 1744." But the architecture of the great temples was for the most part the same with that of the great temple of Mexico, which though of a great height, so as to afford a view of the lake, the cities around, and a great part of the valley of Mexico, and affirmed by eye-witnesses to be the finest prospect in the world—yet, notwithstanding this great height, consisted but of five bodies or stories, perhaps in order to allow space for the plain or upper area on the fifth body, which was . about forty-three perches long and thirty broad, upon which they performed their sacrifices in the view of such an immense concourse of people as this great altitude would afford towards their becoming participants in what was going forward. Nothing architectural could have been more ingeniously contrived to exhibit with all conceivable splendor, not only the spectacle on the platform, but also the processional part, moving

.                                   .

on

on all sides in every plain as it ascended.
But when one reflects that the victims
were human, and that 72,344 of them
were sacrificed on this platform, in one
festival of four days continuance, at the
dedication of this temple, it is not to
be wondered that the Spaniards demo-
lished, and suffered not a stone of it to
remain standing. And yet it had been
better, perhaps, to have adopted a different conduct, and to have suffered the
temple to remain; and, in lieu of the
former horrid butchery, to have performed, in the presence of this mis-
guided people, their own christian, un-
bloody sacrifice, which, from its relation
to the oblation at Calvery of that lamb
which was slain from the beginning, had
happily atoned for all, and precluded
the necessity of any other sacrifice. Such
a substitution would there have been
evangelical indeed; as almost all over
that part of the western hemisphere,
islands, and continent, every man had

a

a chance of becoming an ill-fated prisoner, and consequently one in the dreadful list of victims. But the time presses, and will not admit of much excursion, however agreeable, or even perhaps necessary, towards the just appreciation of certain parts of the subject in hand. Let so much then suffice, as it will sufficiently authorise the observation, that the British Pillar, in the picture of the Thames, possesses every advantage enjoyed in those famed pyramidal, obeliscal, or columnal fabrications of Egypt, Chaldea, Rome, or America, with advantages peculiar to itself, of still higher value than all that it may have in common with those celebrated vestiges of antiquity. This British Naval Pillar, Mausoleum, Observatory, Light-house, or whatever it may be called, as they are all united in the same structure, which, by a very legitimate flight of classical imagination, these Tritons, or sea-gods, have erected to the

the first Naval Power, will admit of
whatever advantages may be obtained
from altitude; and, if the settling of
snow would permit, it may be raised
high enough to see (as Saussure did) the
moon and constellations moving in a jet
black vault at noon day; whilst the easy
unembarrassed road all the way up,
might feast the eye, the mind, and the
heart, with all desirable national, ethi-
cal, or other exemplary useful information. Although this building is at too
great a distance in the picture to afford accurate inspection of detailed
particulars, yet it is near enough for a
general view, as is sufficiently apparent
from the group of figures on the base-
ment, looking at one of the basso-
relievo's, which, by the fleet of ships and
the distant pyramids, might represent
the brave Nelson's victory at the Nile;
whilst some more youthful characters
appear eagerly attentive to what is said
with so much energy, as would appear

by

by the action and stretched-out hands
of the speaker. At the end of the
bridge which connects this building with
the chalky shore, is a triumphal arch,
through which processions might pass;
and, at some distance, under the bridge
is seen a more humble, though not less
endearing prospect of a village church
steeple and fishing-boats, with the men
pulling in their nets. A seventy-four
gun ship is to windward of the Naval
Pillar, stretching out to sea, and a fleet
just appearing in the offing.

In the fifth picture, viz. that of the
Society, Mr. Barry has also introduced
a Tea-kitchen, or Vase for boiling water,
which he offers as an improvement on
those in general use, which in many
respects have been so vulgarly and ill
contrived, that, much as he loves tea,
yet he can never see these complicated,
tasteless urns or vases without disgust,
resting, as they generally do, on a sort
of pedestals with additional feet to them,
handles

handles unaccounted for, but stuck on
merely for the purpose; and the water
issuing from an odious, insulated, de-
fenceless, feeble conveyance, stuck in
like a spigot in a barrel. In lieu of all
this tasteless complicated vulgarity, the
vase, in the picture of the Society, is
of the simplest and least complicated
kind; and if any idea results from its
general appearance, it is the sublime
suggestion of the Grecian cosmogony,
the primæval egg of ancient mother
Night, suspended between two mysterious serpents, the principle of regenera-
ting vitality, the convolutions of whose
bodies, flung in the air, naturally furnish
the handles, and their tails afford the
stable circular foot or basis on which the
whole rests; whilst the passage for the
water of life within, is controuled by
the little Psyche or button in the centre,
where the heads of those serpents meet
at bottom. Perhaps there is nothing in
the immense collection of antique vases

in

in Passeri, or Sir William Hamilton, so classical and completely Grecian as this idea, whilst it is certain that nothing can be more completely adapted to every purpose of security and utility.

There are also some other particulars, of recent introducion, in this picture of the Society, as well as in that of the Elysium; but whatever observations may occur on them will be better reserved for some other time, as this letter is getting too long.

# CONTENTS.

| | Page |
|---|---|
| Preface | |
| Premiums offered in 1801 | 6 |
| Papers in Agriculture | 67 |
| Papers in Chemistry | 189 |
| Papers in Polite Arts | 203 |
| Papers in Manufactures | 233 |
| Papers in Mechanicks | 253 |
| Papers in Colonies and Trade | 341 |
| Rewards bestowed | 369 |
| Presents received | 380 |
| Catalogue of Models and Machines | 386 |
| List of Officers | 389 |
| List of Members | 393 |
| Index | 453 |

# PREMIUMS

OFFERED BY THE

# SOCIETY

INSTITUTED AT LONDON

FOR THE ENCOURAGEMENT OF

# ARTS, MANUFACTURES,

AND

# COMMERCE,

IN

THE YEAR M.DCCCL.

# TO THE PUBLIC.

—

THE chief objects of the SOCIETY are to promote the Arts, Manufactures, and Commerce, of this Kingdom, by giving Rewards for all such useful Inventions, Discoveries, or Improvements (though not mentioned in this book), as tend to that purpose; and, in pursuance of this plan, the SOCIETY have already expended full FORTY THOUSAND POUNDS, advanced by the voluntary subscriptions of their Members, Donations, and Legacies bequeathed.

The manner in which this Money has been distributed may be seen by applying to the Secretary or other Officers of the SOCIETY, at their House in the *Adelphi*. The Register of the Premiums and Bounties they have given will show the very great advantages which the Public have derived from this Institution.

The Meetings of the SOCIETY are held every *Wednesday*, at seven o'clock in the evening, from the fourth *Wednesday* in *October* to the first

Wed-

*Wednesday* in *June*. The several Committees meet on other evenings in the week during the Session.

In order still farther to promote the laudable views of this SOCIETY, it may be necessary to explain the mode by which its Members continue to be elected.

Each Member has the privilege, at any weekly meeting of the SOCIETY, of proposing any person who is desirous to become a Member, provided such proposal is signed by three Members of the SOCIETY.

Peers of the Realm or Lords of Parliament are, on their being proposed, immediately balloted for; and the name, with the addition and place of abode, of every other person proposing to become a Member, is to be delivered to the Secretary, who is to read the same, and properly insert the name in a list, which is to be hung up in the SOCIETY's Room until the next Meeting; at which time such person shall be balloted for: and, if two-thirds of the Members, then voting, ballot in his favour, he shall be deemed a *perpetual Member,* upon payment of *Twenty Guineas* at one payment; or a *subscribing Member*, upon payment of any sum not less than *Two Guineas* annually.

Every

Every Member is entitled to vote and be concerned in all the transactions of the Society, and to attend and vote at the several Committees. He has also the privilege of recommending two persons as Auditors, at the Weekly Meeting of the Society; and, by addressing a note to the Register, of introducing his friends to examine the various Models, Machines, and Productions, in different branches of Arts, Manufactures, and Commerce, for which Rewards have been bestowed; and to inspect the magnificent Series of Moral and Historical Paintings, so happily contrived and completed by James Barry, Esq. which, with some valuable Busts and Statues, decorate the Great Room. He has likewise the use of a valuable Library, and is entitled to the annual Volume of the Society's Transactions.

*Premiums*

## Premiums for Planting and Husbandry.

*The Public are requested to take notice, that the Society abide by the Premiums offered in the 18th Volume of their Transactions, for the setting of Acorns, and planting of Timber-trees, although such Premiums are not here re-printed.*

Class 1. FOREST-TREES. To the person who shall have inclosed and planted, or set, the greatest number of acres (not less than ten) of land, that is incapable of being ploughed, such as the borders of rivers, the sides of precipices, and any land that has too many rocks, or that is not calculated to repay the expense of tillage, owing to the poverty of the soil, the surface being too hilly, mountainous, or otherwise unfit for tillage, with the best sorts of Forest-trees, namely, Oak, Spanish Chesnuts, Ash, Elm, Beech, Alder, Willow, Larch, Spruce and Silver Fir, with or without screens of Scotch Fir, adapted to the soil, and intended for Timber-trees, between the first of October, 1801, and the first of April, 1802; the GOLD MEDAL.

2. For the second greatest quantity of land, not less than seven acres, the SILVER MEDAL, or TWENTY GUINEAS.

3. For the third greatest quantity of land, not less than five acres, the SILVER MEDAL.

A particular ACCOUNT of the methods used in making and managing the plantations, the nature of the soil, the probable number of each sort of plants, together with

proper

proper CERTIFICATES that they were in a healthy and thriving state two years at least after making the plantation, to be delivered to the Society on or before the first Tuesday in November, 1805.

4. ASCERTAINING THE BEST METHOD OF RAISING OAKS. To the person who shall ascertain in the best manner, by actual experiments, the comparative merits of the different modes of raising Oaks for Timber, either from Acorns set on land of the foregoing description, properly dug or tilled, from Acorns set by the spade or dibble, without digging or tillage, either on a smooth surface, or among bushes, fern, or other cover; or from young plants previously raised in nurseries, and transplanted; regard being had to the expence, growth, and other respective advantages of the several methods; the GOLD MEDAL.

The ACCOUNTS and proper CERTIFICATES that not less than one acre has been cultivated in each mode, to be produced to the Society on or before the first Tuesday in November, 1801.

5. The same premium is extended one year farther.

The ACCOUNTS and CERTIFICATES to be produced on or before the first Tuesday in November, 1802.

6. OSIERS. To the person who shall have planted, between the first of October, 1800, and the first of May, 1801, the greatest quantity of land, not less than five acres, with those kinds of Willows, commonly known by the names of Osier, Spaniard, New-kind, or French, fit for the purpose of basket-makers, not fewer than twelve

thousand

thousand plants on each acre; the GOLD MEDAL, or
THIRTY GUINEAS.

7. For the second greatest quantity of land, not less
three acres, the SILVER MEDAL, or TEN GUINEAS.

CERTIFICATES of the planting, and that the plants
were in a thriving state five months at least after the planting, to be produced to the Society on or before the last
Tuesday in November, 1801.

8. The same premiums are extended one year farther.

CERTIFICATES to be produced on or before the last
Tuesday in November, 1802.

*₌* *The Candidates for planting all kinds of Trees are to
certify that the respective Plantations are properly fenced and
secured, and particularly to state the condition the Plants were
in at the time of signing such Certificate.*

*Any information which the Candidates for the foregoing Pre-
miums may choose to communicate, relative to the methods made
use of in forming the Plantation, or promoting the growth of
the several Trees, or any other observations that may have
occurred on the subject, will be thankfully received.*

9. SECURING PLANTATIONS OF TIMBER-
TREES, AND HEDGE-ROWS. To the person who
shall give to the Society the most satisfactory Account,
founded on experience, of the most effectual and least expensive method of securing young plantations of Timber-
trees, and Hedge-rows, from Hares and Rabbits, as well
as Sheep and larger Cattle, which at the same time shall

be

be least subject to the depredations of wood-stealers; the SILVER MEDAL, or TWENTY GUINEAS.

The ACCOUNTS, and CERTIFICATES of the efficacy of the method, to be produced to the Society on or before the first Tuesday in November, 1801.

10. The same premium is extended one year farther.

The ACCOUNTS and CERTIFICATES to be produced on or before the first Tuesday in November, 1802.

11. PREVENTING THE BLIGHT, OR RAVAGES OF INSECTS, ON FRUIT-TREES AND CULINARY PLANTS. To the person who shall discover to the Society the most effectual method of preventing the Blight, or Ravages of Insects, on Fruit-trees and Culinary Plants, superior to any hitherto known or practised, and verified by actual and comparative experiments; the GOLD MEDAL, or THIRTY GUINEAS,

The ACCOUNTS, with proper CERTIFICATES, to be delivered to the Society on or before the second Tuesday in November, 1801.

12. The same premium is extended one year farther.

The ACCOUNTS and CERTIFICATES to be delivered on or before the second Tuesday in November, 1802.

13. REMOVING THE ILL EFFECTS OF BLIGHTS, OR INSECTS. To the Person who shall discover to the Society the most effectual method of removing the ill effects of Blights, or Insects, on Fruit-trees and Culinary Plants, superior to any hitherto known or practised,

practised, and verified by actual and comparative experiments; the GOLD MEDAL, or THIRTY GUINEAS.

The ACCOUNTS and CERTIFICATES to be delivered to the Society on or before the first Tuesday in February, 1802.

14. COMPARATIVE TILLAGE. For the most satisfactory set of experiments, made on not less than eight acres of land, four of which to be trench-ploughed *, and four to be ploughed in the usual manner, in order to ascertain in what cases it may be advisable to shorten the operations of tillage, by adopting one trench-ploughing, for the purpose of burying the weeds, instead of the method, now in common use, of ploughing and harrowing the land three or four times, and raking the weeds together and burning them; the GOLD MEDAL, or FORTY GUINEAS.

It is required that every operation and expense attending each mode of culture be fully and accurately described, and that proper CERTIFICATES of the nature and condition of the land on which the experiments are made, together with a circumstantial account of the appearance of the subsequent crops during their growth, and also of the quantity and weight of the corn and straw under each mode of culture, or, in case of a green crop, the weight of an average sixteen perches, be produced to the Society on or before the first Tuesday in February, 1803.

                                                    15.

* It is a common practice among gardeners, when they have a piece of very foul land, to dig it two spits, or about eighteen inches deep, shovelling the weeds to the bottom. This they call trenching.

15. COMPARATIVE CULTURE OF WHEAT, BROAD-CAST, DRILLED, AND DIBBLED. For the best set of experiments made on not less than twelve acres, four of which to be sown broad-cast, four drilled, and four dibbled, the two latter in equidistant rows, in order fully to ascertain which is the most advantageous mode of cultivating Wheat; the Gold Medal, or Forty Guineas.

It is required that every operation and expense of each mode of culture be fully described; and that proper Certificates of the nature and condition of the land on which the experiments are made, together with an Account of the produce of the Corn, the weight per bushel, and also of the straw, be produced to the Society, on or before the first Tuesday in February, 1803.

16. SPRING WHEAT. To the person who, in the year 1801, shall cultivate the greatest quantity of Spring-Wheat, not less than ten acres, the Silver Medal, or Twenty Guineas.

It is required that the time of sowing and reaping be noticed; also a particular Account of the species, cultivation, and expense attending it, with proper Certificates of the nature and condition of the land on which the experiments were made, and the name of the crop, if any, which the same land bore the preceding year; together with an account of the produce, the weight per Winchester bushel; and a sample, not less than a quart; be produced to the Society, on or before the second Tuesday in December, 1801,

It is supposed that sowing wheat early in the spring will not only allow more time to till the land, but less for
the

the growth of weeds; thus rendering the wheat as clear as
a barley crop, and exhausting the soil much less than autumnal sowing. It may be seen in this volume that the
wheat usually sown in autumn may be put into the ground,
with great success, so late as February or March, thus
giving time to clear the ground from turnips, or to avoid
a bad season.

17. BEANS AND WHEAT. To the person who
shall have dibbled or drilled, between the first of December, 1801, and the first of April, 1802, the greatest
quantity of land, not less than ten acres, with Beans, in
equidistant rows, and hoed the intervals twice or oftener,
and shall have sown the same land with wheat in the autumn of the year 1802; the Silver Medal, or Twenty
Guineas.

It is required that an account of the sort and quantity
of Beans, the time of dibbling or drilling, and of reaping or mowing them, the produce per acre threshed, the
application of the straw, the expense of dibbling or drilling, hand or horse hoeing, the distance of the rows, and
the quality of the soil, together with Certificates of
the number of acres, and that the land was afterwards
actually sown with wheat, be produced on or before the
second Tuesday in March, 1803.

18. BEANS. To the person who, in the year 1801,
shall discover and cultivate, either by the drill or dibbling-
method, on not less than five acres, a species of Horse
Beans or Tick Beans, that will ripen their seeds before the
first of August; the Silver Medal, or Twenty
Guineas.

It

It is required that a particular account of the Bean, the cultivation, and the expence attending it, with proper CERTIFICATES of the nature and condition of the land on which the experiments are made, together with an account of the produce, the weight per Winchester bushel, and a sample of not less than a quart, be produced to the Society, on or before the first Tuesday in December, 1801.

It is apprehended that if a Bean should be brought into cultivation with the habits of the Hotspur or other early Peas, that it would, in a great measure, escape the danger arising from the Collier insect, or other insects, and allow more time for the farmers to till the land for the subsequent crop of Wheat.

The ACCOUNTS and CERTIFICATES to be delivered on or before the first Tuesday in December, 1801.

19. The same premium is extended one year farther.

The ACCOUNTS and CERTIFICATES to be delivered on or before the first Tuesday in December, 1802.

20. COMPARATIVE CULTURE OF TURNIPS. For the best set of experiments made on not less than eight acres of land, four of which to be sown broad-cast, and four drilled, to ascertain whether it is most advantageous to cultivate Turnips by sowing them broad-cast and twice hand-hoeing them, or by drilling them in equidistant rows and horse-hoeing the intervals; the SILVER MEDAL, or TWENTY GUINEAS.

It is required that every operation and expense of each mode of culture be fully described, and that proper CERTIFICATES of the nature and condition of the land on which the experiments were made, together with the

weight

weight of the turnips grown, on a fair average sixteen perches of land, under each mode of culture, be produced to the Society on or before the first Tuesday in March, 1802.

21. PARSNIPS. To the person who, in the year 1801, shall cultivate the greatest quantity of land, not less than five acres, with Parsnips, for the sole purpose of feeding Cattle or Sheep; the GOLD MEDAL, or THIRTY GUINEAS.

CERTIFICATES of the quantity of land so cultivated, with a particular account of the nature of the soil and weight of the produce on sixteen perches, and also of the condition of the Cattle or Sheep fed with the Parsnips, and the advantages resulting from the practice, to be produced to the Society on or before the second Tuesday in February, 1802.·

22. ROTATION OF CROPS. To the person who shall, between the tenth of August, 1801, and the tenth of September, 1803, cultivate the greatest quantity of land, not less than sixty acres, in the following rotation, *viz.* first, Winter-Tares; second, Turnips; and third, Wheat; and apply the two former crops in the best and most farmer-like manner, to the rearing, supporting, and fattening, Cattle and Sheep, on the land which produced the crops; the GOLD MEDAL, or ONE HUNDRED GUINEAS.

23. For the next in quantity and merit, on not less than forty acres; the SILVER MEDAL, or FIFTY GUINEAS.

24.

24. For the next in quantity and merit, on not less than twenty acres, the SILVER MEDAL.

It is required that every operation and expense be fully described, and that satisfactory CERTIFICATES of the nature and condition of the soil on which the crops have grown, together with an account of their appearance, the number and kinds of Cattle fed by the two green crops, and, as near as possible, the improved value of the live stock by the consumption of those crops, and also the quantity and weight of the wheat and straw, be produced to the Society on or before the first day of March, 1804.

It is presumed that very great advantages will arise to such agriculturists as shall adopt this rotation of crops on a dry soil: they will be enabled, with the addition of a few acres of turnip-rooted Cabbage for spring-food, to keep such large flocks of Sheep, and herds of neat Cattle, as may secure a sufficient quantity of manure to fertilize their land in the highest degree, and in every situation.

It is farther conceived that Wheats which will bear sowing in the spring will be particularly suitable for this premium.

25. The same premium is extended one year farther.

CERTIFICATES to be delivered on or before the first day of March, 1805.

26. PRESERVING TURNIPS. To the person who shall discover to the Society the best and cheapest method of preserving Turnips perfectly sound, and in every respect fit for the purpose of supporting and fattening Sheep and neat Cattle, during the months of February, March, and April; the GOLD MEDAL, or THIRTY GUINEAS.

It

It is required that a full and accurate account of the method employed, and the expense attending the process; together with CERTIFICATES that the produce of four acres at the least has been preserved according to the method described, and applied to the feeding of Sheep and neat Cattle; that the whole were drawn out of the ground before the first day of February, in order to clear the greater part of it previous to its being prepared for Corn, and to save the soil from being exhausted by the Turnips; and also of the weight of an average sixteen perches of the crop; be produced to the Society on or before the first Tuesday in November, 1802.

*N. B. It is recommended to those who may be induced to try the necessary experiments for obtaining this and the following four premiums, to consider the method employed for the preservation of potatoes in ridges (which the growers call pies), and also the propriety of adopting a similar method in cases where they are previously frozen. It is supposed that, in the latter instance, the addition of ice or snow, and the construction of the ridges upon a large scale, may be sufficient to preserve the freezing temperature till the vegetables are wanted for the use of Cattle or Sheep, at which time they may be thawed by immersion in cold water, and the rot which a sudden thaw produces may be prevented.*

27.　For the next in quantity and merit, on not less than two acres, the SILVER MEDAL, or FIFTEEN GUINEAS.

28.　PRESERVING CABBAGES. To the person who shall discover to the Society the best and cheapest method of preserving drum-headed Cabbages perfectly sound, and in every respect fit for the purpose of support-

ing

ing and fattening Sheep and neat Cattle during the months of February, March, and April; the GOLD MEDAL, or THIRTY GUINEAS.

29. For the next in quantity and merit, on not less than two acres, the SILVER MEDAL, or FIFTEEN GUINEAS.

Conditions the same as for preserving Turnips, *Cl.* 26.

The ACCOUNTS to be produced on or before the first Tuesday in November, 1802.

30. PRESERVING CARROTS, PARSNIPS, OR BEETS. To the person who shall discover to the Society the best and cheapest method of preserving Carrots, Parsnips, or Beets, perfectly sound, and in every respect fit for the purpose of supporting and fattening Sheep and neat Cattle during the months of February, March, and April; the SILVER MEDAL, or FIFTEEN GUINEAS.

Conditions the same as for preserving Turnips, *Cl.* 26.

The ACCOUNTS to be delivered in, on or before the first Tuesday in November, 1802.

31. PRESERVING POTATOES. To the person who shall discover to the Society the best and cheapest method of preserving Potatoes, two or more years, perfectly sound, without vegetating, and in every other respect fit for the purpose of sets and the use of the table, and, consequently, of supporting and fattening Cattle; the SILVER MEDAL, or TWENTY GUINEAS.

It is required, that a full and accurate ACCOUNT of the method employed, and the expense attending the process,

C

with

with CERTIFICATES that one hundred bushels, at the least, have been preserved according to the method described, and that one or more bushels of the same Potatoes have been set, and produced a crop without any apparent diminution of their vegetative power; and also that they have been used at table with entire satisfaction to the persons who eat of them, together with a sample of one bushel; be sent to the Society on or before the first Tuesday in November, 1804.

32. MAKING MEADOW HAY IN WET WEATHER. To the person who shall discover to the Society the best and cheapest method, superior to any hitherto practised, of making Meadow Hay in Wet Weather; the GOLD MEDAL, or THIRTY GUINEAS.

A full account of the method employed, and of the expense attending the process, with not less than fifty-six pounds of the Hay; and Certificates that at least the produce of six acres of land has been made according to the method described, and that the whole is of equal quality with the samples; to be produced on or before the first Tuesday in January, 1802.

33. HARVESTING CORN IN WET WEATHER. To the person who shall discover to the Society the best and cheapest method, superior to any hitherto practised, of harvesting Corn in Wet Weather; the GOLD MEDAL, or THIRTY GUINEAS.

A full account of the method employed, and of the expense attending the process, with not less than two sheaves of the Corn, and Certificates that at least the produce of ten acres has been harvested according to the
method

method described, and that the whole is of equal quality with the samples, to be produced on or before the first Tuesday in January, 1802.

34. ASCERTAINING THE COMPONENT PARTS OF ARABLE LAND. To the person who shall produce to the Society the most satisfactory set of experiments, to ascertain the due proportion of the several component parts of Arable Land, in one or more Counties in Great Britain, by an accurate analysis of it; and who, having made a like analysis of some poor land, shall, by comparing the component parts of each, and thereby ascertaining the deficiencies of the poor soil, improve a quantity of it, not less than one acre, by the addition of such parts as the former experiments shall have discovered to be wanting therein, and therefore probably the cause of its sterility; the GOLD MEDAL, or FORTY GUINEAS.

It is required that the manurings, ploughings, and crops of the improved land, be the same after the improvement as before; and that a minute account of the produce in each state, of the weather, and of the various influencing circumstances, together with the method made use of in analysing the soils, be produced, with proper CERTIFI-CATES, and the chemical results of the analysis, which are to remain the property of the Society, on or before the last Tuesday in November, 1802.

It is expected that a quantity, not less than six pounds, of the rich, of the poor, and of the improved soils, be produced with the Certificates.

35. IMPROVING LAND LYING WASTE. For the most satisfactory account of the best method of im-

proving

proving any of the following soils, being land lying waste
or uncultivated, viz. Clay, Gravel, Sand, Chalk, Peat-
earth, and Bog, verified by experiments on not less than
fifty acres of land; the GOLD MEDAL, or THIRTY
GUINEAS.

36. For the next greatest quantity, not less than thirty
acres, the SILVER MEDAL, or TWENTY GUINEAS.

It is required that the land before such improvement be
absolutely uncultivated, and in a great measure useless;
and that, in its improved state, it be enclosed, cultivated,
and divided into closes.

CERTIFICATES of the number of acres, of the quality
of the land so improved, with a full account of every
operation and expense attending such improvement, the
state it is in as to the proportion of grass to arable, and
the average value thereof, to be produced on or before the
first Tuesday in February, 1803.

37. MANURES. For the most satisfactory set of ex-
periments, to ascertain the comparative advantages of the
following Manures, used as Top-dressings, on Grass or
Corn Land, viz. Soot, Coal-ashes, Wood-ashes, Lime,
Gypsum, Night-soil, or any other fit article; the GOLD
MEDAL, or the SILVER MEDAL and TWENTY GUI-
NEAS.

It is required that the above experiments be made between two or more of the above-mentioned Manures, and
that not less than two acres of land be dressed with each
Manure. An account of the nature of the soil, quantity
and expense of the Manure and Crops, with CERTIFI-
CATES, to be produced on or before the last Tuesday in
February, 1802.

38 The

38. The same premium is extended one year farther.

The Accounts and Certificates to be produced on or before the last Tuesday in February, 1803.

39. GAINING LAND FROM THE SEA. To the person who shall produce to the Society an account of the best method, verified by actual experiment, of gaining Land from the Sea, not less than twenty acres, on the coast of Great Britain; the Gold Medal.

Certificates of the quantity of Land, and that the experiments were begun after the first of January, 1796, to be produced to the Society on or before the first Tuesday in October, 1801.

40. The same premium is extended one year farther.

Certificates to be produced on or before the first Tuesday in October, 1802.

41. The same premium is extended one year farther.

Certificates to be produced on or before the first Tuesday in October, 1803.

42. MACHINE FOR DIBBLING WHEAT. To the person who shall invent the best Machine, to answer the purpose of Dibbling Wheat, by which the holes for receiving the Grain may be made at equal distances and proper depths, the grain regularly delivered therein, and effectually covered; the Silver Medal, or Twenty Guineas.

The Machine, with Certificates that at least three acres have been dibbled by it, to be produced to the Society on or before the second Tuesday in January, 1802.

Simplicity

Simplicity and cheapness in the construction will be considered as principal parts of its merit.

43. MACHINE FOR REAPING OR MOWING CORN. For inventing a Machine to answer the purpose of mowing or reaping Wheat, Rye, Barley, Oats, or Beans, by which it may be done more expeditiously and cheaper than by any method now practised, provided it does not shed the corn or pulse more than the methods in common practice, and that it lays the straw in such a manner that it may be easily gathered up for binding; the GOLD MEDAL, or THIRTY GUINEAS.

The MACHINE, with CERTIFICATES that at least three acres have been cut by it, to be produced to the Society on or before the second Tuesday in December, 1801. Simplicity and cheapness in the construction will be considered as principal parts of its merit.

44. THRESHING MACHINE. To the person who who shall invent a Machine by which Corn of all sorts may be threshed more expeditiously, effectually, and at a less expense, than by any method now in use; the GOLD MEDAL, or THIRTY GUINEAS.

The MACHINE or a Model, with proper CERTIFICATES that such a machine has been usefully applied, that at least thirty quarters have been threshed by it, and of the time employed in the operation, to be produced to the Society on or before the last Tuesday in February, 1802.

45. DESTROYING THE GRUB OF THE COCK-CHAFER. To the person who shall discover to the Society

Society an effectual method, verified by repeated and satisfactory trials, of destroying the Grub of the Cock-chafer, or of preventing or checking the destructive effects which always attend Corn, Peas, Beans, and Turnips, when attacked by those insects; the GOLD MEDAL, or THIRTY GUINEAS.

The ACCOUNTS, with proper CERTIFICATES, to be produced on or before the first Tuesday in January, 1802.

46. DESTROYING WORMS. To the person who shall discover to the Society an effectual method, verified by repeated and satisfactory trials, of destroying Worms, or of preventing the destructive effects they occasion on Corn, Beans, Peas, or other Pulse; the GOLD MEDAL, or THIRTY GUINEAS.

The ACCOUNTS, with proper CERTIFICATES, to be produced to the Society on or before the first Tuesday in January, 1802.

47. DESTROYING THE FLY ON HOPS. To the person who shall discover to the Society an easy and efficacious method of destroying the Fly on Hops, superior to any hitherto known or practised, on not less than six acres of Hop-ground; the GOLD MEDAL, or THIRTY GUINEAS.

ACCOUNTS and CERTIFICATES to be delivered to the Society on or before the first Tuesday in February, 1802.

48. CURE OF THE ROT IN SHEEP. To the person who shall discover to the Society the best and most effectual method of curing the Rot in Sheep, verified by

C 4 repeated

repeated and satisfactory experiments; the GOLD MEDAL, or FIFTY GUINEAS.

It is expected that the Candidates furnish accurate accounts of the symptoms and cure of the disease, together with the imputed cause thereof, and the actual or probable means of prevention, which, with proper CERTIFICATES, must be delivered to the Society on or before the first Tuesday in February, 1802.

49. PREVENTING THE ILL EFFECTS OF FLIES ON SHEEP. To the person who shall discover to the Society the most effectual method of protecting Sheep from being disturbed and injured by Flies; the SILVER MEDAL, or TWENTY GUINEAS.

It is required that the method be ascertained by repeated experiments, and that a CERTIFICATE of its efficacy be delivered to the Society on or before the first Tuesday in December, 1801.

50. PROTECTING SHEEP. To the person who, in the year 1801, shall protect the greatest number of Sheep, not fewer than one hundred, by hovels, sheds, or any other means, and give the most satisfactory account, verified by experiment, of the advantages arising from the practice of protecting Sheep from the inclemency of the weather, by hovels, sheds, or any other means; the SILVER MEDAL, or TWENTY GUINEAS.

A particular account of the experiments made, with the advantages arising therefrom, together with the expense, and CERTIFICATES of its utility, to be produced to the Society on or before the first Tuesday in March, 1802.

51.

**51.** The same premium is extended one year farther.

The ACCOUNTS and CERTIFICATES to be delivered on or before the first Tuesday in March, 1803.

*N. B.* It is required that the CERTIFICATES shall specify the length of time the Sheep were so protected, and the manner in which they were maintained during that time; together with the general method of managing them.

**52.** IMPROVING THE CONDITION OF THE LABOURING POOR, BY ERECTING COTTAGES, AND APPORTIONING LAND. To the person who, in the year 1801, shall erect the greatest number of Cottages for the accommodation of the Labouring Poor, and apportion not less than two acres of Land to each Cottage; the GOLD MEDAL.

The ACCOUNTS and CERTIFICATES to be delivered to the Society on or before the first Tuesday in February, 1802.

**53.** The same premium is extended one year farther.

The ACCOUNTS and CERTIFICATES to be delivered to the Society on or before the first Tuesday in February, 1803.

**54.** The same premium is extended one year farther.

The ACCOUNTS and CERTIFICATES to be delivered to the Society on or before the first Tuesday in February, 1804.

**55.** IMPROVING THE CONDITION OF THE LABOURING POOR, BY APPORTIONING LAND
TO

repeated and satisfactory experiments; the GOLD MEDAL, or FIFTY GUINEAS.

It is expected that the Candidates furnish accurate accounts of the symptoms and cure of the disease, together with the imputed cause thereof, and the actual or probable means of prevention, which, with proper CERTIFICATES, must be delivered to the Society on or before the first Tuesday in February, 1802.

49.　PREVENTING THE ILL EFFECTS OF FLIES ON SHEEP. To the person who shall discover to the Society the most effectual method of protecting Sheep from being disturbed and injured by Flies; the SILVER MEDAL, or TWENTY GUINEAS.

It is required that the method be ascertained by repeated experiments, and that a CERTIFICATE of its efficacy be delivered to the Society on or before the first Tuesday in December, 1801.

50.　PROTECTING SHEEP. To the person who, in the year 1801, shall protect the greatest number of Sheep, not fewer than one hundred, by hovels, sheds, or any other means, and give the most satisfactory account, verified by experiment, of the advantages arising from the practice of protecting Sheep from the inclemency of the weather, by hovels, sheds, or any other means; the SILVER MEDAL, or TWENTY GUINEAS.

A particular account of the experiments made, with the advantages arising therefrom, together with the expense, and CERTIFICATES of its utility, to the Society on or before ...
1802.

51. The same premium is extended one year farther.

The ACCOUNTS and CERTIFICATES to be delivered on or before the first Tuesday in March, 1803.

*N. B.* It is required that the CERTIFICATES shall specify the length of time the Sheep were so protected, and the manner in which they were maintained during that time; together with the general method of managing them.

52. IMPROVING THE CONDITION OF THE LABOURING POOR, BY ERECTING COTTAGES, AND APPORTIONING LAND. To the person who, in the year 1801, shall erect the greatest number of Cottages for the accommodation of the Labouring Poor, and apportion not less than two acres of Land to each Cottage; the GOLD MEDAL.

The ACCOUNTS and CERTIFICATES to be delivered to the Society on or before the first Tuesday in February, 1802.

53. The same premium is extended one year farther.

The ACCOUNTS and CERTIFICATES to be delivered to the Society on or before the first Tuesday in February, 1803.

e premium is extended one year farther.

TES to be delivered esday in February,

THE
ND
TO

It is required that a full and accurate account of the method employed, and the expense attending the process; together with CERTIFICATES that the produce of four acres at the least has been preserved according to the method described, and applied to the feeding of Sheep and neat Cattle; that the whole were drawn out of the ground before the first day of February, in order to clear the greater part of it previous to its being prepared for Corn, and to save the soil from being exhausted by the Turnips; and also of the weight of an average sixteen perches of the crop; be produced to the Society on or before the first Tuesday in November, 1802.

N. B. *It is recommended to those who may be induced to try the necessary experiments for obtaining this and the following four premiums, to consider the method employed for the preservation of potatoes in ridges (which the growers call pies), and also the propriety of adopting a similar method in cases where they are previously frozen. It is supposed that, in the latter instance, the addition of ice or snow, and the construction of the ridges upon a large scale, may be sufficient to preserve the freezing temperature till the vegetables are wanted for the use of Cattle or Sheep, at which time they may be thawed by immersion in cold water, and the rot which a sudden thaw produces may be prevented.*

27. For the next in quantity and merit, on not less than two acres, the SILVER MEDAL, or FIFTEEN GUINEAS.

28. PRESERVING CABBAGES. To the person who shall discover to the Society the best and cheapest method of preserving drum-headed Cabbages perfectly sound, and in every respect fit for the purpose of supporting

ing and fattening Sheep and neat Cattle during the months of February, March, and April; the GOLD MEDAL, or THIRTY GUINEAS.

29. For the next in quantity and merit, on not less than two acres; the SILVER MEDAL, or FIFTEEN GUINEAS.

Conditions the same as for preserving Turnips, *Cl.* 26.

The ACCOUNTS to be produced on or before the first Tuesday in November, 1802.

30. PRESERVING CARROTS, PARSNIPS, OR BEETS. To the person who shall discover to the Society the best and cheapest method of preserving Carrots, Parsnips, or Beets, perfectly sound, and in every respect fit for the purpose of supporting and fattening Sheep and neat Cattle during the months of February, March, and April; the SILVER MEDAL, or FIFTEEN GUINEAS.

Conditions the same as for preserving Turnips, *Cl.* 26.

The ACCOUNTS to be delivered in, on or before the first Tuesday in November, 1802.

31. PRESERVING POTATOES. To the person who shall discover to the Society the best and cheapest method of preserving Potatoes, two or more years, perfectly sound, without vegetating, and in every other respect fit for the purpose of sets and the use of the table, and, consequently, of supporting and fattening Cattle; the SILVER MEDAL, or TWENTY GUINEAS.

It is required, that a full and accurate ACCOUNT of the method employed, and the expense attending the process,

C

with

with CERTIFICATES that one hundred bushels, at the least, have been preserved according to the method described, and that one or more bushels of the same Potatoes have been set, and produced a crop without any apparent diminution of their vegetative power; and also that they have been used at table with entire satisfaction to the persons who eat of them, together with a sample of one bushel; be sent to the Society on or before the first Tuesday in November, 1804.

32. MAKING MEADOW HAY IN WET WEA-THER. To the person who shall discover to the Society the best and cheapest method, superior to any hitherto practised, of making Meadow Hay in Wet Weather; the GOLD MEDAL, or THIRTY GUINEAS.

A full account of the method employed, and of the expense attending the process, with not less than fifty-six pounds of the Hay; and Certificates that at least the produce of six acres of land has been made according to the method described, and that the whole is of equal quality with the samples; to be produced on or before the first Tuesday in January, 1802.

33. HARVESTING CORN IN WET WEATHER. To the person who shall discover to the Society the best and cheapest method, superior to any hitherto practised, of harvesting Corn in Wet Weather; the GOLD MEDAL, or THIRTY GUINEAS.

A full account of the method employed,. and of the expense attending the process, with not less than two sheaves of the Corn, and Certificates that at least the produce of ten acres has been harvested according to the
method

method described, and that the whole is of equal quality with the samples, to be produced on or before the first Tuesday in January, 1802.

34. ASCERTAINING THE COMPONENT PARTS OF ARABLE LAND. To the person who shall produce to the Society the most satisfactory set of experiments, to ascertain the due proportion of the several component parts of Arable Land, in one or more Counties in Great Britain, by an accurate analysis of it; and who, having made a like analysis of some poor land, shall, by comparing the component parts of each, and thereby ascertaining the deficiencies of the poor soil, improve a quantity of it, not less than one acre, by the addition of such parts as the former experiments shall have discovered to be wanting therein, and therefore probably the cause of its sterility; the GOLD MEDAL, or FORTY GUINEAS.

It is required that the manurings, ploughings, and crops of the improved land, be the same after the improvement as before; and that a minute account of the produce in each state, of the weather, and of the various influencing circumstances, together with the method made use of in analysing the soils, be produced, with proper CERTIFICATES, and the chemical results of the analysis, which are to remain the property of the Society, on or before the last Tuesday in November, 1802.

It is expected that a quantity, not less than six pounds, of the rich, of the poor, and of the improved soils, be produced with the Certificates.

35. IMPROVING LAND LYING WASTE. For the most satisfactory account of the best method of im-

proving

proving any of the following soils, being land lying waste or uncultivated, viz. Clay, Gravel, Sand, Chalk, Peat-earth, and Bog, verified by experiments on not less than fifty acres of land; the GOLD MEDAL, or THIRTY GUINEAS.

36.   For the next greatest quantity, not less than thirty acres, the SILVER MEDAL, or TWENTY GUINEAS.

It is required that the land before such improvement be absolutely uncultivated, and in a great measure useless; and that, in its improved state, it be enclosed, cultivated, and divided into closes.

CERTIFICATES of the number of acres, of the quality of the land so improved, with a full account of every operation and expense attending such improvement, the state it is in as to the proportion of grass to arable, and the average value thereof, to be produced on or before the first Tuesday in February, 1803.

37.   MANURES.   For the most satisfactory set of experiments, to ascertain the comparative advantages of the following Manures, used as Top-dressings, on Grass or Corn Land, viz. Soot, Coal-ashes, Wood-ashes, Lime, Gypsum, Night-soil, or any other fit article; the GOLD MEDAL, or the SILVER MEDAL and TWENTY GUINEAS.

It is required that the above experiments be made between two or more of the above-mentioned Manures, and that not less than two acres of land be dressed with each Manure.   An account of the nature of the soil, quantity and expense of the Manure and Crops, with CERTIFICATES, to be produced on or before the last Tuesday in February, 1802.

38   The

The Accounts and Certificates to be produced on or before the last Tuesday in February, 1803.

39. GAINING LAND FROM THE SEA. To the person who shall produce to the Society an account of the best method, verified by actual experiment, of gaining Land from the Sea, not less than twenty acres, on the coast of Great Britain; the Gold Medal.

Certificates of the quantity of Land, and that the experiments were begun after the first of January, 1796, to be produced to the Society on or before the first Tuesday in October, 1801.

40. The same premium is extended one year farther.

Certificates to be produced on or before the first Tuesday in October, 1802.

41. The same premium is extended one year farther.

Certificates to be produced on or before the first Tuesday in October, 1803.

42. MACHINE FOR DIBBLING WHEAT. To the person who shall invent the best Machine, to answer the purpose of Dibbling Wheat, by which the holes for receiving the Grain may be made at equal distances and proper depths, the grain regularly delivered therein, and effectually covered; the Silver Medal, or Twenty Guineas.

The Machine, with Certificates that at least three acres have been dibbled by it, to be produced to the Society on or before the second Tuesday in January, 1802.

　　　　　　　　Simplicity

Simplicity and cheapness in the construction will be considered as principal parts of its merit.

43. MACHINE FOR REAPING OR MOWING CORN. For inventing a Machine to answer the purpose of mowing or reaping Wheat, Rye, Barley, Oats, or Beans, by which it may be done more expeditiously and cheaper than by any method now practised, provided it does not shed the corn or pulse more than the methods in common practice, and that it lays the straw in such a manner that it may be easily gathered up for binding; the GOLD MEDAL, or THIRTY GUINEAS.

The MACHINE, with CERTIFICATES that at least three acres have been cut by it, to be produced to the Society on or before the second Tuesday in December, 1801. Simplicity and cheapness in the construction will be considered as principal parts of its merit.

44. THRESHING MACHINE. To the person who who shall invent a Machine by which Corn of all sorts may be threshed more expeditiously, effectually, and at a less expense, than by any method now in use; the GOLD MEDAL, or THIRTY GUINEAS.

The MACHINE or a Model, with proper CERTIFICATES that such a machine has been usefully applied, that at least thirty quarters have been threshed by it, and of the time employed in the operation, to be produced to the Society on or before the last Tuesday in February, 1802.

45. DESTROYING THE GRUB OF THE COCK-CHAFER. To the person who shall discover to the Society

Society an effectual method, verified by repeated and satisfactory trials, of destroying the Grub of the Cock-chafer, or of preventing or checking the destructive effects which always attend Corn, Peas, Beans, and Turnips, when attacked by those insects; the GOLD MEDAL, or THIRTY GUINEAS.

The ACCOUNTS, with proper CERTIFICATES, to be produced on or before the first Tuesday in January, 1802.

46. DESTROYING WORMS. To the person who shall discover to the Society an effectual method, verified by repeated and satisfactory trials, of destroying Worms, or of preventing the destructive effects they occasion on Corn, Beans, Peas, or other Pulse; the GOLD MEDAL, or THIRTY GUINEAS.

The ACCOUNTS, with proper CERTIFICATES, to be produced to the Society on or before the first Tuesday in January, 1802.

47. DESTROYING THE FLY ON HOPS. To the person who shall discover to the Society an easy and efficacious method of destroying the Fly on Hops, superior to any hitherto known or practised, on not less than six acres of Hop-ground; the GOLD MEDAL, or THIRTY GUINEAS.

ACCOUNTS and CERTIFICATES to be delivered to the Society on or before the first Tuesday in February, 1802.

48. CURE OF THE ROT IN SHEEP. To the person who shall discover to the Society the best and most effectual method of curing the Rot in Sheep, verified by

C 4         repeated

repeated and satisfactory experiments; the GOLD MEDAL, or FIFTY GUINEAS.

It is expected that the Candidates furnish accurate accounts of the symptoms and cure of the disease, together with the imputed cause thereof, and the actual or probable means of prevention, which, with proper CERTIFICATES, must be delivered to the Society on or before the first Tuesday in February, 1802.

49. PREVENTING THE ILL EFFECTS OF FLIES ON SHEEP. To the person who shall discover to the Society the most effectual method of protecting Sheep from being disturbed and injured by Flies; the SILVER MEDAL, or TWENTY GUINEAS.

It is required that the method be ascertained by repeated experiments, and that a CERTIFICATE of its efficacy be delivered to the Society on or before the first Tuesday in December, 1801.

50. PROTECTING SHEEP. To the person who, in the year 1801, shall protect the greatest number of Sheep, not fewer than one hundred, by hovels, sheds, or any other means, and give the most satisfactory account, verified by experiment, of the advantages arising from the practice of protecting Sheep from the inclemency of the weather, by hovels, sheds, or any other means; the SILVER MEDAL, or TWENTY GUINEAS.

A particular account of the experiments made, with the advantages arising therefrom, together with the expense, and CERTIFICATES of its utility, to be produced to the Society on or before the first Tuesday in March, 1802.

51.

51. The same premium is extended one year farther.

The Accounts and Certificates to be delivered on or before the first Tuesday in March, 1803.

*N. B.* It is required that the Certificates shall specify the length of time the Sheep were so protected, and the manner in which they were maintained during that time; together with the general method of managing them.

52. IMPROVING THE CONDITION OF THE LABOURING POOR, BY ERECTING COTTAGES, AND APPORTIONING LAND. To the person who, in the year 1801, shall erect the greatest number of Cottages for the accommodation of the Labouring Poor, and apportion not less than two acres of Land to each Cottage; the Gold Medal.

The Accounts and Certificates to be delivered to the Society on or before the first Tuesday in February, 1802.

53. The same premium is extended one year farther.

The Accounts and Certificates to be delivered to the Society on or before the first Tuesday in February, 1803.

54. The same premium is extended one year farther.

The Accounts and Certificates to be delivered to the Society on or before the first Tuesday in February, 1804.

55. IMPROVING THE CONDITION OF THE LABOURING POOR, BY APPORTIONING LAND

TO

TO COTTAGES. To the person who, in the year
1801, shall apportion to the greatest number of Cottages, already built upon his or her estate, any quantity
of Land, not less than two acres to each Cottage, for the
better accommodation of the respective Inhabitants; the
GOLD MEDAL.

The ACCOUNTS of the number of Cottages, and of the
quantity of Land apportioned to each, to be delivered to
the Society, with proper CERTIFICATES, on or before
the first Tuesday in February, 1802.

56. The same premium is extended one year farther.

The ACCOUNTS and CERTIFICATES to be delivered
on or before the first Tuesday in February, 1803.

57. The same premium is extended one year farther.

The ACCOUNTS and CERTIFICATES to be delivered on
or before the first Tuesday in February, 1804.

58. PRESERVING SEEDS OF VEGETABLES.
For the best method of preserving the Seeds of Plants in a state fit for Vegetation a longer time than has hitherto been practised, such method being superior to any known to the public, and verified by sufficient trial; to be communicated to the Society on or before the first Tuesday in December, 1801; the GOLD MEDAL, or THIRTY GUINEAS.

59. PREVENTING THE DRY-ROT IN TIMBER.
To the person who shall discover to the Society the cause of the Dry-rot in Timber, and disclose a certain method of prevention, superior to any hitherto known; the GOLD MEDAL, or THIRTY GUINEAS.

The ACCOUNTS of the cause, and method of prevention, confirmed by repeated experiments, to be produced to the Society on or before the second Tuesday in December, 1801.

60. PRESERVING FRESH WATER SWEET.
To the person who shall produce to the Society the best Account, verified by satisfactory trials, of an efficacious method of preserving Fresh Water sweet, during long voyages; the GOLD MEDAL, or FIFTY GUINEAS.

ACCOUNTS, and full descriptions of the methods made use of, in order that it may be known that nothing injurious enters therein, to be produced to the Society, with at least

thirty

thirty gallons of water so preserved, and proper CER-
TIFICATES, on or before the last Tuesday in December,
1801.

61.  PRESERVING SALTED PROVISIONS FROM
BECOMING RANCID OR RUSTY.   To the person
who shall discover to the Society the best, cheapest, and
most efficacious method of preserving Salted Provisions
from growing Rancid or Rusty; the GOLD MEDAL, or
THIRTY GUINEAS.

A full description of the method, with proper CERTI-
FICATES that it has been found, on repeated trials, to
answer the purpose intended, to be produced to the Society on or before the first Tuesday in February, 1802.

62.  CLEARING  FEATHERS  FROM  THEIR
ANIMAL OIL.   To the person who shall discover to the
Society the best and most expeditious method, superior to
any hitherto practised, of clearing Goose-feathers from
their offensive animal Oil, for the use of upholders, in
making beds, cushions, &c. the SILVER MEDAL, or
TWENTY GUINEAS.

A quantity of such Feathers unstripped and so cleaned,
not less than forty pounds weight, with a full account of
the process, to be produced to the Society on or before the
first Tuesday in February, 1802.

63.  REFINING WHALE OR SEAL OIL.   For disclosing to the Society an effectual method of purifying
Whale or Seal Oil from the glutinous matter that incrusts
the wicks of lamps and extinguishes the light, though
fully supplied with Oil; the GOLD MEDAL, or FIFTY
GUINEAS.

It

It is required that the whole of the process be fully and fairly disclosed, in order that satisfactory experiments may be made by the Society, to determine the validity of the claim; and CERTIFICATES that not less than twenty gallons have been purified according to the process delivered in, together with two gallons of the Oil in its unpurified state, and two gallons so refined, be produced to the Society on or before the second Tuesday in February, 1802.

### 64. MANUFACTURING TALLOW CANDLES.

To the person who shall discover to the Society a method of hardening or otherwise preparing Tallow, so that Candles may be made of it, which will burn as clear and with as small a wick as wax candles without running, and may be afforded at a less expense than any at present made with spermaceti; the GOLD MEDAL, or THIRTY GUINEAS.

CERTIFICATES that one hundred and twelve pounds of such Tallow have been made into Candles, and twelve pounds of the Candles made thereof, to be produced to the Society on or before the second Tuesday in January, 1802.

### 65. CANDLES FROM RESIN OR OTHER SUBSTANCES.

To the person who shall discover to the Society the best method of making Candles of Resin, or any other substance, fit for common use, at a price much inferior to those made of Tallow only; the GOLD MEDAL, or THIRTY GUINEAS.

Six pounds at least of the Candles so prepared, with an ACCOUNT of the process, to be delivered to the Society on or before the first Tuesday in December, 1801.

66.

**66. METHOD OF SEPARATING SUGAR IN A SOLID FORM FROM TREACLE.** To the person who shall discover to the Society the best method of separating Sugar from Treacle in a solid form, at such an expense as will render it advantageous to the public; the GOLD MEDAL, or FIFTY GUINEAS.

A quantity of the Sugar so prepared in a solid form, not less than thirty pounds weight, with an account of the process, and CERTIFICATES that not less than one hundred weight has been prepared, to be produced to the Society on or before the first Tuesday in February, 1802.

**67. PROOF SPIRIT.** To the distiller who, in the year 1801, shall make the greatest quantity, not less than one hundred gallons, of a clean marketable Spirit, from articles not the food of man or cattle, equal in strength or quality to the Proof Spirit now in use, and at a rate not higher than the spirit produced from Corn or Melasses; the GOLD MEDAL, or ONE HUNDRED GUINEAS.

Ten gallons of the Spirit, together with proper CERTIFICATES, and a full account of the expense and mode of making it, to be produced to the Society on or before the first Tuesday in January, 1802.

**68. INCREASING STEAM.** To the person who shall invent and discover to the Society a method, verified by actual experiments, of increasing the quantity or force of Steam, in Steam-engines, with less fuel than has hitherto been employed, provided that in general the whole amount of the expenses in using Steam-engines may be considerably lessened; the GOLD MEDAL, or THIRTY GUINEAS.

To

To be communicated to the Society on or before the first Tuesday in January, 1802.

69. DESTROYING SMOKE. For the best account, ascertained by proper experiments, of a cheap method of burning the Smoke of Fires belonging to Steam-engines, Furnaces employed in calcining or smelting metals, or other large works, in order to prevent annoyance to the neighbourhood; the GOLD MEDAL, or THIRTY GUINEAS.

To be produced on or before the first Tuesday in January, 1802.

70. CONDENSING SMOKE. To the person who shall invent the best method by which the Smoke of Steam-engines, Brewhouses, Sugar-houses, or Furnaces, may be advantageously condensed and collected in the form of tar, or some other useful material; the GOLD MEDAL, or FIFTY GUINEAS.

₰ The ACCOUNTS, with proper CERTIFICATES of the method having been successfully employed, and specimens of the materials produced, to be delivered to the Society on or before the first Tuesday in January, 1802.

71. SUBSTITUTE FOR TAR. To the person who shall invent and discover to the Society the best substitute for Vegetable Tar, equal in all its properties to the best Stockholm Tar, and prepared from materials the produce of Great Britain; the GOLD MEDAL, or ONE HUNDRED GUINEAS.

A quantity of the Substitute, not less than one hundred weight, with CERTIFICATES that at least one ton has been
manu-

manufactured, and that it can be afforded at a price not exceeding that of the best foreign Tar, together with an account of the process, to be delivered to the Society on or before the first Tuesday in March, 1802.

72. PREPARATION OF TAN. To the person who shall prepare in the most concentrated form, so as to be easily portable, and at a price applicable to the purposes of manufacturers, the largest quantity, not less than one hundred weight, of the principle called by the French *Tannin*, which abounds in Oak-bark and many other vegetable substances; the GOLD MEDAL, or FIFTY GUINEAS.

CERTIFICATES of the above quantity having been prepared, and a sample of not less than twenty-eight pounds, to be produced to the Society on or before the last Tuesday in January, 1802.

73. PREPARATION OF A RED STAIN FOR COTTON CLOTH. To the person who shall communicate to the Society the cheapest and most effectual method of Printing or Staining Cotton Cloths with a Red Colour, by an immediate application of the colouring-matter to the cloth, equally beautiful and durable with the red colours now generally procured from decoctions of madder; the Gold MEDAL, or THIRTY GUINEAS.

CERTIFICATES that the above process has been advantageously used on ten pieces of calico, each twenty-one yards or upwards in length, one piece of the calico so printed, a quart of the colour in a liquid state, and a full account of the preparation and application, to be produced to the Society on or before the second Tuesday in January, 1802.

74.

74. PREPARATION OF A GREEN COLOUR FOR PRINTING COTTON CLOTH. To the person who shall communicate to the Society the best and cheapest method of Printing with a full Green Colour on Cotton Cloth, by an immediate application of the colouring-matter from a wooden block to the Cloth, equally beautiful and durable as the colours now formed from the complicated process of the decoction of weld on alumine and the solutions of indigo by earths or alcaline salts; the GOLD MEDAL, or THIRTY GUINEAS.

CERTIFICATES and conditions as for premium 73.

75. SUBSTITUTE FOR THE BASIS OF PAINT. To the person who shall produce to the Society the best Substitute, superior to any hitherto known, for the Basis of Paint, equally proper for the purpose as the White Lead now employed; such Substitute not to be of a noxious quality, and to be afforded at a price not materially higher than that of White Lead; the GOLD MEDAL, or ONE HUNDRED GUINEAS.

A quantity of the Substitute, not less than fifty pounds weight, with an ACCOUNT of the process used in preparing it, and CERTIFICATES that at least one hundred weight has been manufactured, to be produced to the Society on or before the first Tuesday in January, 1802.

76. RED PIGMENT. To the person who shall discover to the Society a full and satisfactory process for preparing a Red Pigment, fit for use, in oil or water, equal in tone or brilliancy to the best Carmines and Lakes

D now

now known or in use, and perfectly durable; the GOLD MEDAL, or THIRTY GUINEAS.

One pound weight of such Colour, and a full disclosure of its preparation, to be produced to the Society on or before the first Tuesday in February, 1802.

*N. B.* It is not required that the Colour should resist the action of fire or chemical applications, but remain unaltered by the common exposure to strong light, damps, and noisome vapours.

77. ULTRAMARINE. To the person who shall prepare an artificial Ultramarine, equal in colour, brilliancy, and durability, to the best prepared from Lapis Lazuli, and which may be afforded at a cheap rate; the GOLD MEDAL, or THIRTY GUINEAS.

The conditions are the same as in the preceding premium for the Red Pigment.

78. ANALYSIS OF BRITISH MINERALS. To the person who shall communicate to the Society the most correct Analysis of any Mineral production of Great Britain, hitherto either unexamined, or not examined with accuracy; the GOLD MEDAL.

The Analysis and sufficient specimens to be produced to the Society on or before the first Tuesday in January, 1802.

79. PREPARATION OF SULPHURIC ACID FROM SULPHUR, WITHOUT THE USE OF ANY NITRIC SALT. To the person who shall prepare the
largest

largest quantity (not less than one ton) of Sulphuric Acid from Sulphur, without any Nitric Salt, of a specific gravity, not inferior to the best Sulphuric Acid of commerce; the GOLD MEDAL, or FIFTY GUINEAS.

CERTIFICATES that not less than the above quantity of such an Acid has been prepared, together with a sample, to be produced to the Society on or before the first Tuesday in January, 1802.

80. PREPARATION OF ANY ALKALINE OR EARTHY NITRATE. To the person who shall prepare, in Great Britain, the largest quantity, not less than one hundred weight, of any salt of Nitric Acid, with either earths or alkalies, by a method superior to those hitherto practised; the GOLD MEDAL, or ONE HUNDRED GUINEAS.

CERTIFICATES of the above quantity having been prepared, and a sample of not less than twenty-eight pounds, to be produced to the Society on or before the last Tuesday in January, 1802.

81. FINE BAR-IRON. To the person, in Great Britain, who shall make the greatest quantity of Bar-Iron, not less than ten tons, with Coak, from Coak-Pigs, equal in quality to the best iron imported from Sweden or Russia, and as fit for converting into steel; the GOLD MEDAL, or FIFTY GUINEAS.

Samples, not less than one hundred weight, with CERTIFICATES that the whole quantity is of equal quality, to be produced to the Society on or before the first Tuesday in January, 1802.

**82. PRESERVING IRON FROM RUST.** To the person who shall invent and discover to the Society a cheap composition, superior to any now in use, which shall effectually preserve Wrought Iron from Rust; the GOLD MEDAL, or FIFTY GUINEAS.

A full description of the method of preparing the composition, with CERTIFICATES that it has stood at least two years unimpaired, being exposed to the atmosphere during the whole time, to be produced to the Society, with ten pounds weight of the composition, on or before the first Tuesday in January, 1802.

83. The same premium is extended one year farther.

The description and CERTIFICATES to be produced to the Society on or before the last Tuesday in January, 1803.

84. **REFINING BLOCK TIN.** To the person who shall discover to the Society the best method of purifying or refining Block Tin, so as to render it fit for the finest purposes to which Grain Tin is now applied, and not higher in price; the GOLD MEDAL, or FIFTY GUINEAS.

CERTIFICATES that not less than three tons have been refined or purified, with a full detail of the process, and a quantity, not less than one hundred weight, of the Tin so refined, to be produced to the Society on or before the first Tuesday in January, 1802.

85. **GLAZING EARTHEN WARE WITHOUT LEAD.** To the person who shall discover to the Society the cheapest, safest, most durable, and most easily fusible

ble composition, fit for the purpose of Glazing the ordinary kinds of Earthen Ware, without any preparation of Lead, and superior to any hitherto in use; the GOLD MEDAL, or THIRTY GUINEAS.

Specimens of the Ware so glazed, with proper CERTIFICATES of its having succeeded, and a sample of the materials made use of, to be produced to the Society on or before the first Tuesday in February, 1802.

*Premiums for promoting the Polite Arts.*

86. HONORARY PREMIUMS FOR DRAWING, BY NOBILITY. For the best Drawing, of any kind, made with water-colours, crayons, chalk, black lead, pen, Indian ink, or bister, by young Gentlemen under the age of twenty-one, sons or grandsons of Peers, or Peeresses in their own right, of Great Britain or Ireland, to be produced on or before the first Tuesday in March, 1802; the HONORARY MEDAL OF THE SOCIETY IN GOLD.

87. The same in Silver for the next in merit.

88. The same premiums will be given, on the like conditions, to young Ladies, daughters or grand-daughters of Peers, or Peeresses in their own right, of Great-Britain or Ireland.

89. HONORARY PREMIUMS FOR DRAWING, BY GENTLEMEN. For the best Drawing, of any kind, made with water-colours, crayons, chalk, black lead, pen, Indian ink, or bister, by young Gentlemen under the age of twenty-one; to be produced on or before the first Tuesday in March, 1802; the GOLD MEDAL.

90. For the next in merit, the SILVER MEDAL.

91. The same premiums will be given for Drawings by young Ladies.

*N. B.* As the foregoing Honorary Premiums are intended only for such of the Nobility and Gentry as may hereafter become patrons or patronesses of the Arts, persons professing} any branch of the Polite Arts, or any business dependent on the Arts of Design, or the sons or daughters of such persons, will not be admitted Candidates in these Classes.

92. DRAWINGS OF OUTLINES. For the best Outline, after an original group or cast, in Plaster, of Human Figures, by persons of either sex, under the age of sixteen, the principal figure not less than twelve inches; to be produced on or before the third Tuesday in February, 1802; the greater SILVER PALLET.

93. For the next in merit, the lesser SILVER PALLET.

*N. B.* These Drawings are to be made on paper, and the original either to be produced to the Society, or to be referred to for their examination.

94. DRAWINGS OF LANDSCAPES. For the best Drawing of a Landscape after nature, by persons of either sex, under twenty-one years of age, to be produced on or before the third Tuesday in February, 1802; the greater SILVER PALLET.

95. For the next in merit, the lesser SILVER PALLET.

Each candidate must mention, on the front of the Drawing, whence the View was taken; and the Drawings

D 4                                                        mus must be made with Chalk, Pen, Indian Ink, Water-Colours, or Bister.

96. HISTORICAL DRAWINGS. For the best Historical Drawing, being an original composition, of five or more Human Figures; the height of the principal figure not less than eight inches; to be made with crayons, chalk, black lead, pen, Indian ink, water-colours, or Bister, and to be produced on or before the third Tuesday in February, 1802; the GOLD PALLET.

97. For the next in merit, the greater SILVER PALLET.

98. STROKE ENGRAVINGS OF HISTORICAL SUBJECTS. For the best Stroke Engraving, published in the year 1801, of an historical subject, the size of the plate not less than eighteen inches by fourteen; the GOLD MEDAL.

To be produced to the Society on or before the last Tuesday in January, 1802; and the impression to which the premium is adjudged to remain the property of the Society.

99. For the next in merit, the SILVER MEDAL, on similar conditions.

100. CHINTS PATTERNS FOR CALICO-PRINTERS. For the best Original Pattern in a new taste, of light or dark ground Chints for garment-work, fit for the purposes of Calico-Printers, by persons of either sex; the GOLD MEDAL.

To

To be produced to the Society on or before the second Tuesday in January, 1802; the Pattern to which the premium is adjudged to remain the property of the Society.

101. For the next in merit, the SILVER MEDAL, on similar conditions.

102, COPPER-PLATE PATTERNS FOR CALICO PRINTERS. For the best Pattern, in a new style, fit for the *purposes* of Calico-Printers for garment-work, the SILVER MEDAL.

To be produced to the Society on or before the second Tuesday in January, 1802.

The Pattern to which the premium is adjudged to remain the property of the Society.

103. ENGRAVING ON WOOD. For the best Engraving on Wood, for illustrating works in arts or sciences, or for decorating books, and capable of being worked with the letter-press; the SILVER MEDAL.

The Engraving, and two or more impressions from it, to be produced to the Society on or before the second Tuesday in January, 1802; and the impressions from that engraving to which the premium is adjudged to remain the property of the Society.

*The following Premium (Class 104) is offered in conformity to the Will of the late John Stock, of Hampstead, Esq.*

104. SCULPTURE. For the best Basso-relievo in Terra Cotta, the subject taken from the Iliad of Homer,

and

and consisting of not fewer than three human figures, the height of the principal figure not less than twelve inches, to be produced on or before the third Tuesday in February, 1802 ; a SILVER MEDALLION, with the following engraved inscription : *The Premium given by the Society for the Encouragement of Arts, Manufactures, and Commerce, in conformity to the Will of John Stock, of Hampstead, Esq.*

The Basso-relievo to which the premium is adjudged, to remain the property of the Society.

105. BRONZES. For the best Drapery Figure or Group cast in Bronze; if a single Figure, not less than twelve inches high ; and, if a Group, not less than nine inches ; and which will require the least additional labour to repair; the GOLD MEDAL, or the SILVER MEDAL and TWENTY GUINEAS.

The Cast to be exhibited to the Society before it is begun to be repaired, with the original Figure or Group, on or before the first Tuesday in February, 1802, together with a full explanation of the whole process.

106. SURVEYS OF COUNTIES. To the person who, in the year 1801, shall complete and publish an accurate Survey of any one County in England or Wales, on a scale of not less than one inch to a mile, for which rewards have not already been given by the Society ; the GOLD MEDAL, or FIFTY GUINEAS.

CERTIFICATES of the accuracy of the Survey, and that it was begun after the first of June, 1797, together with the Map, to be produced on or before the first Tuesday in January, 1802.

The

The Map to which the premium shall be adjudged, to remain the property of the Society.

*N. B.* The Society is already in possession of Surveys of the following Counties, viz. Bedford, Cheshire, Cornwall, Cumberland, Derbyshire, Devonshire, Dorsetshire, Durham, Hampshire, Herefordshire, Hertfordshire, Huntingdonshire, Lancashire, Leicestershire, Northamptonshire, North Wales (large and small), Nottinghamshire, Oxfordshire, Somersetshire, Staffordshire, Suffolk, Surrey, Sussex, Westmoreland, and Worcestershire.

107. NATURAL HISTORY. To the Author who shall publish, in the year 1801, the Natural History of any County in England or Wales; the GOLD MEDAL, or FIFTY GUINEAS.

It is required that the several natural productions, whether animal, vegetable, or mineral, peculiar to the County, or found therein, be carefully and specifically arranged and described, in order that the public may be enabled to judge what Arts or Manufactures are most likely to succeed in such County.

The Work to be delivered to the Society on or before the last Tuesday in January, 1802.

———

## CONDITIONS FOR THE POLITE ARTS.

No person who has gained the first premium in any Class, will be admitted a Candidate in a Class of an inferior age; and no Candidate shall receive more than one Premium in one year; nor will they, who for two successive years shall gain the first Premium in one Class, be ever again admitted as Candidates in that Class.

No

No person shall ever be admitted a Candidate in any Class, in which he has three times obtained the whole of the first Premium.

No Candidate shall send in more than one Performance in any one Class.

All the Claims which are produced each Session before the Committee of Polite Arts (to which Premiums or Bounties are adjudged) are to remain with the Society till after the public distribution of Rewards in May; and after that re-delivered, unless where mentioned in the Premiums to the contrary.

No Claim for a Premium in the Polite Arts will be admitted, that has obtained, or has been produced in order to obtain, a Premium, Reward, or Gratification, from any other Society, or any Academy or School.

All performances that obtain Premiums in the Polite Arts, must be begun after the publication of such Premiums.

Purposely to encourage real merit, and to prevent any attempts to impose on the Society, by producing drawings which shall have been made or retouched by any other person than the Candidate, the Society is resolved, upon all occasions, with respect to the successful candidates in classes 86 to 97 inclusive, to prove their abilities, by requiring a specimen, made under the inspection of the Committee of Polite Arts, in every instance where such proof can be obtained.

It is required that all Candidates in the Polite Arts do signify, on their Drawings, their age; and whether the performances are originals or copies; and, if copies, whence they were taken.

*Premiums for encouraging and improving Manu- .factures.*

108. **MACHINE FOR CARDING SILK.** For the best Machine, superior to any now in use, for carding Waste Silk equally well as by hand; to be produced, to-gether with a specimen of the Cardings, on or before the first Tuesday in November, 1801; the SILVER MEDAL, or TWENTY GUINEAS.

109. **CLOTH HOP-STALKS OR BINES.** To the person who shall produce to the Society the greatest quan-tity, not less than thirty yards, of Cloth, at least twenty-seven inches wide, made in Great Britain, of Hop-Stalks or Bines, and much finer in quality than any hitherto ma-nufactured in England of that material; the GOLD MEDAL, or THIRTY GUINEAS.

One pound of the Thread of which the Cloth is made, and thirty yards of the Cloth, together with proper CER-TIFICATES that the whole is manufactured from Hop-Stalks or Bines, to be produced to the Society on or before the first Tuesday in December, 1801.

*N. B.* The Society is already in possession of Cloth made in England from Hop-Stalks or Bines, which may be inspected by application to the Register.

110. **WICKS FOR CANDLES OR LAMPS.** To the person who shall discover to the Society a method of manufacturing Hop-Stalks or Bines, or any other cheap material, the growth of Great Britain, so as to render them

them fit for the purpose of supplying the place of Cotton, for Wicks of Candles or Lamps; TWENTY GUINEAS.

SAMPLES, not less than five pounds weight, of the Wicks, so prepared, to be produced to the Society, with CERTIFICATES that the whole quantity is equal in quality to the Sample, on or before the second Tuesday in January, 1802.

111. PAPER FROM RAW VEGETABLE SUB-STANCES. To the person, in Great Britain, who shall, between the first of January, 1801, and the first of January, 1802, make the greatest quantity, and of the best quality, not less than ten reams, of good and useful Paper, from Raw Vegetable Substances, the produce of Great Britain or Ireland, of which one hundred weight has not been used in manufacturing Paper previous to January, 1801, superior to any hitherto manufactured from such Substances, and which can be generally afforded as cheap as paper of equal quality and apppearance now made from rags; TWENTY GUINEAS.

· N. B. The object of the Society being to add to the number and quantity of raw materials used in this manufacture, it is their wish to include every useful sort of Paper, and to introduce such natural products as can be easily and cheaply procured in great quantities. The Society are in possession of two volumes containing a great variety of specimens of Paper made from Raw Vegetable Substances, viz. Nettles, Potatoe-Hawlm, Poplar, Hop-Bines, &c. which volumes may be inspected by any person on application to the Register.

CERTIFICATES of the making such Paper, and one ream of the Paper, to be produced on or before the second Tuesday in January, 1802.

112.

112. TAKING PORPOISES. To the people in any boat or vessel, who, in the year 1801, shall take the greatest number of Porpoises, on the coast of Great Britain, by Gun-Harpoon, or any other method, not fewer than thirty, for the purpose of extracting oil from them; the GOLD MEDAL, or THIRTY POUNDS.

CERTIFICATES of the number, signed by the persons to whom they have been sold or delivered for the purpose of extracting the oil, to be produced to the Society, on or before the last Tuesday in January, 1802.

113. OIL FROM PORPOISES. To the person who shall manufacture the greatest quantity of Oil from Porpoises taken on the coast of Great Britain, in the year 1800, not less thirty tons; the GOLD MEDAL, or THIRTY POUNDS.

*Premiums for Inventions in Mechanics.*

114. TRANSIT-INSTRUMENT. To the person who shall invent and produce to the Society a cheap and portable Transit-instrument, which may easily be converted into a Zenith-sector, capable of being accurately and expeditiously adjusted for the purpose of finding the latitudes and longitudes of places, and superior to any portable Transit-instrument now in use; the GOLD MEDAL, or FORTY GUINEAS.

To be produced on or before the last Tuesday in January, 1802.

115. TAKING WHALES BY THE GUN-HARPOON. To the person who, in the year 1801, shall strike the greatest number of Whales, not fewer than three, with the Gun-harpoon; TEN GUINEAS.

Proper CERTIFICATES of the striking such Whales, and that they were actually taken in the year 1800, signed by the Master, or by the Mate when the Claim is made by the Master, to be produced to the Society on or before the last Tuesday in December, 1801.

116. DRIVING BOLTS INTO SHIPS. To the person who shall invent and produce to the Society a Model, shewing a method of driving Bolts into Ships, particularly those of Copper, without splitting the head or bending them, with more dispatch, in all directions, and tighter, than by any means hitherto known or in use; the GOLD MEDAL, or FORTY GUINEAS.

The

The Model, with Certificates that a Machine on the same construction has been used to advantage, to be produced to the Society on before the first Tuesday in February, 1802.

· 117. PARISH OR FAMILY-MILL. To the person who shall invent and produce o the Society the best constructed Mill for grinding Corn for the use of private Families, or Parish-poor ; the construction to be such as to render the working of the Mill easy and expeditious, and superior to any hitherto in use ; the Gold Medal, or Forty Guineas.

The Mill, and Certificates of its having been used to good effect, to be produced to the Society on or before the first Tuesday in February, 1802.

N. B. Cheapness and simplicity will be considered as essential parts of its merit ; and the Mill, or the Model, to remain with the Society.

118. MACHINE FOR RAISING COALS, ORE, &c. &c. To the person who shall invent a Machine for raising Coals, Ore, &c. from Mines, superior to any hitherto known or in use, and which shall produce the effect at a less expense than those already known or in use ; the Gold Medal, or Fifty Guineas.

A Model of the Machine, made on a scale of not less than one inch to a foot, with a Certificate that a Machine at large on the same construction has been advantageously used, to be produced to the Society on or before the second Tuesday in February, 1802.

119. MACHINE FOR RAISING WATER. To the person who shall invent a Machine on a better, cheaper, and more simple construction than any hitherto known or

E                                    in

in use, for raising Water out of Wells, &c. from a depth of not less than fifty feet; the GOLD MEDAL, or FORTY GUINEAS.

CERTIFICATES of the performance of the Machine, and a Model of it, on a scale of not less than one inch to a foot, to be produced to the Society on or before the first Tuesday in February, 1802.

120. MACHINE FOR MAKING BRICKS. To the person who shall invent the best and cheapest Machine for making Bricks, superior to any hitherto known or in use, whereby the labour and expense of making Bricks in the usual mode, by hand, may be greatly diminished; FORTY GUINEAS.

A Model, with CERTIFICATES that a Machine at large, on the same construction, has been used to good effect for the purpose of making Bricks, and that at least one hundred thousand Statute Bricks have been made therewith, to be produced to the Society on or before the first Tuesday in March, 1802.

121. BORING AND BLASTING ROCKS. To the person who shall discover to the Society a more cheap, simple, and expeditious Method than any hitherto known or in use, of Boring and Blasting Rocks in Mines, Shafts, Wells, &c. the GOLD MEDAL, or FORTY GUINEAS.

CERTIFICATES of the Method having been practised with success, with a full description thereof, to be delivered to the Society on or before the first Tuesday in January, 1802.

122. GUNPOWDER-MILLS. To the person who, in the year 1801, shall invent and bring to perfection the

most

most effectual method of so conducting the works of Gun-powder-Mills, in the business of making Gunpowder as to prevent explosion; the GOLD MEDAL, or ONE HUN-DRED GUINEAS.

CERTIFICATES and ACCOUNTS of the Method having been put in practice in one or more Gunpowder-Mills in this kingdom, and that it promises, in the opinion of the best judges concerned in such works, to answer the pur-pose intended, to be produced to the Society on or before the first Tuesday in February, 1802.

*N. B.* As an encouragement to persons to turn their thoughts to improvements of this nature, if any should be made on the present method of conducting the business of Gunpowder-making, which fall short of the total preven-tion of explosion, and they are sent to the Society, for the sake of humanity the papers so sent in will receive due consideration, and such Bounty or Reward will be be-stowed thereon as they appear to merit.

123. MILL-STONES. To the person who shall dis-cover, in Great Britain, a Quarry of Stone fit for the pur-poses of Mill-stones, for grinding Wheat, and equal in all respects to that stone known by the name of FRENCH BURR; the GOLD MEDAL, or ONE HUNDRED POUNDS.

A pair of Mill-Stones, at least three feet eight inches diameter, with an account of the situation of the Quarry, and CERTIFICATES that not fewer than two pair of such Mill-Stones have been effectually used for grinding Wheat, to be produced to the Society on or before the first Tues-day in February, 1802.

124. HEATING ROOMS FOR THE PURPOSES OF MANUFACTURERS. To the person who shall in-

vent

vent and discover to the Society a Method of Heating
Rooms, superior to any hitherto known or in use, and at
a moderate expense, for the purposes of Painters, Japanners, and other Manufacturers, so as to avoid the necessity
of iron or copper tunnels going through the rooms to convey the smoke, whereby the danger from such tunnels may
be prevented; the GOLD MEDAL, or FORTY GUINEAS.

A Model, or complete Drawing and Description of the
Method, with CERTIFICATES that it has been successfully practised, to be delivered to the Society on or before
the last Tuesday in March, 1802.

125.  IMPROVED VENTILATION.  To the per-
son who shall invent and produce to the Society a mode
of permanently Ventilating the Apartments in Hospitals,
Work-Houses, and other crowded places, superior to any
now known or used; the GOLD MEDAL, or FIFTY
GUINEAS.

A Model of the Apparatus, and a full Account of the
means by which the effect has been produced, with proper
CERTIFICATES, to be delivered to the Society on or before the last Tuesday in February, 1802.

## *Premiums offered for the Advantage of the British Colonies.*

126. NUTMEGS. For the greatest quantity of merchantable Nutmegs, not less than ten pounds weight, being the growth of his Majesty's dominions in the West Indies, or any of the British Settlements on the Coast of Africa, or the several Islands adjacent thereto, and equal to those imported from the Islands of the East Indies; the GOLD MEDAL, or ONE HUNDRED GUINEAS.

Satisfactory CERTIFICATES, from the Governor or Commander in Chief, of the place of growth, with an account of the number of trees, their age, nearly the quantity of fruit on each tree, and the manner of culture, to be produced on or before the first Tuesday in December, 1801.

127. The same premium is extended one year farther.

CERTIFICATES to be produced on or before the second Tuesday in December, 1802.

128. CINNAMON. For importing into the port of London, in the year 1801, the greatest quantity, not less than twenty pounds weight, of Cinnamon, being the growth of some of the Islands in the West Indies belonging to the Crown of Great Britain, or any of the British Settlements on the Coast of Africa, or the several Islands adjacent thereto, and equal in goodness to the Cinnamon brought from the East Indies; the GOLD MEDAL, or FIFTY GUINEAS.

E 3                    SAMPLES,

SAMPLES, not less than two pounds weight, with CER-
TIFICATES that the whole quantity is equal in goodness;
together with satisfactory CERTIFICATES, signed by the
Governor, or Commander in Chief, of the place of
growth, with an account of the number of trees growing
on the spot, their age, and the manner of culture, to be
produced to the Society on or before the first Tuesday in
January, 1802.

129. CLOVES. For importing into the port of London, in the year 1801, the greatest quantity of Cloves,
not less than twenty pounds weight, of the growth of
some of the Islands of the West Indies subject to the
Crown of Great Britain, or any of the British Settlements
on the Coast of Africa, or the several Islands adjacent
thereto, and equal in goodness to the Cloves brought from
the East Indies; the GOLD MEDAL, or FIFTY GUINEAS.

SAMPLES, not less than two pounds weight, with CER-
TIFICATES that the whole quantity is equal in goodness,
together with satisfactory CERTIFICATES, signed by the
Governor, or Commander in Chief, of the place of
growth, with an account of the number of trees growing
on the spot, their age, and the manner of culture, to be
produced to the Society on or before the first Tuesday in
January, 1802.

130. The same premium is extended one year farther.
SAMPLES and CERTIFICATES to be produced on or
before the first Tuesday in January, 1803.

131. PLANTATIONS OF BREAD-FRUIT TREES.
To the person who shall have raised in any of the Islands
of the West Indies, subject to the Crown of Great Britain,

tain, or in any of the British Settlements on the Coast of
Africa, or the several Islands adjacent thereto, between the
first of January, 1800, and the first of January, 1801, the
greatest number of Bread-fruit Trees, not fewer than one
hundred, and have properly fenced and secured the
same, in order to supply the Fruit to the Inhabitants;
the GOLD MEDAL, or THIRTY GUINEAS.

Proper ACCOUNTS and CERTIFICATES, signed by the
Governor, or Commander in Chief, of the methods made
use of in cultivating the Plants and securing the Plantation, and that the trees are in a growing and thriving
state at the time of signing such Certificates, to be produced to the Society, with Samples of Flour from the
Fruit, on or before the first Tuesday in January, 1802.

132.   The same premium is extended one year farther.

The ACCOUNTS and CERTIFICATES to be produced
on or before the first Tuesday in January, 1803.

133. KALI FOR BARILLA.  To the person who
shall have cultivated, in the Bahama Islands, or any other
part of his Majesty's dominions in the West Indies, or any
of the British Settlements on the Coast of Africa, or the
several Islands adjacent thereto, in the year 1798, the
greatest quantity of land, not less than two acres, with
Spanish Kali, fit for the purpose of making Barilla; the
GOLD MEDAL, or THIRTY GUINEAS.

134.   For the next greatest quantity, not less than one
acre, the SILVER MEDAL, or FIFTEEN GUINEAS.

CERTIFICATES, signed by the Governor, or Commander in Chief for the time being, of the quantity of
land so cultivated, and of the state of the plants at the

E 4                      time

time of signing such Certificates, to be delivered to the
Society, with Samples of the Kali, on or before the second
Tuesday in January, 1802.

135, 136. The same premiums are extended one year
farther.

CERTIFICATES to be produced on or before the second
Tuesday in January, 1803.

137, 138. The same premiums are extended one year
farther.

CERTIFICATES to be produced on or before the second
Tuesday in January, 1804.

139. DESTROYING THE INSECT COMMONLY
CALLED THE BORER. To the person who shall
discover to the Society an effectual method of destroying
the Insect commonly called the Borer, which has, of late
years, been very destructive to the Sugar-Canes in the
West-India Islands, the British Settlements on the Coast of
Africa, and the several Islands adjacent thereto; the GOLD
MEDAL, or FIFTY GUINEAS.

The Discovery to be ascertained by satisfactory CER-
TIFICATES, under the hand and seal of the Governor, or
Commander in Chief for the time being, and of some
other respectable persons, inhabitants of the Islands, or
other place, in which the remedy has been successfully
applied; such CERTIFICATES to be delivered to the
Society on or before the first Tuesday in January, 1802.

140. The same premium is extended one year farther.

CERTIFICATES to be delivered on or before the first
Tuesday in January, 1803.

141.

141. BOTANIC GARDEN IN THE BAHAMA ISLANDS. To the person who, before the first of January, 1801, shall have set apart, and, at his own private expense, shall have properly fenced and cultivated the greatest quantity of ground, not less than five acres, in any of the Bahama Islands, as a Botanic Garden, for the purpose of making experiments in the culture of those articles which are the peculiar production of the tropical climates, and which may tend to promote the commerce and manufactures of this country; the GOLD MEDAL; or ONE HUNDRED GUINEAS.

It is required that any person claiming the foregoing premium should produce to the Society, on or before the first Tuesday in January, 1802, a CERTIFICATE from the Governor, or Commander in Chief of the Bahama Islands for the time being, of his having complied with the above requisitions, and that the Garden is in a proper state of culture at the time of signing such Certificate.

*Premiums offered for the Advantage of the British*
*Settlements in the East Indies.*

142. BHAUGULPORE COTTON. To the person
who shall import into the port of London, in the year
1801, the greatest quantity, not less than one ton, of the
Bhaugulpore Cotton, from which clothes are made in imitation of Nankeen, without dying; the GOLD MEDAL.

A quantity of the Cotton, not less than five pounds
weight in the Pod, and five pounds carded, to be produced
to the Society, with proper CERTIFICATES, signed by
the Secretary to the Board of Trade of Bengal or Bombay,
on or before the last Tuesday in February, 1802.

143. The same premium is extended one year farther.
The SAMPLES and CERTIFICATES to be produced to
the Society on or before the last Tuesday in February,
1803.

144. ANNATTO. To the person who, in the year
1801, shall import into the port of London, from any
part of the British Settlements in the East Indies, the
greatest quantity of Annatto, not less than five hundred
weight; the GOLD MEDAL.

A quantity of the Annatto, not less than ten pounds
weight, to be produced to the Society, with proper CER-
TIFICATES, signed by the Secretary of the Board of
Trade of the respective Settlement, that the Annatto is the
produce

produce of such Settlement, on or before the last Tuesday in February, 1802.

145. The same premium is extended one year farther.

The SAMPLES and CERTIFICATES to be produced to the Society on or before the last Tuesday in February, 1803.

146. TRUE COCHINEAL. To the person who, in the year 1801, shall import into the port of London, from any part of *the British* Settlements in the East Indies, the greatest quantity of true Cochineal, not less than five hundred weight; the GOLD MEDAL.

A quantity of the Cochineal, not less than ten pounds weight, with proper CERTIFICATES, signed by the Secretary of the Board of Trade of the respective Settlement, that the Cochineal is the produce of such Settlement, to be produced to the Society on or before the first Tuesday in February, 1802.

147. The same premium is extended one year farther.

The SAMPLES and CERTIFICATES to be produced on or before the first Tuesday in February, 1803.

---

*Additional Premiums in Colonies and Trade.*

148. CULTIVATION OF HEMP IN UPPER AND LOWER CANADA. To the person who shall sow with Hemp (in Drills at least eighteen inches asunder) the greatest quantity of Land in the Province of Upper Canada, not less than ten acres statute measure, in the

year

year 1801; and shall, at the proper season, cause to be plucked the Summer Hemp (or Male Hemp bearing no seed), and continue the Winter Hemp (or Female Hemp bearing seed) on the ground until the seed is ripe; the GOLD MEDAL, or FIFTY GUINEAS.

149. To the person who shall sow with Hemp (in drills at least eighteen inches asunder) the next greatest quantity of land in the same Province of Upper Canada, not less than five acres statute measure, in the year 1801, and shall, at the proper season, cause to be plucked the Summer Hemp (or Male Hemp bearing no seed), and continue the Winter Hemp (or Female Hemp bearing seed) on the ground until the seed is ripe; the SILVER MEDAL, or TWENTY-FIVE GUINEAS.

CERTIFICATES of the number of acres, the distance of the drills, of the plucking of the Hemp, with a general ACCOUNT of the expense, soil, cultivation, and produce, to be transmitted to the Society, certified under the hand and seal of the Governor or Lieutenant-Governor, together with twenty-eight pounds of the Hemp, and two quarts of the Seed, on or before the last Tuesday in February, 1802.

150. To the person, in Upper Canada, who shall sow with Hemp, in the manner above described, and with the same CERTIFICATES and SAMPLES, the next greatest quantity, not less than one acre; the SILVER MEDAL.

It is required that an accurate ACCOUNT of the expense of the culture, the nature of the soil, and quantity of the produce, be sent with the Certificates.

151.

151, 152, 153. The same premiums are extended one year farther.

CERTIFICATES, &c. as before mentioned, to be transmitted to the Society on or before the last Tuesday in February, 1803.

154, 155, 156, 157, 158, 159. Premiums, exactly similar in all respects to those held out for the Province of Upper Canada, are also offered for the Province of Lower Canada, and are extended to the same period.

160. CURING HERRINGS BY THE DUTCH METHOD. To the person or persons who shall, before January, 1802, cure the greatest quantity of White Herrings, not less than thirty barrels, according to the method practised by the Dutch, and equal in all respects to the best Dutch Herrings, the same being caught in the British Seas, and cured in a British Vessel or Port; the GOLD MEDAL, or FIFTY GUINEAS.

161. For the next greatest quantity, not less than fifteen barrels, the SILVER MEDAL, or TWENTY GUINEAS.

A sixteen-gallon barrel of the Herrings to be produced to the Society on or before the first Tuesday in February, 1802, with CERTIFICATES that the conditions of the Premium have been completely fulfilled, and that the whole were cured in the same manner as the specimen, together with a full description of the process employed, in order that the Society may judge how far the Dutch method has been adopted.

Society's Office, Adelphi, *June* 1, 1801.

Ordered,

THAT THE SEVERAL CANDIDATES AND CLAIM-
ANTS TO WHOM THE SOCIETY SHALL ADJUDGE
PREMIUMS OR BOUNTIES DO ATTEND AT THE SO-
CIETY'S OFFICE IN THE ADELPHI, ON THE LAST
TUESDAY IN MAY, 1802, AT TWELVE O'CLOCK AT
NOON PRECISELY, TO RECEIVE THE SAME; THAT DAY
BEING APPOINTED BY THE SOCIETY FOR THE DIS-
TRIBUTION OF THEIR REWARDS: AND, BEFORE
THAT TIME, NO PREMIUM OR BOUNTY WILL BE
DELIVERED, EXCEPTING TO THOSE WHO ARE ABOUT
TO LEAVE THE KINGDOM.

IN CASES WHERE THE SOCIETY MAY THINK FIT
TO ADMIT EXCUSES FOR NOT ATTENDING IN PERSON,
DEPUTIES MAY BE SUBSTITUTED TO RECEIVE THE
REWARDS, PROVIDED SUCH DEPUTIES ARE EITHER
MEMBERS OF THE SOCIETY, OR THE SUPERIOR OF-
FICERS THEREOF.

GENERAL

## GENERAL CONDITIONS.

As the great object of the Society, in rewarding individuals, is to draw forth and give currency to those Inventions and Improvements, which are likely to benefit the Public at large, Candidates are requested to observe, that if the *means*, by which the respective objects are effected, do require an expense or trouble too great for *General Purposes*, the Society will not consider itself as bound to give the offered *Reward*; but, though it thus reserves the power of giving, in all cases, such part only of any Premium as the performance shall be adjudged to deserve, or of withholding the whole if there be no merit, yet the Candidates may be assured the Society will always judge liberally of their several Claims.

It is required that the matters for which Premiums are offered, be delivered in without names, or any intimation to whom they belong; that each particular thing be marked in what manner the Claimant thinks fit, such Claimant sending with it a paper sealed up, having on the outside a corresponding mark, and on the inside the Claimant's name and address: and all Candidates are to take notice, that no Claim for a Premium will be attended to, unless the conditions of the Advertisement are fully complied with.

No papers shall be opened, but such as shall gain Premiums, unless where it appears to the Society absolutely necessary for the determination of the Claim; all the rest shall be returned unopened, with the matters to which they belong, if inquired after by the Mark, within two years; after which time, if not demanded, they

shall

shall be publicly burnt, unopened, at some meeting of the Society.

All Models of Machines, which obtain Premiums or Bounties, shall be the property of the Society; and where a Premium or Bounty is given for any Machine, a perfect Model thereof shall be given to the Society.

All the Premiums of this Society are designed for Great Britain or Ireland, unless expressly mentioned to the contrary.

The Claims shall be determined as soon as possible after the delivery of the specimen.

No person shall receive any Premium, Bounty, or Encouragement from the Society, for any matter for which he has obtained, or purposes to obtain, a patent.

A Candidate for a Premium, or a person applying for a Bounty, being detected in any disingenuous method to impose on the Society, shall forfeit such Bounty, and be deemed incapable of obtaining any for the future.

The Performances which each year obtain Premiums or Bounties are to remain with the Society till after the public distribution of Rewards.

No Member of this Society shall be a Candidate for, or entitled to receive, any Premium, Bounty, or Reward, whatsoever, except the Honorary Medal of the Society. The Candidates are, in all cases, expected to furnish a particular Account of the subject of their Claims; and, where Certificates are required to be produced in claim of Premiums, they should be expressed, as nearly as possible, in the words of the respective advertisements, and be signed by persons who have a positive knowledge of the facts stated.

Where Premiums or Bounties are obtained in consequence of specimens produced, the Society mean to retain such

part

part of those specimens as they may judge necessary, making a reasonable allowance for the same.

No Candidates shall be present at any meetings of the Society or Committees, or admitted at the Society's Rooms, after they have delivered in their Claims, until such Claims are adjudged, unless summoned by the Committee.

*N. B.* The Society farther invite the communications of scientific and practical Men upon any of the subjects for which Premiums are offered, although their experiments may have been conducted upon a smaller scale than the terms of each require, as they may afford ground for more extensive application, and thus materially forward the views of the Society, and contribute to the advantage of the Public. Such communications to be made by letter addressed to the Society, and directed to Mr. CHARLES TAYLOR, the Secretary, at the Society's Office, in the Adelphi, London.

The Models required by the Society should be upon the scale of one inch to a foot. The Winchester bushel is the measure referred to for grain; and, as the acres of different districts vary in extent, it is necessary to observe, that the Society means Statute Acres, of five and a half yards to the rod or pole, when acres are mentioned in their list of premiums; and they request that all communications to them may be made agreeably thereto.

*The Society desire that the Papers on different subjects sent to them may be full, clear, explicit, fit for publication, and rather in the form of Essays than of Letters.*

F                    *₊* In

\*₊\* In case any person should be inclined to leave a sum of money to this Society, by will, the following form is offered for that purpose:

*Item.* I give and bequeath to A. B. and C. D. the sum of　　　　　upon condition and to the intent that they, or one of them, do pay the same to the Collector for the time being of a Society in London, who now call themselves the Society for the Encouragement of Arts, Manufactures, and Commerce; which said sum of I will and desire may be paid out of my personal estate, and applied towards the carrying on the laudable designs of the Society.

By Order of the Society,

CHARLES TAYLOR, Secretary.

☞ The Lists of the Premiums offered by the Society are published annually in the month of June, and may be had GRATIS, either on sheets or in pamphlets, by application to the Register, at the Society's House, in John-Street, Adelphi, London.

# PAPERS

## IN

# AGRICULTURE.

# AGRICULTURE.

THE GOLD MEDAL, being the Premium offered for planting ELMS, was this Session adjudged to HENRY VERNON, Esq. of Hilton-Park near Woolverhampton, from whom the following Account and Certificates were received.

SIR,

I HAVE for many years planted about thirty acres of different sorts of Trees in the course of the year, and my plantations are in the most thriving state.

Ever-green Trees I transplant in the early part of August, and am perfectly convinced, by long experience, it is the most proper season to move them. I have often known gardeners, who have examined them the following year, say,

F 3       " It

" It surely could not be possible they were moved the preceding year." The leading shoot droops on being first transplanted; but, after two or three re-freshing showers, it recovers and throws forth roots, so as to make the Tree firm before winter.

With respect to the distance between my Elms, it depends on the number of other sorts of Trees that I may have to intermix with them. I plant one Tree, as near as possible, four feet from an-other. I intermix Scotch and Spruce Firs with all my Trees, and cut them away when they in the least are observed to injure other plants.

In the plantation below Essington Windmill, I judge the Elms may be about fifteen feet distant from each other; in one of the clumps on Essing-ton Wood, they are, I think, forty feet distant from each other, and the others at least eighty feet, from the number of Trees mixed with them. Should your Society

Society consider the inclosed as entitled to their honorary premium, it will highly flatter,

SIR,

Your obedient Servant,

HENRY VERNON.

*Lower Wimpole-Street,*
*March 26, 1801.*

Mr CHARLES TAYLOR,

THIS is to certify, That between the 24th of June, 1798, and the 24th of June, 1799, the following pieces of Land were planted with English Elms, from three to seven feet high.

One piece of Land, in quantity twelve acres, two roods, twenty-five perches, called the Brick-kiln Plantation, was planted with different sorts of Trees; and amongst others with English Elms. Very few died; and there are now living

F 4                    four

four thousand English Elms, which have a very healthy appearance.

The Brick-kiln Plantation was taken off a Common, called Essington Wood. It was ploughed very deep, about three months before it was planted. The soil is part of it clay, and the other part gravel: those on the latter succeed best in all respects.

Another piece of Land, called the Castle Ring, containing eleven acres, two roods, two perches, was also planted with different sorts of Trees; and amongst them were many English Elms, on which there are now living two thousand in a very thriving state.

The soil is gravel and loam. This plantation was also taken from Essington Wood Common. Nearly one half of it was ploughed very deep, in the August before it was planted; the other part was left in the state in which it was found. The trees succeed best on the ploughed part.

Both

Both these plantations are very effectually secured against every sort of cattle, by a ditch five feet wide and three feet deep, with oak posts and double rails wound with gorse and thorns, and every where quicked with a double row of fine plants seven years old.

There is also a third plantation under Essington Wind-mill Bank, consisting of very rich light loam, and containing seven acres, two roods, eight perches, of old inclosed Land, that had not been in tillage in the memory of man. This I planted between the 24th of June, 1798, and the 24th of June, 1799, with many different kinds of Trees; amongst others, with English Elm, of which there are now living, in a very flourishing state, five thousand six hundred.

These plantations are in the liberty of Essington, and parish of Bushbury, in the county of Stafford. Witness,

LAWRENCE GRAY.

THIS

THIS is to certify, That Henry Vernon, Esq. has planted, on the different Lands mentioned in the county of Stafford, the number of Trees specified by Mr. Lawrence Gray; that I have walked over the Plantation, with the gardener, and found the same in a very thriving state. The plantations are uncommonly and effectually well fenced and secured to grow Timber; as witness my hand, this 24th day of March, 1801.

JOHN CLARE,
Vicar of Bushbury and Essington.

The

The GOLD MEDAL, or THIRTY GUI-
NEAS, at the option of the Candidate,
being the Premium offered for planting Osiers, was this Session adjudged
to Mr. THOMAS SELBY, of Otford
Castle in Kent, from whom the following Account and Certificates were
received, and who made choice of
the Pecuniary Reward.

SIR,

UNDERSTANDING that a Premium
has been offered, by the Society
for the Encouragement of Arts, &c.
for planting the greatest number of
acres with Osiers, I beg leave to offer
myself as a Candidate for that Premium;
and to lay before the Society, the mode I
have adopted in planting a field of twenty-one acres. The soil is very different
in quality. In some places it is a sandy
loam; and, in others, a reddish clay:
in some it is a sandy bog; and, in others,
a black

a black moory bog. The sub-soil consists of very stiff clay, and sharp reddish clay. The plants are of three sorts, the New Kind, the Osier, and the Willow. They are planted in rows two feet by one, and about 20,000 per acre. Those planted in March 1800, flourished five months after, and are in good condition at present. The land, as may be supposed from the description, is very wet; my apology for which is, that it has been in my occupation only one year. I am perfectly convinced that all wet land that is worth farming, is likewise worth draining; and therefore am now draining this piece of land.

The Osier thrives best, the New Kind next, and the Willow the worst. All the three sorts invariably thrive best on the dryest spots in the field. The expence attending the planting and the sets planted was five pounds per acre, by contract, and I prepared the land. I shall be happy, at all times, to answer
any

any questions which you may think fit to propose concerning them, whether I am the successful Candidate or not.

I am, SIR,

Your most obedient

humble Servant,

THOMAS SELBY.

*Otford Castle, near Seven Oaks, Kent,*
*November 18, 1800.*

Mr. C. TAYLOR.

The preceding Statement is confirmed by the Certificates of

NATH. GEORGE WOODROFFE, A. M. Curate of Otford;

WM. WALLER, Churchwarden;

JOHN COOPER, Seven-Oaks, the Planter.

The

The GOLD MEDAL, being the Premium
offered for sowing, planting, and inclosing Timber-trees, was this Session
adjudged to THOMAS JOHNES, M. P.
of Hafod, from whom the following
Accounts were received.

*Account of Trees and Acorns planted by*
THOMAS JOHNES, *Esq. of Hafod, in*
*Cardiganshire.*

FROM June 1796, to June 1797,
250,000 Trees were planted; of
which 20,000 were three-years-old transplanted Alders, 30,000 one-year-old
transplanted Alders; the others were
Elm, Beech, Birch, Ash, and Mountain
Ash.

The mode of planting was as follows:
After the ground was well inclosed, a
man, with a spade, made two cross cuts
in the sod (the ground not being previously ploughed or otherwise prepared);
he

he was followed by a boy with a bundle of the trees; the plants were in size from nine to twelve inches: the boy placed one of them in the gap, caused by the raising of the spade; the man then pressed the sod close down with his feet, which 'completed the business. About 10,000 were planted to the acre.

The soil is various; from a light gravel, to a peat bog. All trees thrive well therein, if properly secured; but Larch and Beech seem to flourish most. *

Between October 1798, and April 1799, fifty-five acres of good ground were

---

* It may be proper to remark that Mr. Johnes had planted in the same year 400,000 Larch Trees, not noted in the above account, as he had received the Gold Medal for them the preceding Session, and an account of them was inserted in the XVIIIth Volume of the Society's Transactions.

A further account of this gentleman's general Plantations and extensive Improvements, will be found in the Preface to the present Volume.

An ingenious Pamphlet by George Cumberland, Esq. entitled " An Attempt to describe Hafod," was printed in 1796, and is sold by T. Egerton, Whitehall.

were set or planted with Acorns, besides 165,000 Trees in the same time.

The Acorns were planted by a man with a spade paring off a thin turf and throwing it over, afterwards driving his spade two or three times into the ground to loosen the earth, then lifting up a spade full, whilst a boy was ready to throw in two or three Acorns; the earth was then gently trod down with the foot. The Acorns were planted two feet asunder.

The greatest part of the plantations is fenced with a stone wall, five feet high; the remainder, with a turf fence, the same height.

Certificates were sent from James Todd, gardener to Mr. Johnes, and the Rev. Lewis Evans, Minister of Eglwys Newydd, confirming the above; and stating that the plants were growing exceedingly well and in full vigour.

The

The SILVER MEDAL or TWENTY GUI-
NEAS, at the option of the Candidate,
being the Premium offered for the
Cultivation of SPRING-WHEAT, was
this Session-adjudged to Mr. ROBERT
BROWN, of Markle, in the Parish of
Preston and County of Haddington,
Scotland, from whom the following
Account and Certificates were re-
ceived, and who made choice of the
Pecuniary Reward.

*₊* *This Communication will particularly demand the attention of the Farmer, when bad seasons prevent the autumnal sowing of Wheat.*

*Samples of the Wheat may be seen, by
application to the Register, at the Rooms
of the Society.*

*An Account of the Management of seve-*
*ral Fields of Spring-Wheat, belonging*
*to Mr. Robert Brown, Farmer, at*
*Markle, near Haddington.*

THE autumn and winter of 1799
being extremely wet, rendered the
sowing of Wheat, except in a few situations, almost impracticable. I therefore determined to postpone sowing my
Wheat-seed till the spring months; trusting, as my ground was in good condition, that if the weather was then
favourable, I could get the business accomplished in a proper manner. The
land was therefore ploughed in as good
order as possible; and from the uncommon frosts which afterwards prevailed,
it turned very mellow and fine when dry
weather arrived.

About the 20th of February, 1800, I
commenced sowing, which was continued, as circumstances permitted, till
the

the middle of March; and in that time one hundred and forty-five acres were sown, besides ten acres afterwards ploughed down. The soil of the greatest part of the land thus sown, was a deep loam incumbent upon clay; and the remainder was a lighter loam upon a gravelly bottom. Thirty acres had been summer-fallowed, limed, and dunged, the preceding year. Ninety-five acres were after a crop of drilled beans, which had been completely horse-hoed. Fourteen acres had been occupied by turnips and potatoes, both drilled and horse-hoed; and six acres had carried summer tares. None of the fields received more than one ploughing, after the preceding crop was removed, except those under summer fallow; which had seven ploughings, and were manured with fourteen double-horse cart-loads of dung, and three hundred bushels of shell-lime per acre.

The kind of Wheat sown was principally the Essex White and Egyptian

G 2                                           Red,

Red, which in shape of head and size of grain are nearly similar. Some of the White Wheat was of the Kentish variety, which from being long sown upon the farm, was much blended with Red Wheat. The crop upon the heavy loams was, with a few trifling exceptions, uniformly good. The light loam was much hurt by the growth of yellow weeds, which last year prevailed upon such soils in an uncommon degree. The whole was ready for the sickle about the first week of September, and was cut from the 3d to the 12th of that month. A sample of the Essex kind accompanies this Paper.

From the small quantity yet threshed, the produce cannot be exactly ascertained; but, from trials which have been made, it is supposed that the fields sown after summer fallow, will yield forty bushels per acre; those sown after beans, thirty-six bushels; and those after tares, potatoes, and turnips, twenty-four bushels.

bushels.  The last being upon the dry soil were much injured by the drought and yellow weeds, while the deep loam was rather benefited by the dry weather.

The weight of the grain already threshed, is nearly sixty-two pounds per Winchester bushel.

The inferences which may be drawn from the above statement, are,

First, That Wheat may be sown with advantage in the spring months, till the middle of March, if the weather is then dry, the land in good condition, and the succeeding summer moderately warm.

Secondly, That under the above circumstances, the period of harvest is not retarded above ten days by the late sowing, especially in favourable seasons.

Thirdly, That the grain produced from spring crops of Wheat is equally good in quality, as that sown in the autumn and winter months.

G 3                    WE

WE, Alexander Dods, farmer in Newmans, and Andrew Somerville, farmer in Athalstoneford-maine, in the parish of Athalstoneford, in the county of Haddington, Scotland, do hereby certify that the several fields of Spring Wheat, mentioned in the statement given in the preceding pages, and belonging to Robert Brown, farmer at Markle in this county, were cultivated and managed as therein stated; and that the different circumstances connected with the management of the said crop of Wheat, are faithfully described; as witness our hands, this 2d of December, 1800.

Alexander Dods.
Andrew Somerville.

THIS is to certify, that I have measured those fields that were sown with Wheat, last spring, upon the farm of Markle in the parish of Preston,

and

and upon the farm of West-Fortune in the parish of Athelstoneford, both in the county of Haddington, as the same are possessed by Robert Brown, Esq. and find the contents, in English statute acres, to be as under, viz.

|  | A. |  |
|---|---|---|
| On the farm of Markle - - | 117 | 90 |
| On West-Fortune - - - - | 27 | 51 |
| Amount in Acres | 145 | 41 |

WILLIAM DICKINSON,
Land Surveyor.

The THANKS of the Society were this
Session voted to Mr. JOHN TAYLOR,
of Manchester, for the following Account of the Method of making Clover-Hay in wet weather, as practised
in Courland.

*An Account of the Method of making*
*Clover-Hay, invented by the Rev. Mr.*
*Klapmeyer, of Wormen, in Courland;*
*communicated to the Secretary, by his*
*Son Mr. John Taylor.*

IN the method of making Hay, recommended by the Rev. Mr. Klapmeyer, not only a number of hands
are saved, but the Hay is better and
more nourishing.  The Hay is prepared by self-fermentation, whereby it
retains its nutritious juices, and only
loses its watery particles; it is dried
more expeditiously by dissipation of its
humidity, and contraction of the sap-
vessels,

vessels, and thus its nutritious juices are concentrated. This process is conducted in the following manner, viz. The sap-vessels are expanded by the circulation of the liquid juices by heat, and the superfluous humidity is exhaled: on cooling, the sap-vessels contract, and thus future intestine fermentation is prevented, and the nutritious quality preserved.

Upon this principle, the Clover intended for Hay, after having been mowed, remains till four o'clock in the afternoon of the following day, in the swath, to dry; it must then be raked together into small coils, and afterwards made into large cocks in the form of a sugar-loaf, and such as would require six or eight horses to remove. To prevent the air from penetrating these cocks, and to produce a quicker fermentation, they must, whilst forming, be trod down by one or two men. If it be a still close warm night, the fermentation

tation will commence in four hours, and manifest itself by a strong honey-like smell : when a proper fermentation is begun, the cocks will, on being opened,. smoke, appear brownish, and may then be spread abroad. If in the morning the sun is warm, and a little wind arises, the Clover-Hay will quickly dry; it may then, towards noon, be turned with the rake or pitch-fork, and, about four in the afternoon, will be sufficiently dried, so that it may be immediately carted into the barn, without any danger of a second fermentation.

By this method of management the Clover will require only three days, from the time of mowing, to its being housed, and very little work: whilst in the common way, even in good weather, it requires six or eight days; in the old method it frequently becomes of a black colour; but in the new method it is only brown, has an agreeable smell, and remains good and unchangeable in the barn.

barn. The farmer has also another advantage, that if he has not carts enough to carry it into the barn, he needs only, at sun-setting, to heap it again into large well-trodden cocks, and thatch them with straw, in which state they will remain the whole summer without damage or loss. This Clover-Hay is not only greedily eaten by sheep and lambs, but also by horses, calves, and cows.

The last in particular prefer it to the best Meadow-Hay : it produces a great quantity of rich milk ; and the butter made from it, is almost as yellow as summer butter.

As this new mode of making Hay depends principally upon two circumstances — first, that the mown Clover, when brought together into large heaps, may ferment equally and expeditiously ; secondly, that if the day succeeding the fermentation be dry, sunny, and windy— on this account it may be proper to point out

out what should be done when circumstances are unfavourable.

Let us suppose, therefore, that the
night after the Clover-Grass has been
placed in the great cocks, be cold,
damp, or rainy, the fermentation will
yet take place, although it may require
a term of twelve, sixteen, or twenty-
four hours to effect it. If it be a second
or third crop, at which season the nights
are colder, it may even require from
thirty-six to forty-eight hours before the
fermentation ensues: it will however
commence, and may be ascertained from
this circumstance, that you can scarcely
bear your hand in the interior of the
cock.

Even if the night be dry, yet if a
strong cold wind blows, the cock may not
ferment equally, but only in the middle
and on the side opposite to the wind;
the other parts may still remain green.
In such a case the following rules must
be attended to:—

First,

First, If the cock has only fermented in the middle, and on that side where the cold wind did not act upon it, the whole heap must nevertheless be opened the following morning. That which has already fermented must be separated and spread to dry; it must be turned towards noon, and may be carted into the barn in the evening: but that part of the cock which has not fermented, must be again put together into large cocks, and fermented in the same manner as the preceding part, after which it may be spread to dry, and brought into the barn.

Secondly, In such cases where a small portion of the cock has fermented thoroughly, but not the greater part, the heap must be spread abroad in the morning, but must be again made into a close cock in the evening, in such a manner that the part which has fermented be placed at the top or outside of the cock, and that which has not fermented

mented be inclosed within it; then on the ensuing morning, or, if the weather be cold and rainy, on the morning afterwards, the Clover heap may be again spread abroad, and the Clover treated as in Case N° I.

Thirdly, If, in spreading the heap abroad, it be found that nearly the whole of the Clover has fermented, it will not be necessary to delay the housing of the whole on account of some small portion; but the Clover may be dried and carted into the barn. The small portion of Clover which remained unfermented, will not occasion any disaster to the other which has fermented; for there is a material difference betwixt hay thus managed, and the meadow grass which is brought whilst damp, or wet with rain, into the barn, which will grow musty and putrid.

Fourthly, In such instances, where some of the cocks of Clover have thoroughly fermented, and it rains on the

the morning, they ought to be spread abroad, for the Clover must be opened and spread, even if it rains violently; since, if it was suffered to remain longer in the heap, it would take fire, or its juices would be injured by too much fermentation; the leaves and stalks would become black, and the Clover unfit for food: therefore, if the rain continues, the spread Clover must be turned from time to time, but not carted into the barn till dry. This drying takes place, if the rain discontinues for a few hours, much more expeditiously with the Clover which has fermented, than with that made in the common way. Besides which, it must be remarked, that the fermented Clover remains good, even if it continues some weeks exposed to the rain, provided it is at last suffered to dry before it is put into the barn; otherwise the wet from the rain will render it musty and bad. The Clover which has been for so long a time exposed

to

to the rain, will not, however, be so nutritious as that which has been well fermented and sooner dried; but it will be far superior to that which has been exposed to the rain, and got up in the common method.

This new mode has been adopted with success, during the years 1798 and 1799, in Silesia, and found, in every respect, preferable to the old manner. On one of the estates there, it rained much during the Hay time; they were obliged to spread the Clover out of the large cocks, owing to its having fermented only in the middle: the parts which had not fermented were carefully separated and made again into large cocks, which fermented at the expiration of thirty-six hours, rainy weather and cold nights continuing during this period; after which time it was again spread abroad. The former, as well as the latter, remained for three days exposed to the rain, during which period it was turned

turned several times; the rain ceased on
the fourth day, so that the Clover-Hay
was turned towards noon, and carted into
the barn that evening. This Clover-
Hay remained in the hay-loft without
change, and was a very nutritious food.
Several milch-cows were fed with it, who
not only eat it greedily, but also increased in their milk. Lambs and calves
also thrived with it greatly. This method of making Clover-Hay prevents its
taking fire; for Clover which has been
once well fermented and dried, does not
change or spoil in the hay-loft.

Thus far I have given you the practice
related by Mr. Klapmeyer; and if the
hay season be wet in Lancashire, as is
generally the case, I recommend you to
make the trial on your farm.

If the weather should be remarkably
hot, you may, by adopting this plan, prevent a frequent accident; for grass hastily
made into hay, however dry it may appear
to the hand, contains within its fibres

H          much

much humidity; and when trod down in the stack will ferment rapidly, from this humidity endeavouring to escape, which often fires the stack. A certain degree of fermentation is necessary in the making of Hay, in order to develop its saccharine qualities, and make nutritious food. This saccharine fermentation is evident, from the smell and colour of the Hay in common stacks; and from tasting an infusion of it, it resembles, in some degree, the process of making malt from barley, and requires a similar attention. I have no doubt that the method above related will prove generally advantageous, in making Clover-Lucerne and Meadow-Hay in England, and lead to valuable improvements in Agriculture.

I remain

Yours very affectionately,

JOHN TAYLOR.

Leipsig, June 4, 1800.

Mr.

Mr. JOHN PALMER, of Maxstock near Coleshill, in Warwickshire, furnished the following Communication of a Method of HARVESTING CORN in WET WEATHER. Mr. PALMER did not comply with the Conditions prescribed for the whole of the Premium offered; but as the Society were of opinion that the Method he used would be serviceable, if more generally known, the SILVER MEDAL was adjudged to him as a Bounty.

SIR,

I MUST request the favour of you to lay before the Society for the Encouragement of Arts, &c. the following Account and Certificates, in claim of the Premium offered for the best and cheapest method of harvesting Corn in wet weather. The mode I have adopted is simple and effectual, and will, I hope, be approved.

H 2                         The

The weather proving extremely rainy, and my Corn then standing taking much damage, I determined upon cutting it wet, and thrashing it immediately, and then drying it on a kiln : in consequence of this, I collected as many men as were sufficient for the purpose, and employed them as follows, viz.

I caused a part of my men to cut the Corn in the common method with sickles, and bind it into sheaves. A second part I employed to load it on waggons, and carry it to the barn; and as many as could work in the barn, to thrash it. The next morning I winnowed it, and carried it to a malt-kiln to be dried ; which operation was always completed in less than twenty-four hours.

As it is impossible for me to send you two sheaves of the Corn harvested as above described, I have sent you the produce of two sheaves and upwards, which I declare to be a fair sample of the produce of four acres and upwards.

.A timber

A timber-stove, or a hop-kiln, will answer the purpose of drying Corn equally well as a malt-kiln.

*The Expense per Acre was as under stated.*

| | £. | s. | d. |
|---|---|---|---|
| Reaping and carrying to the barn | 0 | 12 | 0 |
| Thrashing and winnowing - - | 0 | 12 | 0 |
| Kiln-drying - - - - - - - | 0 | 5 | 0 |
| | 1 | 9 | 0 |

N. B. Only a part of the above sum should be charged to my new method of harvesting Corn, viz. the extra expence, which is as follows:

Five shillings per acre for drying, and four shillings for the extra trouble of thrashing it.

After the Wheat above mentioned was thrashed in the common method with flails, and dried, I so far completed a machine for thrashing, that I thrashed a very considerable quantity of Wheat,

H 3 and

and ten acres of Barley with it, carried
from the field in November; and it was
dried in the manner described in my
claim. I did not however state this to
the Society, because I had taken out a
patent, dated the 6th of December, 1799,
for my thrashing-machine; and was that
day going to London to give in my
specification, dated the 4th of January,
1800.

Part of the straw of the four acres,
described in my claim, was used for
thatch immediately after it was thrashed;
and part stacked in small narrow ridges,
for litter for my fold-yard.

The grain was very well separated
from the straw by the flails; but that
thrashed by the machine was completely
cleared, though in a very wet state.
This would not be the case with the
common machines of the North.

The quantity of Wheat upon an acre,
was about twenty-one bushels, which is
nearly as much as there would have been,

if

if it had been dried by fine weather. When the advantage of getting in an acre of Wheat per day, in seasons like the last, is properly considered, and making it immediately useful, at the small additional expence of nine shillings per acre, there can be but little doubt respecting its utility; for probably these men could not be employed at any other work.

I am, Sir,

Your humble servant,

JOHN PALMER.

*Maxstock, 24th May, 1800.*

Mr. CHARLES TAYLOR.

The above letter was accompanied with three Certificates; one from Mr. Edward Palmer, of Maxstock in the county of Warwick; another from the Rev. John Dilke, of Maxstock Castle; and the third from Mr. William Twam-

ley,

ley, of Sutton Colfield in the county
of Warwick, miller: which testify that
Mr. John Palmer did harvest four acres
of Wheat and upwards, in the year 1799;
that his plan is likely to be of general
advantage; and that his thrashing machine is in high repute, and answers every
end proposed.

The

The Gold Medal, being the Premium offered for improving Land lying waste, was this Session adjudged to Thomas Fogg, Esq. of Bolton in the Moors, Lancashire, from whom the following Account and Certificates were received.

### SIR,

THIS is to certify, that Mr. Thomas Fogg, of Bolton in the Moors, in the county of Lancaster, manufacturer, has made the following improvements upon some Waste Land belonging to him, situated in Edgeworth, in the said county, viz.

|  | £. | s. | d. |
|---|---|---|---|
| Expences—In walling fences 500 roods, 8 yards to the rood, from 5 to 6 feet in height, at 8s. 6d. - - - | 212 | 10 | 10 |
| Expences—6¼ statute acres covered with stone drains, at 3s. per rood, 8 yards to the rood | | | |
| The same ditto with black soil, lime, and dung, at 6s. per rood, in all 9s. per rood - - - | 221 | 17 | 0 |
| Carried over £.434 | | 7 | 10 |

|  | £. | s. | d. |
|---|---|---|---|
| Brought over    - | 434 | 7 | 10 |

This land was worth about 5s. per
statute acre in its original state, being
of the nature of black soil, producing bent, and is now good meadow
and pasture land, and valued at £3.
per statute acre.

Expences of 13 statute acres covered with
black soil and lime, of sufficient
depth to have carried a crop of oats,
which was sown with grass seeds,
supposed to have cost 6s. per rood,    294  18  0

This land was worth about 3s. per
acre in its original state, being of
the nature of black and hazel soil,
and producing black heath and bent,
and is worth about £2 : 2s. per
acre.

Expences—2 statute acres of land fenced out,
and sets found for many poor people
to plant for potatoes, at £.10 per
acre    -    -    -    -    -    20   0   0

This land was worth about 2s. per acre
in its original state, being of the nature of black soil, and producing nothing but rushes, and is now worth
about £2 ; 2s. per acre.

£.749   5  10

<table>
<tr><td></td><td>£.</td><td>s.</td><td>d.</td></tr>
</table>

|  | £. | s. | d. |
|---|---|---|---|
| Brought over - | 749 | 5 | 10 |

Expences—3 statute acres of land planted with timber of different descriptions, which seem to be in a flourishing condition. This land is fenced with double rails and brush-wood, to keep the west and north winds from the trees. It cost more than £.20 per acre - - - - - -    60   0   0

This land was worth about 2s. per acre in its original state, being of the nature of black soil, producing bent grass.

Expences—26 statute acres levelled and drained with open and covered drains, at present very dry, and the next spring will be ready for any sort of manure, which we believe cost about £200. - - -    200   0   0

This land was worth about 2s. per acre in its original state, being of the nature of black soil, and producing black heath and bent grass, and is now worth about £1. 11s. 6d. per acre.

Total - £.1009   5   10

*N. B.* We believe that there are not less than 500 cart loads of soil collected, and ready to be laid on the said 26 acres

acres of land, the next spring, together with other manure ; also that the above improvements have been made, and money expended, since the beginning of the year 1794.

The above account of expenses upon the above Land, as shewn to us by the said Mr. Thomas Fogg, we believe to be true; and the improvement of the Land we are well acquainted with; as .witness our hands, this 4th day of December, 1800.

> Amos Ogden, Minister of Turton.
> John Horrocks.
> John Ashworth.

Signed in the presence of
Edward Crompton.

SIR,

I HEREWITH send you a description of the Waste Land I have inclosed from the Common called Edgworth Moor, in the parish of Bolton, and county of Lancashire, by an act of Parliament,

granted

granted for that purpose; and also an account of the Method which I have taken for the improvement of the said Waste.

Upon one of the small plots I have built a farm-house, cow-house, and a room above for hay.

Five of the plots were all of similar black soils; the situation, a gentle descent to the south, of about one inch to the yard. One of these plots I manured upon the green swarth; but the soil being too wet, it did not answer my expectations. I then drained all the five plots with stone, laying bottoms underneath. The main-drains opened about two feet square, and smaller drains are directed into them. I afterwards covered the land with compost made from lime, soil, and black dung, which answered very well; and they are now as good meadow and pasture lands as any in the neighbourhood.

On

On a small plot I have walled out a nursery for plants, in which I have about 6000 two-year-old and one-year-old trees: these I take up and plant out as I have occasion.

Two of the plots were alike very bad and bare of soil, they produced nothing but bent-grass. On many parts of them there was no soil, large beds of rocks appearing on the surface: these I got up, and made part of the walls with them, levelling the land at a great expense. I then covered the ground with a compost of lime and rich black soil, produced from decayed timber and vegetables; which soil I dug out of one part of the premises. With the above compost I covered the two plots, from three to four inches thick. The cattle seem to like this pasture better than any of my old inclosures. It has a south aspect, falling from north to south three or four inches in a yard.

Another

Another plot I have improved upon the same plan as the two last, and have no doubt of its answering : but as it has been only done this year, I must attend until the next year to ascertain it. It has a north-east aspect, with a fall of about one inch to the yard from the south.

Two other plots were very boggy and full of small pits, whence peat had been got. Many places were not passable, being full of water: these lots I have levelled and drained with open drains, at a great expense, as they would not bear the cattle to tread upon them. I first made a large drain, which answers the purpose of a fence: it is three yards wide at top, one at the bottom, and two deep. I then cut small drains directed into it, about four yards asunder; with the soil from which I filled up the pits, and where the land wanted I put it sometimes on the middle of the butts, after hacking it small. These small
drains

drains are about one foot in width, and from twelve to eighteen inches deep; taking care not to go into the clay. These small drains are cut by a line: I paid for them 1½d. per rood, of eight yards. These plots have a north-east aspect, with a gentle inclination from the south. They are now as dry as any land I have, and fit for any manure; I have about 500 loads of soil heaped up for that purpose, which I mean to mix with lime next spring.

Another plot, which is nearly flat, I have drained with open drains, and levelled the land, which is now dry enough for tillage.

Another part I have planted with Black Italian Poplar, Lombardy Poplar, Beech, Scotch-Fir, Larch, Sycamore, Ash, Alder, Huntingdon-Willows, and a few Oaks; they flourish well in general: the Larches seem to thrive best, and the Sycamore next. This plantation is double-railed to the west: I have platted brush-

brush-wood in the rails, and fastened it in the ground.

I drained other parts of the land which were mossy, and planted one plot thereof, which had from three to four feet deep of good black soil, with potatoes. A person of the name of Duckworth, who is unacquainted with my application to your Society, told Mr. John Ashworth, of Turton, the Secretary to the Manchester Agricultural Society, that he had weighed the potatoes grown in two different places of it, and the produce was above $7\frac{1}{4}$lb. to a square yard upon the average.

I remain, Sir,

Your most obedient servant,

Thomas Fogg.

Bolton,
December 31, 1800.

Mr. Charles Taylor.

I

Sir,

SIR,

I WAS duly favoured with yours, acquainting me that the Society of Arts had adjudged me the Gold Medal, or the Silver Medal and Twenty Guineas, for my Improvement of Waste Land. I beg leave to inform you that I shall make choice of the Gold Medal, both for the honour it confers, and the good effect it may have on others, in this part, by stimulating some of my neighbours who hold a large quantity of the same description of Waste Land, and who can well afford to improve it.

About Christmas last I begun to prepare about three acres of Waste Land, adjoining to what I had last year in potatoes, which will make about five acres. As I mean to plant the old ground also, I caused the fresh land to be dug up, which appears to be much mellowed by the frost, which has been of great service to it. Potatoes are very dear at

present

present in this neighbourhood. Last year, in order to save the principal part of the root for the use of the table, I procured what is called a cheese-tryer, by which I had the best of the eyes taken out, with little damage to the potatoe.

With those sets I planted about twenty roods upon Bolton-Moor, along with others cut according to the custom of this part; that is, the whole root cut away to the eyes. This method the growers in general most approve of; but those cut out by the cheese-tryer, were equally as good a crop as the others. A neighbour of mine, Mr. James Carlile, pared a quantity so deep as to take the eye fairly out, last year, and planted them; first cutting from the eye nearly all the parings. These, he says, answered, and were as good a crop as those cut upon the old method. I have such confidence in seed thus cut, that what has been used for some time in my house, has been pared

that

that way. I am of opinion, that the parings, if put either in dry sand or ashes, will be preserved till they are wanted. I mean to give them a fair trial this season, and shall take the liberty of communicating the result to the Society.

I remain, SIR,

Your most obedient

humble servant,

THOMAS FOGG.

*Bolton,*
*February 28, 1801.*

Mr. CHARLES TAYLOR.

The

The Thanks of the Society were this
Session voted to his Grace the DUKE
OF BRIDGEWATER, for a Model of a
Drain-Plough, presented by him to
them, and sent with the following
Communication from his Grace's
Agent, Mr. Thomas Bury, of Worsley
Mills, near Manchester.

The Model, which is made upon a scale
of one inch to a foot, is placed in
the Society's Repository for public
inspection.

SIR,

I AM favoured with yours of the 15th
instant. The model of the Gutter-
ing-Plough sent you, was a present to
the Society from his Grace the Duke of
Bridgewater, made by Robert -Tom-
linson, one of his Grace's constant
workmen.

I procured the following account this morning from the Duke's farmer:—In clay or stiff land that lies flat, the plough cannot go too deep; but if it lies on a declivity, about five inches deep is sufficient. In soft light soil, the Plough should go as deep as it can in all situations, because the sides moulder into the gutters. The best time of draining is about Michaelmas, or as soon as the grass is eaten; and the whole should be accomplished betwixt that time and Christmas.

In clay ground that has never been drained, six good horses will be requisite to draw the Plough. In every following year the Plough should be run through the same gutters, and four horses will then be sufficient.

I am, Sir,

Your most obedient servant,

THOMAS BURY.

P. S The

*P. S.* The Share of the Plough must be well steeled, and should be ground sharp.

*Worsley,*
*September 18, 1800.*

Mr. CHARLES TAYLOR.

\*₊\* At Broughton, in the neighbourhood of Manchester, considerable quantities of stiff clay, pasture, and meadow land, have been much improved, under the inspection of the Secretary of the Society, by the use of this Plough.

After the cattle were housed for the winter, three horses were employed to form drains with the Plough at proper intervals: the small drains were made at the distance of about nine yards from each other, in old furrows of the ground, and about five inches deep: the sod, when cut out by the Plough, was of a wedge-like form, and turned out by it

I 4    upon

upon the ridges of the land, entirely
separated from the drain or gutter.
These sods were afterwards divided
across, by a spade, into lengths of about
two feet each, then tossed by a pitch-
fork into a cart, and placed in a heap in
the field, along with strata of quick lime
in a powdery state : the whole mass was
reduced to a compost by the frost during the winter, and in the following
spring was laid upon the surface of the
land, and formed an excellent top-
dressing.

The water from the small drains was
directed into larger drains, made by
lowering the share of the Plough to the
depth of nine or more inches. Little or
no loss of land arose from the small
drains, as natural grasses were produced
therein, early in the spring. It will be
highly advantageous to repeat the operation every winter : it is easily and expeditiously performed ; and no person,
without an actual experiment of the
fact,

fact, can form a sufficient judgment of the great benefit arising to vegetation by the removal of cold stagnant water, during the winter, from land of every description.

*Description of the Duke of Bridgewater's Drain-Plough*, Plate I. Fig. 1.

A B. The beam of the Plough.

C D. The handles.

  E.  The share or sock.

  F.  The coulter, or first cutter of the sod; which coulter is fixed to the share.

  G.  The other coulter, or second cutter, which separates the sod from the land, and directs it through the open space betwixt F and G. This coulter is connected with the share and the beam.

H I.  The sheath of the plough.

  K.  The bridle or muzzle, to which the swingle-tree is to be fixed.

L M. Two

LM. Two wheels of cast iron, which
may be raised or lowered by
screws at N, pressing upon the
flat irons O O, to which the
axis of each wheel is fixed.
These wheels regulate the depth
which the share is to penetrate
into the earth.

P. A chain with an iron pin, to move
the screws at O,

The

The SILVER MEDAL was this Session
voted to THOMAS ANDREW KNIGHT,
Esq. of Elton, near Ludlow, for his
Invention of a DRILL MACHINE for
sowing Turnip-seed; a Plate of which
is annexed to the following Description of its form and mode of application. A complete Machine was
presented by him, and is placed in
the Society's Repository.

S R,

I HAVE sent you a small instrument
for sowing Turnips, which I have
tried on several different soils, and think
I can venture to assert, that it will sow
the seed and cover it perfectly well, in
any soil that is nearly in a proper state
to receive it. It is necessary either to
harrow the ground *across*, or to roll it,
previously to the instrument being used,
that the labourer may see the rows he

has

has made; but I have always found the crop to succeed better after the roller than after the harrow, though the ground has been very strong.

The instrument is so extremely simple in its construction, that it is almost unnecessary to give a description of its mode of action; but as parts of it may probably be broken in carriage, I have added the following sketch :—*See Plate I. Fig. 2.* A, the iron wheel, which, running on its edge, formed by two concave sides, makes the groove into which the seeds fall. I have sometimes used a wheel with strait sides; but I think that concave sides, when well executed, are to be preferred in strong soils, and indeed in any soil. B is a wheel moving on the same axis with A, and turning the wheel C (which gives out the seed) by means of a strap. I have several sizes of the wheel B, in order to increase or diminish the rapidity of C; and consequently to sow more or less seed. D, the

the tube through which the seed passes; and falls into the channel made by the iron wheel. E, the feet of the instrument. F, six lengths of jack-chain; which I find cover the seed remarkably well. The chain is perhaps preferable to any kind of harrow, because it can never become encumbered by loose straw, which is almost always found on or close to the surface, when the ground has been manured; and the iron cutting-wheel has a similar advantage over any kind of share. G I, the seed-box. H H, the handles of the machine.

The labour of using the instrument is very small. My workman usually accomplishes four statute acres or something more in a day: and last night, with the one I send, he sowed an acre and a half after six o'clock in the evening. There are two holes before the axis of the great wheel, to receive two pieces of cane, which point out the proper width of the intervals between the rows.

rows. I usually place my rows at eighteen or twenty inches distance; and I wish my plants to stand at not more than six inches apart in the row; for I find that three small turnips weigh about as much as one large turnip, are more solid, and I think more nutricious, and certainly are much less apt to suffer by unfavourable weather. The ground between the rows is, of course, worked with the hoe. Should the Society, at their next meeting, approve of the instrument, and will afford it a place in their Repository, I will beg them to accept it; if not, I will request you to return it at your leisure.

I am, Sir,

Your most obedient servant,

THOMAS ANDREW KNIGHT.

*Elton, near Ludlow,*
*June 22,* 1800.

Mr. CHARLES TAYLOR.

N. B.

*N. B.* The angle which forms the edge of the wheel A, must be made more or less acute; and the instrument more or less heavy, proportional to the strength of the soil. I have sometimes added weights of lead over the axis of the wheel, but it will rarely be found necessary. I have tried the instrument on different soils, and I think it will answer on any. A great advantage may be derived by sowing turnips with it, at a time when horses, now commonly used for the same purpose, are engaged in other employments. A few days are frequently of importance in sowing turnips, which by fortunate rains have got a wonderful start of those which have been sown a day or two later.

*Fig. 3.* is a section, on a larger scale, of the seed-box G, in *fig. 2.* The wheel, marked C, is also the same as in that figure: it is fixed upon the axis of the cylinder I, which is pierced upon the surface with holes at K, for

the

the seed. This cylinder turns round within a groove at the bottom of the box, and is so well fitted therein, that no seed falls from the box but what is delivered by the holes K. A small brush, marked L, rubs against the cylinder, to clear out any seeds which may remain in the holes.

The seeds fall into the tube underneath the cylinder, and from thence into the channel, made by the indenting rim of the iron wheel.

The loose chains which follow, cover the seeds with earth, as before mentioned.

Fig. 4. a front view of the wheel, exhibiting its edge.

The

The Duke of Bridgewater's Drain Plough.

Fig. 1.

Mr. F. A. Knight's Drill Machine.

Fig. 2.

H

H

The Thanks of the Society were this Session voted to THOMAS ANDREW KNIGHT, Esq. of Elton, near Ludlow, for the following ingenious Communication on the destructive Effects of the APHIS, and BLIGHTS on FRUIT-TREES; with useful Observations for preventing them.

SIR,

SO many writers on gardening, and on general agriculture, have treated on Blights, and so many different theories have been offered to the Public, that the subject may appear to many, to have been already sufficiently investigated. The Society, however, entertained a contrary opinion; and having expressed a wish to receive further information, I avail myself of this opportunity to lay before them some remarks, which I have at different times made, during several

K                                    years

years of rather close attention to the subject.

What are usually termed Blights, in ·the vague and extensive signification of that word, appear to me to originate from three distinct causes :—From insects, from parasitical plants, and from unfavourable seasons.

The destructive effects of the Aphis on wall-trees are so well known to every gardener, as scarcely to require description. The leaves curl up, the fruit drops off, and the progress of vegetation is almost totally suspended. Much ill-applied labour is often used by the gardener to destroy these insects, though they are not very tenacious of life. Another more extensive, but less fatal disease in plants, the honey-dew, is produced by this insect (as described by the Abbé Boissier de Sauvages). It has, however, been contended, that the honey-dew is not produced by the Aphis, but that it is a morbid exudation from -the

plant;

plant; at least that there are two kinds
of it; because the leaves are often covered with honey on trees where the
Aphis is not found, and because the
Aphis is sometimes found without the
honey-dew. But to this it may be objected, that honey, not being a volatile
substance, will remain on the leaves,
till it be washed off by the rain; and,
when moistened by the dew, will leave
the appearance of a recent exudation;
and that the Aphis certainly does not
afford honey at any period of its existence. I have frequently placed plates
of glass and of talc under the leaves of
fruit-trees, on which different species of
the Aphis abounded, and I have found
these substances to be in a few hours
covered with honey: and I have at other
times distinctly seen the honey fall from
the under-sides of the leaves, where
these insects abounded, by the following
means. Having placed a small branch,
containing a numerous colony of insects,

in the window of my study, where the
sun shone strongly upon it, I closed the
shutters so as to exclude all the light,
but that which fell directly on the branch.
In this situation the descending drops of
honey became extremely visible by re-
fraction, and appeared evidently to be
emitted from the insect with considerable force.    Each drop contained many
minute white points, which I considered
as the eggs of the Aphis; but as I knew
that the modes of generation in this
singular insect had much engaged the
attention of naturalists, I did not examine with sufficient attention to decide
that point.  This species of insect appears to require a previous disposition
in the tree to receive it; and its first
attacks may thence be considered as
symptomatic of a previous ill habit in
the tree; for I have found that trees
which have lately been transplanted,
have totally escaped its attacks, when
every other tree of the same kind of
                                    fruit,

fruit, growing in the same situation, has been nearly destroyed. And I can assert from many experiments, that if every peach and nectarine tree was to be dug up once in every five or six years, and to be replanted with some fresh mould round the roots (which should be as little injured as possible), a much larger quantity of fruit, and of very superior quality, would be obtained. It is unnecessary to inform the experienced gardener, that the tree should be removed early in the autumn; that its branches should be considerably retrenched, and that it should not be suffered to bear a heavy crop of fruit in the succeeding season. I have never found any species amongst the numerous and prolific genus of the Aphis, which was not readily destroyed on the wall-tree by covering it with a sheet of canvas, and under that introducing the smoke of tobacco. It is, however, necessary that the fumigation should be

K 3                    repeated

repeated twice or thrice, with intervals
of four or five days.  I have often seen
the addition of sulphur recommended,
and have known it tried, but always
with fatal consequences to the tree, as
well as to the insects.

The blossoms of apple and pear-trees
are often said by farmers to be blighted,
when they are destroyed by insects,
which breed within them, or in their
fruit; and the same term is used, when
the leaves have been eaten by the cater-
pillar: but as the insects themselves, as
well as the manner in which their depredations are made, are extremely obvious,
they do not properly come under our
observation when treating of Blights.

The species of parasitical plants which
are found in the form of disease on other
plants, appear to me greatly to exceed
the number of those I have any where
seen described by botanical writers.  Of
these the mildew is the most common
and obvious.  If a branch, infected
with

with this disease, be struck by the hand
in calm dry weather, a quantity of white
powder will be found to fly from it; and
if this be received on a plate of talc, or
of glass, and examined by the micros-
cope, it will be found to consist of very
numerous oval bodies, evidently orga-
nized. There is another plant similar to
this in every thing but colour (being of a
tawney brown), which is not unfrequently
found on the leaves of young apple-trees.
Both these plants appear to me to be
evidently species of mucor; and as
much the greater number of species of
this genus of plants is found to flourish
in damp air, and in situations deprived
of light, it may be supposed that the
foregoing diseases might be prevented or
removed, by placing the plants at proper distances: but I have not found this
to be the case. They, however, abound
most in low and sheltered situations; but
they are not unfrequently seen in those
of an opposite kind. The red and white

K 4                          mould

mould on hops, and the black spots on stalks of wheat (the rubigo of Virgil), and many other diseases of plants, will, I think, be found to arise from the attacks of minute plants of this genus, which appears to me to possess qualities somewhat similar to the digestive powers of animals.

The most common and extensive causes of what are termed blights, remain still to be described, and evidently exist in the defects and sudden variations of our unsteady climate. Whatever be the cause by which the sap is raised and propelled to the extremities of trees, it is well known that its progress is accelerated by heat, and that it is checked, or totally suspended, by cold; and it has been ascertained by others, as well as by myself, and indeed is known to every experienced gardener, that a plant under the most skilful management, does not readily recover its former vigour, when it has been injured by exposure,

for

for a few hours, to a temperature much below that to which it has been previously accustomed. It frequently happens in this climate, when the blossoms of our fruit-trees are just expanding, that a very warm day succeeds a night whose temperature has been some degrees below the freezing point of water. In such a day the evaporation from the unfolding leaves and blossoms will be greatly increased by the agency of heat and light, whilst the supply of nourishment is in a great measure cut off by the ill effects of the preceding night. The blossoms will nevertheless unfold themselves, but will be unproductive, from the want of due nourishment; whilst the hazy appearance of the air, which almost always accompanies such weather in the spring, will induce the gardener unjustly to infer that the ill effects he observes have arisen from some quality in the air (distinct from excess of heat and cold), which he denominates a Blight.

The

The best defence against this kind of weather for wall-trees, that I believe has yet been tried, is a covering of a double and triple net; for by this the tree is in some degree protected from frost; and the excess of evaporation, in the succeeding day, is in a very considerable degree prevented. Lightning is supposed by many to be very highly injurious to the blossoms of trees; but I believe that the ill effects which appear sometimes to accompany it, may be more justly attributed to excessive heat. The careful gardener often covers his trees with mats, or something of this kind; and by almost totally depriving the tree of light, creates that blight which he is anxious to exclude.

As the blossoms of every tree are formed during the preceding summer and autumn, they will evidently be more perfect in proportion as those seasons have been favourable, and as the management of the gardener has been judicious:

dicious: and as the power of bearing
unfavourable weather will be proportional to their vigour, and to the
maturity of the annual wood, through
which the sap passes to support them,
the gardener should be (though he rarely
is) extremely attentive to keep his trees
in such a state, and the branches at such
distances from each other, that they may
receive the greatest possible benefit from
the portion of light and heat which our
shadowy climate affords them.    It frequently happens in pruning, that too
much bearing-wood is left on the tree.
Every gardener ought to know, that
where a hundred fruits are a sufficient
crop for a tree, he has a better chance
to obtain that hundred from one thousand blossoms, to which the whole nourishment of the tree is directed, than when
the same quantity of nourishment has to
support a hundred thousand.

In standard fruit-trees, where no advantages can be derived from covering
them,

them, much may be done by the judicious application of the pruning-knife. The branches of a tree of this kind ought to be much thinned towards their extremities, so that the light may be admitted into the centre of the tree; but the internal parts of it should never be so thin as to admit of a free current of air through it. When a tree has been properly pruned, blossoms and fruit will be found on every part of it; and, in unfavourable seasons, the internal blossoms will receive protection from the external branches, which will be unfruitful.

It is particularly the interest of every planter, to take care that the varieties of fruit which he plants be sufficiently hardy for the situation in which he places them; for, if this be not attended to, little benefit will be derived from the foregoing observations. I could say much more on the subject; but, as my letter is already of considerable extent, I shall only

add,

add, that if the Society should receive (as they probably will) a more satisfactory account of the cause of Blight, than will be found in the preceding letter, they may dispose of it as they think proper.

I am, Sir,

.Your most obedient servant,

Thomas Andrew Knight.

. P. S. I do not send this paper as a claim for any premium, but to prevent attempts of imposition, from any pretender to the proposed reward.

*Elton, near Ludlow,*
*November* 4, 1800.

Mr. Charles Taylor.

The

The SILVER MEDAL was this Session
presented to Mr. WILLIAM LESTER,
of Northampton, for his Invention
of an Implement in Husbandry,
named by him a CULTIVATOR; from
whom the following Account and Certificate were received, along with a
Model, which is reserved in the Society's Repository.

SIR,

AS the health and luxuriance of
Corn depend, in a great measure,
on the pulverization of the soil previous
to the seed being sown, the Society of
Arts will, I am persuaded, give every
encouragement in their power to the
introduction of any implement that promises an abridgement of labour; and
as all tenacious soils are pulverized in
the best manner in dry weather, when
their particles are the most disjointed,
and

and their contact broken, the propriety of taking the advantage of working them in that state will be obvious: and at the same time it follows, that an improved implement for the abridgement of labour would be a desirable thing, in a climate like England, where the seasons are so uncertain.

In working on a rough fallow, my Cultivator should be set at its greatest expansion, and contracted in proportion as the clods are reduced. I am confident that one man, a boy, and six horses, will move as much land in a day, and as effectually, as six ploughs; I mean land in a fallow state, that has been previously ploughed.

It will be requisite in some states of the soil to alter the breadth of the shares; but of this, I presume, the farmer will always be a proper judge. By the expansion and contraction of the Cultivator, the points of the shares are, in a small degree, moved out of the direct line;

line; but this is so trifling, that it is no impediment to its working.

I am, SIR,

    Your most obedient servant,

        WILLIAM LESTER.

*Northampton,*
*February* 10, 1801.

Mr. C. TAYLOR.

A Certificate from Mr. William Shaw, of Cotton-End, near Northampton, accompanied this letter; in which he states, that he had used Mr. Lester's Cultivator upon a turnip fallow last summer, and that he believes it to be a very useful implement for cultivating the land in a fallow state, by its working or scuffling off seven acres per day, with six horses. He adds, that, from its property of contracting and expanding, it is calculated to work the same land in a rough or fine state, by which mean it unites the principles

ciples of two implements in one; and by the index on the axis, it may be worked at any given depth required.

## Description of Mr. Lester's Cultivator, Plate II. Fig. 1.

A.   The beam.

B B.   The handles.

C C.   A cross-bar of a semicircular form, containing a number of holes, which allow the two bars D D, to be placed nearer or further from each other.

D D.   Are two strong bars, moveable at one end, upon a pivot E, and extending from thence in a triangular form to the cross-bar C. In these bars are square holes, which allow the shares F, placed therein, to be fixed to any height required.

L                     The

The seven shares marked F, are shaped at their lower extremities like small trowels: the upper parts of them are square iron bars.

G G ⎱ Are three iron wheels, on which the
  G. ⎰ machine is moved; they may be raised or lowered at pleasure.

H.   The iron hook to which the swingle-tree and horses are to be fixed.

When the machine is first employed on the land, the bars D D are expanded as much as possible. As the soil is more loosened, they are brought nearer to the centre: the shares then occupy a less space, and the soil will consequently be better pulverized.

The

The GOLD MEDAL, or the SILVER MEDAL and TEN GUINEAS, at the option of the Candidate, being the Premium offered for the best Account of Experiments, to determine the comparative advantage of the Drill or Broad-cast Method in the Cultivation of TURNIPS, was this Session adjudged to the Rev. T. C. MUN-NINGS, of East Dereham, in Norfolk, from whom the following Account and Certificates were received, and who made choice of the SILVER MEDAL and TEN GUINEAS.

A Plate and Description of the Drill-Machine, used in sowing the Turnip-Seed, is annexed, and the Machine is placed in the Repository of the Society.

SIR,

RESIDING in a country in which the Turnip-crop is very deservedly considered as the basis of its husbandry, I

L 2                    have

have, for some time, directed my attention, and made some experiments, relative to the improvement of the cultivation
of that valuable vegetable; conceiving
that in whatever degree I could more
advantageously produce Turnips, or,
when produced, could provide for a
more economical expenditure of the
crop, I might fairly be regarded as in
the same degree promoting the general
and lasting interests of the community.
With this view I have made repeated
trials, to ascertain " *The comparative
advantage of the. Drill or Broad-cast
method, in the Cultivation of Turnips;*"
and as the result of an experiment which
I made last year, has not only been satisfactory to myself, but also to all who
have witnessed the effects of it, I am
induced to offer myself a candidate for
the Premium held out by the Society for
the Encouragement of Arts, &c.

But, before I proceed to a detail of
my experiments, I think it right to observe

serve that I have, *by way of preparation for Turnips*, given my land a *deeper* ploughing in the winter, than is customary with the neighbouring farmers. For this purpose I make use of a Scotch foot-plough; and I think that by *such* ploughing I bring land into action, which has been for some time *dormant*; and which is therefore better suited to the Turnip, than land which has been exhausted by the production of other crops. In every other respect my previous management of my land corresponds with the common practice of my neighbours.

My land *(a field of nine statute acres)*, being thus prepared, instead of sowing the Turnips *Broad-cast*, in the usual method, I invented a DRILL for this purpose, simple in its construction, and of easy management. It consists of a tin box, in the shape of a barrel, affixed to the axis of a wheel about twenty-two inches in diameter, vertical with the

L 3 same,

same, and, in its revolutions, dropping the seed through small apertures in the middle of the barrel.' The holes through which the seed falls, are distant from the wheel about fourteen inches. *(See the engraving and description thereof annexed)*.

I began by having the tops of the different ridges set out with the common Norfolk *two-horse plough* : and, when the same plough took up the furrow next to the top, I immediately followed with my Drill, and dropped the seeds upon the fresh mould the instant it was turned up. I was then followed by a one-horse plough, the over-shot mould of which as quickly buried the seeds. I was thus enabled to sow my seeds as fast as the land was ploughed, and to deposit them in regular and strait rows, at equal distances of about eighteen inches; after which I harrowed or rolled my land, in the same direction in which it was ploughed: and the consequence has been

that

that my crop has grown as regularly as a gardener could plant cabbages. Nearly six acres of my field were thus drilled, and on the same day (in the third week of June) the remainder of the field, or something more than three acres, was sown Broad-cast, after the usual practice of the country, and precisely at the same time when the farmers around me were sowing their lands in a similar manner.

In the course of my observations on the Turnip-crop, I had frequently lamented, that when the crop was indeed abundant, the advantages derived from its expenditure were far from correspondent; because no effectual method has yet been adopted, to protect the Turnips from the severity of a winter's frost. This, in the common method of *Broad-cast* sowing, I considered as impracticable, and therefore resolved to attempt it in my drilled crop; and, in that crop, I have been enabled, by

L 4                            pulling

pulling up the alternate rows, to leave
regular rows about a yard apart; and
have had the land so ploughed, with a
one-horse plough, as to mould up the
Turnips, on each side, most effectually,
and to assume the appearance of what
is called *two-furrow work*.   I have therefore half my crop so buried, as to lessen
very materially, if not absolutely to
prevent the danger arising from the
frequently fatal effects of a cutting
frost.

I am truly happy that the mildness of
the present season prevents my speaking
with greater confidence, as to the success of this part of my experiment,
though the very complete manner in
which the Turnips are now buried, leaves
me without much doubt but that it will
fully answer my expectations.   Many
very experienced farmers, who have
witnessed my proceedings, honour them
with their entire approbation, and look
upon my method of protecting my
plants

plants as a grand discovery, in the management of the Turnip-crop. I am certainly aware that I am not the first person who has drilled Turnips; but I know of no one who has before done it in so simple a manner—in a manner attended with less expence—in a manner admitting of so much ease, in future operations for the defence of the plants—or in a manner more likely to be clearly understood by all who may be desirous of making similar experiments. Of the superior produce of the drilled crop over the broad-cast, on equal quantities of land, every experiment that I have made has most powerfully convinced me; and I have the universal opinion of all who have viewed my present crop, to confirm my sentiments. It has been observed by Mr. Kent, in his General View of the Agriculture of the County of Norfolk, that the ground does not relish Turnips so well as formerly: and

be

he supposes (in my opinion with much justice) that the present comparative ignorance of the use of Turnips amongst the Hanoverians, has arisen from the ground in that country being injured by repeated crops of them. It is certainly a very obvious truth, that Turnips will grow in the greatest abundance on land not accustomed to bear them: but it has frequently occurred to me, that one material reason of failure in a crop of Turnips sown broad-cast, has arisen from the seed not being sown soon enough after the plough; as I have, in numberless instances, taken notice of Turnips vegetating very partially, when only a few furrows have been ploughed between one sowing and another: and, in such cases, I have always thought that, if the seed could have been deposited immediately after the plough, it would not have failed to grow uniformly. I trust it will be found that my experiment

ment powerfully tends to confirm this conclusion.

Of the following advantages, attending my method of drilling Turnips, I am satisfactorily persuaded:—In a dry time, as was the case last season, the seed, by being immediately dropped upon the fresh turned-up mould, has consequently an increased probability of successful vegetation. By being buried somewhat deeper than in the broad-cast method, it receives more moisture in its infant state of vegetation; and by having, if I may so say, new hold of the earth, is less liable to injury, from the effects of continued drought. In confirmation of these persuasions I must state, that Turnips sown on the same day, in the same field, broad-cast, on land in every other respect treated previously in the same way, have not produced one half or one third of a crop, and that the same has been very generally the case with Turnips sown broad-cast;

cast; but that every row of my drilled
plants has succeeded to admiration. The
advantages in the subsequent management of the crop, I have already spoken
of.  If therefore it be desirable to grow
Turnips to advantage ; if it be desirable
to protect them when grown, and by
such protection be enabled to give Stock,
sound, uninjured Turnips, instead of
what may be more than half-rotten, or
frost-nipt almost to putrefaction; I
would willingly flatter myself that the
Society for the Encouragement of Arts
will be convinced that, as far as any
conclusion can be drawn from a single
experiment in favour of one method
rather than another, I have, beyond dis-
pute, established the superiority of the
Drill method of cultivating Turnips.
And as, in addition thereto, I have in
part effected what seems to me the object
of the Society, in the latter part of the
*Nota bene* subjoined to Premium 95,
the preservation of Turnips upon the
                                    ground

ground when grown, I am induced to hope that the Society will think me entitled to the Premium for which I am a candidate.

Of my previous experiments I am not able to furnish the Society with any satisfactory particulars; yet I would by no means omit to declare, that each has been the mean of persuading me, that the Broad-cast method of cultivating Turnips can never be so advantageous as that of the Drill, when properly managed; and I have much satisfaction in assuring the Society, that, from the extraordinary success of my last year's experiment, many of my neighbours have expressed a resolution to drill, and to protect their Turnips for the time to come. Any other particulars into which the Society may be inclined to enquire, will be answered with readiness and pleasure by, Sir,

Your obedient servant,

T. C. Munnings.

P. S. I beg leave to observe, in addition to the advantages I have before stated, that my drilled plants growing in such very strait and equidistant rows, any noxious weeds, such as *charlock*, *thistles*, or *red-weed*, may be destroyed in the infant state of the plants, by hoeing the intermediate spaces; that when the alternate rows are removed, and the land ploughed for the defence of the remaining rows, it receives most of the benefits of a winter's frost, and is very much forwarded in preparation for the barley-crop; and that, above all, from my complete success, I have roused a spirit of emulation in the cultivation of turnips, among the farmers of the county of Norfolk.

With regard to my Turnips it would be easy to multiply Certificates, and be diffuse in my observations, because no agriculturist has viewed them without being surprised both at the abundance of the crop (considering the quality of the

my land), and at the very obvious simplicity of my management of it, from
beginning to end. I shall only farther
observe, that it is now in my power to
sow my seed at equal distances of nine,
eighteen, twenty-seven, thirty-six inches,
or at any given distance of inches, of
which nine are an aliquot part; and
that I consider this as no trifling convenience.

I am, Sir,

Your obedient servant,

T. C. Munnings.

*East Dereham, Norfolk,*
*March 12, 1801.*

Mr. Charles Taylor.

SIR,

SINCE I wrote to you on the subject
of my drilled Turnips, I have been
powerfully struck with some advantages
of the drill method, which I now beg
permission to state to you.

In

In a part of my field from which the alternate rows have not yet been taken, I have, with very great effect, used the hoe-plough, and have not only cut and destroyed whatever weeds were growing between the rows, but have also partially moulded up the apples of the Turnips; and I am induced to believe that even so partial a moulding up, executed in the autumnal months, would have a strong tendency to protect the plants, to facilitate a more complete moulding-up when part of the crop is removed, and to admit the full benefit resulting from the exposure of the earth to a winter's frost.   I am persuaded that such use of the hoe-plough serves likewise to retain necessary moisture, and to produce future pulverization with much less than common labour.  But I have more particularly noticed the very superior verdure of the moulded-up plants, compared with what are not so, and with the larger and almost uninjured tops

tops of the former, in comparison with the latter; for, during some late frosts, the effects of which were very perceptible in the exposed plants, those moulded up have continued to grow, and to branch luxuriantly, with all the vigour of vernal vegetation. I attribute this to the bulbs of such plants not having their juices stagnated by the keenness of the weather.

As I am anxious to have this subject fully submitted to the Society for the Encouragement of Arts, &c. allow me to say, that I consider my Drill for Turnips as much superior to any other, from the single circumstance of its depositing the seed so *instantly* after the plough, as entirely to preserve the good effects of the first evaporation; and that I conceive such evaporation produces the uniform vegetation of such minute seeds. So remarkably uniform was the vegetation last year, that in the six acres of my drilled plants, I believe there was

M                            not

not a deficiency of six square yards; though on three acres of broad-cast, before rain fell, not one half, perhaps not one third part of the seeds vegetated. I am indeed fully persuaded that the Drill method, in the cultivation of Turnips, will in all seasons be superior to the Broad-cast; but that the very great and striking difference between the two methods will most effectually be perceived in a season of uncommon drought; and it is for this reason that I am solicitous to procure for the Drill method an extensive and impartial trial, that agriculturists in general may be satifactorily convinced of its important advantages.

I am, Sir,

Your obedient servant,

T. C. Munnings.

*March* 14, 1801.

Mr. Charles Taylor.

Certificates

Certificates accompanied these letters, from Mr. James Blomfield, of Billingford; Mr. St. John Priest, Master of Scarning School; Mr. William Salter, and Mr. Daniel Reeve, of Beetley; John Tuck, and the Rev. George Preston, Curate of East Dereham; all which confirm the above accounts.

*Description of Mr. T. C. Munnings's Drill Machine. Plate II. Fig. 2.*

A. The wheel with an iron rim.

B. The tin barrel, or seed-box, fixed to the axis of the above wheel.

C. The aperture by which the seed is introduced into the box:—this aperture is afterwards closed by a cover.

D. A semicircular plate of tin, to prevent any dirt falling upon the seed-box.

E E. The two handles of the machine.

*Plate*

*Plate II. Fig. 3.*

F. Represents the seed-box on a larger
scale.

G. The holes in the tin box, through
which the seed falls upon the
land.

H. Part of the axis of the wheel, to
which the seed-box is fixed.

The

The Thanks of the Society were this Session voted to THOMAS ECCLES- TON, Esq. of Scaresbrick-Hall, in Lancashire, for his Invention of an AUGRE, or PEAT-BORER, for drain- ing Boggy Land. A Model of this Implement was presented by him to the Society, along with the following Communication, and is placed in their Repository.

SIR,

THE greatest obstacle to the effectual draining of many boggy lands, con- sists in the earth in the bottoms of the ditches or drains when newly cut, and more especially if made to any consi- derable depth, rising from the pressure of the waters contained in the bog, by which the new-cut drains and ditches are frequently so nearly filled up, as to im- pede the flowing of the water they were

M 3 intended

intended to carry off, and thereby rendering the work comparatively ineffectual.

There are different layers, or strata, in moss or peat lands, which will not allow the water easily to filtrate through them, yet are of so soft and spongy a nature as to rise from the pressure of the water contained in the bog.

It becomes necessary to give a free vent to the above confined water, effectually to drain such lands. This has been most successfully done by the Augre, a model of which I have herewith presented to the Society.

A common augre, or even a pole, will force a passage, and give vent to the water for a short time; but owing to the peat being only pressed sideways, and not cut out, the parts soon join again, and the passage of the water of course becomes completely obstructed; but by means of this Augre, a cylindrical column of peat of six inches diameter will

be

be clearly cut out and taken thence, and a free passage maintained for a very considerable space of time.

The first experiment made, produced a clear augre-hole of the above dimensions, four yards in depth, in one hour; and the water, which had been pent up in the bog, rose above the level of the bottom of the ditch, from four to six inches; and the bottom of the ditch, which was previously very soft, and had begun to swell and rise, in a few days became more firm and solid, and this in so great a degree, that when cleared it remained without swelling or rising in the least. It will considerably reduce the expense of draining such lands, by rendering them so firm as to cause the first end-drains to stand.

The most proper depth to bore, depends on the situation. Where the moss lands lie low, and are in danger of being flooded, no greater depth than what is absolutely necessary for draining the

surface

surface should be bored, as, by deep boring, the land may be sunk so low as to be liable to inundation.

      I am, Sir,

         Your most obedient servant,

            THOMAS ECCLESTON.

*Scarisbrick, Lancashire,*
   *May 25, 1801.*

Mr. CHARLES TAYLOR.

*Description of Mr. Eccleston's Peat-*
   *Borer.*    Plate II. Fig. 4.

A. The cutter of the borer, which pene-
      trates the peat.

B. The body of the borer, six inches in
      diameter.

C. The aperture through which the peat
      introduced by boring is drawn out.

D. A portion of the iron bar of the borer,
      to the upper part of which a cross
      handle is to be fixed.

                     The

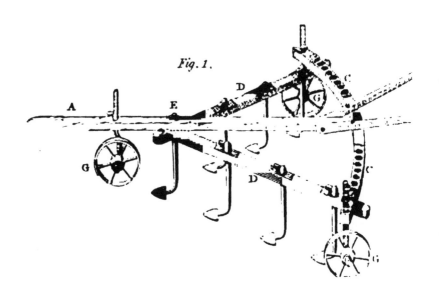

*Fig. 1.*

A    E    D    C

G    G

D    C

G

*Mr. T. C. Munning's Drill Machine.*

E

*Fig. 2.*

E

*Mr. Eccleston's Peat Borer.*

*Fig. 4.*          *Fig. 3.*

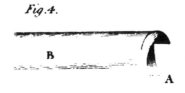

B        C    F

A

The GOLD MEDAL was this Session adjudged to NICHOLAS ASHTON, Esq. of Woolton-Hall, near Liverpool, for planting ONE HUNDRED and THIRTY-THREE ACRES of WASTE MOOR LAND. The following Account and Certificates were received from him.

SIR,

THE Forest of Delamere, in the county of Chester, is of great extent; and from old records appears to have produced much valuable timber, which is nearly all destroyed; and the land, which is now productive of little more than heath, affords but a scanty provision for a few sheep and rabbits.

The soil is in most parts extremely thin; and under it is a great depth of sand, intermixed with gravel.

From the timber it has produced, I was naturally led to expect, with care and

and proper management, trees might be
again raised, which may prove beneficial not only to the planter, but, if executed on a great scale, to the kingdom
at large; and having waste land adjoining to the forest, of the same quality, I
determined, in the summer of the year
1795, to try the experiment. Accordingly,
for that purpose, I enclosed one hundred
and thirty-three acres of land in two
lots, and surrounded them with posts
and double-railing. I engaged Messrs.
Dickson and Sons, nurserymen, to plant
the same with forest-trees; which they
completed the winter following, very
much to my satisfaction, agreeably to
the Certificate sent herewith, to which I
beg leave to refer. It may be proper to
add, that the plantation was surrounded
with a ditch and copse, and the latter
planted, below the railing, with white
thorns. To make the guard still more
effectual; about four feet from the railing, within the inclosures, I directed a
line

line of French gorse to be sowed in a
drill; and having built a lodge upon
the premises for one of my labourers, I
ordered him to devote his whole time
and attention to preserve the fences, and
protect the trees from injury by sheep,
or otherwise. This, I have the pleasure
to say, he has diligently performed; and
there is every appearance of the plantation succeeding according to my
wishes.

From the very thin layer of vegetable
soil, Messrs. Dickson's were of opinion
that it would be best not to plough the
land; but after burning the heath, at the
close of the summer, to plant the trees
that were small near the surface, expect-
ing they would flourish more than if
planted in the sand. This, however,
proved not to be the case; for the
matted roots of the heath were the first
year detrimental to the young plants;
whereas those which were planted on
sand beds, from which the gravel had
been

been screened, took root immediately, and are easily perceived from the rest of the plantation.

If this experimental proof of success in planting timber-trees on very barren soils, should be an inducement to the public, or individuals, to pursue the same upon a large scale, it will give me very particular pleasure, and, I trust, be of great national advantage.

I am, Sir,

Your most obedient servant,

Nicholas Ashton.

N. B.  I beg leave to add, that the flourishing state of my plantations has induced other gentlemen, in the county of Chester, to plant upon similar soils.

*Woolton-Hall,*
*October* 13, 1800.

This

THIS is to certify that Archibald Dickson and Sons, nurserymen, of Hassendeanburn, near Haurick, Roxburgshire, Scotland, by directions from Nicholas Ashton, Esq. planted, during the months of November and December, 1795, four hundred and eighty-seven thousand and forty forest-trees, viz.

| | |
|---|---:|
| Scots Firs - | 242,600 |
| Larches - | 181,200 |
| Ashes | 4,800 |
| Oak - - | 16,200 |
| Sycamore - | 15,000 |
| Elm - - | 7,200 |
| Beech - | 18,060 |
| Tree Willow | 1,200 |
| Alder - | 600 |
| Laburnum - | 60 |
| Weeping Birch - | 60 |
| Mountain Ash - | 30 |
| Spanish Chesnuts | 30 |
| Total | 487,040 |

And

And the said trees were planted upon one hundred and thirty-three acres of Waste Land, in the township of Weaverham, and adjoining to the Forest of Delamere, in the county of Chester.— And I ARCHIBALD DICKSON do further certify, that I have this day, together with the Rev. John WILLAN, of Weaverham, and Mr. GEORGE OKELL, steward for Nicholas Ashton, Esq. visited and carefully examined the said plantation, and find the trees in a promising and flourishing condition; and to the best of our judgment we conceive, that not more than one twelfth part of the whole has perished.

ARCHIBALD DICKSON.
GEORGE OKELL.
JAMES WILLAN.

The

The Thanks of the Society were this
Session voted to EDWARD JONES, Esq.
of Wepre-Hall, in Flintshire, for the
following Communication, on the Destruction of the GRUB of the COCK-
CHAFER.

### SIR,

THE Society having directed their
attention to the preservation of
herbage from noxious insects, and among
others the Cockchafer, by destroying
its Grub; I beg leave to submit a few
observations on the subject for their consideration.

The Grubs of the Cockchafers (or
brown beetles) are white, about an inch
in length, and of the thickness of a
turkey's quill. When disturbed they
contract their length, and their bodies
dilating, appear like lumps of white fat,*
somewhat oval.

They

* Hence the British name " Earth-Lard."

They inhabit sandy and light loamy soils, lie from about two to six inches deep, and may be found in spring, by paring off the sods.

This place was much infested by brown beetles; but about twelve years ago, some labourers removing a bank of earth, exposed a bed of Grubs, several paces in length. Many of them were scattered among the fallen soil; and one of the men proposed to strip the surface of the bank, which being done, the Grubs were seen lying in irriguous channels, as if the parent insects had dropped the eggs moving in various directions.

The same man informed me that they were the favourite food of moles; and he desired me to observe an end of the bank not stripped (being covered with mole hills); " for there no beetle grubs would be found." When opened, his remark proved true:—the moles had traced all the labyrinths of the grubs.

My

I took the hint for the preservation of my foliage, and have ever since protected the race of moles. The brown beetles gradually decreased, and are now rarely seen here. I have not observed more than one or two stragglers in the two last springs.

Some notice of the habits of moles may be acceptable to the Society, as it has been said " that they penetrate deep into the earth, in dry weather; rarely quit their subterraneous dwellings, and have few enemies ;"—and " that they do great mischief in gardens and corn-grounds."

I have always found that in hay and pasture grounds, as soon as the grass is high enough to cover them, they run upon the surface, where they find their food in the numerous caterpillars and insects which in the early part of the summer crawl out of the earth; and they continue above ground till the harvest.

N

vest. They are frequently cut by the
scythe; and I have seen them at various
times come out of deep hay grass into
places recently mown, and, perceiving
their exposure, endeavour to conceal
themselves in the shorn grass.

I have also often seen moles on very
close mown grass, and bare spots in pasture land, plunge, when alarmed, among
the roots; following their path (which
was discernible by the heaving of the
surface), I have forced them out occasionally, to try the depth of the covering, which was only a few shreds of
roots.

There are two circumstances that may
oblige moles sometimes to penetrate
deeply:—disturbed soils in summer, such
as in gardens; and ploughed light lands,
where the moles delve in pursuit of
worms; and, in their course, they must
unroot and destroy some plants; but a
vigilant gardener and husbandman will
prevent much damage.

The

The other cause of their digging deep is frost, which they avoid, or it would kill them. I have found them in winter, in peat soil, two and three feet below the surface; and in the hard frost of 1794-5 (cutting deep trenches to separate grounds), I found moles several mornings, that had worked through and fallen into the trenches, frozen to death.

Their summer emersion is proved by the birds of prey: they destroy great numbers of moles. This year there were taken out of one kite's nest twenty-two moles, and out of another fifteen, some of which were putrid; besides many frogs and unfledged birds.

The rapacity of the kites shews that they are destructive enemies to the moles, which, if moles are serviceable to man, should be known, that he may stay his arm.

Moles are frequently found dead upon the grass in summer, with marks of

N 2                    having

having been bitten, as if to suck their blood, but with no part of their bodies consumed. This, I suppose, is done by weasels; and the following (not very common) occurrence, which happened in the summer of 1789, tends to prove it :—

A kite was observed rising from the ground with some prey, and instead of flying to an adjoining wood, he soared almost perpendicularly. After remaining a short time stationary, he came gradually down, with his wings extended and motionless, and dropt very near the place from which he had risen *.

Several persons who were near, and saw the flight and descent, ran immediately to the spot, and a weasel darted from the kite, which they found dead; and they discovered, on examination, that the kite had been bit in the throat, and

* A similar circumstance was mentioned in the Chester papers, three or four years ago.

and bled to death. Near it they found a dead mole, yet warm, which was bitten in the neck; and they concluded that the weasel had caused the death of both.

In several parts of the kingdom where I have met with a great number of brown beetles, moles were regularly destroyed; and in Staffordshire, being shown several large trees covered by beetles, and totally defoliated, I enquired whether they destroyed the moles? The answer was, that they did, or they should be over-run with them.

The loss of foliage not being of great consequence to the farmer, he is satisfied that his turkeys make him amends in other respects, by eating the brown beetles, of which they are very fond, and which they swallow voraciously.

A gentleman informed me lately, that rooks also eat the beetles.

But these means are confined to the winged beetle. It appears to me that

N 3                              the

the mole is the only certain destroyer of the grub.

My hay and pasture grounds are, every spring, thickly studded with mole hillocks. They are scattered in the usual manner; and when the grasses are up, the moles cease to work, and scarce a hillock appears till after harvest.

I remain, SIR,

Your most obedient servant,

EDWARD JONES.

*Wepre-Hall,*
*December* 24, 1799.

Mr. CHARLES TAYLOR.

The

The SILVER MEDAL was this Session
presented to Mr. JOHN HORRIDGE,
of Raikes, near Bolton in the Moors,
Lancashire, for the following Communication on the Preparation and
Application of COMPOSTS for MA-
NURE.

### SIR,

PERMIT me to request you to lay
before the Society for the Encouragement of Arts, &c. the following
memorial of the improvements and 'experiments which I have made in a quantity of land.

In the first place, I must solicit your
attention to a new and cheap method
of planting potatoes, and which I never
knew to be attempted by any one but
myself. The following is the manner in
which I tried the experiment:—A quantity of land in my farm wanted draining,

and .

and I had occasion, for a large main-
drain for that purpose; in the cutting
thereof I found a quantity of earth, in
a solid bed, resembling peat, but of a
more solid substance than peat generally
is. I threw it into heaps, and, after the
ochery water had left it, mixed it with
lime, which appeared to me to form
with it an excellent manure. After this,
I fallowed a field of a gravelly soil,
drilled it for potatoes, and put the same
quantity of this Compost into the drills,
as I should otherwise have done of black
dung; and the produce from eight statute acres was 864 loads, of thirteen
score to the load. I then ploughed it
for wheat, and had a most excellent
crop; sowed it with white clover and
grass seeds, and let it lie for grass: it
has been, and is now, one of the best
pastures in the neighbourhood. The
land, before the improvement, was worth
about £1. 10s. an acre, and, after taking
two very great crops from it, is now
                                    worth

worth about £3. per acre. The general opinion of the country was against the use of lime, in the setting of potatoes: it has, however, answered beyond expectation; and had I been under the necessity of procuring dung for my potatoes, instead of this Compost, it would have cost me six times as much money.

Having made the above experiment with potatoes and wheat, I was inclined to try the same sort of Compost upon grass-lands. In a little valley between two small hills in my farm, I found a very large bed of peat, composed of decayed vegetable substances, which was boggy, and in some places upwards of nine feet in depth. This I drained and drew off the stagnant water with which it was filled: it appeared to me the whole bed, in consequence of being laid dry, had fermented; for when we afterwards cut it, we found it converted to very fine mould. I caused it to be

trenched

trenched to the next stratum, which was
marl, and mixed it with lime hot from
the kiln; but very soon found that I
must slack the lime before mixing, or it
would have burnt it to ashes, by under-
going a fresh degree of fermentation.
The quantity I mixed was nine thousand
tons, with 1327 horse-loads of lime, which
cost me about £160, and I gave one
penny per cubic yard for the trenching
and mixing: and having about thirty
acres of gravelly soil, I begun in October to cover my land with this Compost,
which, in a very short time, proved advantageous; for the grass began to
spring as if it had been April, and soon
produced a very luxuriant pasture of
about four acres in extent. This I covered first, and turned into it eight milch
cows, about the 15th of December. They
fed thereon till the 1st of March, and
gave me a very great quantity of milk
and butter; and the butter was rich and
yellow, like spring butter. The cows,
while

while in this pasture, had very little hay, and that during the night, of which they would eat only a very few pounds. Since I took out my cows, I have pastured the land with twenty in-lamb ewes, of the large white-faced or Malham breed.— They are now pasturing; and I doubt not but it would feed sheep very fat. I have now covered about twenty-six acres more, which promise to be as successful as the other, and amounting to, in the whole, thirty acres. This, prior to the improvements, was worth £2 : 10s. per acre, and is now worth £4 per acre.

This Compost is, I believe, equal to the best manure I could obtain, and the advantage arising from peat compost with lime, when laid upon gravel, sandy, or clay soils, is almost invaluable. The quantity of this Compost which I have now ready prepared, together with what I have used, amounts to nine thousand tons, which has been raised since last summer;

summer; and the total expense is £530. The quantity per acre is one hundred and forty tons, which cost me about £8 per acre. Had it been dunged the common way, it would have cost me sixteen guineas per acre, and would not have answered so well. The remainder of my compost is upwards of four thousand tons; I have thirty acres more to cover, the greatest quantity of which I intend to plant with potatoes. By the statement above, you will see the annual value of the land at present, and what its value was prior to those improvements.

I remain, SIR,

Yours respectfully,

JOHN HORRIDGE.

*Raikes, near Bolton le Moors,*
*Lancashire.*

Mr. CHARLES TAYLOR.

Certified the 11th of March, 1801, by

THOMAS BANCROFT, Vicar of Bolton.
RA. FLETCHER.    PETER SMITH.

# PAPERS

## IN

# CHEMISTRY.

# CHEMISTRY.

The GOLD MEDAL, being the Premium
offered for preserving FRESH WATER
SWEET during long Voyages, was this
Session adjudged to SAMUEL BEN-
THAM, Esq. of Queen's Square, West-
minster, from whom the following
Account and Certificates were re-
ceived.

SIR,

THE Society for the Encouragement
of Arts, &c. having thought proper to offer a premium in order to ascertain, for the use of the public, the best
mode of preserving Fresh Water sweet at
Sea, I request you to lay before the
Society an account of the method which
I have employed for this purpose on
board two ships, and which has been
attended

attended with all the success that can be
reasonably expected.

The mode in which I conceived Fresh
Water might be preserved sweet, was
merely by keeping it in vessels of which
the interior lining at least should be of
such a substance as should not be acted
upon by the water, so as to become a
cause of contamination. Accordingly,
on board the two ships here alluded to,
the greater part of the water was kept,
not in casks, but in cases or tanks,
which, though they were made of wood,
on account of strength, were lined with
metallic plates, of the kind manufactured by Mr. Charles Wyatt of Bridge-
street, under the denomination of tinned
copper-sheets; and the junctures of the
plates or sheets were soldered together,
so that the tightness of the cases depended entirely on the lining, the water
having no where access to the wood.
The shape of these cases was adapted to
that of the hold of the ship, some of
them

them being made to fit close under the platform, by which means the quantity of water stowed was considerably greater than could have been stowed, in the same space, by means of casks; and thereby the stowage room on board ship was very much increased.

The quantity of water kept in this manner on board each ship, was about forty tons divided into sixteen tanks; and there was likewise, on board each of the ships, about thirty tons stowed in casks as usual.

As the stowing the water in tanks was considered as an experiment, the water in the casks was used in preference; that in the tanks being reserved for occasions of necessity, excepting that a small quantity of it was used occasionally for the purpose of ascertaining its purity, or when the water in the casks was deemed, when compared with that in tanks, too bad for use.

O                                    The

The water in thirteen of the tanks, on board one ship, and in all the tanks on board the other, was always as sweet as when first taken from the source; but in the other three of the tanks, on board one ship, the water was found to be more or less tainted as in the casks. This difference, however, is easily accounted for, by supposing that the water of these tanks was contaminated before it was put into them; for in fact the whole of the water was brought on board in casks, for the purpose of filling the tanks, and no particular care was taken, to taste the water at the time of taking it on board.

After the water kept in this manner had remained on board a length of time which was deemed sufficient for experiment, it was used out, and the tanks were replenished as occasion required: but in some of the tanks, on board one ship at least, the original water had remained

mained three years and a half, as appears by the certificates herewith inclosed. About twenty-five gallons of the water, which had remained this length of time in the ship, are sent to the Society, in two vessels made of the same sort of tinned copper with which the tanks were lined.

I am, Sir,

Your obedient servant,

Samuel Bentham.

A certificate from Captain William Bolton, commander of the said vessel, dated Sheerness, 28th of June, 1800, accompanied this letter, stating that the water delivered to the Society was taken from a tank holding about seven hundred gallons, and which his predecessor Captain Portlock had informed him had been poured into this tank in De-

O 2                    cember

cember 1796, except about thirty gallons added in 1798, and had remained
good during the whole time.

The signatures to the above accounts
were certified on the 28th of June, 1800,
by the

Rev. C. Thee, Minister of Sheerness.

In a letter dated January 27, General
Bentham also states, that the water
which had been preserved sweet on
board his Majesty's sloops Arrow and
Dart, and of which he had sent specimens to the Society, was taken from the
well at the King's brewhouse at Weevil,
from whence ships of war lying at or
near Portsmouth are usually supplied
with water for their sea store, as well as
for present use.

The

The Thanks of the Society were this Session voted to the Rev. EDMUND CARTWRIGHT, of Mary-le-Bone, for the following Communication upon the Production of OPIUM from Lettuces.

## SIR,

HAVING lately made a discovery which I have reason to think may in the event lead to consequences of importance, whether considered as an object of science connected with the medical art, or of political economy in influencing an article of commerce, I feel it incumbent upon me to lay it before a Society with whose views it coincides, and to which, from a variety of personal motives, I am zealously attached.

Happening, some time in the month of August last, to read an account of the

O 3 · process

inspissated to admit of taking a solid form, I carried it, amounting to about six grains, to my friend Dr. George Pearson, requesting he would bring its properties, in any way he thought most satisfactory, to the test of experiment. The Doctor has since favoured me with the following letter on the subject.

DEAR SIR,

ACCORDING to your request, I have the pleasure of sending you an account of the effects of the dried milky juice of Lettuce-stalks, in the instance which fell under my observation. This instance was John Sheppy, aged nineteen years, who had been ill with what is called chronic rheumatism about two months, so as to be confined to his chair and bed. He had regularly slept every night from about nine to twelve o'clock; but at two o'clock had been uniformly awaked by considerable pains of his

O 4                    limbs,

limbs, especially of the elbows, and passed the remainder of the night in a sleepless state.

The sufferer had taken, for several nights preceding the exhibition of the dried Lettuce juice, a scruple in weight of Dover's powder without any relief; and, in place of this medicine, I administered the six grains of dried Lettuce juice at nine o'clock. The consequence was, that in twenty minutes he fell asleep, and slept all night soundly till four in the morning, and a great part of the day following. The next night he also had but slight pain, till the third night, when as usual the paroxysm of suffering returned at midnight. The day after the taking this medicine, the patient was affected with head-ache, and felt a little numbness. He had three evacuations by stool the day following.

On the fourth night after the Lettuce juice had been given, he swallowed one

grain

grain of solid Opium, but without any subsequent relief.

On the fifth night *three* grains of solid Opium were given, but still he had a recurrence of pain at night, and passed a restless night, although not so bad as usual; nor by a repetition of opium could the case be effectually relieved. But it was at last cured by frictions with mercurial ointment.

The preceding trial, I apprehend, shews, as decidedly as a single case can do, that the efficacy of dried Lettuce juice, as an *anodyne*, is at least equal to the dried poppy juice, commonly called Opium, if given in adequate doses.

Yours, &c.

G. PEARSON.

If it should be found on subsequent trials, that the milky juice of Lettuce possesses, as possibly it may do, all the valuable properties of the common Opium, Lettuces may become an important article of culture for the sake of their milky juice

juice only. But the cultivation of Lettuces has this further advantage over that of poppies:—after having yielded what milky juice can be obtained from them, Lettuces afford very wholesome and nutritious food for cattle, especially hogs, which are known to be remarkably fond of them.

There have not been wanting instances, as I have been informed, of Lettuces having been sown purposely to be given to hogs, particularly when first weaned.

Since writing the above, I find a similar discovery has recently been made in America, the particulars of which are detailed in the last Volume of the Transactions of the American Philosophical Society just published. The experiments that were there tried corroborate the one made by Dr. Pearson.

Yours, &c.

EDMUND CARTWRIGHT.

*April* 10, 1801.

Mr. CHARLES TAYLOR.

# PAPERS

## ON THE

# POLITE ARTS.

# POLITE ARTS.

The Thanks of the Society were this
Session voted to Mr. TIMOTHY SHEL-
DRAKE, of the Strand, London, for
the following Communication on the
Nature and Preparation of DRYING
OILS for painting Pictures; being an
Addition to his former Remarks, pub-
lished in the Sixteenth and Seventeenth
Volumes of their Transactions.

SIR,

IN the year 1797 I communicated to
the Society, some papers on the preparation of vehicles for painting; the
intention of which was to point out
such as gave brilliancy and duration to
colours, and were probably similar to,
if not actually the same as, those which
were

were used by those artists who were most celebrated for their skill in the art of colouring. As the facts contained in those papers were likely to be useful to such as practised the art of painting, and as I declared that I had no expectations of premium or compensation for this communication, the Society voted me their greater Silver Pallet; and it has been resolved to publish the papers in the order in which they were received from me.

In N° I. I merely stated the fact, that colours mixed with solutions of amber or copal were more brilliant and durable than the same colours when mixed with drying oils ; and I offered to make farther communications to the Society on this subject, if required.

Having been requested to do so, I communicated the following (N° II.) memorandums, On the nature and pre-paration of Drying Oils, composed with

a view

a view to the improvement of such as are used by artists, as vehicles for painting.

The above-mentioned paper was shown to some artists, who gave it as their opinion that the vehicle proposed was not new, and it was thought impossible to paint with it. To this I replied, that I knew it was not new, and believed it to be the vehicle used by many of the older painters, particularly such as were most celebrated for their skill in colouring: and I digested the fruits of my researches on this part of the subject in the paper N° III. entitled, " Conjectures tending to show that the Vehicle described is similar in principle, if not identically the same, as that used by several of the old Painters," &c.

In this paper it is mentioned, that a part of the peculiar effect of the Venetian pictures is occasioned by the method or process used in painting them; and being asked my opinion on this part

of

of the subject, I communicated the paper N° IV. which has been printed in the Sixteenth Volume of the Society's Transactions, page 279, with the title of " Dissertation on Painting in Oil, in a manner similar to that practised in the ancient Venetian School;" and another paper, N° V. containing " An Account of my Method of purifying the Oils, dissolving the Resins, and compounding them together, so as to form Vehicles for Painting or Varnishes." This paper has been published in the Seventeenth Volume of the Society's Transactions, page 283.

It is evident these papers were written singly at the time they were communicated; and though each of them may be thought satisfactory, with respect to the particular subjects of which it treats, yet as a whole they are defective; and are in that respect undoubtedly different from what they would have been, had I arranged my materials so as to form one

dis-

dissertation on the subject. As it is believed that they may convey useful hints to those who are engaged in the Art of Painting, it has been thought advisable to restore them to that connected form in which they were communicated by me, and to thus print them in the Society's Transactions, merely referring in their proper places to those parts which have already appeared in the former volumes.

N° II. *On the Nature and Preparation of Drying Oils; with a View to the Improvement of such as are used by Artists, as Vehicles for Painting.*

Expressed Oils, considered with a view to the painter's use of them, may be divided into two kinds; first, such as are capable of drying in some circumstances by themselves, and always with certain additions; and secondly, such as

P

cannot

cannot be made to dry by any means whatever.

Of the first, which I shall call Drying Oils, there are three in common use, viz. linseed, nut, and poppy oil. The first is darkest coloured, and dries the soonest; the second is lighter, but does not dry so soon; and the third has least colour, and dries slower than either of the others.

By a process, which it is perhaps needless to describe here *(see Vol. xvii. page 281)*, I have succeeded in separating from each of those oils, a mucilage or gum, in a liquid state, and capable of mixing with water in every proportion, though, when thoroughly dry, it would not dissolve in cold water; but my experiments on this head were not carried to any great length. It is to be remarked that linseed oil afforded most of this gum, nut oil the next largest quantity, and poppy oil the least of all.

Olive

Olive oil, when treated in the same manner, afforded none of this mucilaginous substance; whence I was led to conclude that the essential difference between the drying Oils, and those which do not dry, consists in this:—that the latter either contains no mucilage or gum, or that it is so intimately combined with its other principles, that it cannot be separated from them in that peculiar manner which always takes place in Oils which dry by themselves, or when mixed with colours.

If drying Oil is exposed to the air, in a shallow vessel, and left at rest, a pellicle is soon formed on the top, and becomes externally perfectly dry. If this be removed, a second will be formed in the same manner; and if this experiment be repeated many times on the same quantity of oil, without moving or shaking the vessel, it will be found that the second pellicle will require more time to form it than the first, and so on, till

it

it will be found difficult to get it fairly skinned over in a considerable time. The same effect takes place, in a less visible manner, in every quantity of drying Oil which is united with colours in a picture.

From this experiment it is to be concluded, that drying Oils exert that faculty by throwing up their mucilaginous parts, which become solid when at rest, and in contact with the air.

The ingredients added to Oils to make them dry faster, viz. calces of lead, saline substances, earths or gums, are such as unite with and increase the quantity of those parts which float to the top, and form a skin, more or less dark, over the colours originally mixed with them. If we consider the nature of these ingredients, we shall be at once enabled to account for a fact universally known, viz. that in proportion to the strength of the drying Oil used in painting a picture its colour becomes depraved. It

will

will be injured and finally destroyed, by being kept in a damp situation, excluded from a free circulation of air, or placed under a glass.

The desideratum is to prepare Oil or other vehicle for painting, so that the colours, when mixed with it, shall not be debased under any of the above-mentioned circumstances. It must be so prepared or used, that it shall serve as a cement to unite and bind the colours, without skinning over them. It must likewise not contain those principles which always exist in the calces of lead, saline, or earthy substances, which from the first deprave the colours, and attract particles from the air, under peculiar circumstances, which increase that depravity, till at last the appearance of the colours is totally destroyed.

It is only among the resins or bitumens that we can expect to find a substance possessing the properties requisite to give to colours all the brilliancy

P 3                                    and

and durability of which they are suscep-
tible.    My first attempts and experiments were made with solutions of
mastic and sandarac in the painters oils;
but though these compositions possessed
more brilliancy than the common drying
oils, they were liable to a considerable
objection; for they did not dry readily,
and when dry, were easily acted upon
by all the common solvents for resinous
substances, and on that account must
be very deficient in durability, which is
one of the most necessary qualities I
wished to discover.

The difficulty with which amber is in
any way dissolved, suggested the propriety of trying that substance.    Accordingly I dissolved it, in each of the
painters oils, by Dr. Lewis's process,
without injuring its colour; and this
solution was made in the common way.
It was much darker coloured in itself,
but produced scarcely any difference in
effect when mixed with colour.    By experiments

periments with each of these solutions I ascertained the following facts, viz.

Every colour, and all the tints compounded from it, were more brilliant than corresponding tints and colours mixed with the best drying Oils to be procured from the shops.

Colours mixed with amber, after having been shut up in a drawer for several years, lost nothing of their original brilliancy. The same colours tempered with oils, and excluded from the air, were so much altered, that they could scarcely be recognized.

Colours tempered with amber were laid on plates of metal, and exposed (both in the air and close boxes) for a long time, to different degrees of heat, from that of the sun in summer to the strong heat of a stove, without being injured. It is needless to observe that oil colours cannot undergo the same trials without being destroyed.

P 4                    These

These colours, when perfectly dried in any way, were not acted upon by spirit of wine and spirit of turpentine united. They were washed with spirit of sal armoniac, and solutions of pot-ash, for a longer time than would destroy common oil colours, without being injured.

They dry as well in damp as in dry weather, and without any skin upon the surface. They are not liable to crack, and are of a flinty hardness; whence it appears that this vehicle possesses every desirable property, and it is presumed may be a discovery of some importance to artists.

Having succeeded thus far with amber, I tried the same experiments upon solutions of gum copal, which is nearly as hard and insoluble as amber itself. The result of these was the same as the former, except that with copal the colours were something brighter than with amber. As it is extremely troublesome

to

to dissolve the copal and amber, I tried those solutions of them in oil which are sold in the shops. When good, I found them to answer as well as my own. This is a great convenience, as many might be deterred by the difficulty of preparing this vehicle, who may willingly use it, as it thus to be procured without that trouble.

## The Method of using the Solution of Amber or Copal, as a Vehicle for painting.

The cloth or other substance to be painted on, should be prepared with some colour fully saturated with drying oil; or it will be better done with the same vehicle to be used in painting. If it is not fully saturated, it will absorb some of the vehicle from the colours, which is what is commonly termed the colours sinking in.

All the colours which require grinding, should be previously ground in spirit of turpentine. All the pure parts should be tempered

tempered with such a quantity of the vehicle as will enable them to lie on the pallet. The white should be tempered as stiff as possible. All the tints should be made by mixing the colours so prepared without any more of the vehicle, but they should be diluted with spirit of turpentine, if necessary for working.

If the ground is properly prepared, and the above caution observed in tempering the colours, it will be found that all the dark colours in the picture will bear their full tone, and have a demi-transparency, which increases their native brilliancy, without the dingy appearance so common in ordinary oil-painting. The admixture of white increases the body of the colours progressively, till there will be left in the lightest parts, only so much of the vehicle as will bind the colours, and give them their full tone, but with very little of a shining appearance. When the picture is perfectly dry, it should be varnished with a

mastic

mastic or similar varnish. Perhaps the best would be copal varnish made by solution in spirit of turpentine, or spirit of wine.

The rationale of this vehicle seems to be this: the amber and copal, when dissolved in oil, form a homogeneous mass, which dries by inspissating, instead of skinning over, like the common drying oils, which consist of heteregeneous parts, some of which separate and dry on the top.

As the amber and copal are not soluble in any of the menstruums which · dissolve most resinous substances, pictures painted with them cannot be injured, if cleaned with those menstruums: and as they are extremely hard, and the most durable substances of their class, they protect the colours from every kind of injury, more effectually than any other known vehicle.

Nº III.

N° III.   *Conjectures tending to show that the vehicle which I have described, is similar in principle, if not identically the same, as that used by several of the older Painters, who were eminent for their skill in Colouring.*

Lomazzo, an eminent painter, and pupil of Leonardo da Vinci, published a Treatise on Painting, in which it is mentioned that linseed or nut oil was generally used for painting: he likewise observes, that powdered glass was used as a dryer.  As Lomazzo was blind when he published his treatise, he could have no motive for keeping any thing which he knew secret; whence it is to be concluded, that those oils were generally used for painting in his time, and that he knew of no exceptions to the practice.

In one part of L. da Vinci's Treatise on Painting, he mentions *nut-oil and*
*amber*

*amber*. As we know that amber gives peculiar brilliancy to colours, that L. da Vinci was peculiarly celebrated for the richness of his colouring, and are informed from his own writings that he was acquainted with solution of amber in nut-oil, it is to be presumed *that* was the vehicle he used. If this supposition is *not* to be admitted, we must believe that he knew how to dissolve amber in nut-oil (a process at that time both tedious and troublesome), without knowing the best use to which he could possibly apply it.

Leonardo's biographer says, " When he was at Rome, Leo X. resolved to employ him. Leonardo hereupon sets himself to the distilling of oils, and the preparing of varnishes to cover his paintings withal: of which the Pope being informed, said, pertly enough, that he could expect nothing of a man who thought of finishing his works before he had begun them. Leonardo therefore

therefore left Rome without having been employed."

I must beg leave to dissent from his Holiness's opinion. If my idea of Leonardo's vehicle be just, it was natural for him to begin the preparation of it as soon as he knew that he was to be employed as a painter: and as the spirit of that time led every one who made any useful discovery, to preserve it as a valuable secret, it was equally natural for him to account for his employment by saying that he was preparing varnishes. Whatever his secrets were, they remained unknown to the world till 1651, when his Treatise on Painting was published.

The next intimation of solutions of amber which I have obtained is from the works of Boyle, who gained much of his information from Italian chemists; whence it is evident that the knowledge of this preparation is of long standing in that country; and its use, if it was

used

used at all in the arts, is to be sought for in the works of Italian artists.

Whoever examines the Venetian pictures with attention, considers that the best artists of that school were remarkable for the facility with which they worked, and reflects on some passages in Lomazzo, will be disposed to admit that the peculiar skill of the Venetian painters depended on three circumstances, viz. the colours they used, their method of using them, and the vehicle they worked with. Of the first, Lomazzo gives positive information: the second can never be known without information equally positive; but of the vehicle some knowledge may be obtained by way of analysis. Till that knowledge is obtained, I may perhaps be excused for hazarding the following conjectures.

If my experiments have not misled me, I am entitled to draw the following conclusions from them. Wherever a picture is found possessing evidently superior

perior brilliancy of colour independent
of what is produced by the painter's
skill in colouring, that brilliancy is derived from the admixture of some resinous substance in the vehicle. If it does
not yield on the application of spirit of
turpentine and spirit of wine separately
or together, or to such alkalies as are
known to dissolve oils in the same time,
it is to be presumed that vehicle contains
amber or copal, because they are the
only substances known to resist those
menstrua.

I have been told, and some experiments of my own prove the information
to be true, that the Venetian pictures,
considered with respect to vehicle, are of
two kinds: for some are extremely hard,
and not at all affected by any of the
above menstrua; others are similar in
colour, but so tender that it is scarcely
possible to clean them without injury,
and in that respect are little superior to
mere turpentine colours. The first, in
consequence

consequence of the data which I have laid down, incur the suspicion of being painted with amber or copal, but how are we to distinguish with which?

As each of these substances resists equally the common menstrua, perhaps the distinction can only be made by ascertaining the date of the picture. For example:—if it is found to have been painted before copal was known in commerce, it may safely be said to have amber for its basis; but if it has been painted after that period, I know of no method of distinguishing which of the two was made use of. As copal could not have been known, as an article of trade, before the seventeenth century, it follows that all pictures painted before that period, and possessing the properties I have described, must have amber for the basis of their vehicle. As this exception necessarily includes all the Venetian artists of the first class, we are therefore authorised to conclude that, if the works

Q

of

of these artists can bear the test of the menstrua I have mentioned, amber was the basis of the vehicle with which they were painted.

I once saw a recipe for dissolving copal, said to have been brought from Venice towards the close of the last century. The process was, to melt Venice turpentine upon the fire, to add gradually copal powdered, stirring them together to be united in fusion, and afterwards spirit of turpentine, in order to dilute it to the consistence of varnish. I tried this process, but it did not succeed.

Upon inquiry I found that the Venice turpentine of the shops was only common resin, dissolved in spirit of turpentine to a proper consistence; whence the cause of my failure was evident. Reflecting on the commercial pursuits of the Venetians in the fifteenth and sixteenth centuries, I was led to conjecture that the substance called originally Venice

nice turpentine was the product of some country intimately connected with them. Pursuing this idea, I procured, with much difficulty, some Chio turpentine, repeated my experiment, and succeeded completely. Besides the property of uniting easily with copal, it had others that excited my attention. Common resins, if exposed to fire, burn with extreme fierceness and rapidity; but when some of this was laid on the point of a knife, and held in the flame of a candle, it melted and dropped down before it began to burn. It emitted a peculiarly grateful smell; was of a most beautiful pale gold colour; was more brilliant than any turpentine I had ever seen; and when diluted to the consistence of varnish, perfectly resembled in colour, a solution of copal which I made in spirit of turpentine with camphor.

I showed some of this to a gentleman who was conversant in such subjects. He told me that, when at Venice, he fre-

Q 2

quently

quently rubbed pictures violently with
his handkerchief, to try if he could discover what they were painted with; and
when so rubbed, they smelt exactly like
what I then produced to him.

As I had previously perfected what I
thought to be a superior vehicle, with
which this could not vie in hardness and
durability, I did not prosecute my experiments with this any farther; but as
it unites rapidly with copal, and possesses all its visible properties, I may be
permitted to conjecture that it would
have similar effects when mixed with
colours: and if there was any second,
inferior, and common vehicle, similar in
its visible properties to the last, and so
much within the reach of the most ordinary painters, as to give their works one
common mark with those of the first
artists, it would be difficult to point out
a substance more likely to afford it than
this which must have been common in
their own country, since its name is still
attached

attached to substances of the same class throughout Europe, though its real properties are now but little known.

If this was the basis of the common Venetian vehicle, it might have been used with or without oil. If the latter, the works of the common Venetian painters must have been mere varnish painting : if the former, it must have been compounded with the oil, according to the principles I have already explained. I am inclined towards the latter opinion, from having heard an observation attributed to Bombelli, a celebrated Venetian painter, who said, *" That he wished his pictures to dry as fast as possible, that the oil in them might not rise to the surface, and turn yellow."*

To this conjecture it may be objected that turpentines and compounds from them do not dry well. I am not prepared to answer this objection, as I have made no experiments relative to

it;

it; but it certainly is not conclusive, as such compounds may not dry well in this country, though they may in the warm climate of Italy.

In the *Maniere d'imprimer les Tableaux*, published by Le Blond at Paris, 1740, is a recipe for the varnish he used on the coloured prints executed by him, in this country, before he went to France. It is as follows:—" Take four parts of balsam of capivi and one of copal. Powder and sift the copal; and throw it by degrees into the balsam of capivi, stirring it well each time it is put in: I say each time; for the powdered copal must be put in by degrees, day after day, in at least, fifteen different parts. The vessel must be close stopped, and exposed to the heat of the sun, or a similar degree of heat, during the whole time; and when the whole is reduced uniformly to the consistence of honey, add a quantity of warm turpentine; *Chio turpentine is the best*."

Le Blond's

Le Blond's prints were long neglected, and are now forgotten. Whatever difference of opinion may prevail respecting them, there can be none respecting his varnish, as I have seen some of these prints in perfect condition, notwithstanding they had been thrown carelessly about for nearly sixty years.

Le Blond was a pupil of Carlo Maratti. He died at a very advanced age, leaving behind him the character of an ingenious projector. It is probable that he might collect much information analogous to his pursuits during a long life; but it is more probable that he obtained much of it where he received his education. Thus, wherever we find notices of the use of these substances in the Arts, they invariably lead us towards Italy, where they certainly were first known.

I have thus detailed the circumstances which impress me with a conviction that the vehicle I have offered to public notice

is,

is, in substance, the same as that used by the best colourists of the Italian schools. What impression the facts I have enumerated may make upon others I know not: but still the truth of my opinion must be determined by experience; for it would be of small consequence to prove that this vehicle was used in former times, unless it can likewise be made evident that it will be useful to the present race of Artists.

Yours, &c.

TIMOTHY SHELDRAKE.

*Strand,*
*February,* 1801.

Mr. CHARLES TAYLOR.

# PAPERS

## IN

# MANUFACTURES.

SPECIMEN of PAPER

FROM THE

PAUT-PLANT.

# MANUFACTURES.

The Sum of TWENTY GUINEAS, being the Premium offered for making PAPER from raw VEGETABLE SUBSTANCES superior to any hitherto manufactured from such Substances, was this Session adjudged to Mr. THOMAS WILLMOTT, of Shoreham in Kent; from whom the following Accounts and Certificates were received.

SIR,

AT the particular request of Mr. Sewell, bookseller, in Cornhill, I made some Paper from Gunny-bags, he having very much wished something might be done to reduce the high price of rags.

I was afterwards informed that a Premium of Twenty Guineas was offered by the Society of Arts, &c. for ten

reams

reams of useful Paper made from raw Vegetable Substances. I had made only six reams from the above article; and on mentioning it to Mr. Sewell, he told me, he was apprehensive the Society would not allow the Premium for what I had made, it not being the quantity specified, nor made from the raw material; he therefore undertook to get me a quantity of the raw material from which Gunny-bags are made, that I might make the ten reams as specified. I have now made that quantity, and have sent one ream to the Society, and the other nine I have left with Mr. Sewell.

If the Society should think I merit the Premium, or any part of it, for the pains and trouble I have taken, I shall think myself much honoured by such mark of their favour.

I remain, Sir,

Your humble servant,

T. Willmott.

*Shoreham, Kent,*
*November 6, 1800.*

Certificates were sent from William Strip and John Penfold, confirming the above; and that they had prepared the article, and saw it made into paper, and sent back to London on the 31st of October.

THIS is to certify, that I, JOHN SEWELL, of N° 32, Cornhill, having had a hint from a literary gentleman, long resident in India, that a specimen of paper which I had approved, was made in the East Indies from a vegetable called the Paut Plant, I applied to some of the principal persons in the Company's warehouse for that article, and was informed that a large quantity had been imported into England about seven years ago; that the whole was sold at from 18s. to 20s. per cwt. to various persons concerned in the sail, hammock, sack, and packthread business; that some went to Manchester and Scotland,

Scotland, but that none then remained in the Company's warehouse except samples.

From such samples, and what remained with the brokers, I collected enough to make the few reams of Paper manufactured by Mr. Thomas Willmott.

The first attempt failed, by the Paper being spoiled in bleaching; the Paper now sent, is the result of a second trial.

From further experiments made in my presence, by an ingenious chemist well skilled in the manufactory, it is found that gunny-bags, ropes, and other waste materials made from the same substance, will make a better paper.

It is also found by experience, that old rags, which have been used on the table, bed, or for apparel, make better paper than new flax or hemp.

Gunny-bags may be had from most grocers, gunpowder-makers, and dealers in in India goods; as the Company send nearly all their importations in those bags. They may be bought in almost any quantity, at so cheap a rate as from a farthing to a penny per pound; and if introduced for manufacturing wrapping and other inferior Papers, they cannot fail to reduce the present high price of rags.

JOHN SEWELL.

*Cornhill,*
*November 6, 1800.*

## Mr. CHARLES TAYLOR.

SIR,

SINCE I saw you, it has occurred to me, that the circumstance of ships being engaged to bring home rice from Bengal, may afford a better opportunity, than I first imagined, for bringing over a considerable quantity of *paut*. Experience has shewn that some ships cannot take such heavy articles as rice and

sugar,

sugar, to the extent of their chartered tonnage. As *paut* may be shipped from Bengal at about 4s. per cwt. if it is put on board without being packed into bales, it seems an advantageous article to occupy that space in the upper part of rice ships, which must otherwise remain entirely vacant. As none of the *paut* hitherto brought over, has sold for less than 20s. per cwt. there appears to be ample room for profit to the importer, and very little capital risked.

It is procured at the lowest prices, and in the greatest abundance, at Maulda and Buddaul, where it costs barely 3s. per cwt.; in Calcutta the prices are higher. This article must be carefully distinguished from the *sun* which is deemed hemp, and is liable to a heavy duty. *Paut* is only liable to a small duty : it is known in India, and has been sent to Europe, by the name of *jute*, and may be characterised as the article

article with which gunnies are always made in Bengal.

I remain, SIR,

Your very humble servant,

H. W. GOODHALL.

To Mr. SEWELL.

\*\*\* The Society have been informed by Mr. Sewell, that two varieties of the Paut plant have been cultivated at Calcutta, viz.

Bhungee Paat, the Corchorus Olitorius of Linnæus, and the Ghee Naltha Paat, or Corchorus Capsularis.

R                    The

The CHICOREE PLANT having for some years past been cultivated upon a very extensive Scale in Germany, for the use of its Root as an excellent Substitute for Coffee, and for the advantage of its Herbage in feeding Cattle, the following Account of the Culture of the Plant, and Method of manufacturing Coffee from its Root, was sent from Germany, by Mr. JOHN TAYLOR, to the Secretary; with some of the Seed, and Samples of the Root in different Stages of its Preparation, which are placed in the Society's Repository for public inspection.

*Mode of cultivating the English Chicoree Plant, Cichorium Intybus of Linnæus, Cichorien Wurzel, or Hindlœufte, of the Germans, as recommended by the Chicoree Coffee Manufacturers at Dresden.*

FOR cultivating the Chicoree Plant a sandy or loamy soil answers best, clay or heavy soil is not proper, because the

the roots cannot penetrate a sufficient depth, and because in such ground they are more difficult to be pulled up, the roots being usually half-a-yard in length. The ground must be either delved a spade or more in depth, or ploughed very deep by two ploughs following each other in the same furrow; this work is best done in autumn. The land must afterwards be lightly ploughed at the time of sowing; but it may be ploughed in like manner in spring, if omitted in autumn, then harrowed and immediately sown. Chicoree does not properly require stable manure, because the roots do not taste so well where cattle dung is used as in land unmanured. Fallow land, or land on which one crop has been grown, is very proper. If the ground be poor, marl, gypsum, lime, or the mud from ponds, are recommended as manures, or composts may be formed from two thirds of loam, and one third of dung for sandy soil; or of

two

two thirds sand and one third dung for loamy soil; by putting the mixture in a heap for some months, watering it repeatedly, and turning it with the spade some weeks before used. By adopting this method the Chicoree will be excellent, and the ground greatly improved for future cultivation.

As the roots run deep, the dung, when used, should be laid low. Changing the land each year is better for the Chicoree, and also for the ground, as by the weeding and working it is in good order for other crops. If the Chicoree be drilled and potatoes grown betwixt the rows, Chicoree may be planted two years together. As potatoes require to be well manured, a crop of corn may then be taken from the land, and Chicoree again planted for one year.

The seed of the preceding year should be chosen for sowing: it should be cleaned from the seeds of weeds, and be mixed with ashes and earth, to enable

it

it to be sown in such a manner that the roots may stand from four to six inches asunder.

Some persons steep the seed for twenty-four hours, in a solution made from three quarts of dung-liquor, six quarts of water, four ounces of common salt, and three ounces of saltpetre, to three pounds of seed; and if that quantity of water be not sufficient to moisten it, add more. After the seed has been steeped therein for eighteen or twenty-four hours, it may be mixed with ashes and earth as above mentioned, and sown on ground laid out in large flats previously harrowed: after sowing, it must be harrowed with one harrow, in the manner that clover and rape seed is covered.

On a Dresden acre of 300 square perches, of something more than fifteen English feet each, containing in the whole 67,500 square feet, three pounds

R 3                    and

and a half to four pounds of seed are sown, according to the goodness of the seed.

The seed may be sown from the middle of April to the middle of June, so that towards autumn the roots may be drawn in succession as the land was sown sooner or later.

After the seed is sown, nothing more is required than to keep it clear from weeds, and either .to draw out the thickest plants in August for use, to allow more room for the smaller ones, or to pluck out the smaller plants, which is the better way, as it will occasion the larger ones to increase until September and October, when they may be dug up to advantage.

The roots, when taken up, must be separated from the stalks, leaves, and fibres, which are commonly used for feeding cattle; the Chicoree Coffee manufacturers pay from 3s. to 4s. per cwt. for such green roots.

Those

Those who wish to raise seed for themselves on a small scale, must preserve some of the strongest roots in a hole in the earth during the winter, and plant them out in the spring: but those who grow the plants in quantities may reserve a plot of the best plants for that purpose; remembering to pluck out any bad plants from amongst them, as the best seed is only produced from good plants.

The seed must be gathered when the greatest part is ripe, by cutting off the stalk and placing it upright for some days in the sun, binding the top round with a little straw to guard the seed from the birds, and to allow it to ripen more perfectly. It is then beat or thrashed out, according as the quantity may require.

*Additional Observations on the Culture and Preparation of Chicoree.*

THE plants flourish best when they have been thinly sown and remain in such state; but where any vacancies occur, those may be filled up with transplanted roots, placed from four to six inches asunder. When the roots are taken up in the autumn, they are first washed, and then cut by a machine into thin slices; afterwards dried partly in the air, and the drying completed on a malt-kiln. They are then laid aside till roasted: when roasted, they will keep for a year or two in a dry place.

Such roots are best whose thicknesses are from one to two inches; if thicker, they are too coarse; and if thinner, have but little taste. In general the leaves are cut off, and used as food for cattle, some weeks previous to the roots being

plucked

plucked up. Some persons strip the leaves several times during the summer, but then there is less produce of the roots.

The roots, when drawn and washed, should be sliced by the hand, or by a machine: they should then be thinly laid upon hurdles in an airy room, and often turned, to prevent them from rotting, and to assist the air in drying them before they are carried to the malt-kiln. If the quantity is small, they may be dried by the common stoves of the room. No more roots should be dug up at once than can be washed and sliced on the same day, if possible.

---

## Manufacture of the Coffee from dried Chicoree Roots.

THE dried Roots are roasted in iron coffee-drums, containing from half a bushel to one bushel each; these drums are placed within brick furnaces, in which

which a space of half a foot is left betwixt the brick-work and the drum, on every side, so that the heat may be equally divided: within the drum are thin bars of iron, running lengthways, to shake or divide the roots whilst roasting; during which operation the drum is constantly kept turning by a handle placed on its axis. The criterion of the roots being properly roasted, is, that they are not too dark as if burnt, nor too light-coloured for want of sufficient roasting: the large and small slices should be roasted separately.

After this operation the roots are ground in the manner of flour, in similar mills, and the fine reserved for use; but the coarser part is again returned to the mill, to be finer ground: it is then packed in casks, or put up in paper bags, as may be thought necessary, and preserved dry.

This powder is the Coffee, and may be prepared alone, as common coffee-
berries,

berries, when ground for use; or it may be mixed with one quarter or one half of its weight of genuine West India or Turkey coffee, at discretion. The price at which it is sold, is usually from five-pence to eight-pence per lb. Raw coffee-berries, mixed with the root whilst roasting, improve its odour and quality.

Large manufactories of the Chicoree Coffee are established, with considerable profit to the proprietors, at Berlin, Magdeburg, Brunswick, Dresden, and other parts of the Continent.

The article is become in general demand and use throughout Germany, as a pleasant and wholesome nourishment, in place of West-India coffee, which formed a considerable part of the diet of the inhabitants.

*Leipsig,*
*June* 4, 1800.

# PAPERS

## IN

## MECHANICKS.

# MECHANICKS.

The SILVER MEDAL was this session adjudged to Mr. H. SARJEANT, of Whitehaven, in Cumberland, for a MACHINE FOR RAISING WATER; from whom the following Account, Description, and Certificates, were received, together with a Drawing of the Machine.

SIR,

I AM sensible that the little Engine, a drawing of which accompanies this letter, can lay no great claim to novelty in its principle; nevertheless it is respectfully submitted to the consideration of the Society, how far its simplicity, and cheapness of construction, may render it worthy of their attention, with a view

to

to its being more generally known and used in similar cases.

Irton-Hall, the seat of E. L. Irton, Esq. is situated on an ascent of sixty or sixty-one feet perpendicular height; at the foot of which, at the distance of about 140 yards from the offices, runs a small stream of water. The object was to raise this to the house for domestic purposes.

To this end a dam was made at a short distance above, so as to cause a fall of about four feet; and the water was brought by a wooden trough, into which was inserted a piece of two-inch leaden pipe, a part of which is seen at A.

The stream of this pipe is so directed as to run into the bucket B, when the bucket is elevated; but so soon as it begins to descend, the stream flows over it, and goes to supply the wooden trough or well in which the foot of the forcing pump C stands, of three inches bore.

D,

D, is an iron cylinder attached to the pump rod, which passes through it. It is filled with lead, and weighs about 240 lbs. This is the power which works the pump, and forces the water through 420 feet of inch pipe from the pump up to the house.

At E is fixed a cord which, when the bucket comes to within four or five inches of its lowest projection, becomes stretched and opens a valve in the bottom of it, through which the water empties itself.

I beg leave to add, that an engine, in a great degree similar to this, was erected some years ago by the late James Spedding, Esq. for a lead-mine near Keswick, with the addition of a smaller bucket which empied itself into the larger, near the beginning of its descent, without which addition it was found that the beam only acquired a libratory motion, without making a full and effective stroke.

S

To

To answer this purpose in a more simple way, I constructed the small Engine in such manner as to finish its stroke (speaking of the bucket end), when the beam comes into an horizontal position, or a little below it.  By this means the lever is virtually lengthened in its descent in the proportion of the radius to the cosine, of about thirty degrees, or as seven to six nearly, and consequently its power is increased in an equal proportion.

It is evident that the opening of the valve might have been effected, perhaps better, by a projecting pin at the bottom; but I chose to give an exact description of the Engine as it stands. It has now been six months in use, and completely answers the purpose intended.

The only artists employed, except the plumber, were a country blacksmith and carpenter; and the whole cost, exclusive

clusive of the pump and pipes, did not amount to £5.

I am, SIR,

Your humble servant,

H. SARJEANT.

*Warwick Court, Holborn.*

Mr. CHARLES TAYLOR.

In another letter, dated Whitehaven, April 28, 1801, Mr. Sarjeant further observes that the pump requires about eighteen gallons of water in the bucket to raise the counter-weight, and make a fresh stroke in the pump; that it makes three strokes in a minute, and gives about a half-gallon into the cistern at each stroke. He adds, " I speak of what it did in the dryest part of last summer; when it supplied a large family, together with work-people, &c. with water for all purposes, in a situation

S 2                     where

where none was to be had before, except some bad water from a common pump which has been since removed. But the above supply being more than sufficient, the Machine is occasionally stopped to prevent wear, which is done by merely casting off the string of the bucket-valve."

*P. S.* I have just been informed that a drawing of the Engine, which I had communicated to a person in this neighbourhood, was sent to a Colliery near Swansea some months ago, and that it has already been applied to use there; it is not however sufficiently powerful for the coal-works in this neighbourhood.

*The following Certificate accompanied these Letters.*

I DO hereby certify, that the Water-Engine constructed near my house, under the direction of Mr. Sarjeant, has been

been eight months in use, and fully answers the purpose intended.

EDMUND L. IRTON.

*Irton-Hall,*
*March* 18, 1801.

I DO also certify the above to be true.

ROBERT WILKINSON,

One of his Majesty's Justices of the Peace for
the County of Cumberland.

*March* 13, 1801.

The

The Sum of TEN GUINEAS, being the Premium offered for taking Whales by the GUN HARPOON, was this Session adjudged to Mr. ROBERT HAYS, Harpooner of the ship Ipswich, fitted out by Mr. T. Wilkinson, of Wapping, from whom the following Account and Certificates were received.

SIR,

I BEG leave to present you with the inclosed Certificate from Captain Robert Kay, commander of my ship Ipswich, employed in the Greenland fisheries, on behalf of Robert Hays, harpooner of the said ship, for the Premium offered by the Society of Arts, &c. for the taking of Whales, he having struck three.

I am, SIR,

Your obedient servant,

T. WILKINSON.

N° 258, *Wapping,*
*November* 24, 1800.

Mr. CHARLES TAYLOR.

. SIR,

BEING, on the 16th of May, 1800, in the latitude of 80° north, and longitude 6° 30′ east from London, I, ROBERT HAYS, harpooner, shot a Whale about ten or eleven fathoms from the boat, which run nine lines out before we got another harpoon fixed in her : it was four hours from the time she was shot until dead. The length of bone was seven feet four inches. Hackluyt's Head-land bearing E. S. E. distant, by estimation, eighteen leagues.

May 26, 1800, being in latitude 79° 40′ north, and longitude 7° east from London, I shot a Whale about nine fathoms from the boat, which run eight lines out before fastened by another harpoon. It was two hours from the time she was struck until dead. The length of bone was nine feet six inches.

June 18, 1800, being in latitude 79° 30′ north, and longitude 7° 30′ east, I shot

S 4                    a Whale

a Whale about eight fathoms distant from the boat, which run eleven lines out before we got another harpoon fixed in her. It was four hours from the time she was shot until dead.

Hackluyt's Head-land bearing E.N.E. distant, by estimation, seven or eight leagues.

The above-mentioned three Whales were struck by me,

ROBERT HAYS.

Witness to the signature,

JOHN WILKINSON,

THIS is to certify the above statement from Robert Hays, harpooner, of the ship Ipswich under my command, is a perfect true and just account; as witness my hand, this 24th of November, 1800.

ROBERT KAY.

No. 11, *Princes-street,*
    *Rotherhithe.*

The

The Sum of TEN GUINEAS was this Session adjudged, as a Bounty, to Mrs. J. BESANT, of Brompton, for a new-invented Undershot WATER-WHEEL; from whom the following Account was received, together with Models, upon the new and old construction, for comparative experiments.

SIR,

I BEG leave to lay before the Society some observations respecting the common Undershot Water-wheel, and to point out the superiority of that of my invention.

First,—In common Water-wheels more than half the water passes from the gate through the wheel, without giving it any assistance.

Secondly,—The floats coming out of the tail-water are resisted with almost the

the whole weight of the atmosphere, at
the instant they leave the surface of the
water.

Thirdly,—The same quantity of water
which passed between the floats at the
head, must of course pass between them
at the tail, and consequently impede the
motion of the wheel.

In the Water-wheel of my invention,

First,—No water can pass but what
acts, with all its force, on the extremity
of the wheel.

Secondly,—The floats coming out of
the water in an oblique direction, prevent the weight of the atmosphere from
taking any effect.

Thirdly,—Although the New Water-
wheel is heavier than that on the old construction, yet it runs lighter on its axis,
the water having a tendency to float it.

Fourthly,—By experiments made with
the models, proofs have been shown, that
the new Wheel has many advantages
over

over the common wheel, and that, when it works in deep tail water, it will carry weights in proportion of three to one, so that it will be particularly serviceable for tide-mills.

I hope on trial, before the Society, my invention will prove successful, and am,

SIR,

Your obedient servant,

J. BESANT.

No. 26, *Brompton*.

To the SECRETARY of the
Society of Arts, &c.

\*<sub>\*</sub>\* Repeated experiments of the above Invention were made by the Committee; from the result of which it appeared to possess some advantages over the common Wheel, and to have a greater power of action.

*Description*

*Description of the late Mr. Besant's Water-wheel.* **Plate IV. Fig. 1 & 2.**

A. The body of the Water-wheel, which is hollow in the form of a drum, and is so constructed as to be proof against the admission of water within it.

B. The axis on which it turns.

C. The float boards, placed on the periphery of the wheel. Each board is obliquely fixed firm to the rim of it, and to the body of the drum.

D. The reservoir, containing the water.

E. The penstock, which regulates the quantity of water running to the wheel.

F. The current of water which has passed the wheel.

*Fig.* 2. Is a front view of the Water-wheel, shewing the oblique direction in which the float boards C are placed on the face of the wheel.

The

The GOLD MEDAL, or FORTY GUINEAS, at the option of the Candidate, being the Premium offered for an Improvement in the Method of DRIVING BOLTS INTO SHIPS, was this Session adjudged to Mr. RICHARD PHILLIPS, of Bristol; from whom the following Account and Certificates were received, and who made choice of the Pecuniary Reward. Models of the Machine are placed in the Society's Repository.

MR. RICHARD PHILLIPS, of Bristol, in several letters sent to the Society, states, that he had invented a method of driving Copper Bolts into Ships, without splitting the heads or bending them; and that by means of tubes contrived by him, for the purpose, this could be effected without difficulty, and had been satisfactorily executed in the presence

sence of several of the principal ship-builders of Bristol.

A Certificate accompanied these letters, from Mr. William James, and Mr. Samuel Hast, ship-builders, and also from Mr. George Winter, of Bristol, testifying that they had tried the experiment of driving Copper Bolts through the jointed Cylinder invented by Mr. Phillips; and that they so far approve of it, that they mean to adopt the general use of them, for driving Bolts in all directions, particularly on the outside of Ships, whether iron or copper; as this method not only prevents the Bolts from bending, but keeps the heads from splitting, and enables the Bolts to be driven much tighter, than by any other means with which they were acquainted. They further add, that by the application of Mr. Phillips's Cylinder and Punch, a Copper Bolt which had been crippled at the edge of the hole, and which could not be started by a mall, went up with

ease

ease in a perpendicular direction in the flat of a ship's bottom, not four feet from the ground.

This Certificate was witnessed by

MR. WILLIAM HOLDEN.

The same facts are also certified by Mr. Thomas Walker, and Mr. James M. Hillhouse, of Bristol, who add their opinion, that the adoption of this invention, in the different dock-yards of the kingdom, will prove very advantageous.

\*\*\* Since Mr. Phillips's first application to the Society for a premium, he has made a considerable improvement in the construction of his Tubes. The description and engraving hereunto annexed are of the improved kind: models of both are, however, preserved in the Society's Repository, for public inspection.

The

The instrument employed for driving the Bolts, consists of a hollow tube formed from separate pieces of cast iron, which are placed upon the heads of each other, and firmly held thereto by iron circles or rings over the joints of the tube. The lowest ring is pointed, to keep the tube steady upon the wood. The Bolt being entered into the end of the hole bored in the wood of the ship, and completely covered by the iron tube, is driven forward within the cylinder by an iron or steel punch, placed against the head of the Bolt, which punch is struck by a mall: and as the bolt goes further into the wood, parts of the tubes are unscrewed and taken off, till the Bolt is driven home into its place up to the head.

The tubes are about five inches in circumference, and will admit a Bolt of seven eighths of an inch in diameter.

*Reference*

*Reference to the Engraving of Mr. R. Phillips's Method of driving Bolts into Ships.* Plate IV. Fig. 3, 4, 5, 6.

### Fig. 3.

A.　The copper bolt, with one end entered into the wood, previous to fixing the tube.

B.　A piece of timber, or ship's side, into which the bolt is intended to be driven.

### Fig. 4.

CCCC.　The parts of the iron tube fastened together, ready to be put on the bolt A.

DDDDD. Iron or brass rings with thumb-screws, placed over the joints of the tube, to hold them firm together.

EEEEE. The thumb-screws, which keep the rings and tubes firm in their proper places.

T　　　　　F. Two

F.  Two points formed on the lower
      ring: they are to stick into the
      timber, and to enable the tube
      to be held firm in its place.

### Fig. 5.

Shows the separation of the parts
  of the tube which is effected
  by slackening the thumb-screws
  and rings.

To put them together, you slide
  the rings over the joints, placed
  as close as possible; then, by
  tightening the thumb-screws,
  you will have them firm together, and may continue the
  tubes to any length, from one
  foot to whatever number is
  required.

### Fig. 6.

GH.  Two steel punches or drifts, to
      be placed on the head of the
      copper bolt within the tube,
      whilst driving. The blow given
                              upon

Mr. R. Phillips's Tubes for driving Bo
into Ships.

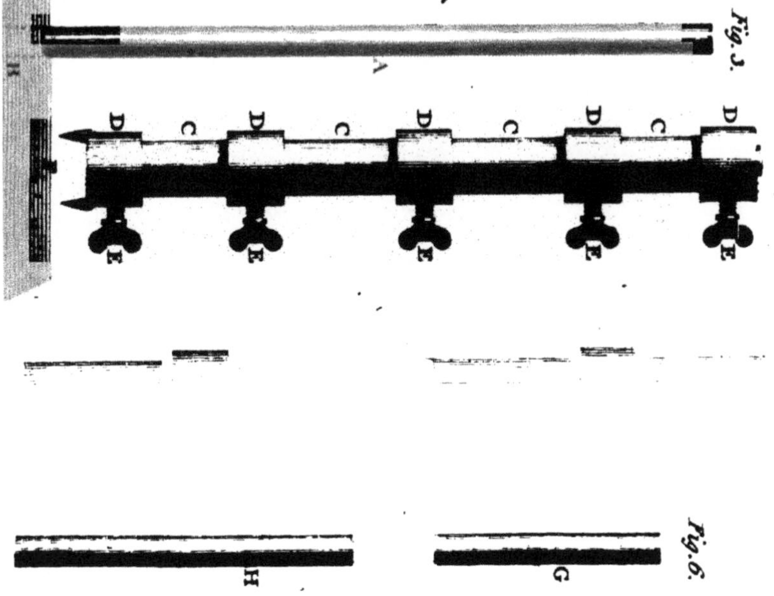

Fig. 1.

Fig. 6.

upon the punch drives forward the bolt. The shortest of them should be used first, and, when driven nearly to its head, should be taken out of the tube, and the longer punch applied in its place.

A Bounty of TWENTY-FIVE GUINEAS was this Session voted to Mr. THOMAS ARKWRIGHT, of Kendal, for his Invention of a Machine for RAISING ORE, &c. from Mines; a Plate and Description of which Machine are hereunto annexed, and a complete Model reserved in the Society's Repository, for the inspection and use of the Public.

SIR,

KNOWING that the Society of Arts, &c. always stand forward in support of ingenuity, I take the liberty of sending you the Model of a Machine, for raising Ore from Mines, and likewise for raising Water, by the same operation, if required, which I beg you will present to the Society.

I am, SIR,

Your most obedient servant,

THOMAS ARKWRIGHT.

*Kendal, in Westmoreland,*
*January 22, 1801.*

*Description.*

*Description of Mr. T. Arkwright's Machine, for raising Ore from Mines.* Plate V.

A.      An endless chain formed of thin plates of iron, through the ends of which plates iron bolts are passed, which keep the sides of the chain at a certain distance asunder, and on which the buckets to contain the ore are suspended.

BCDE.      The buckets suspended on the iron bolts.

GHI.      Three cylinders, round which the chain and buckets revolve. The two cylinders GH are placed above the shaft; the cylinder I within the mine. Their rims are so much higher than the body of the cylinders, as to admit the buckets to lie within the rims.

As the endless chain and buckets are moved forwards by a power applied to the axis of the cylinder G, the bolts of

T 3          the

the chain fall into notches made at regular distances in the rims of that cylinder, which preserve the chain from slipping.

As each empty bucket passes under the axis of the bottom cylinder I, it loads itself with ore instantaneously from a large box K, constantly filling by the workmen below, which box rests on two moveable pins L, at that end furthest from the wheel, and on an iron catch M at the other. The bucket thus filled ascends to the top of the cylinder G; and, in its passage betwixt the cylinders G and H, discharges its contents into a channel or receiver placed betwixt them, from whence they slide into a cart or receptacle placed underneath the inclined trough N. The empty bucket passes over the cylinder H, descends on the opposite side under the cylinder I, and loads itself again at K, as before mentioned; the buckets regularly loading and discharging themselves, whilst the cylinder G is kept in motion.

O is

.1.

C
G
O
H
N
D
B
A
M K
L
E

Fig 2.
K
P

O is a racket-wheel on the cylinder, to prevent a retrograde motion in the chain.

*Fig.* 2. shows, upon a larger scale, the manner in which the box K above mentioned loads the buckets. P is an iron tooth projecting from the endless chain, which, pressing upon the catch R, underneath the box K, occasions that part of the box next the chain to sink down, and discharge into the bucket beneath it a quantity of ore sufficient to fill it. As the loaded bucket rises, it lifts the box K to its former place, till the operation is repeated by the next tooth upon the chain.

\*\*\* The model remaining with the Society contains two machines put in motion by the same power, one of which is for raising ore, the other for clearing mines from water. The machine for raising ore was the object for which the Bounty was given; therefore only that part is engraved and described.

T 4                The

The Sum of FIFTY POUNDS was this
Session voted, as a Bounty, to Mr.
FIELD EVANS, of Pool-Quay, Mont-
gomeryshire, for the Discovery of a
Quarry of BURR-STONE proper for
Mill-stones, from whom the following
Account and Certificates were received,
along with a pair of Mill-stones.

SIR,

BEING informed that the Society for
the Encouragement of Arts, &c.
had offered a Premium to the person
who should discover a quarry of stone
fit for the purpose of Mill-stones, and
of the same quality as French Burr-
stones, and having myself discovered
such a quarry, in a hill called Moel y
Golfa, in the parish of Buttington, in
this county, I have accordingly sent a
pair of Mill-stones to the Society, before
whom

whom I request you to lay my claim as soon as convenient.

I am, Sir,

Your obedient servant,

Field Evans.

*Pool-Quay, Montgomeryshire,*
10th May, 1800.

Mr. Charles Taylor,

The following Certificates accompanied this letter, viz. from Mr. Henry Gardner, mill-stone manufacturer, Liverpool, dated the 1st of March last, stating, that he had manufactured into mill-stones several tons of the Moel-y-Golfa-Hill Burr-stones, and believes them to be a good substitute for French Burr.

From Elisha Williams, dated the 29th of April last, of the parish of Erbistock, in the county of Denbigh, stating, that he had used a pair of Burr mill-stones from

from Moel-y-Golfa quarry in Montgomeryshire, which he had found equal to the French Burr mill-stones, and that they would with ease grind eight measures in one hour.

From John Allport, steward to the Montgomery and Pool House of Industry, dated the 30th of April last, stating, that he had used at the Gaer-mills near Montgomery, one pair of Mill-stones from Moel-y-Golfa quarry, and that he finds them equal to the French Burr mill-stones. The above is also attested by Amb. Gettyn, and Morris Jones, Directors of the Corporation of Guardians of the Poor of the Montgomery and Pool united district, and W. Williams, miller.

From Lewis Evans, Esq. of Esgairgiliog, in the county of Montgomery, stating, that he had used a pair of Mill-stones from the Moel-y-Golfa quarry, for grinding

grinding wheat, and found them equal to the French Burrs. The said Certicate is attested by Hugh Evans, Esq. and Robert Jones, miller, on the 2d of May last.

From W. Heighway, dated Pontesford the 6th of May, 1800, stating, that he had used two pair of Mill-stones at his mills, in the county of Salop, for grinding wheat; that they came from Moel-y-Golfa quarry; and that he found them equal to the French Burrs.

From John Davies, New Mills, dated the 7th of May last, stating that the Mill-stones usually obtained on the Moel-y-Golfa Hills answer very well, and that he had used them himself.

In a letter dated the 5th of March last, Mr. Field Evans states, that the specimens of Stone which he has sent may not probably appear so porous as the French Burrs,

Burrs, the pores being in a great measure filled with a soft chalky substance, which, when worked, clears out, and is not found to injure the flour; and that the stones become harder in using. That the quarry lies in the south-west end of the hill, about 300 yards from the foot or bottom of it, the vein being in some parts three yards wide, in others not more than four feet; that it makes its appearance on the surface from south-west to north-east, from 400 to 600 yards, and then disappears on the surface for about a mile north-east, where the vein is much wider than before mentioned; that the quarry has been worked from fifteen to twenty feet deep, without any appearance of a bottom; and that there is likewise a great quantity of Burrs promiscuously in the soil, which are of a good quality, particularly on the east side.

Mr. Field Evans also, in the above-mentioned letter, furnishes a particular account

account how he discovered the said Burr-stones, in October 1797; that he noticed them in about two months afterwards to Robert Lambert, a mill-wright; and that, about June 1798, he employed Thomas Webster to make him a pair of Mill-stones from the said Burrs. He further observes, that the said Mill-stones have been almost in constant use, at Mr. Evans's mill, for about two years and a half; that he has since kept from one to three persons constantly employed in making Mill-stones from the said quarry, who have made above twenty pairs; and that he has sold fourteen pair and a half thereof, and fifty-seven ton of the stone, and has not heard any complaints respecting their quality.

A certificate, dated the 4th of March, 1801, from the Rev. William Davies, of Buttington, and Richard Williams, and Thomas Brown, churchwardens, testified that

that Mr. Field Evans was the first person that discovered the quarry in Moel-y-golfa Hill, and applied the Burrs to the making of Mill-stones.

Mr. J. Probert of Powis Castle, in a note, dated the 5th of March, 1801, states, that the mountain which produces these Mill-stones, is situated on the western confines of the county of Montgomery, bordering upon Shropshire, about a mile and a half distant from the river Severn, by means whereof they may be sent to Bristol, as well as to the interior parts of the kingdom, along the canal joining the Severn with the Thames; that the Montgomeryshire Canal branches out of that of Ellesmere, along which they may be conveyed to Chester, Liverpool, &c.

The

The SILVER MEDAL was this Session adjudged to Mr. GARNET TERRY, of the City-Road, Finsbury-Square, for an improved MILL FOR GRINDING HARD SUBSTANCES; a Plate and Description of which are annexed, and a complete Model reserved in the Society's Repository.

### SIR,

I HAVE taken the liberty of sending, for the inspection of the Society for the Encouragement of Arts, &c. a small Mill calculated for the purpose of grinding hard Substances.

I have made one on a large scale, and find it answers the purpose of reducing to powder, Coffee, Bones, Ashes, and other such things: it has also been tried, and found effectual and expeditious, in breaking down Beans, Peas, Malt, Barley, &c. If it is worth the notice of the Public,

Public, I beg you will make such use of it as the Society may think proper.

I am, with respect, .

SIR,

Your humble servant,

GARNET TERRY.

Nº 20, *City Road, Finsbury-square,*
*March* 3, 1801.      .

Mr. CHARLES TAYLOR.

*Description of Mr. Garnet Terry's Mill.* .
Plate VI.  Fig. 1.

A.  The hopper, or receptacle of the articles which are intended to be ground.
B.  A spiral wire, in the form of a reversed cone, to regulate the delivery of them.
C.  An inclined iron plate, hung upon a pin on its higher end: the
lower

lower end rests on the grooved axis D, and agitates the wire B.

D. The grooved axis, or grinding cylinder, which acts against the channelled iron plate E.

F. A screw on the side of the mill, by means of which the iron plate E is brought nearer to or removed further from the axis D, according as the article is wanted finer or coarser.

G. The handle, by which motion is given to the axis.

H. The tube from whence the articles, when ground, are received.

*.* The front of the mill is taken off, in order to show its interior construction.

A Bounty of FIFTEEN GUINEAS was this
Session voted to Mr. WILLIAM BUL-
LOCK, of Portland-street, for an im-
proved DRAWBACK LOCK for House-
Doors; a Plate and Description of
which are hereunto annexed, and a
complete Lock reserved in the Society's
Repository.

SIR,

I HAVE herewith sent, for the inspection of the Society, an improved Drawback Lock for House Doors,
&c. which improvement is in latching
the door; for it is well known, particularly in damp weather, that the air
drawing through it, rusts the head or
bevel of the bolt, by which means it
requires great force to shut the door,
and occasions a disagreeable noise, besides shaking the building.

It has frequently happened that the
house has been exposed to robbery from
the

the door being left unlatched, when supposed to be fast. This improvement
removes all those inconveniences, as it
lets the bolt shoot into the staple immediately when the door closes, but not
before; and the reliever works so very
easy, that the door is made fast with one
twenty-fourth part of the force required
with locks upon the common construction.

By an experiment with the Lock
sent herewith, it will be proved that two
ounces added to the reliever, will shoot
the Lock with more ease than three
pounds will do, applied to the bevel bolt;
and if the lock is .rusty, the advantage
will be much more in favour of the new
method. I flatter myself it will be of
great utility to the public, as its construction is simple and cheap. It may
be added to any old lock, as may be
seen from that now sent. It may be
advantageously applied to French windows and glass doors, as it prevents the

door

door from being strained, or the glass broke, by the force applied to shut them. I have fixed several Locks, upon this new principle, which answer well; and if the invention meets with the approbation of the Society, I hope to be rewarded according to its merit.

I remain, with respect,

SIR,

Your most obedient servant,

WILLIAM BULLOCK,

Nº 6, *Portland-street, Soho,*
*May 5,* 1801.

Mr. CHARLES TAYLOR,

*Pl VI*

*Mr Garnet Terry's Mill*

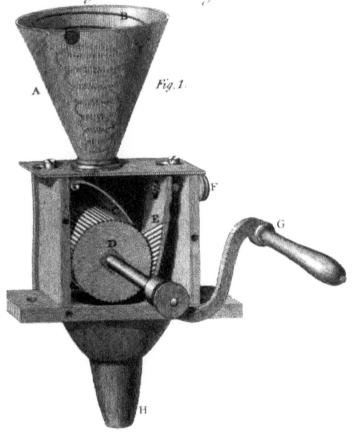

*Fig. 1.*

*Mr Bullock's Drawback Lock*

*Fig. 2.*

*Description of Mr. William Bullock's improved Drawback Lock.* **Plate VI. Fig. 2.**

**A.** Is the new iron latch here affixed to an old common drawback house lock.

**B.** An iron pin at one end of the latch, on which pin it is moveable.

**C.** A projecting part of the latch, which, when the common spring bolt **D** of the lock is drawn back, in the usual manner, is forced into the nick on its higher part at **E**, by the spring **F**, underneath the latch.

The bolt **D** then remains within the lock, until, on closing the door, the reliever **G** gently presses on the lock box, fixed in the common way on the door cheek; which pressure draws the projecting part **C** out of the nick **E**, and permits the end of the bolt **D**, by the force of the spring **G**, to slide into the lock box, and fasten the door.

The

The Sum of FIFTEEN GUINEAS was this Session voted as a Bounty to Mr. THOMAS GENT, of Homerton, for a new-invented CRANE, for raising and delivering heavy Bodies. A Plate and Description are annexed, and a Model of the Machine may be seen in the Society's Repository.

### SIR,

AN offer of encouragement being published by the Society, to any person producing a model of an improved Machine for drawing up Ore, &c. from mines and pits; I beg leave to submit to your consideration a model of a Crane, which I hope will answer for that purpose; also for sinking Wells, clearing Canals, and raising Casks or other heavy Weights out of Cellars. I flatter myself that a Machine on the principle of this model, is calculated

better

better for this purpose than any I have seen, it having a two-fold principle, viz. first, that of making a perpendicular draft, and discharging the load at the same time (without any intermediate space); and, secondly, raising the same a sufficient height, so as to place the article in a cart, or other carriage, for conveyance. I leave the merit of the plan to the judgment of the Society, and shall be pleased with such encouragement as they may award.

I am, Sir,

Your obedient humble servant,

Thomas Gent.

Nº 5, *Lower Terrace, Homerton,*
*April* 14, 1801.

Mr. Charles Taylor.

*Descrip-*

*Description of Mr. Thomas Gent's Crane.*
Plate VII.   Fig. 1 and 2.

A.   The crane, three feet in length from the centre B.

B.   The centre, upon which it turns under the cross-beam.

C.   The quadrant, two feet eight inches in length from the centre B.

D,   A chain, which works upon the quadrant, and communicates with the roller E, on which is a toothed wheel put in motion by a small pinion on the axis of the winch-handle F.

G.   A rope, which passes over the pulley H at the end of the crane. The weight to be raised is fastened to the block I, and is lifted up by the other end of the rope winding round the roller K.

K.

K. Is a roller, on which a toothed
wheel is placed, and worked
by a pinion fixed on the axis L,
moved by the handle M.

NN. Are catches, which are slided
occasionally into the teeth of
the wheels on the rollers, to
keep them stationary.

O. The cross-beam of the machine,
from which the crane is suspended underneath.

PP. Two upright posts, which support
the cross-beam.

When a weight is to be lifted from
within the shaft of a mine, over which
the machine is to be placed, the pulley
H should be drawn down, and the point
of the quadrant C raised upright in a
perpendicular line; then, by working
the handle M, the weight is raised from
within the shaft, until it clears the surface of the ground, at which period, by
turning the handle F, the point of the
quadrant

quadrant C is brought gradually into an horizontal line, which projects the crane and weight so far from the shaft, as to allow a cart to be placed underneath to convey the article which has been thus raised.

*Fig.* 2. shews the method by which the chain is connected with the roller.

D. The same chain as in the former figure, but in a different point of view.

E. The roller mentioned in the former figure.

SS. A double cord, the two extremities of which are fastened at TV to the roller E, and joined to the lower end of the chain at W : this double cord serves to keep the chain regularly in the centre of the quadrant.

The

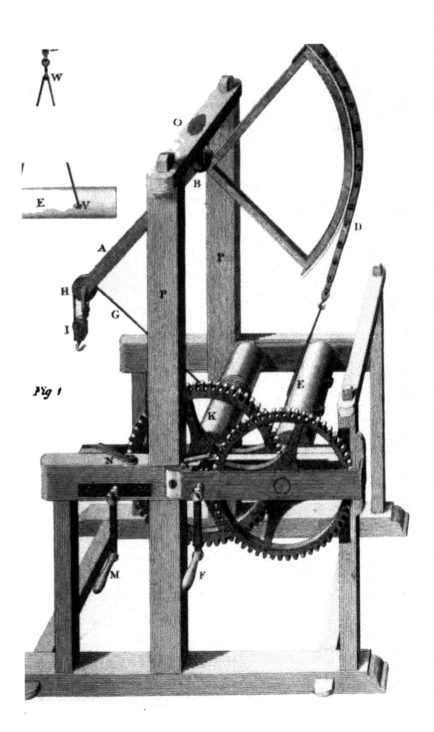

*Fig 1*

Lowry .

The Thanks of the Society were this Session voted to Sir George Onesiphorus Paul, Baronet, of Grosvenor-Street, for the following valuable Communication of the method invented by him, and used under his direction, for the Ventilation of Hospitals, &c. Actuated by his usual philanthropy, he has also presented to the Society Models of the Machinery he employed, and which are reserved in the Society's Repository, for public inspection. Engravings and a Description of them are hereunto annexed.

SIR,

I HAVE been favoured with your letter, stating the terms of a Premium offered by the Society of Arts, &c. for "A Mode of permanently ventilating the Apartments in Hospitals, Gaols, and other

other crowded places, superior to any now known or used;" and that the Society had done me the honour " to direct you to express their wish to receive from me communications on this subject."

I not only agree with the Society, that " the subject is important to the health of persons destined to inhabit such places" as are specifically mentioned in the proposal for the Premium; but I also believe that the morbid effects of impure air are felt in all situations of life where education, business, or social intercourse, may aggregate mankind.

From observations made during a pursuit which of late years may be said to be habitual to me, I fear I must *also* admit that Ventilation is improperly performed, by the means now generally employed,—where those means act on persons in a sickly or convalescent state, or accustomed to delicate habits of life.

The

The transverse passage of outward air, through a room (which I shall term free Ventilation), is no *doubtful* mode of obtaining vital air; yet, certainly, if the attendant consequences render such a mode inadmissible (to an efficient degree) in the abodes of sickness or infirmity, the Society are justified in considering the subject as open to much further improvement.

Desiring to be understood as not addressing the Society as a claimant of their Premium; I conceive I may assist them in the pursuit of their laudable purpose, by submitting to their perusal some practical observations on the modes of Ventilation hitherto practised, and by communicating the outline of a design already conceived, and in a limited degree adopted, for correcting their admitted imperfections.

It may be necessary to premise, that the peculiar enquiry, the result of which will be detailed in the following pages,

was

was excited by some objections, originating in a most respectable quarter, and directed against a system, on which I had heretofore *solely* depended, in providing for the Ventilation of such public establishments as have been placed more particularly under my direction.

It may be inferred from the note annexed to the proposed Premium, that similar objections are entertained by the Society: I shall therefore, as you requested, submit my observations, without that delay which would necessarily be occasioned by my modelling them in conformity to the rules you have communicated, and waiting for certificates to accompany them. If there really does not exist a doubt as to principle or fact, on a question so important, should not that doubt be made the subject of a previous special consideration, so that a point of direction may be given to the mechanical exertions intended to be excited?

Although

Although particular conclusions may be controverted, I may venture to assume as the basis of all observations on this subject,

First,—That a certain and frequently renewed supply of vital air is essential to the purposes of animal life; and the more regular and uninterrupted that supply, the more favourable will it be to health.

Secondly,—That where the quantity of atmospheric air introduced into an apartment, is less than nature has bestowed in free circulation, her purpose is in a degree counteracted; and although the breathing impure air (*i. e.* air despoiled of its natural proportion of vital air) for a short time may not produce an immediate sensible effect, an injury may arise to the constitution, proportionate to the extent of that time. And further, when (as in the ordinary intercourses of society in London) persons are in the habit of placing themselves

selves, during a considerable portion of every twenty-four hours, in a situation to breathe in this defective atmosphere, the accumulated consequences may be serious and important.

Thirdly,—That in rooms from which currents of fresh air may not be excluded, they may be so injudiciously directed as to be useless and injurious. And,

Fourthly,—That if, in addition to the consumption of vital air by the lungs, the persons of those assembled in any apartment should be filthy,—should their clothing (particularly that made of woollen) have been so long worn as to have absorbed any considerable portion of the perspiration of the body,—or should the apartment itself be damp and foul, the vital properties of the air will be contaminated, and although instant death may not ensue (which has been known to be a consequence), the fevers emphatically termed the Gaol, Hospital,

or

or Ship Fever, from its usually originating in these places, will be generated with a degree of malignancy proportionate to its causes, and, being so generated, will become infectious with a like degree of malignancy.

It is about twenty years since the deleterious consequences of inattention to Ventilation were set forth by Mr. Howard. So strong and so general was the conviction of the public mind, not only as to the evil pointed out, but regarding the remedies proposed by that indefatigable philanthropist, that the Legislature thought fit to adopt the whole of his principles, and to make them the basis of several positive laws, under the direction of which the greater number of prisons of the kingdom have since been reconstructed, and the remainder (with few exceptions) altered in conformity to the principle recommended by him, namely, *that of introducing cur-*

X *rents*

*rents of fresh air* INTO *and* THROUGH *every apartment.*

In these prisons, where attention is also paid to personal cleanliness, I venture to say, the Gaol Fever is unknown, unless brought into them by prisoners committed in a state of previous infection.

By equal exertion on the like principles, the healthiness of the ships of war has been so improved, that they are no longer sources of this desolating pestilence.

Regarding hospitals, I fear it cannot be proved that a relief so complete has been effected. Mr. Howard was not sparing in his strictures on the management of this important branch of our public institutions; but the improvement he suggested went no farther than simply the introduction of fresh air. The reconciling this advantage with that generally diffused warmth, necessary in sick

sick rooms, seems to have escaped his contemplation.

Of the several hospitals constructed since his observations were made public, most have been planned with a view to facilitate the passage of outward air through the wards. The Directors of old hospitals have adopted alterations more or less tending to the same purpose; but all seem to have rested at this point: yet, considering the importance of pure air to patients, during the tedious cure of compound fractures, and other accidents or diseases, together with the no less important object of securing them from currents of cold air, it cannot be denied that much still remains to be effected.

In the construction of the larger Workhouses, termed Hundred-houses, similar principles of Ventilation have been attended to with evident success, in preserving the health of the inhabitants; but with respect to Parish Workhouses

on the *lesser* scale—School-rooms (both
for boys and girls in every rank of life),
Manufactories—Apartments for Public
Lectures—and Ladies Assembly-rooms—
these, together with the circumscribed
Cottages of the Poor, remain in a state
most dangerous to health from imperfect
Ventilation. To these sources, and to
no other, may be traced the few putrid
and contagious diseases which occasionally show themselves amongst us;
and which, to the credit of *free Ventilation*, can no longer justly be called
Gaol or Ship Fever.

At a period of demonstrated success
of the doctrine recommended by Mr.
Howard, and adopted by his disciples,
the valuable essays and experiments of
Count Rumford appeared before the
public: whilst opening to the world a
new and most useful system of domestic
philosophy, he has advanced opinions unfavourable to those means by which these
important effects have been produced.

In

In theory this ingenious philosopher and friend of mankind has decidedly negatived the necessity and questioned the propriety of Ventilation, by the admission of currents of air. In the construction of those buildings most immediately under his direction, he has certainly adopted a *practice* of a direct opposite tendency.

Opinions of such authority could not fail to be respected: they must at least raise a doubt in the mind of the most confident advocate of an opposite theory.

As the Count's observations and practice tended to invalidate a material part of that system, in the pursuit of which immense sums had been *confidently* expended in the kingdom, and respecting which I bear more than a common share of responsibility, I felt myself peculiarly called upon to scrutinize his objections, and to obviate such as should appear to be denied by experience; but, at the same time, certainly to

X 3      abandon

abandon whatever ground could not be fairly maintained by a result.

As my conclusions on the point disputed are formed on circumstantial observations made within a Prison and Hospital immediately under my own eye, and as these particular institutions have not unfrequently been resorted to as examples for imitation, a detailed reasoning regarding them may serve for general application.

The County Gaol at Gloucester is constructed on the principles of admitting air to pass into and through it in strait lines, from one extremity to the other. There is no obstruction to a freedom of current, other than as the streams of air passing through the long passages, open at each end, move with the greater velocity, they of necessity carry with them the weaker currents, passing into and through the cells at right angles.

From

From the time this prison was opened in 1791, until the year 1800, about 1300 persons were committed to it; and, on the average, about one hundred prisoners were constantly confined in it. In these nine years the number of deaths has been thirteen; and of these, four sunk under the effects of disease brought into prisons with them. During the last year, the prison has been crowded in an uncommon and very improper degree: two hundred and fourteen have been confined; and the average number has been one hundred and sixty-seven. One prisoner only has died (a woman aged sixty) in the month of October last. At the opening of the Spring Assizes, 1801, (the time of the greatest numbers) there was not one prisoner sick, or in the hospital ward.

By this statement it appears, that the proportion of deaths is so much below the common average, in the ordinary situations of life, that the healthiness of

X 4                                    this

this abode may be said to be peculiar; and it is in proof, that however currents of air may be found injurious to particular constitutions, they are not unfavourable to general health.

Every prisoner in this gaol, when not in the infirmary-ward, sleeps in a room containing from fifty-two to fifty-seven feet of superficial space, built with brick, resting on an arch, and arched over; so that no air can enter it but through the openness provided for it. As air is constantly passing immediately under it, and round it on every side, it is necessarily dry: it is ventilated by opposite openings near the crown of the arch.  To that opening which is towards the outward air, there is a shutter, which the occupant may close at will; but it is so imperfectly fitted, that, when closed, a considerable portion of air must enter by its sides. The opposite opening to the passage, the prisoner has no means of closing in any degree.

During

During the ten years these rooms have been inhabited, there have been three winters in which the cold has been intense. As I had considerable apprehensions of the effects of this situation in severe weather, I directed the surgeon of the gaol to be constant in his attention; and particularly in the report of his observations during the inclemency of these seasons. I also made a point frequently to visit the prison, and to examine every prisoner as to the effects apprehended; and, as much to my surprise as to my satisfaction, notwithstanding the querulous disposition of persons in their situation, I never heard a complaint from old or young, from male or female, suffering by cold in the night apartments.* And further, it is
· the

---

* Fahrenheit's thermometer has never been observed to be below 33° in the severest nights, in the middle region of a cell in which a prisoner was sleeping; whereas, in the ordinary apartments of a dwelling-house, water is frequently known to freeze by a bed-side.

the decided opinion of the two able
physicians who have most liberally un-
dertaken to superintend the health of
this prison, that no ill consequences have
arisen from prisoners sleeping in the
situation above described.

I must contend, therefore, it is a fact
established by experience, that in a room
containing not more than from 415 to
439 cubical feet of air, in which there
is no fire, the body of a person sleeping
under a proper allowance of woollen
bed-clothes will so far warm the atmosphere around him, or to speak more
conformable to modern doctrine, so
little of the heat generated in the body
will be carried off by the surrounding
air, that he will not suffer by a current *
passing at a distance over him, provided
the apartment be secured from damp.

On

---

* The term "current" is not to be understood in a
stronger sense than merely to signify that species of circulation of air, which is directed in strait lines from point to
point, by the action of any efficient cause.

On the points, therefore, of warmth and Ventilation *combined* it must surely be allowed (regarding rooms so constructed) there is no farther *desideratum.*

Prisoners, on their rising in the morning, are removed into small working-rooms or wards situated on the ground-floor. These day apartments are, in like manner, constructed with cross openings near the ceiling or crown of the arch; but there is also in each of them an open fire-place. Respecting these apartments, my observations tend to *confirm* Count Rumford's objection to open fires, and his preference to closed stoves. Nay, farther, I am disposed to admit, that openings for free Ventilation are incompatible with strong fires in open fire-places.

It is certain that, in rooms so provided, the danger arising from impure air is completely guarded against; yet this advantage is gained at the risk of another

another evil, which, though not so important, should, if possible, be avoided.

The air which in the same room without an open fire-place would pass inwards by one opening, and outwards by the other, being attracted by the fire to supply the constant rarefaction in the chimney, passes inwards from both openings towards the fire place, and the body of a person placed near it, being in its current, is exposed to the danger of partial chill. To this circumstance, in these apartments, I am inclined to attribute the few complaints of a dysentery or aguish tendency, which have occasionally interrupted the general health of this prison.

In the hospital, the scene of my observations, the morbid effects of foul air in the wards have, until lately, been no otherwise relieved than,

First,—By introducing currents of fresh air by the windows, with an improved

proved mode of hanging the upper sash, peculiar to this hospital, by the effect of which the current of air admitted is turned upwards to the ceiling, and prevented from descending on the patients, whose beds are placed under the windows;

Secondly,—By piercing holes in the ceiling of the wards, and by means of plaistered channels or wood funnels, leading the foul air, rising into them, to the roof.

In warm weather, when the doors of the wards are open, and the fires low, these channels or funnels operate with considerable effect. Much foul air will by its relative specific lightness (not being counteracted by a stronger power), ascend them and escape; a further portion will pass off by the windows opening to the leeward, and Ventilation may be duly effected.

But, on the contrary, when the doors are shut, and strong fires are made, these

these will inevitably attract the currents of air *inwards* and towards them, from all the openings; and should patients be situated in their course, the effect cannot fail to be injurious.

Besides, as the windows are generally closed in the night (the most important time for Ventilation), no other change of air takes place, but what is effected by the open fires, which, whilst supplied immediately from the middle region, are constantly consuming the best air of the room.

Hence it appears that free Ventilation, or the transverse passage of outward air, may be inconsistent with the general warmth required in the apartments of the sick; and that channels for the escape of foul air, unassisted by a power more constant and decisive than the relative specific lightness of that air, is a mean inefficient to preserving a healthful respiration in the crowded wards of an hospital.

As

As a remedy to these apparent defects in the ordinary mode of Ventilation, it has been imagined that the draft, or determination of the air, to the funnels in the ceiling of the rooms requiring Ventilation, is accelerated by the operation of fire; and by causing an increased degree of rarefaction, at the termination of the funnel, to discharge the air rising to the ceiling in a degree depending on the correct application of the apparatus and quantity of fuel consumed.

In all rooms or apartments requiring Ventilation, it is presumed that (according to the old system) channels or funnels are provided for the discharge of air ascending into them. These channels or funnels, so provided, should be rendered air-tight, and brought to terminate immediately under the fire intended to work them. The ash-pit and fire-place should be so closed, by doors, as to prevent the fire from drawing the

the air from the room surrounding it. The whole draft or consumption occasioned by the fire will then be supplied from the further termination of the channel or funnel.

This effect may be applied according to circumstances, either to the ceiling of the room in which the fire is made, to the room below, or to that above it; and, draught thus produced may, by a proper apparatus, be increased or diminished at will.

In the hospital in which I have made the first experiment of this design, I have caused a stove to be so formed as to answer the culinary purposes of the ward in which it is fixed, and at the same time to ventilate the ward beneath it; and no additional expense is created in fuel by the operation.

By a fire made in one of these stoves, a ward beneath it, containing about 18,000 cubical feet, filled with patients (and which, in spite of all former means,

was

was ever remarkably offensive) was in a few minutes so relieved of contaminated air, as to be sensibly felt by all the patients in it, without their perceiving any increased current.

The principle of the means of Ventilation adopted in this hospital may be be applied with perfect facility to ships.

By carrying the funnel from a cabin or ship stove, of any kind or dimension (observing *only* to exclude the admission of surrounding air), to the hold or underdecks, they may be as completely ventilated as the wards of an infirmary. In stormy weather, when the decks of a ship must of necessity be closed, the fires would perform a service which could no otherwise be attained; whilst, by the nature of the apparatus, the fire itself would be secured from the effects of the wind.

If the stove or grate over a lady's drawing-room were properly fitted to this purpose, on the evening of her assembly,

Y it

it might be set in action, and the room beneath cleared of its impure air, without recourse being had to the openings of windows: the openings in the ceiling might be rendered ornamental.

By applying the same principle to German or other closed stoves, the chief objection to their use in crowded rooms would be obviated; and I should then agree with Count Rumford, that in all rooms, where the indulgence of the habit of open fires was not in question, such stoves (if constructed of earthen materials) would afford a more " genial warmth," and a " due circulation be at the same time effected."

So fitted and constructed, they would be incontestably better than open fires for the wards of Hospitals, Poor-houses, Manufactories, Theatres for Lectures, School-rooms, and Prisons. Respecting the last-mentioned structures, I must further observe, that if public Kitchens were a sutler appointed, under due regulations, the present necessity of open fires for prisoners to cook individually for themselves, would be superseded much to their advantage.

On the other hand, I must also observe, that if closed stoves, acting on this principle, were adopted, Count Rumford's objections to the introduction of fresh air would be obviated, with regard to any room in which they should be in action, provided the opening through which it entered was made on a level with the ceiling.

Air entering at this level would, in the absence of open fires, be acted upon by no other draft than the mouth of the funnel in the ceiling, and could not descend in currents to the lower region of the room.

In a room so filled with company as to vitiate the air within it, the atmospheric air entering, being specifically heavier, would indeed descend, and be replaced

by

by the ascending impure air; but, as it would not descend by a stronger impulse than its difference of specific weight, it must be slow in its motion, and would produce no sensible current.

Should the above observations and conclusions be thought worthy attention, I shall, with great pleasure, direct Models of the improved Hospital-Sashes, and of the Stoves for accelerating Ventilation by the action of fire, to be made for the use of the Society.

I am,

Your very obedient servant,

G. O. PAUL.

*Grosvenor-Street,*
*May 30, 1801.*

CHARLES TAYLOR, Esq.
Secretary to the Society of Arts, &c. *Adelphi.*

*A*

*A perspective View of Sir G. O. Paul's Stove, for ventilating the Wards · of Hospitals.*

### Plate VIII. Fig. 1.

A A.  A chimney-piece, of ordinary dimensions.

B.   A Bath-stove, made to fit the chimney: the hobbs of which, NN, project two inches and a half before the fire-grate.

C C.  Folding-doors to close the fronts of the ash-pit, and to fall back against the hobbs.

D D.  Folding-doors to close the front of the fire-grate, and to fall back against the hobbs.

E.   A door to close the top of the fire-grate, when a very strong draught is required. When put down, the smoke is directed through the open space H, and the door is used as a hot table for

Y 3                    culinary

culinary purposes; when open, it serves as a chimney back.

F.   A flat bar projecting two inches and a half before the fire-grate as a stop to the upper and lower doors.

G G.  Holes left in the castings of the ash-pit, to receive the mouths of air-tunnels in the back, or on either side, as circumstances may require.

H.   The opening to the back flue, used as a passage for the smoke, when the top door is closed on the fire-grate.

I I.  A double register:—first, to close the back flue when the fire-grate is open; secondly, to close the front flue when the back draught is necessary; and, thirdly, to prevent the heat being carried up the chimney.

Fig. 2. A back view of the ventilating stove, on which similar letters are

are marked as denote the same parts already mentioned in *Fig.* 1.

KK. Are shoulders for tunnels cast with the ash-pit, fixed at the openings G G, mentioned in *Fig.* 1.

*N. B.* There should be doors or regulators to the mouths of the air-tunnels K K, to close them when the doors of the stove are open, otherwise (there being at that time little or no draught by the tunnels towards the fire), the dust will pass by them into the rooms with which they communicate.

L L. Air-tunnels are to be fixed on the shoulders K K, and to be prolonged in any direction required, either downwards to any room below, which wants ventilating, or upwards to the ceiling of the room in which the fire is made, or

Y 4                                    to

to any rooms above it requiring ventilation.

*N. B.* The direction of the first length or piece of the tunnel should, in all cases, be upwards, to prevent sparks of fire, which may fly into it, being conveyed into a room ventilated by a descending tunnel.

The tunnel should, at least, rise so far that the lower edge of it may be higher than the upper edge of the shoulder on which it is fixed.

M. A back flue to conduct the smoke when all the doors are closed, and the stove made to act with its utmost force.

NN. The hobbs on each side the fireplace.

*Fig.* 3. A side view of the ventilating stove, in which the letters correspond as before.

*Fig.*

*Fig. 4.* A view from above of the two chimneys which convey away the smoke, and of the register which closes one or other of them, as occasion may require.

*Description of the Sash-Window for an Hospital.* Plate VIII. Fig. 5.

*aaaa.* A common sash-window frame, the upper extremity of which should be level with the ceiling of the room.

*b.* The lower sash fixed.

*c.* The upper sash working inwards on the pivots *e e*, at each side of its lower end.

*dd.* Inclined edges fixed, with a proper inclination inwards, on the jambs to which the sash is fitted. These jambs and ledges should be made as exactly as possible to fit the sash in its working, to prevent air from passing inwards by its sides.

*e e.*

*e e.* The pivots on which the upper sash-frames move.

*f.* A regulator, notched on its lower part, and moving in a groove *g*. At the extremity of the regulator is a loop or ring *h*, to receive a hook fixed to a long pole; by which the sash may be worked by the apothecary or nurse. The notches in the regulator resting on the groove, admit the sash to be placed at any intermediate distance required.

The pole may be afterwards removed out of the reach of the patients.

A

_w for Hospitals._

**Fig. 6.**

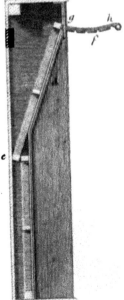

_Lowry sculp._

A Bounty of THIRTY GUINEAS was this Session voted to Mr. JOHN DE LAFONS, for his communication of a new ESCAPEMENT for WATCHES, a Plate and Description of which are hereunto annexed, and a complete Model reserved in the Society's Repository for the inspection and use of the Public.

SIR,

HAVING considered the perfection of Chronometers to consist more in giving an equal impulse to the balance than to any other general cause, I present, in hopes of the approbation of the Society, the model of a new Escapement, which has not only the property of correcting the errors of the main-spring, train of wheels, &c. and giving an equal power to the balance, but likewise the wheels are locked, without spring-work, perfectly

perfectly safe from getting out of order, and are unlocked with less power than in any Escapement I know, as the wheels do not bear against the locking with more than a tenth part of the whole pressure from the main-spring; a circumstance I believe to be perfectly new.

Although the giving an equal impulse to the balance has been already most ingeniously done by Mr. Mudge, and by Mr. Haley (from whose great merit I would not wish to detract), yet the extreme difficulty and expense attending the first, and the very compound locking of the second, render them far from completing the desired perfection. Presuming I have simplified the above ideas, I leave it to the Society's judgment to determine the merit of mine.

I am, Sir,

Your obedient servant,

JOHN DE LAFONS.

*April* 13, 1801.

Mr. CHARLES TAYLOR.

*Observations on, and Description of, an improved Escapement.*    Plate IX. Fig. 1, 2, 3, 4, 5.

HIGHLY flattered by the honourable patronage my mechanical attempt has received, after returning my most ardent thanks for the favour of the great attention paid by the Gentlemen of the Committee, I feel it incumbent on me to point out the perfections and advantages arising from my improvements on the Remontoire detached Escapement for Chronometers, which gives a perfectly equal impulse to the balance, and not only entirely removes whatever irregularities arise from the different states of fluidity in the oil, from the train of wheels, or from the main-spring, but does it in a simpler way than any with which I am acquainted. I trust it will not be thought improper in me to answer some objections made at the examination before

before the Committee, as I am fully persuaded the more mathematically and critically the improvements are investigated, the more perfect they will prove to be.

It was first observed, that my method did not so completely detach the train of wheels from the balance as another Escapement then referred to. I beg leave to remark, that the train of wheels in mine is prevented from pressing against the locking, by the whole power of the remontoire-spring; so that the balance has only to remove the small remaining pressure, which does away that objection, and also that of the disadvantage of detents, as this locking may be compared to a light balance turning on fine pivots, without a pendulum-spring; and has not only the advantage of banking safe at two turns of the balance, and of being firmer and less liable to be out of repair than any locking where spring work is used, but likewise

likewise of unlocking with much less power.—It was then observed, it required more power to make it go than usual. Permit me to say, it requires no more power than any other Remontoire Escapement, as the power is applied in the most mechanical manner possible.—And lastly, it was said, that it set or required the balance to vibrate an unusually large arch before the piece would go. This depends on the accuracy of the execution, the proportionate diameter and weight of the balance, the strength of the remontoire-spring, and the length of the pallets. If these circumstances are well attended to, it will set but little more than the most generally detached Escapements.

I proceed

I proceed to describe mine as follows :

A. The scape-wheel.

B. The lever pallet, on an arbor with fine pivots, having at the lower end

C. The remontoire or spiral spring fixed with a collar and stud, as pendulum-springs are.

D. The pallet of the verge, having a roller turning in small pivots for the lever pallet to act against.

E. Pallets to discharge the locking, with a roller between, as in *Fig.* 4.

F. The arm of the locking pallets continued at the other end to make it poise, having studs and screws to adjust and bank the quantity of motion.

a & b. The locking pallets, being portions of circles, fastened on an arbor turning on fine pivots.

G. The triple fork, at the end of the arm of the locking pallets.

The

The centre of the lever-pallet in the draft, is in a right line between the centre of the scape-wheel and the centre of the verge, though in the model it is not; but may be made so or not, as best suits the calliper, &c.

The scape-wheel A, with the tooth 1, is acting on the lever-pallet B, and has wound up the spring C; the verge-pallet D (turning the way represented by the arrow) the moment it comes within the reach of the lever-pallet, the discharging-pallet E, taking hold of one prong of the fork, removes the arm F, and relieves the tooth 3 from the convex part of the lock $a$. The wheel goes forward a little, just sufficient to permit the lever-pallet to pass, while the other end gives the impulse to the balance : the tooth 4 of the wheel is then locked on the concave side of the lock $b$, and the lever-pallet is stopped against the tooth 5, as in *Fig.* 3. So far the operation of giving the impulse, in order again to

Z                    wind

wind the remontoire-spring (the other
pallet at E, in the return, removing
the arm F the contrary direction), relieves the tooth 3 from the lock *b*. The
wheel again goes forward, almost the
whole space, from tooth to tooth, winds
the spiral-spring again, and comes into
the situation of *Fig.* 1. and thus the
whole performance is completed. The
end of the lower pallet B resting on
the point of the tooth 1, prevents the
wheel exerting its full force on the
lock *a*, as in *Fig.* 1. The same effect
is produced by the pallet laying on
the tooth 5, by preventing the wheel
from pressing on *b*; and thus the locking becomes the tightest possible. Thi
Escapement may be much simplified by
putting a spring with a pallet made in
it, as in *Fig.* 5. instead of the lever
pallet and spiral-spring. The operation
will be in other respects exactly th
same, avoiding the friction of the pivots
of the lever-pallet. This method I prefer

*Fig 5.*

*Fig.3.*

*Fig.1.*

*Fig.2.*

*Fig.4.*

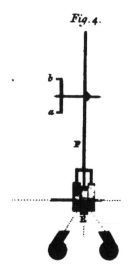

fer
as
the
ait

of
re

fer for a piece to be in a state of rest, as a clock; but the disadvantage, from the weight of the spring in different positions, is obvious.

The locking may be on any two teeth of the wheel, as may be found most convenient.

JOHN DE LAFONS.

L Mr. CHARLES TAYLOR,

# PAPERS

## IN

## COLONIES AND TRADE.

## COLONIES AND TRADE.

The following Communications on the
production and application of Myrabolans, and their use as a substitute for
Aleppo Galls, originated from the late
Dr. Alexander Johnson, of Charlotte-
Street, Portland-Place, who laid before the Society several other articles
the products of the East Indies, with
a view to the general advantage of
Great Britain and her Colonies. Samples of the Myrabolans, and Specimens of the Colours they yield in
dying, may be seen in the Repository
of the Society.

On the 6th of February, 1793, Dr.
Johnson laid before the Society samples
of an article which he had received from
Mr. Hellenus Scott, of Bombay, under

the

the name of East-India Galls; the Committee to whose examination they were referred, found them to be the larger species of Myrabolans, and that they possessed many qualities similar to the Gall-Nuts of the Levant, both the pulp and outer bark striking a good black colour with Martial Vitriol. The following letter was afterwards sent by Dr. Johnson to the Secretary.

---

*Charlotte-Street, Portland-Place.*

**SIR,**

THE India nut Myrabolan, like our Walnut, contains its tinging quality only in its fruits or parenchymous part. Its astringent essence, far stronger than that of our Walnut, strikes a strong black colour with the feculæ of iron, and fine browns with weaker solutions of copperas, while with allum it makes buff colours and their class.

Unac-

Unacquainted with the component parts of this nut, the tradesmen who were to use it required it to be coarsely ground, which, to satisfy them, was done, but proved wrong; on the one hand useless, and on the other loss of substance: a part of the fruit remaining on the grind-stones and clogging them, and another part became so adhesive to the broken shells and kernels, as scarcely to be disengaged from them by boiling.

From those and other circumstances, the idea arising that the fruity part alone was the useful, it became necessary to ascertain it by experiment. Three ounces of the nuts were therefore taken, put into an earthen pan, had warm soft water poured upon them, and with a slight cover were placed on the hobb of of a kitchen-range to stew. The evaporating water was replaced from a kettle usually upon that fire; and the next day, when examined and rubbed upon a board, the cover of the nut came easily off,

off, leaving only some pulp adhesive to the shell, which then was put again into the pan, and stewed in the same manner as before. The greater part of the pulp came off in the water; but some still sticking fast, the nuts, with the clearest of the last water, were then thrown into a small tub, and therein rubbed with a hearth brush or small broom, until they became quite clean. They were then dried, and the next day bruised and broken, and set again to stew as before; the decoction became of a light brown: which colour it kept unaltered, notwithstanding a frequent addition of a solution of iron filings, and of copperas.

I am, Sir,

Your most obedient servant,

ALEXANDER JOHNSON.

Mr. CHARLES TAYLOR.

The

The Committee sent Samples of the article to several principal dyers and callico-printers in different parts of the kingdom, for their opinion of its quality: the answers to which were, that the Myrabolans possessed very strong astringent powers, and would be a very desirable substitute for Galls, if the price of them was moderate. The Committee, therefore, declared to the Society, that the Myrabolans would be useful in various manufactures, and serve as a good substitute for Galls. The Society finding that the Myrabolans, though the product of a British Colony, paid heavier duties on importation than Galls sent from Turkey, presented a memorial to the Lords of the Treasury, stating that the importation of this and other useful products of our Settlements, are in effect discouraged by being subject to high duties, while articles from foreign countries, possessing similar properties, are admitted on more favourable terms; and

peti-

petitioning, that some steps might be taken to remove a discouragement so detrimental to the trade and manufactures of this country.

Although it does not appear that the petition of the Society has yet been complied with, there is reason to hope that so important a business will engage the attention of Government, and prevent large sums of money being sent to foreign states for similar articles.

The following is an abstract of a letter received by the Secretary, along with samples of two kinds of Myrabolans, in answer to an application made by him to Mr. William Pope, of Mahometpore, near Cassumbazer, in Bengal, for information on Myrabolans, and other products of India.

SIR,

SIR,

I AM induced to send you the following articles, being part of those
mentioned in your letter to Mr. Pope,
on which you required information.

Myrabolans, or a specimen of dried
fruit which I suppose to be the article
described under the name of Myrabolans. The Bengal name for this fruit is
Hurrah P'hul, the largest being called
Burrah Hurrah, and the smallest Choota
Hurrah. They are sold in the common
Bazar; the large at one rupee and a
half per maund, or 82lb. avoirdupoise,
and the small at four rupees per
maund.

They are of a very astringent quality,
and much used by the natives of India
in fixing colours. They are also used
for giving a black dye to leather, which
is done by mixing the powder of the
larger sort with a certain proportion of
iron filings and water,

The

The smaller kind, from every information which I have been able to procure, is more used in medicine than dying, although from the acid astringency of both kinds, their properties must be nearly the same.

I am, Sir,

Your obedient servant,

J. Machlachlan,

Council-House, Calcutta.

Mr. Charles Taylor.

\*\*\* From the different experiments laid before the Society, this conclusion may be drawn, that Myrabolans will furnish various shades of buff colours, ash, brown, and black, according to the mordants employed; that all the dyes from them are very permanent, and that they have the quality of giving a fullness and firmness to the goods dyed therewith.

Some

Some hundred weights of them have been already used at Manchester, in stead of Galls, in the Turkey red-dye, and in other branches of business. The colouring matter of Myrabolans is easily extracted by boiling them, after they have been bruised in a mortar, without the trouble of separating the stone or kernel. In their common state and appearance, when imported, Myrabolans resemble dried plums, and are equal in value to half their weight of galls; but if the fruity or outer part could be sent from India in a dry state, without the stone or kernel, which is of little or no use, the article would be more valuable than Aleppo Galls.

*June* 4, 1801.

Five sorts of Myrabolans have been distinguished in the shops, all which have similar qualities; but the sort used in the above trials appears to be the fruit of the *Phyllanthus Emblica* of Linnæus, thus described, *Phyllanthus foliis pinnatis floriferis caule arboreo, fructu baccato.*

The Silver Medal was this Session voted to Andrew Stephens, Esq. of Keerpoy, in Bengal, for the following Communication on Lake made by him from fresh Stick Lack, and sent to the Society with a quantity of the Lake, which is placed in their Repository.

Accounts of experiments made on this Lake by Dr. Bancroft are also annexed, which demonstrate that the Lake is a useful substitute for Cochineal in various cases, as may be seen from patterns of dyes prepared from it, and remaining for public inspection.

SIR,

AS Lake from the Stick-Lack just gathered from the trees, is an addition to the catalogue of dying-drugs, I consider it not unworthy the attention

of

of the Society for the Encouragement of Arts, &c. and therefore beg leave to present a sample for their inspection, and humbly request they will be pleased to give it to some member of the Society experienced in the art of dying scarlet, to examine and report upon it.

I have reason to suppose that it is little inferior to Cochineal; and, as it may be afforded much cheaper, I hope it will be found a valuable article to the dyer.

But, should it even be found unequal to Cochineal, I am certain it will give a much better dye than can be obtained from Stick-Lack in England, as that article is liable to heat, and decay on the passage; and it suffers so much from age alone, that the dyers in Bengal cannot obtain colours so bright from Lack gathered only six or eight months, as they can from the fresh.

My situation is favourable for procuring the article. I have already delivered

A a                    18,000 lb.

18,000lb. weight to the Company; but no accounts of sales, or any reports thereon, have as yet reached the Board of Trade here.

As the extracting the colouring matter from Lack, and sending it home in the form of Lake, may justly be considered as a useful invention, and has been declared by Dr. Bancroft to be a *desideratum*, it will not, I trust, be deemed presumption in me, to hope for some mark of approbation from a Society of Gentlemen to whom the manufactures of England are already so much indebted.

I am, Sir,

Your most obedient servant,

ANDREW STEPHENS.
Assistant Surgeon, Bengal Establishment.

*Keerpoy,*
*March* 22, 1799.

To the SECRETARY of the
Society of Arts, &c.

The

The following letter from Dr. Bancroft to the Committee of Chemistry, was sent in answer to a request made by them on the 22d of February last. It states the natural history of Lacca, the mode of separating the colouring matter from it, and various methods of applying the colour for the purposes of Dyers; illustrated by specimens of woollen-cloth dyed by the Doctor, and which may be seen at the Society's Repository.

*To the Committee of Chemistry of the Society of Arts, &c.*

GENTLEMEN,

LACCA or Gum-lac is, as you doubtless know, produced abundantly by an insect of the Coccus genus, of which very satisfactory accounts have been given, first by Mr. James Kerr, in the Philosophical Transactions for the year 1781, and afterwards by Dr. Roxburgh,

A a 2      in

in those of the year 1791. These insects, when young, place themselves upon the succulent extremities of the branches of certain shrubs growing in different places, and more especially upon the uncultivated mountains on both sides of the Ganges, where they soon produce and involve themselves in a spissid sub-pellucid liquid, which seems to glue them to the branches where they are placed ; and, by a gradual accumulation of this liquid, each insect acquires, and becomes inclosed in a perfect cell, where, at maturity it appears like a small oval red bag, without life, and full of a *beautiful red fluid.* The whole mass of these cells, and of the insects contained therein, while adhering externally to the sticks or branches in question, is called *stick* lac; but when detached from the sticks, and garbled, it takes the name of *seed* lac: and this last being boiled in water to separate the colouring matter, then strained, and formed into thin plates

plates (while liquified by heat), becomes *shell* lac, and constitutes the principal part of sealing-wax, when well made.

Dr. Roxburgh found that these insects gave to water a much more *beautiful red colour* while fresh, than after being dried; and thence concluded that it might be well for persons living where lac is most abundant, to endeavour to extract the colouring-matter while fresh and moist, in such a manner as to render it capable of being afterwards preserved without injury.

About three years before the publication of Dr. Roxburgh's paper, I had received from Mr. P—, a gentleman who had lately returned to this country from India, a sample of colouring-matter, which he called East-India cochineal, and which very nearly resembled that of Mexico, when it has been reduced to powder. With this substance I made several experiments, which convinced me that it was the colouring mat-

A a 3

ter

ter of lac, extracted most probably by hot water, and precipitated by alum. Of these experiments I gave an account in the first volume of my publication, upon the Philosophy of Permanent Colours.

On the 7th of July, 1796, Mr. Fleming, Inspector of Drugs at Calcutta, wrote a letter to the Bengal Board of Trade, of which the following is an extract, viz.

" Dr. Bancroft, in a very instructive work, which he has lately published on the subject of Dying, mentions as a *desideratum*, a method of extracting the colouring matter of lac, and thinks that if it could be formed into Lake, and sent home in that state, it would be a far preferable method to that of sending the stick lac. Encouraged by so good an authority, I herewith send for your inspection two bottles of a preparation which I have received from Mr. Stephens, at Keerpoy, and which appeared

to

to me to be exactly what the Doctor desires. Mr. Stephens informs me, that he prepared it from *fresh* lac, by a method discovered by himself; and that if it should be found to answer on trial, he will be able to provide a considerable quantity of it every year. I therefore beg leave to recommend that the accompanying sample may be sent home by the ship Dart, with a request to the Honourable Court of Directors, that it may be forwarded to Dr. Bancroft, for his opinion of its value," &c.

This recommendation the Board of Trade thought proper to adopt, and transmitted the same with the samples in question by the Dart, as appears by their letter of the 9th of July, 1796, to the Court of Directors, by whose order they were afterwards forwarded to me, for the purpose mentioned by Mr. Fleming. With these samples I made some successful experiments, and gave such an account of them, as, joined to the

A a 4                    then

then high price of Cochineal, induced the East-India Company, as I have been informed, to purchase a considerable quantity of the Lake, or preparation in question, from Mr. Stephens, and at a very handsome price; though I believe few or no steps have been taken here to bring it into use among the Dyers, Morocco-leather manufacturers, Paper-stainers, &c.

Mr. Stephens having lately addressed the Society of Arts, &c. on the subject of this Lake, and sent them a sample of it, and I having been requested at a Committee of Chemistry, to whom Mr. Stephens's communication was referred, to repeat my experiments with a part of the sample sent to the Society, I have done so; and now beg leave to offer the Committee some specimens of colours dyed therewith, and an account of the means and process by which they were so dyed.

In

In the first volume of my publication on Permanent Colours, I have described and recommended a method of dying the scarlet colour from Cochineal upon a *new* principle; and this method has enabled me to produce a better scarlet with Mr. Stephens's Lake, than I have yet been able to do by the ordinary method. Perhaps my failures in this respect may be owing to a cause which I did not suspect until very lately, and the existence or non-existence of which I have not since had leisure to ascertain, though I hope soon to do it. In the mean time I shall endeavour as shortly as possible to enable the Committee to understand the nature and principle of the new method just mentioned. I had found, more than twelve years ago, that the *true* or *natural* colour of Cochineal when given to wool by dying, with the common solution, or nitro-muriate of tin, which the Dyers invariably employ for dying scarlet, was not a *scarlet*, but a bright a bright *rose* colour, as N° I. of the samples which accompany this paper; and that in the usual process it only became a scarlet from the chemical action of the acid of a considerable portion of tartar, which the Dyers invariably use; though without knowing the particular effect resulting from it.

N° II. is a sample of a very beautiful *scarlet*, dyed by the successor of the late Mr. Nash, in Gloucestershire, and like all *true* scarlets is a *compound* colour, of about three portions of the rose of N° I. and one portion of pure yellow; though in this instance the effect or colour results not from the addition of a *foreign yellow*, but from such a conversion of the cochineal rose colour towards the yellow, as is equivalent to about one fourth of the whole. Reflecting on this fact, and considering the great difference in price between the colouring-matter of Cochineal and that of the purest known *yellows*, I concluded that a

great

great saving of expense might be obtained by employing the former without
tartar, so as only to produce that portion, which is necessary, of the *rose* colour,
and superadding a suitable portion of
yellow from some of the cheaper yellow
dying-drugs; among which the *quercitron-bark* naturally occurred to me as
producing, with the solutions of tin, one
of the purest and brightest yellow colours; of which a sample may be seen
at N° III.   Upon this principle the
sample N° IV. has been dyed; by first
giving the cloth a yellow ground, with
a suitable quantity of the usual solution,
or nitre-muriate of tin, and of the quercitron-bark, and then superadding the
cochineal *rose* colour, by dying it in the
usual way with cochineal, and a like
solution of tin as for a scarlet; taking
care only to *omit the tartar,* which would
otherwise have carried the colour so
much farther towards the *yellow hue* as to
produce an *aurora.*

It

It is upon this principle that the samples N° V. and N° VI. have been dyed, from Mr. Stephens's *Lac-Lake*. Both were first dyed yellow, with the quercitron-bark, as at N° III. and afterwards dyed with the Lake: but for N° V. I employed, along with the Bark and Lake, a suitable portion of the solution of tin, commonly used by scarlet-dyers in the nitro-muriate of that metal: and for N° VI. I substituted the murio-sulphate, which I have in my first volume recommended as cheaper, and in some respects preferable, to the nitro-muriate of tin. I must, however, observe, that the colouring-matter of Mr. Stephens's Lake, having, as I believe, been precipitated by alum, cannot be disengaged from the aluminous earth, and dissolved even by boiling-water alone. Pure pot-ash, or pure soda, should be added in nearly an equal quantity to the Lake employed, in order to produce a complete separation, and solution of the colouring-matter,

matter; and the water should be made hot, and kept nearly at a boiling heat for half an hour; after which the clear liquor may be decanted from the sediment.

It will be perceived that the samples N° V. and N° VI. are a little less vivid and beautiful than the Gloucestershire scarlet N° II. or that dyed, or rather compounded, from cochineal and quercitron-bark N° IV. But it is probable that the colours from Lac-Lake may prove rather more durable than those from cochineal, and in that way they may compensate for their little inferiority in brightness. It is difficult to measure the quantity or amount of the colouring-matter afforded by the Lac-Lake, with accuracy, in experiments made upon so small a scale as mine; but I think there is reason to conclude, that four pounds of the Lake will yield about as much colour as one pound of fine cochineal.

I have

I have the honour to be, very respectfully,

GENTLEMEN,

Your most obedient servant,

EDWARD BANCROFT.

May 29, 1801.

P. S. Mr. Stephens has not explained
the means or process employed by him
to produce the Lake in question. I am,
however, convinced, that after extracting the colouring-matter by hot water,
he has precipitated it by alum; which
appears to me not to be the most eligible
method of obtaining what is wanted from
the Lac.

Probably the colouring-matter might
be more advantageously procured by
extracting it with the help of boiling-
water, and afterwards evaporating the
decoction to complete dryness, in the
ways, and with the precautions, usually
employed for the like purposes. But if

it

it should be found expedient to employ any means of precipitation, I think some of the solutions of tin, which have been found suitable for dying scarlet, would prove more efficacious than alum in this way; because the calx of tin is of greater specific gravity than alumine: and it would moreover prove advantageous to the scarlet dye, because, by adding any suitable acid, this calx, and the colouring-matter precipitated by it, might be redissolved in a state fit for *immediate use*, without the necessity, which now exists, of employing an alkali, to detach the colouring-matter from the aluminous precipitant; and also without the danger of redissolving a portion of alumine along with the colouring-matter of the Lac, by which the scarlet might probably be rendered less vivid than it would be with a basis obtained wholly from tin.

*⁎* Ex-

*.* Experiments made by other persons confirm Dr. Bancroft's observations. It appears that the effects of this Lake for dying cotton-cloth, staining leather, and printing upon paper, are analogous to those of cochineal, but require three or four times the weight, to produce similar intensity of colour.

The price of the article is such as will probably bring this Lake into general use, among Painters, Manufacturers, Printers, and Dyers.

---

# REWARDS

### BESTOWED BY THE

# SOCIETY,

From October, 1800,

To June, 1801.

---

# REWARDS

## BESTOWED IN

# AGRICULTURE.

Class 25.    TO Henry Vernon, Esq. of Hilton-Park, in Staffordshire, for having planted eleven thousand six hundred English Elms, the Gold Medal.  See page 69.

Class 49.    To Mr. Thomas Selby, of Otford Castle, in Kent, for having planted twenty-one acres with Osiers, Thirty Guineas.  See page 75.

Class 67.    To Thomas Johnes, Esq. of Hafod, in Cardiganshire, for extensive Plantations of Timber-trees, the Gold Medal.  See page 78, and Preface.

Class 88.        To Mr. ROBERT BROWN,
of Markle, in Scotland, for
cultivating one huudred and
forty-five acres of Spring-
Wheat, TWENTY GUINEAS.
See page 81.

Class 93.        To the Rev. T. C. MUN-
NINGS, of East Dereham, in
Norfolk, for comparative experiments in the growth of
Turnips, the SILVER MEDAL
and TEN GUINEAS.    See
page 147.

Class 103.    To Mr. THOMAS FOGG, of
Bolton, Lancashire, for improving fifty acres and a half
of Land lying waste, the
GOLD MEDAL.    See page
105.

        To Mr. JOHN PALMER, of
Maxstock Castle, near Coles-
hill, in Warwickshire, for
Harvesting Corn in Wet
Weather, the SILVER ME-
DAL.    See page 99.

                        To

To Mr. JOHN HORRIDGE, of Raikes, Lancashire, for his preparation and application of Manures, the SILVER MEDAL. See page 183.

To NICHOLAS ASHTON, Esq. of Woolton-Hall, in Lancashire, for planting one hundred and . thirty-three acres of Waste Moor Land, the GOLD MEDAL See page 169.

To Mr. WILLIAM LESTER, of Northampton, for an implement in husbandry called by him a Cultivator, the SILVER MEDAL. See page 142.

To THOMAS ANDREW KNIGHT, Esq. of Elton, near Ludlow, for a Drill Machine for sowing Turnip-seed, the SILVER MEDAL. See page 123.

## IN CHEMISTRY.

Class 147.     To Samuel Bentham, Esq. Queen's-Square, for preserving Fresh Water Sweet during long Voyages, the Gold Medal. See page 191.

## IN POLITE ARTS.

Class 185.     To Mr. T. Kilburn, of Wallington, for a Drawing of Flowers, the Silver Medal.

Class 187.     To Miss Sarah Matilda Parry, of Bath, for an original Sketch from Nature, being a View on the River Wye, the Silver Medal.

Class 189.     To Mr. William Mulready, of Langley-Street, for a Drawing of Outlines, the Greater Silver Pallet.

Class

Class 190.    To Mr. PETER JOSEPH BONE, Hanover-Street, for a Drawing of Outlines, the LESSER SILVER PALLET.

Class 191.    To Mr. FRANCIS JOHN SARJEANT, Berkeley-Square, for a View from the Red-Lane, near Reading, in Berkshire; being an original Drawing from Nature, the GREATER SILVER PALLET.

Class 194.    To Mr. H. MOSES, of Greenwich, for an Historical Drawing of the Continence of Scipio, the GREATER SILVER PALLET.

To Miss LOUISA CHARLOTTE LLOYD, of Aston, in Staffordshire, for a Drawing of the Head of Galen, from a Cast in Plaster, the SILVER MEDAL.

To Miss MARY SMIRKE, Charlotte-Street, Fitzroy-Sq.

B b 4                    for

for a Painting, being a View from Nature, taken near Finchley, the GOLD MEDAL.

To Miss BEAUCHAMP, of Langley Park, for a Copy of a Painting from Salvator Rosa, the SILVER MEDAL.

To Miss ANDRAS, of Pall-Mall, for two Models, being her Royal Highness Princess Charlotte, and Lord Nelson, taken from life, the GREATER SILVER PALLET.

To Mrs. REBECKAH LOWRY, of Titchfield-Street, for two Paintings on Glass, the SILVER MEDAL.

## IN MANUFACTURES.

Class 207.    To Mr. THOMAS WILLMOT, of Shoreham, Kent, for Paper made from raw Vegetable Substances, TWENTY GUINEAS. See page 235.

See page 235.

                                IN

## IN MECHANICKS.

Class 212.   To Mr. ROBERT HAYES, of Wapping, for taking three Whales by the Gun Harpoon, TEN GUINEAS. See page 262.

Class 213.   To Mr. RICHARD PHILLIPS, of Bristol, for his improved Mode of driving Bolts into Ships, FORTY GUINEAS. See page 269.

Class 222.   To Mr. FIELD EVANS, of Pool Quay, Montgomeryshire, for discovering a Quarry of Burr-stone proper for Mill-Stones, FIFTY POUNDS. See page 280.

To Mr. THOMAS ARKWRIGHT, of Kendal, for a Machine for raising Minerals, TWENTY-FIVE GUINEAS. See page 276.

To

To Mr. HENRY SAR-
JEANT, of Whitehaven, in
Cumberland, for a Machine
for raising Water, the SILVER
MEDAL. See page 255.

To Mr. THOMAS GHENT,
of Homerton, for an im-
proved Crane, FIFTEEN
GUINEAS. See page 294.

To Mr. WILLIAM BUL-
LOCK, of Portland-Street,
for an improvement in Drawback Locks, FIFTEEN GUI-
NEAS. See page 290.

To Mrs. BESANT, Bromp-
ton-Row, for an improved
Water-Wheel, TEN GUINEAS.
See page 265.

To Mr. DE LAFONS, for a
Watch Escapement, THIRTY
GUINEAS. See page 331.

To Mr. GARNET TERRY,
of the Bank, for a Steel Mill
for grinding hard Substances,
the

the SILVER MEDAL. See
page 287.

## IN COLONIES AND TRADE.

To ANDREW STEPHENS,
Esq. of Calcutta, for making 18,000 lb. of Lake from
Stick-Lack, the SILVER MEDAL. See page 352.

# PRESENTS

# SOCIETY,

SINCE THE PUBLICATION OF THE EIGHTEENTH
VOLUME OF THESE TRANSACTIONS.

With the Names of the Donors.

———————————

## THE ROYAL SOCIETY.

THE Second Part of the 89th, and the First, Second, and Third Parts of the 90th Volume of the Philosophical Transactions.

## THE SOCIETY OF ANTIQUARIES.

The 13th Volume of the Archæologia, and a Copy of the Royal Charter and Statutes of that Society.

THE

THE LEIPSICK SOCIETY.

Three Numbers of the Transactions of that Society.

THE MANCHESTER AGRICULTURAL SOCIETY.

The Rules, Orders, and Premiums, of that Society.

SOCIETY FOR BETTERING THE CONDITION OF THE POOR.

The 1st and 2d Volume of the Reports of that Society, and the two First Numbers of the 3d Volume, presented by Dr. Garthshore from the Committee.

BOARD OF NAVAL ARCHITECTURE.

The Report of the Committee for conducting the Experiments of the Society for the Improvement of Naval Architecture, presented from that Board by Thomas Mortimer, Esq.

DR.

### Dr. James Anderson.

The 15th to the 26th Number inclusive, of Recreations in Agriculture.

### James Barry, Esq.

Several Prints, illustrative of the Paintings in the Great Room.

### William Dalrymple, Esq.

A Pamphlet entitled a Treatise on the Culture of Wheat, with an Appendix, containing an Account of the Growth of Wheat with Beans, and a plan of improved Seed Harrows.

### Mr. R. Dodd.

A Quarto Pamphlet, on the intended Grand Surry Canal.

### Dr. Garnet.

An Octavo Volume, in Boards, entitled Outlines of a Course of Lectures on Chemistry.

JOHN

JOHN HINCKLEY, Esq.

Three Octavo Volumes, entitled Rinaldo Rinaldini, translated from the German.

The late JOHN HOLLIDAY, Esq.

A Quarto Volume, entitled The Life of Lord Mansfield.

JOHN HOLLINGSHED, Esq.

Three Pamphlets, entitled Hints to Country Gentlemen and Farmers, on the Importance of using Salt as a general Manure.

THOMAS JOHNES, Esq. M. P.

An Octavo Volume, entitled A Cardiganshire Landlord's Advice to his Tenants.

JAMES MALTON, Esq.

A Quarto Volume, entitled The young Painter's Maulstick.

DR.

### DR. ROLLO.

An Octavo Pamphlet, entitled An Account of the Royal Artillery Hospital, Woolwich.

### THE REV. H. P. STACEY.

A Pamphlet, entitled Observations on the Failure of Turnip Crops.

### Mr. WILLIAM STICKNEY.

An Octavo Pamphlet, entitled Observations respecting the Grub.

### Mr. THOMAS TAYLOR, the Assistant Secretary.

A Quarto Volume in Boards, entitled The Metaphysics of Aristotle, translated from the Greek.

### JOHN WYATT, Esq.

The 66th to the 84th Number inclusive, of the Repertory of Arts and Manufactures.

Mr.

Mr. John Taylor.

Samples of Chicoree Seed, of Chicoree Roots, in different states, and of Coffee prepared from them.

# A CATALOGUE

## OF THE

# MODELS AND MACHINES

Received since the Publication of the Eighteenth Volume of the Society's Transactions, with the Numbers as they are arranged, in the Class to which they belong.

———

## AGRICULTURE. CLASS I.

No. LXXXVII.  A MODEL of a Drain-Plough, by his Grace the Duke of Bridgewater. See Page 117.

LXXXVIII.  A Drill-Machine for Sowing Turnip-Seed, by Thomas Andrew Knight, Esq. See Page 123.

LXXXIX.

LXXXIX.   A Model of a Cultivator for pulverizing ploughed Fallows. See Page 142.

XC.   A Drill-Machine for Sowing Turnip-Seed, by the Rev. T. C. Munnings. See Page 147.

XCI.   A Model of an Augre, or Peat-Borer, for draining Boggy Land, by Thomas Eccleston, Esq. See Page 165.

MECHANICKS.   CLASS IV.

CLXXXIV.   A Model of a Water-Wheel, by the late Mr. Besant. See Page 265.

CLXXXVI.   Two Models of Machines for driving Bolts into Ships, by Mr. R. Phillips. See Page 269.

CLXXXVII.   A Model of a Machine for raising Ore from Mines, by Mr. Thomas Arkwright. See Page 276.

CLXXXVIII.  A Model of a Mill for grinding Hard Substances, by Mr. Garnet Terry. See Page 277.

CLXXXIX.  A Drawback Lock for House Doors, by Mr. William Bullock. See Page 290.

CXC.  A Crane for raising and delivering heavy Bodies See Page 294.

CXCI.  A Model of a Stove for Ventilation, and a Model of a Sash Frame, recommended for Hospitals, by Sir G. O. Paul, Bart. See Page 299.

CXCII.  An Escapement for Watches, by M. John De Lafons. See Page 331.

OF THE

# OFFICERS of the SOCIETY,

AND

# CHAIRMEN

OF THE SEVERAL

# COMMITTEES,

Elected March 23, 1801.

———

### PRESIDENT.

CHARLES Duke of Norfolk, F. R. and A. S.

### VICE-PRESIDENTS.

Charles Duke of Richmond, K. G. F. R. and A. S.

William Henry Duke of Portland, K. G. F. R. and A. S.

C c 3        Hugh

Hugh Duke of Northumberland, K. G.
F. R. and A. S.
Jacob Earl of Radnor, F. R. and A. S.
Charles Earl of Liverpool, LL. D.
Charles Earl of Romney, F. R. S.
Hon. Robert Clifford, F. R. and A. S.
Sir William Dolben, Bart.
Sir Watkin Lewes, Knt.
Thomas Pitt, Esq. F. A. S.
Caleb Whitefoord, Esq. F. R. and A. S.
Thomas Skip Dyot Bucknall, Esq. M. P.

### SECRETARY.

Mr. Charles Taylor.

### ASSISTANT-SECRETARY.

Mr. Thomas Taylor,

### REGISTER.

Mr. George Cockings.

### COLLECTOR.

Mr. Stephen Theodore Borman.

CHAIR-

# CHAIRMEN OF THE SEVERAL COMMITTEES.

Elected March 23, 1801.

---

### ACCOMPTS.

James Hebert, Esq.
William Lumley, Esq.

### CORRESPONDENCE AND PAPERS.

Edward Bancroft, M. D. F. R. S.
Richard Powell, M. D.

### POLITB ARTS.

Matthew Michell, Esq.
George Meredith, Esq. F. A. S. P. R. I.

### AGRICULTURE.

Rev. Stephen Eaton, A. M. and F. A. S.
John Middleton, Esq.

C c 4     MANU-

### MANUFACTURES.

John Hinckley, Esq.
Joseph Colen, Esq.

### MECHANICKS.

John Read, Esq.
George Howe Browne, Esq.

### CHEMISTRY.

Edward Howard, Esq. F. R. S.
Henry Coxwell, Esq.

### COLONIES AND TRADE.

John Baker, Esq.
William Meredith, Esq.

### MISCELLANEOUS MATTERS.

Joseph Jacob, Esq.
William Kirkby, Esq.

# L I S T

OF

# CONTRIBUTING MEMBERS.

### NOVEMBER, 1801.

*N. B.* Thofe marked with ** pay Five Guineas annually; those marked with *, Three Guineas annually; those with P, are Perpetual members; those with †† have served the office of Steward; and those marked with † are Stewards elect.

### A.

ARGYLL, John Duke of
   Athol, John Duke of, F. R. S.
Anspach, Elizabeth Margravine of Brandenburgh
Alvanley, Richard Lord, *Great George-street*
†Anderson, Sir John William, Bart. M. P. *Adelphi Terrace*
††P Abbot, Charles, Esq. *Pall-mall*, M. P. F. R. and A. S.

Abercromby,

Abercromby, John, Esq. *Claygate, near Esher, Surrey*

Abdy, Rev. Thomas Abdy, *Cooper-sale, Essex*

Adair, Alexander, Esq. *Pall-mall*

††Adam, William, Esq. *Albemarle-street*

Adam, William, Esq. *Lincoln's-inn-fields*

Adam, Joseph, M. D.

Adams, William, Esq. M. P. *Craven-street*

Adams, John, Esq. *Ely-place*

Adams, Dudley, Esq. *Fleet-street*

Adamson, Mr. David, *Oxford-street*

Affleck, Col. James, *Vere-street, Cavendish-square*

Agace, Daniel, Esq. *Gower-street*

D'Aguilar, Honourable Ephraim Baron, *Broad-street-buildings*

Aickin, James, Esq. *Denmark-street, Soho*

Ainslie, Henry, M. D. *Dover-street*

Ainsworth, Mr. Richard, *Moss Bank, near Bolton*

Albin, William, Esq. *Tokenhouse-yard*

P Alexander Claud, Esq.

††Alexander, Mr. Daniel, *Lawrence-Poultney-lane*

††Allen, Edward, Esq. *Clifford's-inn*

††Allen, John, Esq. F. R. S. *Clement's-inn*

††Allen, William, Esq. *Lewisham, Kent*

Allix, John Peter, Esq. *Swaffham-house, Cambridge-shire*

Anderson, David, Esq.

Anderson, James, LL. D. *Islington*

P Andrew, Thomas Harrison, Esq. *Moss Hall, Finchley*

Andrews, Magnus, Esq. *Sackville-street, Piccadilly*

Angerstein, John Julius, Esq. *Pall-mall*

P Annesly,

P Annesly, Honourable Richard, Esq. *Dublin*

P Antrobus, Edmund, Esq. *New-street, Spring-gar-dens*

Arbuthnot, George, Esq. *King-street, Golden-square*

Arkwright, Richard, Esq. *Cromford, Derbyshire*

Armstrong, Mr. John, *Pimlico*

P Ashby, Shuckbrugh, Esq. F. R. S. *Great Ormond-street*

Ashby, Henry, Esq. *St. Andrew's-court, Holborn*

Ashton, Nicholas, Esq. *Woolton Hall, near Liverpool*

Ashton, Mr. Isaac, *Billiter-lane*

Aslet, Mr. Robert, *Bank*

Astley, Jacob Henry, Esq. M. P. *Burgh Hall, Norfolk*

††Atcheson, Nathaniel, Esq. F. S. A. P. R. I. *Ely-place*

††Atlee, Mr. John, *Wandsworth*

††Atlee, Mr. James, *Thames street*

††P Aubert, Alexander, Esq. F. R. and A. S. *Austin-friars*

### B.

P Bedford, Francis Duke of

**Buccleugh, Henry Duke of

P Bute, John Earl of, F. A. S.

P Buchan, David Earl of, LL. D. F. R. and A. S.

Bristol, Right Rev. Frederick Earl of, F. R. S.

P Beverley, Algernon Earl of

Barrington, the Right Hon. Lord Viscount

P Brownlow, Lord, F. R. and A. S.

Braybrooke,

Braybrooke, Richard Lord, *Lower Grosvenor-street*

Bolton, Thomas Lord, F. A. S.

P Balgonie, Lord

P Bouillon, Prince of, Philip D'Auvergne, Captain in the Royal Navy, F. R. and A. S.

Bruhl, his Excellency Count de, *Old Burlington-street*

Bruce, the Honourable Major-General, M. P.

Bowes, the Honourable George

Bowes, the Honourable Thomas, *Redbourn, near St. Albans*

P Blacket, Sir Thomas, Bart.

Banks, the Right Honourable Sir Joseph, Bart. President of the Royal Society, K. B. and F. A. S. *Soho-square*

Baring, Sir Francis, Bart. M. P. *Devonshire-square*

Burgess, Sir James Bland, Bart. *Duke-street, Westminster*

Bruce, Governor James

††P Bacon, John, Esq. F. A. S. *Temple*

P Bacon, John, Esq. *Newman-street*

††Bacon, Anthony, Esq.

Bailey, Charles, Esq. *Swallowfield, Berks*

Bailey, James, Esq. *Lambeth*

††Baker, John, Esq. 12, *Grosvenor-street*

P Baker, William, Esq. *ditto*

Bancroft, Edward, M. D. and F. R. S. *Francis-street, Tottenham-court-road*

P Barclay, David, Esq. *Walthamstow*

Barclay, Robert, Esq. F. L. S. *Terrace, Clapham*

＊ Barclay, Robert, Esq. *Lombard-street*

Baring,

Baring, John, Esq. M. P. *Devonshire-square*

Barker, Richard, Esq. *Tavistock-street, Bedford-square*

Barker, Mr. Charles, *Chandos-street*

Barlow, Mr. J. *Great Surrey-street, Blackfriars*

P Barnard, William, Esq. *Deptford*

P Barnard, Edward, Esq. *ditto*

Barnard, Mr. Thomas, *Adelphi*

Barnard, Josiah, Esq. *Cornhill*

Barnard, Leonard, Esq. *Bucklersbury*

††Barnardiston, Nathaniel, Esq. *Harpur-street*

Barnet, Edward, Esq. *Soho-square*

Barrett, Miss Eliza, *Stockwell*

Barrington, the Rev. George, *Durham*

Barry, Henry Alexander, Esq. *Eversley Lodge, Hants*

Barry, James, Esq. *Castle-street, Oxford-street*

Bartlett, Patrick, Esq.

P Bartolozzi, Francis, Esq. R. A. *North-end*

Barton, Rev. John, Chaplain to the House of Commons

Bates, Mr. George Ferne, *No. 73, Hatton Garden*

Bate, John, Esq. *Bedford-row*

Batson, Edward David, Esq. *Lombard-street*

Baverstock, Mr. James, *Windsor*

††Beale, Daniel, Esq. *Fitzroy-square*

P Bean, Mr. Nathaniel, *King's-road, Bedford-row*

P Bean, Mr. Isaac, *ditto*

Bearcroft, Philip, R. Esq. *Vere-street*

Beatson, Robert, Esq. *Kilrick, Scotland*

Beaumont, Daniel, Esq. *Great Russel-street*

†† Beard,

††Beard, John, Esq. F. A. S. *Doctors-commons*

· Beazely, Charles, Esq. P. R. I. *Blackfriars-road*

Beddall, Mr. John, *Jekyls, Fenchingfield, Essex*

Belisario, Mr. John, *Gerard's Cross, Bucks*

Bell, William, Esq. *Norfolk-street, Strand*

Bell, Mr. Anthony, *Charlotte-street, Pimlico*

Bellew, Christopher K. Esq. *Inner-Temple*

Belches, Robert, Esq.

Bennett, James, Esq. *Bedford-square*

Bent, Mr. William, *St. Martin's lane*

Bentham, General Samuel, *Queen's-square, West-minster*

Bentley, Robert, Esq. *Bedford-street, Covent-garden*

††Benwell, Joseph, Esq. *Battersea*

Berwick, Joseph, Esq. *Hollow-park, near Worcester*

Biddulph, Robert, Esq. M. P. *Arlington-street*

Bignell, William, Esq. *Seething-lane*

† Bingley, Thomas, jun. Esq. *Coleman-street*

Bingley, Mr. John, *John-street, Tottenham-court-road*

Birch, Thomas James, Esq. Captain of the 1st Regiment of Life Guards

Birchill, Mr. Matthew, *Fulham*

Birkett, Daniel, Esq. *Trinity-square, Tower-hill*

††Birkhead, Charles, Esq. *Ryegate, Surrey*

Bishop, Nathaniel, Esq. *Yorkshire*

Bisset, Capt. Robert, Commissary-General, *Great Pulteney-street*

Blaauws, William, Esq. *Queen-Ann-street, West*

††Blades, John, Esq. *Ludgate-hill*

Black, Mr. George, *Princes-street, Bank*

Blackburne,

Blackburne, John, Esq. M. P. F. R. S. *Park-street Westminster*

Blair, Alexander, Esq. *Devonshire-place*

††Blake, William, Esq. *Aldersgate-street*

Blandy, John, Esq. *Reading*

Blandy, William, Esq. *Reading*

Blane, William, Esq. F. R. S.

Blicke, Charles Tufton, Esq. *Billiter-square*

Blizard, Mr. William, F. R. and A. S.

Blomefield, Colonel, *Shooter's-hill*

Boddington, Thomas, Esq. *Mark-lane*

P Boehm, Edmund, Esq. *Broad-street*

Boddy, Mr. Francis, *Warwick-lane*

Boddy, John, Esq. *Thames-street*

Bonar, Thompson, Esq *Broad-street-buildings*

Booth, John, Esq. *Devonshire-street, Queen-square*

Borradaile, R. Esq. *Fenchurch-street*

Borradaile, William, *ditto*

Borman, Mr. William, *Winchester*

Borron, Arthur, Esq. *Warrington*

Bostock, the Rev. John, *Windsor*

Bostock, Samuel, Esq. *Borough*

P Bosville, William, Esq. F. R. S. *Gunthwaite Hall, Yorkshire*

Botfield, Thomas, jun. Esq. *Ditton, near Bewdley, Worcestershire*

Bovi, Mr. Mariano, *Piccadilly*

Boulton, Matthew, Esq. F. R. S. *Soho, near Birmingham*

Bousfield, George, Esq. *King's-bench Walk*

††Bowzer

††Bowzer, Richard, Esq. *No.* 3, *Bedford-row*

††Boydell, John, Esq. and Alderman, *Cheapside*

Bracken, Rev. Thomas, *Jermyn-street, St. James's*

Braithwaite, Daniel, Esq. F. R. and A. S. *Post-Office, and Grenville-street, Brunswick-square*

Braithwaite, Mr. John, *Brook-street, Tottenham-court-road*

Bramah, Mr. Joseph, *Piccadilly*

Brettingham, Robert, Esq. *Grosvenor-place*

Brewer, Mr. John, jun. *Ludgate-hill*

P Brickwood, John, Esq. *Billiter-square*

Brickwood, Mr. Nathaniel, *Thames-street*

Bridge, Mr. Thomas, *Southwark*

Bridgman, William, Esq. *No.* 76, *Old Broad-street*

††P Broadhead, Theodore Henry, Esq. F. A. S. *Portland-place*

Broadwood, James, Esq. *Charlotte-street, Portland-place*

Brockbank, Mr. Joseph, *Crescent, New Bridge-street, Blackfriars*

Brodie, Alexander, Esq. M. P.

††Brodie, Alexander, Esq. *Carey-street*

Brodie, Mr. John, *Clifford's-inn*

✱P Brooke, Richard Brooke de Capell, Colonel, F.R.S, *Great Oakley, Northamptonshire*

Brounlie, John, M. D. *Carey-street, Lincoln's-inn*

Brown, Thomas, Esq. *Adelphi*

Brown, John, Esq. *John-street, Adelphi*

Browne, Isaac Hawkins, Esq. M. P. F. R. S, *South Audley-street*

Browne,

Browne, Francis John, Esq. M. P.

Browne, George Howe, Esq. *Bedford-street, Covent-garden*

Browne, Mr. Robert, *Kew*

Browne, Thomas, Esq. No. 134, *New Bridge-street*

Bryan, Michael, Esq. *Pall-mall*

Bryer, Mr. Robert, No. 58, *Strand*

††Bucknall, Thomas Skip Dyot, Esq. M. P. *Baker-street, Portman-square*

Buckell, George, Esq. jun. *Chepstow, Monmouth-shire*

Buller, John, Esq. *Morval, Cornwall, and Gloucester place, Portman-square*

Burdon, Mr. William, *St. Andrew's court, Holborn*

Burgess, John, Esq. *Brook Farm, Hants, or* 107, *Strand*

† Burgoyne, Montague, Esq. *Mark Hall, Harlow, Essex*

Burnett, Robert, jun. Esq. *Vauxhall*

P Burney, Charles, M. D. *Greenwich*

Burton, Launcelot, Esq. *Newcastle-street, Strand*

Bury, Edward, Esq. *Walthamstow*

Butt, Mr. James Strode, *Paragon, Kent-road*

Butts, John, Esq. *Chatham-square*

Byerley, Mr. Thomas, *York-street, St. James's square*

††Byfield, George, Esq. *Craven-street*

Byfield, Mr. George, *Craig's-court, Charing-cross*

C.

## C.

Clermont, Earl

††Chetwynd, Richard Lord Viscount

Conyngham, Right Honourable William, F. A. S.

Cavendish, Hon. Henry, F. R. and A. S. *Gower-street, Bedford-row*

*††Clifford, the Honourable Robert, V. P. F. A. S. and P. R. I. *Edward-street, Portman-square*

Coghill, Sir John, Bart. *Coghill Hall, Yorkshire*

P Carnegie, Sir David, Bart. M. P.

Caldwell, Ralph, Esq. *Hilborough, Norfolk*

††Caley, John, Esq. F. A. S. *Gray's-inn*

Callender, John, Esq. M. P. *Cumberland-place*

Caldecott, John, Esq. *Rugby, Warwickshire*

Calverley, Thomas, Esq. *Elm-court, Temple*

Campbell, Governor William

Campbell, Duncan, Esq. *Great Queen-street*

Carden, James, Esq. *John-street, Adelphi*

Carew, Reginald Pole, Esq. M. P. F. R. and A. S. *New Cavendish-street, Portland-place*

Carpenter, Charles, Esq. *Moditonham, Cornwall*

Cartwright, Charles, Esq. *India-house*

Cartwright, Rev. Edmund, *Marybone Park*

Cartwright, Rev. Edmund, jun. *Baliol College, Oxford*

††P Cater, Mr. Richard, *Bread-street, Cheapside*

Chadwick, Thomas, Esq. *Hampton, Middlesex*

Chalie, John, Esq. *Bedford-square*

Chamberlayne, John, Esq. *Bromley*

Champernoun,

Champernoun, John, Esq. *Totness, Devon*
Champney, Joseph, Esq. *Cheapside*
Charington, John, Esq. *Mile-end*
Cheek, J. M. G. Esq. *Evesham, Worcestershire*
Cherry, Benjamin, Esq. *Hertford*
Chippendale, Mr. Thomas, *St. Martin's lane*
Christie, Daniel Beat, Esq. *Finedon, near Welling-borough*
✝ Christian, John Giles, Esq. *Doctors-commons*
Christian, John, Esq. *Lincoln's-inn*
Claridge, John, Esq. *Upton-on-Severn, Worcestershire*
P Clark, Mr. James
✝✝Clarke, Richard, Esq. Chamberlain, *Bridge-street-Blackfriars*
Clarke, Mr. Henry, *Gracechurch-street*
Clarke, Richard, Esq. *Worcester*
Clarke, John, Esq. *Edinburgh*
Clarke, William, Esq. *Tynemouth, Northumberland*
Clark, James, Esq. M. D. *Tavistock-street, Covent-garden*
Clay, Henry, Esq. *Birmingham*
✝ Cleland, Walter, Esq. *Adelphi Terrace*
Cleveland, William, Esq. *Dowgate-hill*
Close, Rev. Henry John, *Ipswich*
Cockett, Thomas, Esq. *Inner Temple*
P Coggan, Captain John, *East-India House*
Closs, Thomas, Esq. *Bermondsey-street*
Cole, Benjamin, Esq. *Battersea-rise, Surrey*
Cole, Robert, Esq. *Windsor*
Cole, Thomas Comyns, Esq. *Woodstock-street, Bond-street*

Coleman,

Coleman, Edward, Esq. Professor at the Veterinary College

P Colen, Joseph, Esq. Governor of York Fort, *Hudson's Bay*

Collier, Mr. Joshua, *Dartmouth-street, Westminster*

††Collins, Thomas, Esq. F. A. S. *Berners-street*

Collins, Benjamin Charles, Esq. *Salisbury*

Collow, William, Esq. *Broad-street-buildings*

Colquhoun, Patrick, Esq.

Combe, Harvey Christian, Esq. Alderman, M. P. *Great Russell-street, Bloomsbury*

Combrune, Gideon, Esq. *Berners-street*

Compton, Mr. Henry, *Charlotte-street, Pimlico*

††Conant, Nathaniel, Esq. *Great Marlborough-street,*

P Coningham, James, Esq.

Constable, M. M. Esq. *Evringham, Yorkshire*

Cook, Charles Gomond, Esq. *Southampton-street, Covent-garden*

† Cooke, Mr. John Kenworthy, *Red-lion-square*

Cookney, Charles, Esq. *Staples-inn*

Cooper, Mr. Benjamin, *Earl's-street, Blackfriars*

Coore, John, Esq. *Winchester-street*

Cope, William, Esq. *Sanctuary, Westminster*

Copely, Thomas, Esq. *Netherall, near Doncaster, Yorkshire*

P Coppens, B. M. D. *Ghent, Flanders*

Corbyn, Mr. John, *Holborn*

Cosser, Stephen, Esq. *Abingdon-street*

Cotton, Richard, Esq. *Duke-street, St. James's square*

Coussmaker, Lannoy Richard, Esq. *Gower-street, Bedford-square*

Coussmaker,

Coussmaker, William Kops, Esq. *Brunswick-square*
Cowell, George, Esq. *America-square*
Cox, Robert Albion, Esq. *Little Britain*
Cox, Rev. Thomas, F. A. S. *Harley-street*
Cox, Mr. William, *Beaufort-buildings*
††Coxwell, Henry, Esq. *Fleet-street*
Cradock, Joseph, Esq. M. A. and F. A. S. *Gumley, Leicestershire*
Craig, Charles Alexander, Esq. *Great Scotland-yard*
Crawford, John, Esq. *Newman-street*
††Crawshay, Richard, Esq. *George-yard, Thames-street*
††Crawshay, William, Esq. *ditto*
Crawley, Samuel, Esq. *Ragnall, Nottinghamshire*
Crichton, John, Esq. *Stephen-street, Rathbone-place*
Crillan, J. F. Esq. *of the Isle of Man*
††Criswell, William, Esq. *Bedford-row*
Crocker, Benjamin, Esq. Surveyor, *Bath*
Crocker, Mr. Abraham, *Froome, Somersetshire*
Crook, Thomas, Esq. *Tytherton, near Chippenham, Wilts.*
Crook, John, Esq.
Cross, William, Esq. *Thorngrove House, Worcester*
Crowder, William Henry, Esq. *Frederick's-place, Old Jewry*
††Crowther, Philip Wyatt, Esq. *Guildhall*
Cunningham, William, Esq.
Curwen, John Christian, Esq. M. P.

## D.

**Devonshire, William Duke of

P Dartmouth, George Earl of, F. R. and A. S. and F. L. S.

Dundas, Thomas Lord, F. R. and A. S.

P Dolben, Sir William, Bart. V. P. M. P. *Bridge-court, Channel-row, Westminster*

Denham, Sir James Stewart, Bart. M. P.

Durno, Sir James

Douglass, Admiral John, *Chichester*

Dallison, Mr. Thomas, *Wapping*

Dalton, Mr. John, *Bread-street, Cheapside*

Dampier, Edward, Esq. *Grove-place, Hackney, and Harpur-street*

Dancer, Mr. John, *Doncaster*

††P Daniel, John, Esq. *Mincing-lane*

Daniell, James, Esq. *Upper Wimpole-street*

Davis, Mr. Thomas

Davies, the Rev. J. D.D. F. R. and A. S. Provost, *Eaton*

Davies, Rees, Esq. *Swansea*

Davis, Thomas, Esq. *Mark-lane*

Davison, Rev. Thomas Hartburn, *Northumberland*

Davison, Alexander, Esq. *Swarford, Northumberland, and St. James's square*

Dawes, John, Esq. *Pall-mall*

Dawson, Mr. Robert, *St. Paul's Church-yard*

††Day, Thomas, Esq. *Leicester-place, Leicester-fields*

Deane, John, Esq. *Hartley Court, Reading*

† Deane,

† Deane, Mr. Matthias, *No.* 19, *Carey-street*

Delafield, Joseph, Esq. *Castle-street, Long-acre*

Devalaud, George, Esq. *Bloomsbury-place*

De l'Hoste, Lieut. Colonel, *Weymouth-street, Portland-place*

††Dent, Robert, Esq. F. A. S. *Temple-bar*

Dent, John, Esq. M. P. F. A. S. *ditto*

P††Dent, William, Esq. *Battersea-rise*

Desanges, Mr. William, *Wheeler-street, Spitalfields*

Desanges, Mr. John Francis, *ditto*

Devall, Mr. John, *Buckingham-street, Portland-place*

††Devis, Arthur William, Esq. Member of the Asiatic Society, Bengal, *Gerrard-street*

Dickinson, Henry, Esq. *Leadenhall-street*

P Dickinson, Charles, Esq. *Soho-square*

D'Israeli, Isaac, Esq. *James-street, Adelphi*

Ditcher, Philip, Esq. *East Bergholt, Suffolk*

Dixon, John, Esq. *Phillimore-place, Kensington*

Doe, Thomas, Esq. *Bygrave Park, Herts*

Dollond, Mr. Peter, *St. Paul's Church-yard*

Dollond, Mr. John, *ditto*

† Doratt, John, Esq. *Bruton-street*

Douce, Thomas Augustus, Esq. *Townmalling, Kent*

Doughty, John, Esq. *Aldermanbury*

P Douglass, William, Esq. *America-square*

Douglas, John, Esq. *Manchester*

Dowbiggin, Samuel, Esq. *Hatfield-Regis, Herts*

Down, Richard, Esq. *Bartholomew-lane*

Downer, Henry, Esq. *Fleet-street*

Drake, Mr Samuel, *Margaret-street, Westminster*

P Draper,

P Draper, Daniel, Esq. *St. James's street*

Draper, Mr. John, *Clayton-place, Kennington-road*

Drinkwater, Peter, Esq. *Manchester*

Driver, Mr. William, *Surrey-square, Kent-road*

Duberley, James, Esq. *Soho-square*

Duckworth, George, Esq. *Manchester*

Dundas, Robert, Esq. M. P. *Somerset-place*

Dundass, David, Esq. *Richmond, Surrey*

Dunn, Samuel, Esq. *Adelphi*

Duppa, Baldwin Duppa, Esq. *Hollingbourn-place, near Maidstone, Kent*

††*Duval, the Rev. Philip, D. D. F. R. and A. S. *Newman-street*

Dyke, Thomas, Esq. *Doctors Commons*

## E.

††P Egremont, George Wyndham Earl of

Eardley, Sampson Lord, M. P. F. R. and A. S.

P Egerton, Rev. Francis Henry, *Bridgewater-house, Pall-mall*

Einsiedel, his Excellency Count

Elphinstone, the Honourable William

Eden, Sir John, Bart. M. P.

Eden, Sir Frederick Morton, Bart. F. A. S.

Erskine, Sir William, Bart. M. P.

† Eamer, Sir John, *Wood-street, Cheapside*

Erle, Henry, Esq. *Gower-street*

Eaton, Rev. Stephen, A. M. and F. A. S. *St. Ann's, Soho*

P Eaton,

P Eaton, Peter, Esq. *Westford, Essex*

Echardt, Francis Fred. Esq. *Whiteland House, Chelsea*

P Eckersall, John, Esq. *Clareton, near Bath*

Eccles, the Rev. Allan Harrison, *Bow, Middlesex*

P Eccleston, Thomas, Esq. *Scaresbrick, Lancashire*

Edwards, John, Esq. *Warnford-court*

Edwards, Samuel, Esq. *Stamford, Lincolnshire*

Edwards, Mr. John, *at Mr. Wood's, No.* 35, *Broad-street-buildings*

Ellice, Alexander, Esq. *Great Pulteney-street, Bath*

Ellill, John, Esq. *Queen-street, Cheapside*

Elliot, John, Esq. *Pimlico*

Elliot, George, Esq. *South-street, Finsbury-square*

Elsley, Gregory, Esq. *Garden-court, Temple*

P Errington, John, Esq. *Stanhope-street, May-fair*

Esdaile, William, Esq. *Clapham*

Evans, Robert, Esq. *Great Surrey-street*

Evans, B. B. Esq. *Cheapside*

*††Ewer, Samuel, Esq. F. L. S. *Hackney*

P Ewbank, Andrew, Esq. *Upper Grosvenor-street*

F.

††Fife, James Earl of, F. R. and A. S.

††Falmouth, George Evelyn Lord Viscount

Finch, Honourable Captain William, *Albury, near Guildford*

P Fludyer, Sir Samuel, Bart. *Fludyer-street, Westminster*

P Fletcher, Sir Henry, Bart. M. P. *Southampton-row, Bloomsbury*

Farquhar,

Farquhar, Sir Walter, Bart. *Conduit-street*

Fairman, William, Esq. *Lynsted, Kent*

Farmer, Richard, Esq. *Kennington*

\* Favenc, Abraham, Esq. *Size-lane*

Featherstone, Mr. William, *Adelphi*

P Felton, Samuel, Esq. F. R. and A. S. *Titchfield-street, Portland-place*

P Fermor, William, Esq.

††Ferris, Samuel, M. D. F. R. and A. S. *Beacons-field*

Fidler, James, Esq. *Spa-fields*

Field, William, Esq. *Chatham-place*

Fielding, Jeremiah, Esq. *Bread-street, Cheapside*

Fincham, Francis, Esq. *Charing-cross*

Fitzherbert, Thomas, Esq. *Roehampton, Surrey*

Fletcher, James, M. D.

Fludyer, George, Esq. M. P. *Fludyer-street*

Fonblanque, John, Esq. *Lincoln's-inn*

Forrest, Digory, Esq. *No. 28, South Molton-street*

Forde, the Rev. Brownlow, D. D. *St. John's gate*

Forman, William, Esq. *Thames-street*

Forsyth, William, Esq. F. A. S. *Kensington*

Forster, William, Esq. *Hull*

Forster, John, Esq. *Bath*

Fothergill, Mr. John, *No. 85, Fenchurch-street*

Foulston, Mr. John, *No. 18, Frith-street, Soho*

Fowler, Dr. William, *Cecil-street, Strand*

††Fowler, David Burton, Esq. *Fig-tree-court, Temple*

Fox, Mr. John, *Box Hill, Dorking, in Surrey*

P Franco, Jacob, Esq. *St James's square*

Frankland,

Frankland, William, Esq. *Cavendish-square*
Franklin, Captain William
Franklin, James, Esq. *Dean's-place, Berks*
Fraser, Simon, Esq. *King's-arms-yard, Coleman-street*
Fraser, William, Esq. F. R. S, *Queen-square, Holborn*
Fraser, Mr. David, *Great Pulteney-street*
Fremantle, William Henry, Esq. *Stanhope-street, May-fair*
French, George, Esq. *Eastcheap*
Fry, Edmund, Esq. *Type-street, Chiswell-street*
Fry, Mr. Joseph Storrs, *Bristol*
Fullarton, Colonel William, M. P. and F. R. S.
Fuller, Mr. John, *Pentonville*
Fulton, Henry, Esq. *Watling-street*

## G.

Gordon, Alexander Duke of, K. T. and F. R. S.
* Grosvenor, Richard Earl of, F. R. S.
Glasgow, George Earl of, F. R. and A. S.
P Gallaway, Arundell Lord Viscount, M. P. and K. B.
P Greville, Right Hon. Charles, M. P. and F. R. S. *Paddington*
• Greville, the Hon. Robert, F. R. and A. S. *Great Cumberland-street*
Grey, Sir Henry, Bart. *Howick, Northumberland*
††Gascoigne Sir Thomas, Bart. F. A. S. *Partington, in the County of York*

Green,

Green General Sir William, Bart. F. R. and A. S. *Chandos-street, Cavendish-square*

P Geary, Sir William, Bart. M. P. *Oxen Heath, Kent*

Gwillim, Sir Henry, *Madras*

Galloway, James, Esq. *Gower-street*

Garden, Rev. Edmund, *New North-street, Red-Lion-square*

Garnet, Robert, Esq. *Cripplegate*

Garnet, Dr. J. *Great Marlborough-street*

Garthshore, Maxwell, M. D. F. R. and A. S. *St. Martin's lane*

Gee, John, Esq. *Wardour-street, Soho*

† Gellibrand, Thomas, Esq. *Bow*

Gibbes, George Smith, M. B. *Bath*

Gibbs, Harry Leeke, Esq. *No. 1, Clifford-street, New Bond-street*

Gilbert, Mr. Henry, *Holborn*

Giles, Peter, Esq. *Streatham Park, Surrey*

Gillet, Gabriel, Esq. *Guildford-street*

Gisborne, Thomas M. D. *Clifford-street*

Gist, Samuel, Esq. *Gower-street*

Glanville, Mr. Edward, *Broad Sanctuary, Westminster*

P Godschall, William Man, Esq. F. R. and A. S.

Godwin, James, Esq. *Wingfield, Berks*

Goldthwaite, Thomas, jun. Esq.

Goodwyn, Henry, jun. Esq. *East Smithfield*

Gooch, Captain George, *Clapham-road*

Goodchild, Mr. Thomas, *Tooley-street*

Goodhew, William, Esq. *Deptford*

Goodrich, Mr. Simon, *Admiralty, and Upper Eaton-street, Pimlico*

Gotobed, John, Esq. *Norfolk-street, Strand*

Gosling, William, Esq. F. A. S. *Fleet-street*

Gosling, Francis, Esq. *Fleet-street*

Gosling, William, Esq. *Clay Hall, Walker, in Herts*

Gowland, Thomas, Esq. *Belmont-place, Vauxhall*

Grace, Mr. William, *Water-street, Chatham-place*

Graham, George, Esq.

Graham, William, Esq. *Thames-street*

Graham, Aaron, Esq. F. R. S. *Great Russell-street*

Graham, Captain Thomas, *No. 17, New Broad-street*

Grant, General James, *Sackville-street*

Grant, Major John, *Hill-street, Berkeley-square*

††Grant, John, Esq. *Fleet-street*

Grant, Peter, Esq. *Fort Augustus, North Britain*

P††Gray, Walker, Esq. *Fenchurch-street*

Gray, John, Esq. *Somerset-place*

P Green, Rupert, Esq. *Percy-street, Rathbone-place*

Green, Mr. William, *Deptford*

††Greene, Thomas, Esq. F.R. and A.S. *Bedford-square*

Greene, Joseph, Esq. *New Basinghall-street*

Green, James, Esq. *No. 38, Rathbone-place*

Greenwood, Abraham, Esq. *Steining-lane*

P Gregory, Robert, Esq. *Berners-street*

Grenfell, William, Esq. *Copper Office, Thames-street*

Grenfell, John, Esq. *Thames-street*

Gresley, Rev. William

Griffin, John, Esq. *Steward-street, Spitalfields*

Griffin, Edward, Esq. *Tufton-street, Westminster*

P††Griffith, Edward, Esq. *of Caernarvon*

Griffith, John, Esq. *No. 16, Portland-place*

Griffith,

Griffith, Mr. Vaughan, *Paternoster-row*

Groote, George William, Esq. *Dean-street, Soho*

Grosvenor, Richard Erle Drax, Esq. M. P.

P Grote, George, Esq. *Threadneedle-street*

Groves, John, Esq. *Sloane-street, Knightsbridge*

††Grubb, John, Esq. *Lincoln's-inn-fields*

Gruber, Rev. Dr. Michael, *Castle-street, Oxford-market*

Gubbins, Mr. James, *Surrey-street*

Guy, John, Esq. *Twickenham*

### H.

††\*Hardwicke, Philip Earl of, F. R. and A. S.

Hawke, Martin Lord

Heathfield, Francis Augustus Lord

Haslang, his Excellency Count

Harcourt, Honourable General William

Honeywood, Sir John, Bart. M. P.

Hume, Sir Abraham, Bart. F. R. S. *Wormleybury*

Hanmer, Sir Thomas, Bart. *Hanmer, Flintshire*

Heathcote, Sir John, *Edensor, Langton Hall, Staffordshire*

Harley, Rt. Honourable Thomas, Alderman, M. P. *Aldersgate-street*

Hope, the Right Hon. Brigadier-General John

Hope, the Hon. Lieutenant-Colonel Charles

Herne, Sir William, Alderman

Hay, Major-General Alexander

Haring, John, Esq. *George-street, Hanover-square*

Hakewell, Henry, Esq. *Margaret-street, Cavendish-square*

Hall,

Hall, Phineas, Esq.

Hall, James, Esq. *King-street, Holborn*

Hallet, William, Esq. *Farringdon, Berks*

Hamilton, Rev. Anthony, D. D. F. R. and V. P. of A. S. *Bruton-street*

Hamilton, William, Esq. *Blackheath*

Hamilton, William, M. D. *Old Broad-street*

P†Hamerton Charles, Esq. *Whitefriars*

Hammett, John, Esq. *Lombard-street, and New Norfolk-street, Park-lane*

Hammond, Thomas, Esq. *No.* 14, *Margaret-street, Cavendish-square*

Handesyde, Charles, Esq. *Newcastle-upon-Tyne*

Hankey, Joseph, Esq. *Poplar*

Hanmer, Job, Esq. *Holbrook Hall, Sudbury*

Hanson, John, Esq. *Bruton-street*

Hanwell, Captain, *Ratcliff-cross*

Hardcastle, Joseph, Esq. *Duck's-foot-lane*

Harding, John, Esq. *Argyle-street*

P††Harman, Jeremiah, Esq. *Princes-street, Lothbury*

Harness, Dr. *Sloane-street, Knightsbridge*

Harper, Robert John, Esq. *British Museum*

Harris, Robert, Esq. Banker, *Reading*

Harrison, Richardson, Esq. *Freern Barnet, Middlesex*

Harrison, Thomas, Esq. *Wolverton, Bucks*

Harrison, Robert, Esq. *Lincoln's-inn-fields*

Harrop, Joseph, Esq. *Great Marlborough-street*

Harvey, Robert, M. D. F. L. S. P. R. I. *Adelphi*

Harwood, William, Esq. *Hanwell Park*.

Haslam,

Haslam, John, Esq. *Bethlem Hospital*

* Hastings, Warren, Esq.

Hawes, Benjamin, Esq.

Hawkes, George, Esq. *Thames-street*

Hawkins, John, Esq. F. R. S.

Haworth, Richard, Esq. F. A. S. *Chancery-lane*

Hay, Robert, Esq.

Hay, James, Esq.

Heath, Mr. Richard, *No. 8, Finsbury-square*

††Heaviside, Richard, Esq. *Taunton*

††Heaviside, John, Esq. F. R. S. *George-street, Hanover-square*

P††Hebert, James, Esq. *Great Portland-street*

Hele, John, Esq. *Charlotte-street, Rathbone-place*

††Henderson, John, Esq. LL. B. and F. A. S.

Hendrie, Patrick, Esq. *Tichborne-street*

Hennell, David, Esq. *Foster-lane*

Henshaw, Benjamin, *Hoddesdon, Hertfordshire*

Hepworth, John, Esq. *York*

Heron, Patrick, Esq. M. P. *Blackheath*

Heriot, John, Esq. *Catherine-street, Strand*

Hewlet, Mr. William, *Strand*

Hewetſon, John, Esq. *Tower-hill*

Hewett, William Nathan Wright, Esq. *of Belham House, near Doncaster, Yorkshire*

Hewitt, Mr. Henry Thomas, *No. 3, Dover-place, Kent-road*

Hicks, Mr. John, *Brighton*

Higgins, Matthew, Esq.

Hilton, John, Esq. *Ironmonger-lane, Cheapside*

Hill,

Hill, Richard, Esq. *Plymouth, Glamorganshire*

Hill, Edward, Esq. *Albion-street, Blackfriars-road*

✝ Hinckley, John, Esq. *Inner Temple*

P Hoare, Charles, Esq. F. A. S. No. 37, *Fleet-street*

Hoare, Jonathan, Esq. *Stoke Newington*

Hobday, William, Esq. *Holles-street, Cavendish-square*

P Hobson, William, Esq.

Hobson, George, Esq.

Hodgson, Mr. George, *Lambeth-marsh*

Hodges, Mr. Richard, *Scotland-yard*

P Holder, James, Esq. *Ash Park*

P Holland, Henry, Esq. F. A. S. *Sloane-place, Knights-bridge*

Holland, Richard, Esq. *Half-moon-street, Piccadilly*

Holland, Mr. George, *High Holborn*

Hollis, Thomas Brand, Esq. F. R. and A. S. *Chesterfield-street*

Holcombe, Rev. William, *Canon of St. David's*

Holford, John Carteret, Esq. *Richmond*

Holmes, Mr. John, *Whitefriars*

Holme, Mr. William, *Bass-court, Thames-street*

Holroyd, John, Esq. *Scotland-yard*

Home, Patrick, Esq. M. P. *Gower-street*

Homfray, Samuel, Esq. *Mirthir Tidville, Glamorganshire*

Honeybourne, Mr. Robert, *Stourbridge*

Honyman, Captain Robert, M. P. *Royal Navy*

Hooper, Thomas, Esq. *Panty Goitre, Monmouthshire*

E e

Horn,

Horn, Nicholas, Esq. *St. Martin's lane, Cannon-street*

Horner, Thomas, Esq. *Mell's Park, near Froome, Somersetshire*

Horridge, John, Esq. *Raikes, near Bolton*

Horrocks, John, Esq. *Preston, Lancashire, or No. 3, Bucklersbury*

Horton, Mr. William, *Newgate-street*

Hotham, John, Esq. *Middle Temple-lane*

P Houghton, William, Efq. *Conduit-street*

P Howard, Edward, Esq. F. R. S. *Nottingham-place*

Howard, Bernard, Esq. *Farnham, Suffolk*

Howell, Richard, Esq. *Thames-street*

Howell, Mr. John, *Vine-street, Piccadilly*

Howell, James, Esq. *Somerset-place*

Howell, Edward, Esq. *Lindsey-row, Chelsea*

P Hudson, Vansittart, Esq. *Temple*

Hughes, Rev. Edward, Esq. *Kinmell Park, St. Asaph*

Hughes, Henry, Esq. *King's-road, Bedford-row*

Hulme, William, Esq. *Twydale, Kent*

Hunt, Rowland, Esq.

Hunter, John, Esq. M. P. *Bedford-square*

P Hurst, Robert, Esq. *Horsham Park, Sussex*

Hurt, Charles, Esq. *Wirksworth, Derbyshire*

Hussey, William, Esq. M. P. *Salisbury*

Hyde, John, Esq.

I.

P Ilchefter, Henry Thomas Earl of

Johnstone, the Honourable Lieutenant - Colonel Cochrane, M. P.

††Ingilby, Sir John, Bart. M. P. F. R. and A. S.

Johnston, Sir William, Bart. *Glocester-place, New-road*

Inglis, Sir Hugh, Bart. *Bedford-row*

P Jackson, William, Esq. *Dowgate-wharf*

††Jacob, Joseph, Esq. *Greek-street, Soho*

Jamison, Mr. *Charing-crofs*

Jardin, Mr. John, *Throgmorton-street*

P Idle, Christopher, Esq. P. R. I. *Strand*

Jeffery, George, Esq. *Throgmorton-street*

Jefferys, Thomas, Esq. *Cockspur-street*

- Jefferys, Mr. George

P Jenkins, Thomas, Esq. *Rome*

P Jenour, Joshua, Esq. *Fleet-street*

Jennings, Rev. George, *Bottisham Hall, Cambridge*

Jervoise, Jervoise Clark, Esq. M. P. *Hanover-square*

Jervoise, Thomas Clarke, Esq. *Vere-street, Cavendish-square*

Jessup, Mr. William, jun. *Farningham, Kent*

Jeudwine, Thomas, Esq. *Basinghall-street*

Illingworth, Thomas, Esq. *Frith-street, Soho*

Ince, William, Esq. *Broad-street, Carnaby-market*

Innes, Hugh, Esq. *Tavistock-street, Bedford-square*

Johnes,

Johnes, Thomas, Esq. M. P. *Hafod, Cardiganshire*

††Johnson, John, Esq. *Mary-le-bone-street*

Johnson, John, jun. Esq. *Berners-street*

Johnson, James, Esq. *Lambeth-walk*

Johnson, Thomas, Esq. *Ely-place*

Johnston, Alexander, Esq. *Drury-lane*

Jones, Edward, Esq. *Wepre Hall, Flintshire*

Jones, John, Esq.

Jones, John, Esq. *Frankley, Wiltshire*

Jones, Mr. Francis, *Grosvenor-street*

Jones, Mr. John, *Charlotte-street, Mansion-house*

Jones, Griffith, Esq. *Austin-friars*

Jones, Henry, Esq. *Old City Chambers*

Jones, Mr. David, *No. 1, Barton-street, Westminster*

Jones, Thomas, Esq. *Newcastle-street, Strand*

Jourdan, Major Edward, *Harley-street*

Irving, William, Esq. *Great George-street, West-minster*

## K.

⁎ Kinnoull, Robert Drummond Hay Earl of

Kinnaird, George Lord, F. R. and A. S.

Keith, George Lord, M. P. *Harley-street*

Kaye, Rev. Sir Richard, Bart. Dean of Lincoln, LL. D. F. R. and A. S.

Kaye, Mr. Joesph, Architect, *Saville-row*

Keighley, James, Esq.

Kent, Nathaniel, Esq. *Windsor*

Kenyon,

Kenyon, Samuel, Esq. *Lamb's-conduit-street*

††Keysall, John, Esq. *Charlotte-street, Bedford-square*

Kidman, Mr. John, *Fleet-street*

Kiernan, Mr. Thomas, *Church-street, Blackfriars-road*

King, the Rev. Richard, *Worthin, Shropshire*

King, Mr. Thomas, jun.

King, William, Esq. *Cutlers Hall*

King, Mr. Joseph, *No. 7, Caroline-street, Bedford-square*

Kingston, John, Esq. *Stratford-place*

Kirkby, William, Esq. *Exchequer-Office, Temple*

Knill, John, Esq. *Gray's-inn*

Knight, Mr. George, *Cliffe, near Rochester*

Knight, Mr. Joseph, *No. 427, Strand*

Knowles, James M. Esq. *Lombard-street*

Knubley, Richard, Esq. *Bath*

## L.

P Lansdowne, the Most Noble the Marquis of

\* Leicester, George Earl of, F. R. S. and President of the Society of Antiquaries

\*\*Liverpool, Charles Earl of, V. P.

P Lewisham, George Lord Viscount, F. R. and A. S. and F. L. S.

P Leicester, Sir John, Bart. M. P. *Piccadilly*

P Laurent, Sir Francis, Kt.

P Lewes, Sir Watkin, Kt. V. P. *Parliament-street*

P††Lambert, Charles, Esq. F. A. S. *Temple*

Lambert, Anthony, Esq.

Landmann,

Landmann, Isaac, Esq. *Royal Academy, Woolwich*

Langton, Mr. Daniel, Builder, *Wandsworth*

P Larkins, William, Esq. F. R. and A. S. *Blackheath-point*

Law, Thomas, Esq. *Abroad*

Lawrence, Richard, Esq. *Mincing-lane*

Lawrence, Richard James, Esq.

Leach, Mr. Edward, *Cotton Manufactory, Tottenham-court-road*

Lefevre, Charles Shaw, Esq. M. P. *No. 4. Spring-gardens*

Leader, William, Esq. *Wandsworth*

††Leake, William, Esq. *Sackville-street*

Leatham, William, Esq. *Chatham-square, Black-friars*

Leatham, Isaac, Esq. *Burton-le-street, Yorkshire*

Lees, William, Esq. *Office of Ordnance, Tower*

Legh, George John, Esq. *High Legh, Cheshire*

††Legh, John, Esq. *Bedford-square*

Lennon, Captain Walter Caulfield, *Bath*

Lenox, Colonel Alexander, *Charlotte-street, Portland-place*

Lester, Mr. William, *Northampton*

Lettsom, John Coakley, M. D. F. R. and A. S. *Basinghall-street*

Levien, Solomon, Esq. *No. 73, Aldersgate-street*

Levy, Moses Isaac, Esq. F. A. S. *George-street, Hanover-square*

††Lewis, Percival, Esq. *Lincoln's-inn*

††Lewis, William, Esq. F. L. S. *Holborn*

Lewis,

Lewis, Thomas, Esq. *Great James-street, Bedford-row*

Lillingstone, A. Spoone, Esq.

Liptrap, John, Esq. F. A. and L. S. *Whitechape'-road*

Llewellyn, John, Esq. *Penllengane, Glamorganshire*

Loat, Mr. Richard, *Long-acre*

P Lloyd, William, Esq.

Lloyd, Thomas, Esq. *Buckingham-street, Strand*

* Lock, William, Esq.

P Long, Samuel, Esq. M. P. *Hill-street, Berkeley-square*

Longman, Mr. Thomas, *Cheapside*

P Loveden, Edward Loveden, Esq. M. P. *Buskett Park*

' Lowry, Mr. Wilson, *Titchfield-street*

Lowry, Mrs. Rebeckah, *ditto*

Lowten, Thomas, Esq. *Temple*

Lowth, Rev. Robert, *George-street, Hanover-square*

Loxdale, Thomas, Esq. *Braidley Lodge, near Bilson, Staffordshire*

††Lumley, William, Esq. *No. 51, Lincoln's-inn-fields*

† Lynd, James, Esq. *Beaufort-buildings*

### M.

* Macclesfield, George Earl of

* Morton, George Earl of, F. R. and A. S.

P Mount Norris, Earl of, *Stratford-place*

P Malmesbury,

P Malmesbury, James Earl of, K. B. and LL. D.

Milford, Richard Lord, M. P.

**Marsham, the Honourable Charles, M. P.

*PMonckton, the Honourable Edward, M. P. *Port-land-place*

Middleton, Sir Charles, Bart. M. P. *Hertford-street, May-fair*

Mac Pherson, Sir John, Bart. M. P. *Brompton*

Morshead, Sir John, Bart. *Hampton Court*

Monro, Sir Hugh, Bart. *Gloucester-place, Portman-square*

P Mackreth, Sir Robert, M. P. *Cork-street*

Macdonald, John, M. D.

M'Leod, John, Esq.

††Mac George, William, Esq. *New Bond-street*

Mackenzie, Alexander, Esq. *No. 38, Norfolk-street*

Macklin, John, Esq. *No. 139, Cheapside*

Macmurdo, Mr. Edward Longdon, *Bread-street*

P Macnamara, John, Esq. *Baker-street, Portman-square*

Mac Dougal, Mr. James, *No. 418, Oxford-street*

Mac Konochie, A. Lochart, Esq.

Magens, Dorrien, Esq. *Cavendish-square*

Maitland, Ebenezer, Esq. *Coleman-street*

Malcolm, Mr. Jacob, *Stockwell*

Malton, James, Esq. *Norton-street, Portland-place*

Manley, John George, Esq. *Braziers, Oxon*

Mainwaring, Mr. Thomas, *Strand*

Marks, Mr. John, Builder, *Princes-street, Hano-ver-square*

Marriott,

Marriott, John Martin, Esq. *Lamb's-conduit-street*

Marsland, Samuel, Esq. *Manchester* -

Marsh, Mr. William, *South-street, Grosvenor-square*

Marshall, Andrew, M. D. *Bartlett's-buildings*

Marter, William, Esq. *Kensington*

Martin, James, Esq. M. P. *Downing-street*

Martin, Matthew, Esq. *Parliament-street*

Martyn, the Reverend Thomas, B. D. F. R. S. F. L. S. *Professor of Botany, Cambridge*

Martin, Thomas, Esq.

††Maskall, Samuel, Esq. *Mitre-court, Milk-street*

Mason, John, Esq. *Cannon-street*

Masquener, John James, Esq. *Tottenham-street*

Matthews, Edward, Esq. *Sol's-row, Tottenham-court-road*

Mawley, Edward, Esq. *Thornhaugh-street*

Mayhew, John, Esq. *Broad street, Carnaby-market*

Mayhew, James, Esq. *Titchfield-street*

Mayniac, Francis, Esq. *St. John's square*

Meheux, John, Esq. *Hans Place, Sloane-street*

* Melville, General Robert, F. R. and A. S. *Brewer-street*

††Meredith, William, Esq. *Harley-place*

††Meredith, George, Esq. F. A. S. P. R. I. *Nottingham-place*

Merry, William, Esq. *Gower-street*

Mestaer, Peter Everett, Esq. *New Broad-street*

Metcalfe, Christopher Barton, Esq *West-Ham*

Meux, Richard, jun. Esq. *Liquor-pond-street*

††Meyrick,

†† Meyrick, John, Esq. F. A. S. *Great George-street*

Meyrick, Owen Patland, Esq. *Bodalgan, Anglesey*.

†† Michell, Matthew, Esq. *Beaufort-buildings, Strand*

† Middleton, John, Esq. *Lambeth*

Medford, Rev. William, *Hurst, Berks*

Midgley, Mr. George Deakin, Chemist, *Strand*

P Midford, George, M. D. *Reading*

††Mildred, Daniel, Esq. *White-hart-court, Grace-church-street*

Miles, Mr. John, *Birmingham*

Millikin, Mr. Halley Benson

Millington, Langford, Esq. *Tooting, and Berners-street*

Millington, Mr. Thomas, *Golden-square*

P Mills, Abraham, Esq. *Fence House, Macclesfield*

Mills, Mr. George, *Old Swan-stairs*

Mills, Samuel, Esq. *Finsbury-place*

Milles, Thomas, Esq. *No. 4, New-square, Lincoln's-inn*

Miller, John, Esq. *Red-lion-square*

Milnes, Richard Slater, Esq. M. P. *Foiston, near Ferrybridge, Yorkshire*

Minchin, Thomas A. Esq. *Gosport*

Minier, Mr. William, *Strand*

Minier, Mr. Charles, *ditto*

Minish, Mr. William, *Whitechapel*

Mist, Mr. Henry, *Long-acre*

Mitchel, Michael, Esq. *Walthamstow*

Mitchel, William, Esq. M. P.

Mitchell, Robert, Esq. *Newman-street*

Mitford,

, Mitford, Robert, Esq. *Great Portland-street*

Montresor, John, Esq.

Moore, Daniel, Esq. *Lincoln's-inn*

Morley William, Esq. *New Broad-street*

Morse, Leonard, Esq. F. R. S. and A. S. *Great George-street, Westminster*

Morris, Mr. William, *Whitcombe-street*

, Mortimer, Charles, Esq. *Greenhammerton, Yorkshire, and No. 42, Upper Grosvenor-street*

Morton, Thomas, Esq. *John's-street, Adelphi*

Mosely, Walter Michael, Esq. *near Worcester*

††Moser, Mr. John, *Frith-street, Soho*

Munn, Daniel Rolfe, Esq. *Hammersmith*

Murrey, John, M. D. *Bury-street, St. James's*

.Myers, Mr. William, *Aldersgate-street*

Myers, Thomas, Esq. *Park-place*

## N.

P Norfolk, Charles Duke of, President, F. R. and A. S.

\*\*Northumberland, Hugh Duke of, V. P. K. G. F. R. and A. S.

††Northampton, Charles Earl of

Northesk, William Earl of

Nash, Mr. Thomas, *Worcester*

Nash, John, Esq. *Dover-street*

Nepean, Evan, Esq. M. P. Secretary to the Admiralty

Newbury, Jacob, Esq. *New Inn*

Newcombe,

Newcombe, William, Esq. *Bank, and No. 23, Threadneedle-street*

Newman, John, Esq. *No. 80, New Broad-street*

Newnham, the Rev. William Moore, *Boyle-street, Saville-row*

P Newton, Robert, Esq. *Norton-house, Berks*

P Newton, Andrew, Esq.

Newton, William Morris, Esq. *Wallington, Surrey*

Newton, Mr. John, *Lamb's-conduit-street*

De Neyva, Joseph da Cunha Para, Esq. *Artillery-place*

††Nichols, John, Esq. *Red-lion-passage, Fleet-street*

Nicholson, William, Esq. *Bartholomew Hospital*

Nichollson, Samuel, Esq. *Cateaton-street*

Nicolay, Frederick, jun. Esq. *St. James's Palace*

††Nicol, George, Esq. *Pall-mall*

Nixon, Rev. Robert, F. S. A. *Vale Mascal, North-bray, Kent*

Noble, William, Esq. *Pall-mall*

Nollekins, Joseph, Esq. R. A. *Mortimer-street*

Nouaille, Peter, Esq. *Greatness, Kent*

Norman, Robert, Esq. *Cannon-street*

Northey, William, Esq. *Queen-street, May-fair*

Norton, Mr. John, *Tooley-street*

Nutting, Mr. Joseph, *King-street, Covent-garden.*

## O.

P Ossory, John Earl of Upper, F. R. and A. S.

Ogle, Mr. Thomas, *Abroad*

Oldham, John, Esq. *Grafton-street*

Oliver,

Oliver, the Rev. John, *Croombs-hill, Greenwich*
Ord, John, Esq. F. R. and A. S. *Lincoln's-inn-fields*
Orrell, Thomas, Esq. *Winsley-street, Oxford-street*
Osorio, Abraham, Esq. *Theobald's-road*
Ovey, Richard, Esq. *Tavistock-street*

## P.

**Portland, William Henry Duke of, V. P. K. G.
　F. R. and A. S.
**Pitt, the Right Honourable William, M. P.
Pelham, the Right Honourable Thomas, M. P.
　*Stratton-street*
Peel, Sir Robert, Bart. M. P. *Bury, Lancashire*
* Pusey, Honourable Philip, *Grosvenor-square*
Pulteney, Sir William, Bart. M. P. *Bath-house*
Paul, Sir George Onesiphorus, Bart. *Lower
　Grosvenor-street*
Packer, Mr. William, *Charlotte-street, Bloomsbury*
Page, Francis, Esq. M. P. *Atsbon, Oxfordshire*
Page, Francis, Esq. *Newbury, Berks*
Page, Frederick, Esq. *ditto*
††Page, Mr. John, *High Holborn*
P Paice, Mr. Joseph, *Bread-street-hill*
Pakenham, Captain Edward, R. N.
Papworth, Mr. Thomas, *No. 60, Newman-street*
† Parkes, Richard, Esq. *Broad-street, Bloomsbury*
Parkins, Mr. William, *Adelphi-wharf*
Parker, David, Esq. *King's-mews*
Parker, Mr. William, *Fleet-street*
††Parker, Mr. Samuel, *Bridge-street, Blackfriars*

Parker,

Parker, Mr. Thomas, *Fleet-street*

Parker, Samuel Walker, Esq. *White Lead Works,*
*Newcastle-upon-Tyne*

Parkinson, Mr. Thomas, *Bloomsbury-market*

Parnell, Mr. Hugh, *Church-street, Spitalfields*

Parry, William, Esq. *Norton Hall, Wiltshire*

Parson, S. P. LL.D. *Doctors Commons*

Paterson, William, Esq. *Devonshire-place.*

Paxton, Mr. Christopher, *Aldersgate-street*

Patience, Mr. Joseph, *Wormwood-street, Bishopsgate-*
*street*

Payn, James, Esq. *Maidenhead, Berks*

††Payne, Samuel, Esq. *Vauxhall*

Peacock, Mr. Lewis, *Lincoln's-inn-fields*

Pearce, William, Esq. *Craig's-court*

Pearsall, Mr. James, *No.* 54, *Bread-street*

††Pearson, James, Esq. *Basinghall-street*

Peel, Jonathan, Esq. *Lawrence-lane, Cheapside*

Peel, Joseph, Esq. *ditto*

Peirson, Peter, Esq. F. R. and A. S. *Inner Temple*

Pelerin, Henry Ferdinand, Esq. *No.* 12, *New*
*North-street, Red-lion-street*

Pemberton, John, Esq. *Inner Temple*

Penruddock, Charles, Esq.

Penton, Mr George, *New-street-square, Shoe-lane*

Pepys, W. H. jun. Esq. *Poultry*

P Perin, William Philip, Esq. F. R. and A. S.

Perry, John, Esq. *Blackwall*

Perry, James, Esq. *Strand*

Perrott, George, Esq. *Craycombe-house, Worcestershire*

Petrie,

Petrie, William, Esq. M. P. F. R. and A. S. *Hertford-street, May-fair*

Petrie, John, Esq. M. P. *Portland-place*

P Pettiward, Roger, Esq. *Baker-street, Portman-square*

Phillips, John, Esq. *Ely*

Phillips, John, Esq. *No.* 13, *Southampton-street, Bloomsbury*

Phillips, Mr. Samuel, *St. George's-road, Blackfriars-bridge*

Phillips, Mr. Richard, *St. Paul's Church-yard*

Phillips, William, Esq. *Shinfield Park, Berks*

Phillipson, Thomas, Esq. *Harpur-street*

Phipps, Warner, Esq. *Pancras-lane*

Piper, Stephen, Esq. *Haverhill, Essex*

Pitt, William Morton, Esq. M. P. and F. R. S. *Arlington-street*

P✝✝Pitt, Thomas, Esq. V. P. F. A. S. *Wimpole-street*

.. Planta, Joseph, Esq. F. R. S. *British Museum*

Pocock, Charles, Esq. *Sowley, in the County of Southampton*

Pollen, George Augustus, Esq. M. P. *Hill House, Leatherhead*

Pollett, Mr. Robert, *North Weald, near Epping*

P Portman, Edward Berkeley, Esq. *Bryanston, near Blandford, Dorset*

Porter, William, Esq. *Copthall-court, Throgmorton-street*

Pote, Edward Ephraim, Esq. *East-Indies*

P Potter, Christopher, Esq. *Abroad*

Potter, George, Esq. *Charing-cross*

Powell, David, jun. Esq. *Little St. Helen's*

Powell,

Powell, John Clark, Esq. *Little St. Helen's*

††Powell, Arthur Annesly, Esq. *Devonshire-place*

Powell, Richard, M. D. *Essex-street*

Powlett, William Powlett, Esq. M. P. *Sambourne, near Stockbridge*

P Prado, Samuel, Esq. *Grafton-street*

Praed, William, Esq. M. P. *Tyringham, Bucks*

Pratt, Edward Roger, Esq. *Ryston House, Norfolk*

Pratt, John, Esq. *Lower Brook-street*

Prescott, George, Esq. *Cheshunt*

Preston, Mr. Thomas, *Strand*

Preston, Richard, Esq. *Temple*

Pricket, Thomas Esq. *Wanstead, Essex*

Pringle, Mark, Esq. M. P.

Prinsep, John, Esq.

Pryce, Benjamin, Esq. *Bath*

Pugh, David Heron, Efq.

Purser, Mr. William, *Bennett-street, Blackfriars-road*

## Q.

\* Queensberry, William Duke of, K. T.

## R.

\*\*Richmond, Charles Duke of, V. P. K. G. F. R. and A. S.

\*\*Radnor, Jacob Earl of, V. P. F. R. and A. S.

Roslyn, Earl of, *Russel-square*

\*\*Romney, Charles Earl of, V. P. and F. R. S.

\* Ryder, the Right Honourable Dudley, M. P.

††Ridley

††Ridley, Sir Matthew White, Bart. M. P. *Port-land-place*

††Raby, Alexander, Esq. *Broad Sanctuary*

Radcliffe, John, Esq. *No. 2, New-inn*

Rae, John, Esq. *Broad-street-buildings*

Raggett, Richard, Esq. *Odiham, Southampton*

Raikes, Thomas, Esq. *New Broad-street*

P Ramey, John, Esq. *Ormesby, Norfolk*

††Ramsbottom, John, Esq. *Aldersgate-street*

††Ramsbottom, Richard, Esq. *ditto*

Randell, William, Esq. *Belmont Cottage, Vauxhall*

Rastrick, Mr. John, *Morpeth*

Rawlinson, Abraham, Esq. *Lancaster*

Rawlinson, Thomas, Esq. *ditto*

Reaston, Francis Bushell, Esq. *Queen Anne-street West*

‡†Read, John, Esq. *Great James-street, Bedford-row*

Read, General Henry, *Ramsbury, Wiltshire*

Reeves, John, Esq. F. R. and A. S. *Cecil-street, Strand*

Reeves, Mr. William John, *Holborn-bridge*

Reeve, Joshua, Esq. *Dean-street, Canterbury-square*

Reid, Mr. John, *Fan-street, Aldersgate-street*

††Reid, Andrew, Esq. *Cleveland-row, St. James's*

††Reid, John, Esq. *Bedford-square*

Reina, Mr. Peter Anthony, *Great Newport-street*

††Remington, John, Esq. *Milk-street, Cheapside, and Clapton*

Reynolds, Major Thomas Vincent

Ricard, the Rev. Francis, *Jersey*

F f

Riddell,

Riddell, Colonel John

P Ring, Thomas, Esq. *Reading, Berks*

Rivier, Philip, Esq. *Lawrence-Poultney-lane*

Roberts, Colonel Roger Elliott, *No. 46, Albemarle-street*

Roberts, Robert, Esq. *Paragon, Southwark*

Roberts, Thomas, Esq. *Charter-house-square*

Roberts, Rev. William Hancock, D.D. *Lough-borough House*

Robertson, William, M.D. *Golden-square*

Robertson, James, M.D. F.R.S. *Ibbetson's Hotel*

Robinson, Samuel Wakefield, Esq.

††Robinson, George, Esq.

P Robinson, Thomas, Esq. *Bentinck-street, Manchester-square*

Robinson, Mr. John, *Arundel-street, Strand*

Robinson, George, Esq. *Winchester-street*

Robinson, John, Esq. M.P. *Wyke House, Isleworth*

Robins, Mr. John, *Warwick-street*

Robley, John, Esq. *Aldersgate-street*

††Robson, James, Esq. High Bailiff of the City of Westminster, *Conduit-street*

Rodes, Cornelius Heathcote, Esq. *Balborough, Derbyshire*

Rogers, Samuel, Esq. F.R.S. *Paper-buildings, Temple*

Rondeau, James, Esq. *No. 3, Shorter's-court, Throgmorton-street*

Roope, John, Esq. *Yarmouth*

Roper,

Roper, Rev. Francis, *Wexham Parsonage, near Slough, Berks*

Roper, Mr. Robert, *Houndsditch*

Rose, George, Esq. M. P. *Old Palace-yard*

Rose, George Henry, Esq. *St. James's square*

Rose, John, Esq. *Greville-street*

P Ross, Colonel Patrick, F. R. and A. S. *Harley-street*

Rough, William, Esq. *Inner Temple*

Rowcroft, Thomas, Esq. P. R. I. *Lawrence Poultney-lane*

. Rowley, Owsley, Esq. *Hants*

Rowntree, Mr. Thomas, *Great Surrey-street, Black-friars-road*

Rucker, Daniel Henry, Esq. *Broad-street, City*

Ruggles, Thomas, Esq. F. A. and L. S. *Clare, Suffolk*

Runquest, Peter Andrew, Esq. *Bury-court, St. Mary Axe*

Rush, John, Esq. *Sackville-street*

P Russel, Jesse, Esq. *Goodman's-fields*

Russel, William, Esq. *Berwick, Northumberland*


## S.


\* Shrewsbury, Charles Earl of

P Suffolk, John Earl of

P Shaftesbury Anthony Earl of, F. R. and A. S.

Scarborough, George Augustus Earl of

P Stanhope, Charles Earl of, F. R. S.

P St. Vincent, John Earl of
P Scarsdale, Nathaniel Lord
Stuart, the Honourable Charles, M. P.
P St. Aubyn, Sir John, Bart. F. R. and A. S. *Stratford-place*
Sheffield, Sir John, Bart. *Portland-place*
Smith, Sir John, Bart. F. R. and A. S. *Sydling, Dorsetshire*
††Sinclair, Sir John, Bart. M. P. F. R. and A. S.
Stephens, Sir Philip, Bart. M. P. F. R. and A. S.
††Smith, Sir Sidney, Kt. Capt. R. N. Commander Grand Cross of the Order of the Sword
Stirling, Sir Walter, Bart. M. P. *Pall-mall*
Smith, Major-General Edward
St. Barbe, John, Esq. *Seething-lane*
Sadler, Jonathan, Esq. *King's-arms-yard, Coleman-street*
††Salte, William, Esq. *Poultry*
Sanders, John, Esq. *Mortlake, Surrey*
Sandford, Rev. Thomas, *Isle of Man*
Sansom, Philip, Esq. *Fenchurch-street*
Sargeaunt, Mr. John, *Great Queen-street*
Sarel, Andrew Lovering, Esq. *Surrey-street*
Satterthwaite, Mr. John, *Mincing-lane*
Savage, Mr. James, *Great Queen-street*
Saunders, Thomas, Esq. *Haydon-square, Minories*
Saunders, George, Esq. F. A. S. *Oxford-street*
P Saunders, Edward Grey, Esq. *Harley-place*
Saxon, Mr. Samuel, *Parliament-street*
Sayer, Henry J. Esq. *Lincoln's-inn*

Schaw,

Schaw, Lieutenant-Colonel John B.

Scholey, Mr. George, *Old Swan-stairs*

P Scott, David, Esq. *Devonshire-place*

P Scott, John, Esq. *Adelphi Terrace*

Scott, Alexander, Esq. *Suffolk-street, Charing-cross*

Scott, Robert, Esq. *Grosvenor-square*

Scott, Hugh, Esq.

††Seale, Mr. David, *Peckham*

Seddon, Mr. Thomas, *Aldersgate-street*

P Selby, Henry Collingwood, Esq. *No. 2, Gray's-inn-square*

Serra, Isaac, Esq. *King's-road, Bedford-row*

Sewell, Mr. John, *Cornhill*

Sewell, the Reverend George, *Byfleet, near Ripley, Surrey*

Sewell, Mr. George, *London-street, Fitzroy-square*

Shadwell, Henry, Esq. *Beverley, Yorkshire*

Shaw, John, Esq. *Great James-street, Bedford-row*

Sharp, Hercules, Esq. *Chester-place, Kennington*

††Sheldon, Thomas, Esq. F. R. S. *Tottenham-court-road*

Sheldrake, Mr. Timothy, *Strand*

††Sheplee, Richard, Esq. *Horslydown*

Shiffner, Godin, Esq. *Weymouth-street, Portland-place*

P Shipley, Mr. William, Gent. *Maidstone, Kent*

P Shore, Samuel, Esq. *Norton-hall, Derbyshire*

P Shore, Samuel, jun. Esq.

Sibley, Joseph, Esq. *Market-street, Herts*

Simonds, William B. Esq. *Reading*

F f 3                     Simpson,

Simpson, Mr. Thomas, *Chelsea Water-works*

Simpson, John, Esq. *Manchester*

Simpken, Mr. Charles, *Oxford-street*

Simpkin, Mr. Thomas, *Strand*

Skinner, Thomas, Esq. Alderman, *Aldersgate-street*

Skinner, William, Esq. *Finsbury-square*

Slade, John, Esq.

Slade, John Moore, Esq. *Chatham*

Smallwood, William Esq. *Jerusalem Coffee-house*

Smart, Mr. George, *Camden Town*

Smirnove, Rev. James, *Upper Mary-le-bone-street*

\* Smith, George, Esq.

† Smith, John Spencer, Esq.

††Smith, William, Esq. *Lombard-street*

Smith, William, Esq. M. P. *Park-street*

††Smith, Joshua, Esq. M. P. *Great George-street, Westminster*

Smith, Mr. Dedrick, *Gerard-street*

\* Smith, Mr. Nathan, *Knightsbridge, Brighthelmstone*

Smith, Captain William, of the Royal Navy

Smith, Henry, Esq. *Draper's-hall*

Smith, Mr. Richard, *Crown-court, Cheapside*

Smith, Mr. Edward, *Broad-street, City*

††Smith, George, Esq. *Lombard-street*

Smith, Eaglesfield, Esq.

Smith, John Prince, Esq. *No. 11, Lower Thorn-haugh-street*

Smith, Robert, Esq. *Basinghall-street*

Smith, Walthall Ridgway, Esq. *No. 5, New Inn*

Smith,

Smith, Mr. Thomas, *Strand*

Soane, John, Esq. F. A. S. P. R. I. *Lincoln's-inn-fields*

Soley, Mr. Thomas Apreece, *Bloomsbury*

Songa, Anthony, Esq.

Sowerby, John, Esq. *Watling-street*

††Sparks, Robert, Esq. *St. John's street*

Sparks, Thomas, Esq. *Aldersgate-street*

Sparkes, Joseph, Esq. *Red-lion-square*

Sparkes, John, Esq. *Doughty-street*

Sparrow, Robert, Esq. *Portland-place, and Workingham-hall, Suffolk*

Spiller, James, Esq. *Guildford-street*

Spilsbury, Mr. William, *Snowhill*

Spilsbury, Mr. Charles, *ditto*

Splitgerber, Mr. John Christian, *Church-court, Walbrook*

Splitgerber, Mr. Frederick, *ditto*

Spottiswood, John, Esq. *Sackville-street*

Spurrier, Mr. Isaac, *Greek-street, Soho*

Stafford, Robert, Esq. Banker, *Huntingdon*

Standen, the Reverend J. H. Rector of Murston, *Kent*

Standish, Edward Townley, Esq. *Park-street, Westminster, and of Standish-hall, in Lancashire*

Stanhope, Walter Spencer, Esq. *Upper Grosvenor-street*

Stanley, George, Esq. *Ponsonby-hall, Cumberland*

Steell, Robert, Esq. *Finsbury-square*

Steer, Charles, Esq. *Church-street, Spital-fields*

P††Steers,

P††Steers, John William, Esq. F. A. S. *No. 7, Fig-tree-court, Inner Temple*

P. Steers, James, Esq. *ditto*

*††Stephens, Francis, Esq. F. R. and A. S. Commissioner of the Victualling Office

Stephens, James, Esq. *Camerlton-house, near Bath*

Stephens, John, Esq. *Reading*

Stevenson, Thomas, M. D.

Stevenson, James, M. D.

Stiff, Mr. Thomas, *New-street, Covent-garden*

Stirling, William, Esq. *Bread-street, Cheapside*

Still, Mr. Samuel Stanford, *Bankside, Southwark*

Stockwell, John, Esq. *Crutched-friars*

Stockdale, Mr. Jeremiah, *Holborn*

Stodart, William, Esq. *Golden-square*

Stone, Mr. Thomas

††Stone, William, Esq.

Stonard, Nathaniel, Esq. *Bow, Middlesex*

Storey, Robert, Esq. *Bedford-square*

Strachan, James, Esq. *Mincing-lane*

††Strange, James, Esq. M. P. *Bond-street*

Stratton, Mr. William, *Gutter-lane*

Street, Mr. James Wallis, *King-street, Bloomsbury*

Street, John, Esq. *Brunswick-square*

Stretton, William, Esq. *Broad-street, Soho*

Stuart, Andrew, Esq. M. P. and F. A. S. *Lower Grosvenor-street*

Suart, George, Esq. *Lancaster*

P Sulivan, Richard Joseph, Esq. M. P. F. R. and A. S. *Grafton-street*

Sulivan, John, Esq. M. P. *Chesterfield-street, May-fair*

Sumner, George, Esq. M. P. *George-street, West-minster*

†PSutton, Robert, Esq. *Finsbury-square*

Sykes, Mark Masterman, Esq. *Sledmere, Yorkshire*

Sykes, Richard, Esq. *No. 3, Walbrook*

Symmons, John, Esq. F. R. A. S. and L. S. *Pad-dington-house*

## T.

**Thanet, Sackville Earl of

Tabrum, Mr. Robert, *Gracechurch-street*

Tait, William, Esq. *Cardiff*

P Talbot, Thomas Mansel, Esq. *Penrie Castle, Gla-morganshire*

††Tate, William, Esq. *Queen-street, Chelsea*

Taubman, Major John, *Isle of Man*

Taylor, William, Esq. M. P. *No. 32, Pall-mall*

Taylor, William, Esq. *Charlotte-street, Bedford-square*

Taylor, John, Esq. *John-street, Adelphi*

Taylor, Mr. Josiah, *Holborn*

Taylor, Captain Charles

Taylor, Thomas, Esq. *Friday-street, Cheapside*

P Teixiera, Abraham David, Esq. *Mincing-lane*

Tekell, John, Esq. *Lamb's-buildings, Temple*

Templer, James, Esq. *Stover-lodge, Devon*

Tennant,

Tennant, George, Esq. *No. 21, Southampton-row, Bloomsbury*

Test, Potter, Esq. *Great Portland-street*

Test, Thomas, Esq. *No. 7, Leicester-place*

Thomas, David, Esq. *Pay Office, Horse Guards*

Thomson, the Rev. Robert, D. D. *Kensington*

Thomson, Alexander, Esq. *Somerset-street*

P Thompson, William, Esq. *Leeds, Yorkshire*

Thompson, William, Esq. *Thames-street*

Thompson, Mr. George, *Duke-street, York-buildings*

Thompson, Mr. John, *ditto*

Thomson, Mr. Joseph, *Vine-street, Piccadilly*

P Thornton, Samuel, Esq. M. P. *Clapham*

Thornton, William, Esq. Colonel in the 1st Regiment of Foot Guards, *Park-lane*

Thornton, Dr. Robert, *Duke-street, Grosvenor-square*

Tildesley, Thomas, Esq. *Hampton-court*

Tilloch, Alexander, Esq. *Carey-street*

Thoyts, William, Esq. *Southamstead, Berks*

Timbrell, William Hall, Esq. *No. 47, Charlotte-street, Portland-place*

P Timson, Thomas, Esq. *Moon Park, Surrey*

Tomkison, Thomas, Esq. *Dean-street, Soho*

Tomlins, Mr. Thomas, *Lambeth-marsh*

Topham, Edward, Esq.

Totton, Stephens Dinely, Esq. A. M. *Abroad*

Towne, Mr. Francis

Townsend, Francis, Esq. Windsor Herald, *Heralds College*

†† Towry,

††Towry, George Philips, Esq. Commissioner of the Victualling Office

P Travers, Mr. Joseph, *Swithin's-lane*

Trenchard, John, Esq. *Welbeck-street*

Tresham, Henry, Esq. *George-street, Hanover-square*

Trevelyan, Walter, Esq. *Morpeth, Northumberland*

Trotter, John, Esq. *Soho-square*

Trotter, Captain John, *Wimpole-street*

P Tunstall, Marmaduke, Esq. F. R. and A. S. *Wycliffe, Yorkshire*

P Turnbull, John, Esq. F. R. and A. S. *New Broad-street*

Turner, Charles H. Esq. *Limehouse*

Turner, Thomas, Esq. *Caughley-place, near Sheffnall, Shropshire*

P Turner, John Frewen, Esq. *Cold Overton, Leicestershire*

P Tyers, James, Esq. *Little Eastcheap*

Tytler, Henry William, M. D. *Titchfield-street*


U.


P Uxbridge, Henry Earl of, F. A. S.

Udny, Robert, Esq. F. R. and A. S. *Teddington*

Upton, Charles, Esq. *Derby*

# V.

P Valencia, Richard Lord Viscount, F. L. S.

Vernon, George Venables Lord, *Park-place*

P Villiers, Right Honourable J. C. *North Audley-street*

Valangin, Francis, M. D. *Hermes-hill*

Valpy, the Rev. Richard, D. D. and F. A. S. *Reading, Berks*

Vandercomb, Joseph Fitzwilliam, Esq. *Bush-lane, Cannon-street*

Vaughan, Benjamin, Esq.

Vaughan, William, Esq. *Mincing-lane*

Venner, Corbyn Morris, Esq. *King's-bench-walk, Temple*

††Vernon, John, Esq. *Bedford-square*

Vernon, Henry, Esq. *Hilton-park, Wolverhampton, or No.* 10, *Lower Wimpole-street*

Vidal, Emeric, Esq. *Brentford*

Vidler, Mr. John, *Milbank, Westminster*

Vigne, Stephen James, Esq. *Margaret-street, Westminster*

Vivian, John, Esq. *Gray's-inn*

Vivian, John, Esq. *Temple*

## W.

P Warwick, George Earl of, F. R. and A. S.

P Winchelsea, George Earl of, F. A. S.

Westmeath, Right Honourable Earl of

* Williams, Sir Edward, Bart.

P Webb, Sir John, Bart. F. R. and A. S.

Wynn, Sir Watkin Williams, Bart. *St. James's square*

P Willis, Sir Francis, Kt. *Charles-street, Berkeley-square*

Wynne, the Right Hon. Sir William, LL. D. F. R. and A. S. *Doctors-commons*

Wadd, William, Esq. *Basinghall-street*

††Wade, George, Esq. *Southampton-row, Bloomsbury*

Waistell, Mr. Charles, *High Holborn*

Wait, William, Esq. *Lawrence-Pountney-hill*

Wakefield, Mr. Edward, jun.

††Walcot, William, Esq. F. A. S. *Inner Temple*

P Wale, Gregory, Esq. *Shelford, near Cambridge*

Walker, John, Esq. F. R. and A. S. *Gower-street, Bedford-square*

Walker, John, Esq. *Argyll-street*

Walker, Thomas, Esq. *Woodstock, Oxon*

Walker, Mr. Daniel, *Great Pulteney-street*

Walker, Mr. Thomas, *Epsom*

Walker, Thomas, Esq. *Russel-place, Fitzroy-square*

Walker, Thomas, Esq. *Croydon*

Walker, Joshua, Esq. *Rotherham*

Walker,

Walker, Thomas, Esq. Master in Chancery, *Lincoln's-inn-fields*

Walker, Dean, Esq. *Conduit-street*

Waller, Charles, Esq. *West Wickham, Kent*

Waller, William, Esq.

Wallis, John, Esq. *Bodmin, Cornwall*

Wallis, George, M. D. *Red-lion-square*

Walshman, Thomas, M. D. *Physician to the Surrey and Western Dispensaries*

Wansey, Mr. John, *Lothbury*

Wansey, Mr. George, *Warminster; Wilts*

Warburton, the Rev. W. P. *Lambeth-house*

P Ward, Mr. John, *Air-street, Piccadilly*

P Ward, Ralph, Esq. *Great Portland-street*

Ward, John, Esq. *Ludgate-street*

P Waring, Richard Hill, Esq. F. R. S. *Inner Temple*

Watherston, Dalhousie, Esq. *Duchess-street, Portland place*

Watkins, George, Esq. *Featherstone-buildings*

Watkins, Jeremiah, Esq. *Charing-cross*

Watkins, Walter, Esq. *Groyney Works, near Abergavenny*

Watson, John, Esq. *Preston, Lancashire*

Watts, David Pike, Esq. *No. 32, Gower-street*

Watts, John, Esq. *Thames-street*

Webster, John, Esq. *Duke-street, Westminster*

P Wedgwood, John, Esq. F. L. S. *Devonshire-place*

Wedgwood, Josiah, Esq. *Etruria, Staffordshire*

Wedgwood, Thomas, Esq. *ditto*

Wenman,

Wenman, Charles, Esq. *Lambeth Walk*

P††West, Thomas Thompson, Esq. *Crown-court, Cheapside*

††West, Benjamin, Esq. President of the Royal Academy, and F. A. S. *Newman-street*

West, James, Esq. *Queen-Ann-street West*

Westcot, George, Esq. *Chelmsford*

Westmacott, Mr. Richard, *Mount-street, Grosvenor-square*

Weston, John Webbe, Esq. *Sutton-place, near Guildford*

Weymouth, Henry, Esq. *Battersea*

Whipham, Thomas, Esq. *Fleet-street*

White, Thomas, Esq. *Retford, Nottinghamshire*

††White, John, Esq. *Mary-le-bone*

White, John, jun. Esq. *ditto*

White, William Wood, Esq. *Walthamstow*

P White, Rev. Stephen, LL. D.

††Whitefoord, Caleb, Esq. F. R. and A. S. V. P. *Adelphi*

Whitefoord, J. R. Esq. *Gloucester-place, Portman-square*

Whitfield, George, Esq. *Elm-court, Temple*

P Whitefield, Henry Fotherby, Esq. *Rickmansworth, Herts*

Whitehead, George, Esq. *Basinghall-street*

Whittingham, Mr. Charles, *Dean-street, Fetter-lane*

Whyte, John, Esq. *Brewer-street*

Wilberforce,

Wilberforce, William, Esq. M. P. *Palace-yard, Westminster*

Wilder, Lieutenant-Colonel Francis John

Wilkins, Jeffery, Esq. *Brecon*

††Wilkinson, John, Esq. *Brymbo, Denbighshire*

P Wilkinson, William, Esq. *Plasgrona, near Wrexham*

Wilkinson, Charles, Esq. *Soho-square*

Williams, George Griffies, Esq. *Caermarthen*

P††Williams, Thomas, Esq. M.P. *Llanidan, Anglesed*

Williams, Isaac Lloyd, Esq. *Southampton-street, Bloomsbury*

Willich, Dr. A. F. M. *James-street, Covent-garden*

Williams, Mr. Nicholas

Williams, Mr. John, *Cornhill*

Williams, John Lloyd, Esq. *Somerset-street*

Williamson, General Adam

P††Willis, William, Esq. *Lombard-street*

P\*Willis, Robert, M. D. *Tenterden-street, Hanover-square*

Willet, John Willet, Esq. F. R. and A. S. *Grosvenor-square*

††Willock, John, Esq. *Golden-square*

Wilmot, John, Esq. *John-street, Bedford-row*

Wilson, Mr. Edward, *Strand*

Wilson, Thomas, Esq. *Navy Pay Office, Somerset-house*

Wilson, Rev. Mr. *Hall-place, Dartford, Kent*

Wilson, Thomas Esq. F. L. S. *Gower-street*

Wilson, Matthew, Esq. *Red-lion-square*

Wilson,

Wilson, Joseph, Esq. *Milk-street*

Wilson, Mr. Thomas, *Fullwell Lodge, Twickenham*

Wilson, Mr. John, *Bedford-street, Covent-garden*

Wilson, Mr. Thomas, *St. John's College, Oxford, or Catherine-court, Trinity-square*

Wilsonne, Mr. William, *Basinghall-street*

Winder, Mr. John, *Shell Farm, Lenham, Kent*

Windus, William P. Esq. *Oxford-street*

P Winne, Captain Ifaac Lascelles

Winslow, Mr. Thomas, *Fullwell Lodge, Twickenham*

Winter, George, Esq. *Charlton, near Bristol*

Winter, James, Esq. *Inner Temple*

Winter, John, Esq. *St. James's street*

Wise, Matthew Blacket, Esq.

† Wisset, Robert, Esq. *India House*

Wood, George, Esq. *New Broad-street-buildings*

Wood, John, Esq. *Cardiff*

Wood, William, Esq. *Cork-street*

Wood, John, Esq. *North-Cove, Yorkshire*

Wood, John, Esq. *St. Bartholomew's Hospital*

Woodburn, Mr. William, *St. Martin's lane*

Woodfall, Mr. George, *Paternoster-row*

P Woodhull, Michael, Esq.

Worrall, Jonathan, Esq. *Micklam, near Dorking, Surrey,* or at Mr. John Bond's, *St. Mary-axe*

Worthington, Thomas G. Esq. *Jefferies-square, St. Mary-axe*

P Wotton, William Samuel, Esq.

††Wright, Nathaniel, Esq. *Hatton-street*

G g     P††Wright,

P†† Wright, Peter, Esq. *Lamb's-conduit-street*

Wright, J. Esq. *Market Drayton, Shropshire*

Wright, Mr. William, *Strand*

Wrighte, Rev. Thomas William, A. M. F. A. S. *Somerset-place*

Wyatt, Edgell, Esq. *Inner Temple*

Wyatt, Samuel, Esq. *Albion Mills*

Wyatt, John, Esq. *Fleet-street*

Wyatt, James, Esq. R. R. *Queen Ann-street East*

Wyatt, Jeffery, Esq. *Harley-street* .

†† Wynne, John, Esq. *Fig-tree-court, Temple*

†† Wyndham, Thomas, Esq. M. P. *Dunraven, Gla-morganshire*


## Y.


†† Young, Sir William, Bart. M. P. F. R. and A. S.

Young, Mr. Lake, *Watling-street*

P Young, Arthur, Esq. F. R. S. &c. *Bradfield-hall, Suffolk*

Young, Samuel, Esq. F. R. and A. S. *Gower-street*

Young, Mr. Thomas, *Little Britain*

Z.

## Z.

Zenobio, Right Honourable Count Alvise
P Zachary, John, Esq. F. A. S. *Arely, Worcestershire*

### CORRESPONDING MEMBER.

Berczy, William, Esq. *of York and Berczy, in Upper Canada*

---

# INDEX.

### A.

Page

ACID SULPHURIC, premium for a preparation of   34
ACORNS, premiums offered for planting   6
AGRICULTURE, premiums in   ibid.
           Papers in   69
AIR FOUL, the morbid effects of, how relieved in an
   hospital   316
     VITAL, a supply of, essential to animal life   303
AMBER, the solution of, how to be used as a vehicle
   for painting   217
ANNATTO, premium for   58
APHIS, on the destructive effects of the   129
     first attacks of, how to be considered   132
     Trees lately transplanted escaped the attacks
       of the   ibid.
     how destroyed   133
ARKWRIGHT, Mr. Thomas, a bounty of Twenty-five
   Guineas to   276
                 description of a machine
                   by, for raising Ores   277
ASHTON, Nicholas, Esq. the Gold Medal to   169

B.

## B.

BANCROFT, Dr. accounts of experiments made by,
on Lake from Stick-Lack     355

BAR-IRON FINE, premium for making     35

BARRY JAMES, Esq. account of his additional improvements in the Pictures in the Society's Great
Room     .     xxxvii

BEANS, premiums for the cultivation of     12

       and Wheat, premiums for the cultivation of     12

BENTHAM, Samuel, Esq. the Gold Medal to     191

BESANT, Mrs. a bounty of Ten Guineas to     265

BLIGHTS, premiums for removing the ill effects of     9

       on Fruit-Trees, a paper on     129

       originate from three causes     130

       the most common and extensive causes of     136

BLOND LE, an ingenious projector     231

BOGGY Land, a paper on Draining     165

       what the greatest obstacle to draining     ibid.

BOLTS, premium for driving, into Ships     48

       accounts of a method of driving, into Ships,
by Mr. Phillips     269

       reference to the engraving of Mr. Phillips's
method     273

BOMBELLI, a celebrated Venetian painter, an observation of, respecting his Pictures     229

       a recipe of, for Varnish     230

BORER, premium for destroying the     56

BOTANIC Garden in the Bahama Islands, premium
for the cultivation of the     57

BREAD-FRUIT Trees, plantation of, a premium for     54

BRICKS, machine for making, premium for     50

BRIDGEWATER, the Duke of, thanks to     117

                           BRONZES,

BRONZES, premium for    42

BROWN, Mr. Robert, Twenty Guineas to    81

BULLOCK, Mr. William, a bounty of Fifteen Guineas
to    290

BURR-STONE for Mill-Stones, an account of the discovery of a Quarry of    280

### C.

CABBAGES, preserving, premiums for    16

CALICO-Printers, premiums for copper-plate patterns for    41

CANDLES, Tallow, premium for manufacturing    29

CARROTS, PARSNIPS, or BEETS, premium for preserving    17

CARTWRIGHT, the Rev. Edmund, thanks to the, for a paper on the production of Opium from Lettuces    197

CHEESE-TRYER used with advantage in taking out the eyes of potatoes    115

CHEMISTRY, premiums in    27

Papers in    191

CHICOREE Plant, the, an account of the culture of, and method of manufacturing Coffee from    242—248

CHINTZ Patterns for Calico-Printers, premiums for    40

CINNAMON, premium for    54

CLOTH, Cotton, premium for a Preparation of a Red Stain for    32

for printing, of a green colour    33

CLOVER-HAY, a paper on the method of making    88

how to be managed in unfavourable circumstances    92

new method of making, adopted with success in Silesia    96

Gg 3      CLOVER-

CLOVER-HAY, fermentation necessary in the making
of        98

CLOVES, premium for        54

COALS, machine for raising, premium for      49

COCHINEAL, true, premium for      59

COCKCHAFFER, premium for destroying the Grub
of the      22

       on the destruction of the Grub of the  175

COFFEE, method of making, from the Chicoree Plant  242

     . manufacture of, from dried Chicoree Root  249

COLONIES and TRADE, premiums in      53

              Papers in      343

COLOURS mixed with Amber do not lose their brilliancy  215

COMPARATIVE TILLAGE, premium for      10

CONDITIONS to POLITE ARTS      43

           General      63

COPAL, the solution of, how to be used as a vehicle
for Painting      217

      process for dissolving      226

CORN, premium for harvesting in wet weather      18

            a Machine for reaping or mowing  22

      a paper on harvesting in wet weather    99

      the health and luxuriance of, on what in a
great measure they depend      142

COTTON, Bhaugulpore, premium for      58

COUNTIES, surveys of, premium for      42

CRANE, a new-invented, description of  294—296

CROPS, rotation of, premiums for cultivating      14

CULTIVATOR by Mr. Lester, an account of a    142

D.

## D.

DE LAFONS, Mr. Thirty Guineas to 331
DRAIN-PLOUGH from the Duke of Bridgewater, a
  paper on the 117
                  Description of the 121
DRAWING, honorary premium for 38
       of Outlines, a premium for 39
       Landscapes, a premium for ibid.
       Historical, premium for 40
DRILL-MACHINE for sowing Turnip-seed, description
  of a 123
           by Mr. Munnings, description of a 163
DRILLING Turnips, the advantages of 155

## E.

ECCLESTON, Mr. Thomas, thanks to 165
ELMS, a paper on planting 69
ENGRAVING on WOOD, premium for 41
ESCAPEMENT, new, by Mr. De Lafons, a description
  of a 331
EVANS, Mr. Field, a bounty of Fifty Pounds to 280
EVER-GREEN Trees best transplanted in August 69

## F.

FEATHERS, premium for clearing, from their animal
  oil 28
FEVER,

FEVER, Gaol, in what prisons unknown                306

FLEMING, Mr. extract from a letter of, on Lack      358

FOGG, Mr. Thomas, the Gold Medal to                 105

FOREST-TREES, premiums for planting                 6

FRUIT-TREES, premiums offered for preventing the
   Blight of                                          9

### G.

GAOL, county, at Gloucester, how constructed        310

GENT, Mr. Thomas, a bounty of Fifteen Guineas to    294

GRUBS of the Cockchaffers, description of the        175

   the favourite food of Moles                      176

GUNNY-BAGS, account of Paper made from              235

### H.

HAY, Meadow, premium for making, in wet weather     18

HEAT, excessive, highly injurious to the Blossoms of
   Trees                                             138

HEMP, cultivation of, in Canada, premiums for       59

HERRINGS, premium for curing, by the Dutch method                                              . 61

HONEY-DEW produced by the Aphis                     130

HOPS, premium for destroying the Fly on             23

HORRIDGE, Mr. the Silver Medal to                   183

HOWARD, Mr. the principles of, respecting Ventilation, adopted by the Legislature                  305

## I.

JOHNES, Thomas, Esq. the Gold Medal to 78
JOHNSON, Dr. Alexander, a communication from, on
Myrabolans 343
JONES, Edward, Esq. thanks to 175
IRON, premium for preserving from rust 36

## K.

KALI for Barilla, premium for 55
KITES enemies to Moles 179
KNIGHT, Andrew, Esq. the Silver Medal to 123
Thanks to, and communica-
tion from, on Blights 129

## L.

LACCA, or Gum-Lack, how produced 355
LAKE, from Stick-Lack, a paper on 352
supposed little inferior to Cochineal 353
LAND, Arable, premium for ascertaining the compo-
nent parts of 19
lying waste, premium for improving ibid.
Paper on the improvement of 105
gaining, from the Sea, premium for 21
Waste Moor, a paper on planting 169
LESTER,

LESTER, Mr. William, the Silver Medal to        142
LETTUCES, advantage of the cultivation of, over that
    of Poppies        202
LOCK, drawback, description of an improved, by
    Mr. Bullock        290—293
LOMAZZO, observations of, on painting        220


                    M.


MACHLACHLAN, Mr. a letter from, on Myrabolans  350
MANUFACTURES, premiums in        45
                Papers in        235
MANURE, a paper on the preparation and application
    of composts for        183
MECHANICKS, premiums in        48
                Papers in        255
MEMBERS, a list of the        393
MILDEW, consists of numerous oval bodies evidently
    organized        135
MILL, parish or family, premium for        49
MILLS, gunpowder, premium for        50
MILL-STONES, premium for discovering        51
MILL for grinding hard substances, an account of a   287
MINERALS, British, premium for analysis of        34
MODELS and MACHINES, a catalogue of the        386
MOLES, habits of, described        177
            the only certain destroyer of the Grub        182
MUNNINGS, the Rev. T. C. the Silver Medal and Ten
    Guineas to        147
MYRABOLANS, on the production and application of  343
                            N.

## N.

NATURAL HISTORY, premiums for                             43

NITRATE, alkaline or earthy, premium for preparation of                                               35

NUTMEGS, premium for                                      53

## O.

OAKS, premiums for the best method of raising             7

OIL, Whale, or Seal, premium for refining                28

    from Porpoises, premium for                         47

OILS, drying, on the nature and preparation of           205

    expressed, how divided                             209

OFFICERS, a list of the                                  389

OPIUM from Lettuces, on the production of                197

ORE, an account of a Machine for raising, from
   Mines                                                  276

OSIERS, premiums for planting                              8

    Papers on planting                                  75

## P.

PAINT, premium for a substitute for the basis of         33

PALMER, Mr. John, the Silver Medal to                    99

PAPER from raw Vegetables, premium for         46,      235

    made from Gunny-bags, account of                   235

PARSNIPS,

PARSNIPS, premium for cultivating                14
PAUL, Sir G. O. thanks to                        299
PAUT-Plant, not the same as Sun                  240
PEARSON, Dr. a letter from, on Opium from Lettuces                                          199
PEAT-BORER, by Mr. Eccleston, description of     168
PHILLIPS, Mr. Richard, Forty Guineas to          269
PIGMENT, red, premium for a preparation of        33
POLITE ARTS, premiums in                          38
POOR, the labouring, premium for improving the condition of                                     25
POLITE Arts, papers in the                       205
POTATOES, a new and cheap method of planting     183
PREMIUMS various, offered in the 18th Vol. continued, though not printed                          6
PRESENTS received by the Society                  380
PROVISIONS, salted, premium for preserving        28

## R.

REWARDS bestowed by the Society                  370
ROCKS, premium for boring and blasting            50
ROOMS, premium for heating, for manufacturers     51
RUBGIO, the, of Virgil, what                     136

## S.

SARJEANT, Mr. H. the Silver Medal to             255
SASH-WINDOW for an Hospital, description of a     329
SCULPTURE, premium for                            42
                                          SELBY,

SELBY, Mr. Thomas, Thirty Guineas to 75

SHEEP, premium for the cure of the rot in 83

for preventing the ill effects of flies

on 24

for protecting . ibid.

SHELDRAKE, Mr. Timothy, thanks to 204

conjectures by, respecting .

his vehicle for painting 220

SILK Machine for carding, premium for 45

SMOKE, premium for destroying 31

condensing ibid.

SPIRIT Proof, premium for making 30

SPRING WHEAT, premium for cultivating 12

Paper on the cultivation of 81

STEAM, premium for increasing 30

STEPHENS, Andrew, Esq. the Silver Medal to, and

a paper from, on Lack 352

STOVE-Timber, a, will dry corn as well as a malt-kiln 101

for ventilating Hospitals, by Sir G. O. Paul, a

perspective view of the 325

engraving of historical subjects, premium for 40

SUGAR, premium for separating, in a solid form, from

treacle 30

## T.

TAN, premium for the preparation of 32

TAR, premium for substitute for 31

TAYLOR, Mr. John, thanks to 88

Paper from, on the culture of the

Chicoree plant 242

TERRY,

TERRY, Mr. Garnet, the Silver Medal to     287

THRESHING Machine, premium for     22

TIMBER-TREES, premiums offered for planting     6

             for securing plan-
             tations of     8

TIMBER, premium for preventing the dry rot in     27

    Trees, paper on planting     78

TIN, Block, premium for refining     36

TRANSIT Instrument, premium for a     48

TURNIPS, premium for comparative culture of     13

         for preserving     15

    on the cultivation of, by the drill method     147

    cause of the failure of, when sown broad-
    cast     154

TURPENTINE, Venice, of the shops, of what composed     226

## U.

ULTRAMARINE, premium for a preparation of     34

## V.

VEGETABLES, premium for preserving the seeds of     27

VENETIAN Pictures, part of the peculiar effect of,
  how occasioned     207

         with respect to vehicles of two
         kinds     224

    Painters, skill of the, on what it depended   223

                   VENTILATION,

VENTILATION, improved, premium for 52

of Hospitals, &c. a paper on the, by
Sir G. O. Paul 299

imperfect, the source of putrid diseases 308

propriety of, by currents of air,
questioned by Count Rumford 309

free, when improper 318

how to be applied to ships 321

VERNON, Henry, Esq. the Gold Medal to 69


W.


WARE, Earthen, premium for glazing without lead 36

WATER, Fresh, premium for preserving sweet 27

method of preserving sweet 191

Machine for raising, premium for 49

an account of Mr. Sarjeant's machine for
raising 255

Wheel, undershot, account of a new-invented 265

WHALES, premium for taking, by the Gun-Harpoon 48

WHEAT, comparative culture of, premium for the 11

Machine for dibbling, premium for 21

may be sown with advantage in spring 85

WICKS for Candles or Lamps, premium for 45

WILLMOTT, Mr. Thomas, Twenty Guineas to 235

WORMS, premium for destroying 23

H h

*Printed by W. and C. Spilsbury, No. 57, Snowhill, London.*

# ERRATA.

Page 302, line 18, for *does not exist*, read *does exist*.
——— 303, — 23, for *intercourses*, read *intercourse*.
——— 304, — 23, for *fevers*, read *fever*.
——— 310, — 13, for *principles*, read *principle*.
——— 311, — 5, for *these*, read *the*.
——— —, — 9, for *prisons*, read *prison*.
——— 312, — 12, for *openness*, read *openings*.
——— 313, — 8, for *particularly*, read *particular*.
——— 316, — 15, for *dysentery*, read *dysenteric*.
——— 319, — 3, for *that the draft*, read *to accelerate the draft*.
——— —, — 6, dele *is accelerated*.
——— 329, — 16, for *edges*, read *ledges*.

# Society for the Encouragement of Arts, Manufactures, and Commerce.

ADELPHI, Jan. 14, 1802.

THE SOCIETY for the ENCOURAGEMENT of ARTS, MANUFACTURES, and COMMERCE, wishing to encourage the growth of HEMP for the use of the Navy, in certain parts of Scotland, comprehending the whole county of Argyle; that part of Perthshire, situate to the North of the river Tay, and West of the Military Road (See Ainslie's Map of Scotland) leading from Logierait to the county of Inverness; and such other parts of Scotland as lie North of Inverness-shire—offers to the Person who shall sow with Hemp, in drills at least eighteen inches asunder, the greatest quantity of Land in the above-mentioned district, not less than Fifty Acres, statute measure, in the year 1802, and shall at the proper season cause to be plucked the Summer-Hemp (or Male Hemp, bearing no seed), and continue the Winter-Hemp (or Female Hemp, bearing seed) on the ground, until the seed is ripe — the GOLD MEDAL, or FIFTY GUINEAS.

To the Person who shall sow with Hemp (in drills at least eighteen inches asunder) the next greatest quantity of Land in the same above-mentioned district, not less than Twenty-five Acres, statute measure, in the year 1802, and shall at the proper season cause the same to be plucked as above mentioned — the SILVER MEDAL, or TWENTY-FIVE GUINEAS.

*Certificates* of the number of Acres, of the distance of the drills, of the plucking of the Hemp, with a general Account of the soil, cultivation, and produce, to be delivered to the Society, along with fourteen pounds of the Hemp, and two quarts of the Seed, on or before the second Tuesday in January 1803; addressed to the Secretary, at the Society's House, in the Adelphi, London.

By Order of the Society,

CHARLES TAYLOR, Sec.

# DIRECTIONS to the BOOKBINDER.

Place the Print of O. S. Brereton, Esq. as Frontispiece of the Volume, to face the Title-page.

The Plate, No. I. of the Duke of Bridgewater's Drain-Plough, and Mr. Knight's Drill-Machine, to face page 128.

The Plate, No. II. of Mr. Lester's Cultivator, the Rev. T. C. Munnings's Drill-Machine, and Mr. Eccleston's Peat-Borer, to face page 168.

A Sample of the Paper made from the Paut-Plant, to face page 234.

The Plate, No. III. of Mr. Sarjeant's Machine to raise Water, to face page 260.

The Plate, No. IV. of the late Mr. Besant's Water Wheel, and Mr. Phillips's Tubes for driving Bolts into Ships, to face page 274.

The Plate, No. V. of Mr. Arkwright's Machine to raise Ore from Mines, to face page 278.

The Plate, No. VI. of Mr. Garnet Terry's Mill and Mr. Bullock's Drawback Lock, to face page 292.

The Plate, No. VII. of Mr. Gent's Crane, to face page 298.

The Plate, No. VIII. of Sir G. O. Paul's Stove and Sash Frame, to face page 330.

The Plate, No. IX. of Mr. De Lafon's Watch Escapement, to face page 338.

FRANCIS EDWARD GREGORY ESQ.

Drawn & Engraved by W<sup>m</sup> Evans.

Published as the Act directs Nov 1. 1804.

# TRANSACTIONS

OF THE

# SOCIETY

INSTITUTED AT LONDON,

FOR THE

# ENCOURAGEMENT

OF

# ARTS, MANUFACTURES,

## and COMMERCE;

WITH THE

PREMIUMS offered in the YEAR 1802.

## VOL. XX.

———————

LONDON:

Printed by W and C. SPILSBURY, Snowhill.

Sold by the REGISTER, at the SOCIETY's HOUSE, in the ADELPHI;
and by Meffrs. ROBSON, J. WHITE, BECKET, JOHNSON, CADELL
and DAVIES, PAYNE and MACKINLAY, WALTER, RICHARDSON,
SEWELL, and TAYLOR.

[ Price TEN SHILLINGS and SIX-PENCE. ]

M.DCCCII.

# PREFACE.

THE Society instituted at London, in the year 1753, for the encouragement of Arts, Manufactures, and Commerce, is founded upon principles so liberal and advantageous to the Public, as probably not to be excelled by any similar establishment in Europe.

To encourage merit in every department of Arts, Manufactures, and Commerce, is the professed object of its Members, and to which they especially call the attention of the Public. Their annual list of Premiums shows some particular subjects which they notice : but their views are not bounded by that list, nor is their patronage confined by its catalogue ; for other matters, which are likely to prove in any way useful to

mankind,

mankind, are received for their consideration, and are often liberally rewarded by Bounties.

It should be well remembered, that this Society does not confine its exhibition of valuable Paintings and Models to a few individuals; but, on the contrary, their Rooms and Repositories are open gratuitously to any person, on the recommendation of a Member, from ten till two o'clock daily, Sundays and Wednesdays excepted; and Sketches of the implements are allowed to be taken, for others to be made from them.

The annual Volume of the Society, to which every Member is entitled, contains an account of the principal Improvements or Inventions rewarded each year; but, independent of these, there are many interesting Models in the Society's Repository, of which no description has yet been published.

It may be necessary to remark, that no Patent Machines are admitted to a place

# PREFACE.

place in their Repository: it is one of the conditions on which the gifts of the Society are conferred, that the inventor accepts the reward and honourable mention of the Society, in full compensation for a patent right: the inventor has, however, full liberty to make and vend his inventions; and it is natural to suppose, that the applications of the Public for such articles will be made to him, in preference to others; and that the sanction of the Society will bring his merits forward to the world, in a manner likely to procure him much future benefit.

Several decisions lately made in the Courts of Justice, show upon what futile grounds many of the Patents stand which have been granted, and that, instead of producing any profit to the Patentee, they have involved him in great expense and trouble; whereas the rewards of this Society are granted free of every expense, and the inventor's

name

name is recorded and handed down to posterity.

To add their tribute of especial regret and veneration to the public voice, the Society have adorned the present Volume with a Portrait of his Grace the late Francis Duke of Bedford, drawn and engraved, (with the permission of his illustrious successor), by Mr. Evans, from a Bust executed by Mr. Nollekens. His Grace was elected a member of this Society in the year 1797.

The name of this lamented Nobleman, so lately lost to the world, will excite those recollections of his character, talents, and pursuits, which the language of panegyric would but ill express; the value of his efforts, and their influence upon the present state of society, will live in the pages of the historian. It is for us, while the memory of his well-spent life is fresh, and ere, like most human events, it is softened into the general mass by the shades of distance,

to

to endeavour to perpetuate its influence, by holding forth the bright example for the imitation as well as the admiration of others.

Under the List of Premiums offered by the Society for the present Session, will be found several modifications of the former premiums, and introduction of others. . Amongst those which are new, may be noticed the *Cultivation of Buck Wheat — Raising Grass Seeds — Raising Water for the Irrigation of Land—Culture of Hemp in certain parts of Scotland—Refining Copper from the Ore—Mineralogical Maps of England, Wales, Ireland, and Scotland—Line Engravings of Landscapes—Modelling in Clay or Plaster—Ornamental Drawings for Architectural Designs—Perspective Drawings of Machines—Discovery of Statuary Marble—Manufacturing Transparent Paper—Preparing British Mill-stones — Preventing Accidents from Horses falling with Two-wheeled Carriages—and Improvement of Turnpike Roads.*

The

. The Premiums offered for the Cultivation of Hemp in Canada, have been modified, on account of much interesting information received from different parts of Canada on the subject. From experiments made on some samples received from thence, it appears the quality is excellent for the purposes of the Navy; that the culture of it in that country is thought to be an object deserving attention by the government of this Empire; that the premiums offered by the Society have excited a spirit of noble emulation amongst the inhabitants of Canada; and that there is good reason to expect the time is approaching, when this Kingdom will be rendered independent of the Northern Powers for so essential an article, of which the average of the last seven years importation has been above thirty thousand tons per annum.

· The plan of curtailing the long Certificates, which occupied a considerable

able part of the former Volumes, has been attended to in the present; and the articles offered to the Public will be found interesting and useful. A few explanatory. remarks, on the several subjects in the order they occur, may probably not be unimportant.

Under the class of Agriculture, the Gold Medal of the Society was presented to John Hunter, Esq. of Gubbins, in Hertfordshire; a gentleman considerably advanced in years, and who had devoted much of his time to improvements in Agriculture; actuated by public spirit, he had lately made a plantation of forty thousand Oaks, using at the same time this memorable expression, " I have long " employed myself in such agricultural " pursuits as have yielded to me some " advantages; I will now bequeath a le- " gacy, which will be a benefit to my " country." It is with concern we notice the subsequent decease of this worthy character, after he had been highly gratified

gratified with the attention paid by the Society to his merit.

The observations of the Rev. Richard Yates, F. A. S. on the culture and growth of Oaks, convey information of great importance on the subject ; and it is hoped will be considered with much attention.

The extensive plantations of Larch Trees, by John Christian Curwen, Esq. M. P. deserve public approbation ; the quick growth of the Larch, and durability of the timber, when in use, entitle it to the particular attention of all persons concerned in plantations. Mr. Curwen has extended the views of the Society, by additional experiments on fattening Cattle with potatoes ; and it is hoped that this object will be further pursued.

Henry Vernon, Esq. of Hilton Park, continues, as will be seen from his Paper on Silver Firs, to extend his beautiful plantations.

The

- The communications from Mr. F. C. Cherry, of Stoke d'Aubernon, and Mr. Seth Bull, of Ely, give much satisfactory information, on the planting and growth of Osiers. The advantages derived from them by the planters, the great consumption of them by the basket-makers, and employment afforded by them to the industrious poor, make them a desirable object of a more extended encouragement and patronage.

The utility of Elm-timber has been long experienced; and it affords a pleasing reflexion to observe that Charles Gibson, Esq. of Quermore Park, has formed an extensive plantation, on such a plan as to intermix the beauties of foliage with valuable timber-trees.

It having been too frequently observed, by the Committee of Agriculture, that the management of Fallows, upon the careless principle of mere uncultivation, prevailed too generally throughout the kingdom, they have endeavoured,

in

in their premiums, to correct so perni-
cious a system, by preventing the growth
of weeds, and using what are usually
termed meliorating crops; the production of a crop of beans, previous to the
sowing of wheat, and during that time
in which land is frequently allowed to
lie idle, shows, in a strong point of view,
from the communication of Mr. Robert
Brown, of Markle, the utility of the
measure, and the necessity of its being.
more generally attended to.

Of the great assiduity of Thomas Skip
Dyot Bucknall, Esq. frequent honourable mention has been made in many
preceding Volumes of the Society's Transactions; his curious detail of the Hampton Court Vine, and his communication
on the nature of the varieties of engrafted
Fruit-trees, in the present Volume, will be
found to contain very important information to Orchardists, and explain many
points which have been heretofore very
imperfectly understood, relative to the

loss

loss of various species of fruits, and will be the means of furnishing orchards with proper kinds for regular production.

Another valuable Paper on the management of Fruit-trees is inserted from William Fairman, Esq.: it is on the subject of engrafting, and entitled, " Extreme Branch Grafting," to distinguish it from that in common use. By Mr. Fairman's method, trees which have been in a vitiated or barren state, have been rendered productive: new grafts having been introduced at the extremity of the branches, the beauty and size of the trees have been preserved; the new grafts have not only become luxuriant, and produced large crops of fruit, but energy and vigour have been by them communicated to the parent stock, and indicated by healthy shoots and branches from every part of the tree.

The

The very great attention paid by Mr. Johnes, of Hafod, to every branch of agricultural improvement, demands particular notice; and have well entitled him to the honorary rewards of the Society. To surmount the difficulty of local prejudice, is almost an Herculean task: we have even been told, that nature, in certain situations, is ungrateful, and that we may court her favours in vain; but Mr. Johnes has shewn the fallacy of this reasoning.

In the Preface to our last Volume, we gave a short sketch of the beautiful scenery created by him at Hafod, and noticed the improvements then taking place in his dairy; he has lately been occupied in collecting together the different breeds of Milch-cows, and ascertaining their comparative merits. He has imported above forty cows from Holland. He has refuted the erroneous notion, that varieties of Cheese could not

be

be produced on the same land. His dairy furnishes him with the kinds so nearly resembling Parmesan, Stilton, Gloucester, Lancashire, Cheshire, &c. and so excellent in quality, as not to be distinguished either in form or taste from those they are intended to imitate.

He has cultivated, upon an extensive scale, wheat, barley, rye, potatoes, and yams; and his crops, have been equal to those of the Southern counties of England. When we consider his exertions, we reflect with pleasure what may be done by individuals for the general service of mankind.

Before our observations are closed under the class of Agriculture, the great additional value made by Mr. Beech in his land, by plantations and drainings, should not pass unnoticed.

Mr. Spencer Cochrane's communication on the culture of wheat sown in the spring, is a further confirmation to
a Paper

a Paper in the last Volume, by
Mr. Brown, of Markle, on this subject;
but though it appears that good wheat
may be produced in the same year from
any kind hitherto tried, it may, nevertheless, be important to ascertain what
particular species of wheat is most early
in its produce, and best adapted for
sowing in the spring.

Under the class of Chemistry will
be found an account by Mr. Thomas
Willis, an ingenious chemist, of his application of the bulbs of the *Hyacinthus
non scriptus*, as a substitute in many
cases for Gum Arabic or Senegal. When
it is considered that these gums have
been sold for many years on an average of 9l. per cwt. it is probable this
substitute will be a valuable acquisition
to the Calico-printers, as the quantity
of gum imported in 1801 was upwards
of two millions of pounds.

The edulcoration of Fish-oil has been
for a long time thought of consequence

to

to this Kingdom; and the establishment of peace renders every object, which can give encouragement to our sailors at this crisis, particularly desirable. In such a view, the Whale Fisheries of this United Empire, and every improvement of the oil when produced, so as to make it answer the purposes of the other foreign oils, is important; the quantity of foreign olive oil imported into Great Britain in the year 1801, being above 1180 tons in weight. Though forty-two years have elapsed since the late Mr. Dossie's paper on the edulcoration of Fish-oil was rewarded by the Society, yet it will be found to contain much information still useful on the subject, and to be equal to other more modern modes for producing similar effects; it will certainly show that the subject was better understood at the time it was written than has been lately supposed.

b It

It is to be observed, that since the establishment of the Royal Academy, the bounties of this Society, in the class of Polite Arts, are chiefly directed to young artists of two descriptions, viz. to those of fortune, whose taste may lead them to become patrons of the Polite Arts, or as a stimulus to others who are likely to become professional artists.

The rewards, therefore, for encouraging rising genius bestowed by the Society under this class, are not usually detailed in the body of the Volume, but may be found in page 386.

The improvements of Great Britain in her Manufactures within a few years, almost surpass belief; and the art of weaving by machinery alone, in a very extensive manner, is likely to be generally adopted, and to render Europe dependent upon this united Empire for manufactures. Every individual manufacturer seems anxious to excel in im-

improve-provements; and the Loom invented by Mr. Clulow, and noticed in this Volume, not only possesses the advantage of Weaving Sacks and similar articles without seams, but its construction is such as to show the means of giving firmness and stability to looms and fabrics of every description.

Under the class of Mechanicks, a variety of articles rewarded by the Society, will be here noted in the order they are printed in the Volume.

The Gun-lock, invented by Mr. Webb, is well calculated to prevent the accidents which frequently happen from the eagerness or carelessness of sportsmen.

In the hurry of passing through a hedge, a twig catching the trigger, often fires a common fowling-piece unintentionally; or a similar gun, left carelessly loaded, is taken up and fired without consideration. In the first instance, the same cause is not likely to produce a similar effect in Mr. Webb's Lock, and

in the second, the compound motion
of the finger and thumb required to discharge the piece, though familiar to the
sportsman, will not be found out so
easily by a novice in the art.

Mr. Knight's improvement for separating stumps of trees, and useless
blocks of wood, by means of gunpowder, will furnish the farmer with many a
comfortable fire, instead of suffering
such logs to remain a nuisance to the
land, as has been frequently the case.

The dreadful ravages occasioned by
the dry-rot in timber, are too well known
to require any comment; and the expense it occasions is enormous.

The Iron Lever invented by Mr. Woart,
and which has been found to answer well
in practice, is likely to check its mischief, and give security to the building
at a very moderate charge. Its simplicity and effect do great credit to this
ingenious workman.

The

The existence of Mill-stone Quarries in Great Britain, to answer the purpose of French Burr-stone for grinding corn, and to preclude the necessity of procuring annually 27,000 Burr-stones from France, has, during the last three years. been so clearly ascertained in Carnarvonshire, Montgomeryshire and Scotland, as to render an offer of further premiums . in that line unnecessary. Mr. James Brownhill, of Alloa, near Stirling, in Scotland, has lately received from the Society a reward of One Hundred Pounds for his discovery of a Quarry of Stone at Abbey Craig, the mill-stones from which, by numerous certificates, are reported to have produced more flour, of a better quality, and in less time, than · has been produced by French burrs from an equal quantity of the same wheat.

In the month of January last, a reward was recommended by a Committee of the Society to Mr. Henry Greathead
for

for his Life-Boat, and their Gold Medal and Fifty Guineas, were adjudged to him immediately afterwards. The subsequent rewards granted to him from Government, also from the Trinity-House, and Merchants at Lloyd's, confirm the opinion of the Society, on the merits of this invention.

The Society have lately voted their Gold Medal to William Hall Timbrel, Esq. for his improvement of Herniary Trusses, and his new-invented Calico Cushion.

In the department of Colonies and Trade, many interesting communications have been made to the Society, during their last Session.

The culture of the Bread-Fruit Tree appears to be generally extended throughout the West-India islands, and likely to be very beneficial. The accounts received from the Honourable Joseph Robley, Governor of Tobago, show an astonishing increase in his plantation,

and

and that his efforts in that line are suc
cessfully continued.

From communications received by
the Society from other correspondents,
it appears, that a dry nourishing food,
resembling Tapioca in appearance and
quality, may be prepared from it. Some
cakes, well flavoured, made from such
flour, have been sent to the Society; and
specimens of the Bread-Fruit, preserved
in various ways, are now in their possession.

The indefatigable exertions of Dr. Anderson, of the Botanical Garden at
St. Vincent, have been rewarded by the
Gold Medal of the Society: the good effects of that establishment have not only
been proved there, but have been extended by him to most of the neighbouring islands, and likewise to Great Britain.

The garden has lately been enriched
by many valuable exotics, procured by
him from Trinidad and Cayenne, of
which

which he has furnished a list to the Society, amongst which, two of the true. Nutmeg Trees are very important acquisitions.

It is understood, that the boundaries of the Garden will soon be enlarged by order of Government, and there is no doubt that proportionable advantages will arise from Dr. Anderson's well-known activity.

The Society desire it to be clearly understood, that, as a body, they are not responsible for any opinion or representation of facts, contained in the following Papers : they have allowed the communications to pass in the language and manner of the several persons concerned, without attempting to make embellishments in the style, which might prejudice the subject matter.

Sundry Presents from different Public Bodies and Individuals, have been received by the Society, the particulars of which are inserted in page 393; they

take

take the present opportunity of returning their thanks for these favours, and of
expressing hopes of their further continuance.

It will be found, that the Rewards of
the Society are not confined to England
and Wales. In the last Session, a claim
of considerable value was conferred on
a person in Scotland. The merits of
some claims from Ireland, remain yet
under consideration. The Dublin Society have favoured this Society with an
account of a reward lately given by
them to Mr. Alexander Johnstone, for
an improvement in the construction of
Malt-Kilns. The mutual efforts of both
Bodies will, doubtless, contribute much
to the general advantage of the United
Empire.

During the last Session, the Society
lost, by death, that very faithful officer,
Mr. George Cockings, their Register,
whose honest zeal in the discharge of his
duty, during a service of thirty years,
entitles his memory to this record of
esteem.

The present Session commenced in October last, and will continue till the month of June. Communications upon subjects relative to Arts, Manufactures, and Commerce, will be immediately laid before the Society, on being addressed to their Secretary, Mr. Charles Taylor, at the Society's House in the Adelphi, London; and ample honorary and pecuniary rewards will be gratuitously conferred, for any inventions or improvements which have merit.

The Society will also esteem any other hints or observations, which may tend to promote the objects of their institution.

The great encouragement which this Society has experienced, for a term of nearly fifty years, and the many worthy characters who continue to be elected Members of it, promise to further, in a high degree, the laudable endeavours of this Establishment, and to insure it, for a long series of years, an honourable distinction amongst the most respectable Societies in Europe.

# CONTENTS.

|  | Page |
|---|---|
| Preface | |
| Premiums offered in 1802 | 1 |
| Papers in Agriculture | 75 |
| Papers in Chemistry | 199 |
| Papers in Mechanicks | 241 |
| Papers in Manufactures | 343 |
| Paper in Colonies and Trade | 355 |
| Rewards bestowed | 381 |
| Presents received | 393 |
| Catalogue of Models and Machines | 400 |
| List of Officers | 403 |
| List of Members | 407 |
| Index | |

OFFERED BY THE

# SOCIETY

INSTITUTED AT LONDON,

FOR THE ENCOURAGEMENT OF

## ARTS, MANUFACTURES,

AND

## COMMERCE,

FOR

THE YEAR M.DCCCII.

# TO THE PUBLIC.

———

JOHN STREET, ADELPHI,
LONDON.

THE chief objects of the SOCIETY are to promote the ARTS, MANUFACTURES, and COMMERCE of this Kingdom, by giving Rewards for all such useful Inventions, Discoveries, and Improvements, (though not mentioned in this Book) as tend to that purpose; and, in pursuance of this plan, the SOCIETY have already expended near FIFTY THOUSAND POUNDS, advanced by voluntary Subscriptions of their Members, and Legacies bequeathed.

The manner in which this money has been distributed may be seen by applying to the Secretary or other Officers of the SOCIETY, at their house in the *Adelphi*. The Register of the Premiums and Bounties they have given will shew the very great advantages which the Public have derived from this Institution.

The

The Meetings of the SOCIETY are held every *Wednesday*, at seven o'clock in the evening, from the fourth *Wednesday* in *October* to the first *Wednesday* in *June*. The several Committees meet on other evenings in the week during the session; and in general cases in the following manner:

Committees of Correspondence and Agriculture, on *Monday*.

Colonies and Trade, and Manufactures, on *Tuesday*.

Mechanicks, on *Thursday*.

Polite Arts, on *Friday*.

Chemistry, on *Saturday*.

Accompts, in the *first Week* of every Month.

In order still farther to promote the laudable views of this SOCIETY, it may be necessary to explain the mode by which its Members continue to be elected.

Each Member has the privilege, at any weekly Meeting of the SOCIETY, of proposing any person who is desirous to become a Member, provided such proposal is signed by three Members of the SOCIETY.

Peers

Peers of the Realm or Lords of Parliament are, on their being proposed, immediately balloted for; and the name, with the addition and place of abode, of every other person proposing to become a Member, is to be delivered to the Secretary, who is to read the same, and properly insert the name in a List, which is to be hung up in the SOCIETY's room until the next Meeting; at which time such person shall be balloted for; and, if two thirds of the Members, then voting, ballot in his favour, he shall be deemed a *perpetual Member*, upon payment of *Twenty Guineas* at one payment; or a *subscribing Member*, upon payment of any sum not less than *Two Guineas* annually.

Every Member is entitled to vote and be concerned in all the transactions of the SOCIETY, and to attend and vote at the several Committees. He has also the privilege of recommending two persons as Auditors, at the weekly Meeting of the SOCIETY; and, by addressing a note to the Housekeeper, of introducing his friends to examine the various Models, Machines, and Productions, in different branches of Arts, Manufactures, and Commerce, for which Rewards have been bestowed; and to inspect the magnificent series of moral and historical Paintings so happily contrived and

B 3                    completed

completed by JAMES BARRY, Esq. which, with some
excellent Busts and Statues, decorate the Great Room.
He has likewise the use of a valuable Library; and
is entitled to the annual Volume of the SOCIETY's
Transactions.

The time appointed for admission to the Paintings
or Models, is from ten to two o'clock, *Sundays* and
*Wednesdays* excepted.

Premiums

# Premiums in Agriculture.

Class 1. FOREST-TREES. To the person who shall have inclosed and planted, or set, the greatest number of acres (not less than ten) of land that is incapable of being ploughed, such as the borders of rivers, the sides of precipices, and any land that has too many rocks, or that is not calculated to repay the expence of tillage, owing to the stiffness or poverty of the soil, the surface being too hilly, mountainous, or otherwise unfit for tillage, with the best sorts of Forest-Trees, namely, Oak, Spanish chesnuts, Ash, Elm, Beech, Alder, Willow, Larch, Spruce and Silver Fir, with or without screens of Scotch Fir, adapted to the soil, and intended for timber trees, between the 1st of October, 1801, and the 1st of April, 1802, the GOLD MEDAL.

2. For the second greatest quantity of land, not less than seven acres, the SILVER MEDAL, or TWENTY GUINEAS.

3. For the third greatest quantity of land, not less than five acres, the SILVER MEDAL.

A particular ACCOUNT of the methods used in making and managing the plantations, the nature of the soil, the probable number of each sort of plants, together with

B 4           proper

proper CERTIFICATES that they were in a healthy and thriving state two years at least after making the plantation, to be delivered to the Society on or before the first Tuesday in November, 1805.

4, 5, 6. The same premiums are extended one year farther.

CERTIFICATES to be produced on or before the first Tuesday in November, 1806.

7. ASCERTAINING THE BEST METHOD OF RAISING OAKS. To the person who shall ascertain in the best manner, by actual experiments, the comparative merits of the different modes of raising Oaks for timber, either from acorns set on land of the foregoing description properly dug or tilled, from acorns set by the spade or dibble, without digging or tillage, either on a smooth surface, or among bushes, fern, or other cover; or from young plants previously raised in nurseries, and transplanted; regard being had to the expence, growth, and other respective advantages of the several methods; the GOLD MEDAL.

The ACCOUNTS, and proper CERTIFICATES that not less than one acre has been cultivated in each mode, to be produced to the Society on or before the first Tuesday in November, 1802.

8. The same premium is extended one year farther.

The ACCOUNTS and CERTIFICATES to be produced on or before the first Tuesday in November, 1803.

9. OSIERS.

9. OSIERS. To the person who shall have planted, between the 1st of October, 1801, and the 1st of May, 1802, the greatest quantity of land, not less than five acres, with those kinds of Willows, commonly known by the names of Osier, Spaniard, New-kind, or French, fit for the purpose of basket-makers, not fewer than twelve thousand plants on each acre; the GOLD MEDAL, or THIRTY GUINEAS.

10. For the second greatest quantity of land, not less than three acres, the SILVER MEDAL, or TEN GUINEAS.

CERTIFICATES of the planting, and that the plants were in a thriving state five months at least after the planting, to be produced to the Society on or before the last Tuesday in November, 1802.

11. The same premiums are extended one year farther.

CERTIFICATES to be produced on or before the last Tuesday in November, 1803.

*₊* *The Candidates for planting all kinds of trees are to produce certificates that the respective plantations are properly fenced and secured, and particularly to state the condition of the plants at the time of signing such certificates. Any information which the Candidates for the foregoing premiums may choose to communicate, relative to the methods made use of in forming the plantations, or promoting the growth of the several trees, or any other observations that may have occurred on the subject, will be thankfully received.*

12. SECURING

12.  SECURING PLANTATIONS OF TIMBER-TREES, AND HEDGE-ROWS.  To the person who shall give to the Society the most satisfactory account, founded on experience, of the most effectual and least expensive method of securing young plantations of Timber-trees, and Hedge-rows, from hares and rabbits, as well as sheep and larger cattle, which at the same time shall be least subject to the depredations of wood-stealers; the SILVER MEDAL, or TWENTY GUINEAS.

The ACCOUNTS, and CERTIFICATES of the efficacy of the methods, to be produced to the Society on or before the first Tuesday in November, 1802.

13.  The same premium is extended one year farther.

The ACCOUNTS and CERTIFICATES to be produced on or before the first Tuesday in November, 1803.

14.  PREVENTING THE BLIGHT, OR RAVAGES OF INSECTS, ON FRUIT-TREES AND CULINARY PLANTS.  To the person who shall discover to the Society the most effectual method of preventing the Blight, or ravages of Insects, on Fruit-trees and Culinary Plants, superior to any hitherto known or practised, and verified by actual and comparative experiments; the GOLD MEDAL, or THIRTY GUINEAS.

The ACCOUNTS, with proper CERTIFICATES, to be delivered to the Society on or before the second Tuesday in November, 1802.

15.  The same premium is extended one year farther.

The ACCOUNTS and CERTIFICATES to be delivered on or before the second Tuesday in November, 1803.

16.  REMOVING

16. REMOVING THE ILL EFFECTS OF BLIGHTS, OR INSECTS. To the person who shall discover to the Society the most effectual method of removing the ill effects of Blights, or Insects, on Fruit-trees and Culinary Plants, superior to any hitherto known and practised, and verified by actual and comparative experiments; the GOLD MEDAL, or THIRTY GUINEAS.

The ACCOUNTS and CERTIFICATES to be delivered to the Society on or before the first Tuesday in February, 1803.

17. COMPARATIVE TILLAGE. For the most satisfactory set of experiments, made on not less than eight acres of land, four of which to be trench-ploughed*, and four to be ploughed in the usual manner, in order to ascertain in what cases it may be adviseable to shorten the operations of Tillage, by adopting one trench-ploughing, for the purpose of burying the weeds, instead of the method, now in common use, of ploughing and harrowing the land three or four times, and raking the weeds together, and burning them; the GOLD MEDAL, or FORTY GUINEAS.

It is required that every operation and expense attending each mode of culture be fully and accurately described, and that proper CERTIFICATES of the nature and condition of the land on which the experiments are made, together with a circumstantial account of the appearance of the subsequent crops during their growth; and also of

* It is a common practice among gardeners, when they have a piece of very foul land, to dig it two spits, or about eighteen inches deep, shovelling the weeds to the bottom. This they call trenching.

the

the quantity and weight of the corn and straw under each mode of culture, or, in case of a green crop, the weight of an average sixteen perches, be produced to the Society on or before the first Tuesday in February, 1803.

18. COMPARATIVE CULTURE OF WHEAT, BROAD-CAST, DRILLED, AND DIBBLED. For the best set of experiments made on not less than twelve acres, four of which to be sown broad-cast, four drilled, and four dibbled, the two latter in equidistant rows, in order fully to ascertain which is the most advantageous mode of cultivating Wheat; the GOLD MEDAL, or FORTY GUINEAS.

It is required that every operation and expense of each mode of culture be fully described; and that proper CERTIFICATES of the nature and condition of the land on which the experiments are made, together with an ACCOUNT of the produce of the corn, the weight per bushel, and also of the straw, be produced to the Society on or before the first Tuesday in February, 1803.

19. SPRING WHEAT. To the person who, between the 10th of January and the 10th of April, 1802, shall cultivate the greatest quantity of Wheat, not less than ten acres; the SILVER MEDAL, or TWENTY GUINEAS.

It is required that the time of sowing and reaping be noticed; also a particular ACCOUNT of the species, cultivation, and expense attending it, with proper CERTIFICATES of the nature and condition of the land on which the experiments were made, and the name of the crop, if any, which the same land bore the preceding year;
together

together with an ACCOUNT of the produce, the weight per Winchester bushel; and a Sample, not less than a quart; be produced to the Society on or before the second Tuesday in February, 1803.

It is supposed that sowing Wheat early in the spring will not only allow more time to till the land, but less for the growth of weeds; thus rendering the wheat as clean as a barley crop, and exhausting the soil much less than autumnal sowing. It may be seen in the 19th Volume, that the Wheat usually sown in autumn may be put into the ground, with great success, so late as February or March, thus giving time to clear the ground from turnips, or to avoid a bad season.

20. BEANS AND WHEAT. To the person who shall have dibbled or drilled, between the 1st of December, 1801, and the 1st of April, 1802, the greatest quantity of land, not less than ten acres, with Beans, in equidistant rows, and hoed the intervals twice or oftener, and shall have sown the same land with Wheat in the autumn of the year 1802; the SILVER MEDAL or TWENTY GUINEAS.

It is required that an account of the sort and quantity of Beans, the time of dibbling or drilling, and of reaping or mowing them, the produce per acre thrashed, the expense of dibbling or drilling, hand or horse hoeing, the distance of the rows, and the quality of the soil, together with CERTIFICATES of the number of acres, and that the land was afterwards actually sown with Wheat, be produced on or before the second Tuesday in March, 1803.

21. BEANS. To the person who, in the year 1801, shall discover and cultivate, either by the drill or dibbling method,

method, on not less than five acres, a species of Horse-Beans or Tick-Beans, that will ripen their seeds before the 21st of August; the SILVER MEDAL or TWENTY GUINEAS.

It is required that a particular ACCOUNT of the Bean, the cultivation, and the expense attending it, with proper CERTIFICATES of the nature and condition of the land on which the experiments are made; together with an Account of the produce, the weight per Winchester bushel, and a sample, of not less than a quart; be produced to the Society on or before the first Tuesday in December, 1802.

It is apprehended that if a Bean should be brought into cultivation with the habits of the hotspur, or other early peas, that it would, in a great measure, escape the danger arising from the collier-insect, or other insects, and allow more time for the farmers to till the land for the subsequent crop of Wheat.

The ACCOUNTS and CERTIFICATES to be delivered on or before the first Tuesday in December, 1802.

22. The same premium is extended one year farther.

The ACCOUNTS and CERTIFICATES to be delivered on, or before the first Tuesday in December, 1803.

23. COMPARATIVE CULTURE OF TURNIPS. For the best set of experiments, made on not less than eight acres of land, four of which to be sown broad-cast, and four drilled, to ascertain whether it is most advantageous to cultivate Turnips by sowing them broad-cast and hand-hoeing them, or by drilling them in equidistant rows, and hand or horse hoeing the intervals; the SILVER MEDAL, or TWENTY GUINEAS.

It is required that every operation and expense of each mode of culture be fully described, and that proper certificates of the nature and condition of the land on which the experiments were made, together with the weight of the Turnips grown, on a fair average sixteen perches of land, under each mode of culture, be produced to the Society on or before the first Tuesday in March, 1803.

The object whith the Society have in view in offering this premium, is experimentally to ascertain the most advantageous method of growing Turnips. To do this in a satisfactory manner, both the drilled and broad-cast crops should have the advantage of the most perfect cultivation; consequently the drilled crops should have the intervals between the rows worked by the horse or hand hoe, or by both these implements; and the rows should be either weeded or hand-hoed, or both weeded and hand-hoed. The broad-cast crop should have every advantage which weeding and hand-hoeing can give it, consistently with leaving the soil a flat surface.

24. The same premium is extended one year farther.

CERTIFICATES to be produced on or before the first Tuesday in March, 1804.

25. PARSNIPS. To the person who, in the year 1802, shall cultivate the greatest quantity of land, not less than five acres, with Parsnips, for the sole purpose of feeding cattle or sheep; the GOLD MEDAL, or THIRTY GUINEAS.

CERTIFICATES of the quantity of land so cultivated, with a particular account of the nature of the soil and weight of the produce on sixteen perches, and also of the

the condition of the cattle or sheep fed with the Parsnips, and the advantages resulting from the practice, to be produced to the Society on or before the second day in November, 1803.

26. BUCK WHEAT. To the person who shall cultivate the greatest quantity of land with Buck Wheat, not less than thirty acres; the GOLD MEDAL.

It is required that the time of sowing and reaping be noticed; also a particular account of the species, cultivation, and expense attending it, the manner of reaping it, thrashing it, and housing the grain; with proper CERTIFICATES of the nature and condition of the land on which the experiments were made, and the name of the crop, if any, which the same land bore the preceding year; together with an ACCOUNT of the produce, and a sample of the seed, not less than a quart; be produced to the Society on or before the second Tuesday in January, 1803.

27. For the next greatest quantity, not less than fifteen acres, on similar conditions; the SILVER MEDAL.

Information respecting its application to the feeding of cattle, hogs, and poultry, and other of its uses, is also desired. It is known to be particularly serviceable. in furnishing honey to bees.

28. RAISING GRASS SEEDS. To the person who shall raise the greatest quantity of each or any of the following named Grass Seeds, viz. — Meadow Fox-tail (Alopecurus Pratensis), Sweet-scented Vernal Grass (Anthoxanthum Odoratum), Timothy Grass, Meadow Fescue Grass, Smooth-stalked Meadow Grass (Poa Pratensis), Rough-stalked Meadow Grass (Poa Trivialis); the SILVER MEDAL, or TEN GUINEAS.                            It

- It is required that certificates from persons who have viewed them in a proper state, to identify that they are one or other of the seeds above mentioned, indicating clearly the particular species, and noticing the quantity produced of such seeds, free from weeds or mixture of other grasses, together with proper Samples of the seeds, be produced to the Society on or before the first day of February, 1803.

29. The same premium is extended one year farther.

CERTIFICATES to be produced on or before the first day of February, 1804.

30. ROTATION OF CROPS. To the person who shall, between the 10th of August, 1801, and the 10th of September, 1803, cultivate the greatest quantity of Land, not less than forty acres, in the following rotation, viz.—1st, Winter-Tares; 2d, Turnips; and 3d, Wheat; and apply the two former crops, in the best and most farmer-like manner, to the rearing, supporting, and fattening horses, cattle, sheep, or hogs, on the land which produced the crops; the GOLD MEDAL, or ONE HUNDRED GUINEAS.

31. For the next in quantity or merit, on not less than thirty acres; the SILVER MEDAL, or FIFTY GUINEAS.

32. For the next in quantity or merit, on not less than twenty acres; the SILVER MEDAL.

It is required that every operation and expense be fully described; and that satisfactory certificates of the nature and condition of the soil on which the crops have grown,

C together

together with an account of their appearance, the number of horses and cattle, sheep or hogs, fed by the two green crops, and, as near as possible, the improved value of the live stock by the consumption of those crops, and also the quantity of wheat per acre, and its weight per bushel, be produced to the Society on or before the first day of November, 1804.

It is presumed that very great advantages will arise to such agriculturists as shall adopt this rotation of crops on a dry soil. They will be enabled, with the addition of a few acres of turnip-rooted cabbage for spring food, to keep such large flocks of sheep and herds of neat cattle as may secure a sufficient quantity of manure to fertilize their land in the highest degree, and in every situation. It is farther conceived that Wheats which will bear sowing in the spring will be particularly suitable for this premium.

33.   The same premium is extended one year farther.

CERTIFICATES to be delivered on or before the first day of November, 1805.

34.   PRESERVING TURNIPS.   To the person who shall discover to the Society the best and cheapest method of preserving Turnips perfectly sound, and in every respect fit for the purpose of supporting and fattening sheep and neat cattle, during the months of February, March, and April; the GOLD MEDAL, or THIRTY GUINEAS.

It is required that a full and accurate account of the method employed, and the expense attending the process, together with certificates that the produce of four acres at the least have been preserved according to the method described,

scribed, and applied to feeding of sheep and neat cattle; that the whole were drawn out of the ground before the first day of February, in order to clear the greater part of it previous to its being prepared for corn, and to save the soil from being exhausted by the turnips; and also of the weight of an average sixteen perches of the crop; be produced to the Society on or before the first Tuesday in November, 1803.

*N. B.* It is recommended to those who may be induced to try the necessary experiments for obtaining this and the following four premiums, to consider the method employed for the preservation of Potatoes in ridges (which the growers call pies), and also the propriety of adopting a similar method in cases where they are previously frozen. It is supposed that, in the latter instance, the addition of ice or snow, and the construction of the ridges upon a large scale, may be sufficient to preserve the freezing temperature till the vegetables are wanted for the use of cattle or sheep, at which time they may be thawed by immersion in cold water, and the *rot* which a sudden thaw produces, may be prevented.

35. For the next in quantity and merit, on not less than two acres, the SILVER MEDAL, or FIFTEEN GUINEAS.

36. PRESERVING CABBAGES. To the person who shall discover to the Society the best and cheapest method of preserving drum-headed Cabbages perfectly sound, and in every respect fit for the purpose of supporting and fattening sheep and neat cattle, during the months of February, March, and April; the GOLD MEDAL, or THIRTY GUINEAS.

C 2

37. For

37. For the next in quantity and merit, on not less than two acres, the SILVER MEDAL, or FIFTEEN GUINEAS.

Conditions the same as for preserving Turnips, Class 34. And the ACCOUNTS to be produced on or before the first Tuesday in November, 1803.

38. PRESERVING CARROTS, PARSNIPS, OR BEETS. To the person who shall discover to the Society the best and cheapest method of preserving Carrots, Parsnips, or Beets, perfectly sound, and in every respect fit for the purpose of supporting horses, and fattening sheep and neat cattle, during the months of February, March, and April; the SILVER MEDAL, or FIFTEEN GUINEAS.

Conditions the same as for preserving Turnips, Class 34. And the ACCOUNTS to be delivered in, on or before the first Tuesday in November, 1803.

39. PRESERVING POTATOES. To the person who shall discover to the Society the best and cheapest method of preserving Potatoes, two or more years, perfectly sound, without vegetating, and in every other respect fit for the purpose of sets and the use of the table, and, consequently, of supporting and fattening cattle; the SILVER MEDAL, or TWENTY GUINEAS.

It is required that a full and accurate ACCOUNT of the method employed, and the expense attending the process, with CERTIFICATES that one hundred bushels at the least have been preserved according to the method described, and that one or more bushels of the same Potatoes have been set, and produced a crop without any apparent dimi-

nution

nution of their vegetative power; and also that they have been used at table, with entire satisfaction to the person who eat of them, together with a sample of one bushel, be sent to the Society on or before the first Tuesday in November, 1804.

40. MAKING MEADOW-HAY IN WET WEA-THER. To the person who shall discover to the Society the best and cheapest method, superior to any hitherto practised, of making Meadow-Hay in Wet Weather; the GOLD MEDAL, or THIRTY GUINEAS.

A full ACCOUNT of the method employed, and of the expense attending the process, with not less than fifty-six pounds of the hay, and CERTIFICATES that at least the produce of six acres of land has been made according to the method described, and that the whole is of equal qua-, lity with the samples, to be produced on or before the first Tuesday in January, 1803.

41. HARVESTING CORN IN WET WEATHER. To the person who shall discover to the Society the best and cheapest method, superior to any hitherto practised, of harvesting Corn in Wet Weather; the GOLD MEDAL, or THIRTY GUINEAS.

A full ACCOUNT of the method employed, and of the expense attending the process, with not less than two sheaves of the corn, and CERTIFICATES that at least the produce of ten acres has been harvested according to the method described, and that the whole is of equal quality with the samples, to be produced on or before the first Tuesday in January, 1803.

C 3

42.

**42. ASCERTAINING THE COMPONENT PARTS OF ARABLE LAND.** To the person who shall produce to the Society the most satisfactory set of experiments, to ascertain the due proportion of the several component parts of rich Arable Land, in one or more Counties in Great Britain, by an accurate analysis of it; and who having made a like analysis of some poor arable land, shall, by comparing the component parts of each, and thereby ascertaining the deficiencies of the poor soil, improve a quantity of it, not less than one acre, by the addition of such parts as the former experiments shall have discovered to be wanting therein, and therefore probably the cause of its sterility; the GOLD MEDAL, or FORTY GUINEAS.

It is required that the manurings, ploughings, and crops, of the improved land, be the same after the improvement as before; and that a minute ACCOUNT of the produce in each state, of the weather, and of the various influencing circumstances, together with the method made use of in analysing the soils, be produced, with proper CERTIFI-CATES and the chemical results of the analysis, which are to remain the property of the Society, on or before the last Tuesday in November, 1803.

It is expected that a quantity, not less than six pounds, of the rich, of the poor, and of the improved soils, be produced with the certificates.

**43. IMPROVING LAND LYING WASTE.** For the most satisfactory ACCOUNT of the best method of improving any of the following soils, being land lying waste or uncultivated, viz. Clay, Gravel, Sand, Chalk, Peat-earth,

and

and Bog, verified by experiments on not less than fifty acres of land; the GOLD MEDAL, or THIRTY GUINEAS.

44, For the next greatest quantity, not less than thirty acres, the SILVER MEDAL, or TWENTY GUINEAS.

It is required that the land before such improvement be absolutely uncultivated, and in a great measure useless; and that, in its improved state, it be inclosed, cultivated, and divided into closes.

CERTIFICATES of the number of acres, of the quality of the land so improved, with a full ACCOUNT of every operation and expense attending such improvement, the state it is in as to the proportion of grass to arable, and the average value thereof, to be produced on or before the first Tuesday in February, 1803.*

45. MANURES. For the most satisfactory set of experiments, to ascertain the comparative advantages of the following Manures, used as top-dressings on grass or corn land, viz. Soot, Coal-ashes, Wood-ashes, Lime, Gypsum, Night-soil, or any other fit article; the GOLD MEDAL, or the SILVER MEDAL and TWENTY GUINEAS.

It is required that the above experiments be made between two or more of the above-mentioned manures, and that not less than two acres of land be dressed with each manure.

An ACCOUNT of the nature of the soil, quantity and expense of the manure, and crops, with CERTIFICATES, to be produced on or before the last Tuesday in February, 1803,

46. The

46. The same premium is extended one year farther.

The ACCOUNTS and CERTIFICATES to be produced on or before the last Tuesday in February, 1804.

47. GAINING LAND FROM THE SEA. To the person who shall produce to the Society an account of the best method, verified by actual experiment, of gaining Land from the Sea, not less than twenty acres, on the coast of Great Britain or Ireland; the GOLD MEDAL.

CERTIFICATES of the quantity of land, and that the experiments were begun after the 1st of January, 1796, to be produced to the Society on or before the first Tuesday in October, 1802.

48. The same premium is extended one year farther.

CERTIFICATES to be produced on or before the first Tuesday in October, 1803.

49. The same premium is extended one year farther.

CERTIFICATES to be produced on or before the first Tuesday in October, 1804.

50. MACHINE FOR DIBBLING WHEAT. To the person who shall invent a Machine, superior to any hitherto known or in use, to answer the purpose of dibbling Wheat, by which the holes for receiving the grain may be made at equal distances and proper depths; the SILVER MEDAL, or TWENTY GUINEAS.

The MACHINE, with CERTIFICATES that at least three acres have been dibbled by it, to be produced to the Society on or before the second Tuesday in January, 1803.

Simplicity

- Simplicity and cheapness in the construction will be considered as principal parts of its merit.

51. MACHINE FOR REAPING OR MOWING CORN. For inventing a Machine to answer the purpose of mowing or reaping Wheat, Rye, Barley, Oats, or Beans, by which it may be done more expeditiously and cheaper than by any method now practised, provided it does not shed the corn or pulse more than the methods in common practice, and that it lays the straw in such a manner that it may be easily gathered up for binding; the GOLD MEDAL, or THIRTY GUINEAS.

The MACHINE, with CERTIFICATES that at least three acres have been cut by it, to be produced to the Society on or before the second Tuesday in December, 1802.

Simplicity and cheapness in the construction will be considered as principal parts of its merit.

52. THRASHING-MACHINE. To the person who shall invent a Machine by which Corn of all sorts may be thrashed more expeditiously, effectually, and at a less expense, than by any method now in use; the GOLD MEDAL, or THIRTY GUINEAS.

The MACHINE, or a Model, with proper CERTIFICATES that such a machine has been usefully applied, that at least thirty quarters have been thrashed by it, and of the time employed in the operation, to be produced to the Society on or before the last Tuesday in February, 1803.

53. DESTROYING THE GRUB OF THE COCK-CHAFER. To the person who shall discover to the Society

ciety an effectual method, verified by repeated and satisfactory trials, of destroying the Grub of the Cockchafer,
or of preventing or checking the destructive effects which
always attend corn, peas, beans, and turnips, when attacked by those insects; the GOLD MEDAL, or THIRTY
GUINEAS.

The ACCOUNTS, with proper CERTIFICATES, to be
produced on or before the first Tuesday in January, 1803.

54. DESTROYING WORMS. To the person who
shall discover to the Society an effectual method, verified
by repeated and satisfactory trials, of destroying Worms,
or of preventing the destructive effects they occasion on
corn, beans, peas, or other pulse; the GOLD MEDAL, or
THIRTY GUINEAS.

The ACCOUNTS, with proper CERTIFICATES, to be
produced to the Society on or before the first Tuesday in
January, 1803.

55. DESTROYING THE FLY ON HOPS. To
the person who shall discover to the Society an easy and
efficacious method of destroying the Fly on Hops, superior
to any hitherto known or practised, on not less than four
acres of hop-ground; the GOLD MEDAL, or THIRTY
GUINEAS.

ACCOUNTS and CERTIFICATES to be delivered to the
Society on or before the first Tuesday in February, 1803.

56. CURE OF THE ROT IN SHEEP. To the
person who shall discover to the Society the best and most
effectual method of curing the Rot in Sheep, verified by

repeated

repeated and satisfactory experiments; the GOLD MEDAL, or FIFTY GUINEAS.

It is expected that the Candidates furnish accurate Accounts of the symptoms and cure of the disease, together with the imputed cause thereof, and the actual or probable means of prevention, which, with proper CERTIFICATES, must be delivered to the Society on or before the first Tuesday in February, 1803.

57. PREVENTING THE ILL EFFECTS OF FLIES ON SHEEP. To the person who shall discover to the Society the most effectual method of protecting Sheep from being disturbed and injured by Flies; the SILVER MEDAL, or TWENTY GUINEAS.

It is required that the method be ascertained by repeated experiments, and that a CERTIFICATE of its efficacy be delivered to the Society on or before the first Tuesday in December, 1802.

58. PROTECTING SHEEP. To the person who, in the year 1802, shall protect the greatest number of Sheep, not fewer than one hundred, by hovels, sheds, or any other means, and give the most satisfactory account, verified by experiment, of the advantages arising from the practice of protecting Sheep from the inclemency of the weather, by hovels, sheds, or any other means; the SILVER MEDAL, or TWENTY GUINEAS.

A particular Account of the experiments made, with the advantages arising therefrom, together with the expense, and CERTIFICATES of its utility, to be produced to the Society on or before the first Tuesday in March, 1803.

59. The

59. The same premium is extended one year farther.

The ACCOUNTS and CERTIFICATES to be delivered on or before the first Tuesday in March, 1804.

*N. B.* It is required that the Certificates shall specify the length of time the sheep were so protected, and the manner in which they were maintained during that time; together with the general method of managing them.

60. IMPROVING THE CONDITION OF THE LABOURING POOR, BY ERECTING COTTAGES, AND APPORTIONING LAND. To the person who, in the year 1801, shall erect the greatest number of Cottages for the accommodation of the labouring Poor, and apportion not less than two acres of Land to each Cottage; the GOLD MEDAL.

. The ACCOUNTS and CERTIFICATES to be delivered to the Society on or before the first Tuesday in February, 1803.

61. The same premium is extended one year farther.

The ACCOUNTS and CERTIFICATES to be delivered to the Society on or before the first Tuesday in February, 1804.

62. The same premium is extended one year farther.

The ACCOUNTS and CERTIFICATES to be delivered to the Society on or before the first Tuesday in February, 1805.

63. IMPROVING THE CONDITION OF THE LABOURING POOR BY APPORTIONING LAND
                                          TO

TO COTTAGES. To the person who, in the year 1802, shall apportion to the greatest number of Cottages, already built upon his or her estate, any quantity of Land, not less than two acres to each Cottage, for the better accommodation of the respective inhabitants; the GOLD MEDAL.

The ACCOUNTS of the number of Cottages, and of the quantity of Land apportioned to each, to be delivered to the Society, with proper CERTIFICATES, on or before the first Tuesday in February, 1803.

64. The same premium is extended one year farther.

The ACCOUNTS and CERTIFICATES to be delivered on or before the first Tuesday in February, 1804.

65. The same premium is extended one year farther.

The ACCOUNTS and CERTIFICATES to be delivered on or before the first Tuesday in February, 1805.

66. RAISING WATER FOR THE IRRIGATION OF LAND. To the person who shall discover to the Society the cheapest and most effectual method of raising Water in quantities sufficient to be beneficially employed for the purposes of irrigating Land, superior to and cheaper than any other method now in use; the GOLD MEDAL, or THIRTY GUINEAS.

A MODEL, on a scale of one inch to a foot, with CERTIFICATES that a machine at large on the same construction has been used, specifying the quantity of water delivered in gallons per hour, and the height to which it was

raised,

raised, to be produced to the Society on or before the first of March, 1803.

66*.   The same premium is extended one year farther.

CERTIFICATES to be produced on or before the first of March, 1804.

67.   CULTURE OF HEMP IN CERTAIN PARTS OF SCOTLAND.  The Society for the Encouragement of Arts, Manufactures, and Commerce, wishing to encourage the growth of Hemp for the use of the Navy, in certain parts of Scotland, comprehending the whole county of Argyle, that part of Perthshire situated to the north of the river Tay, and west of the Military Road (see Ainslie's Map of Scotland) leading from Logierait to the county of Inverness, and such other parts of Scotland as lie north of Inverness-shire, offers to the person who shall sow with Hemp, in drills at least eighteen inches asunder, the greatest quantity of land in the above-mentioned district, not less than fifty acres statute measure, in the year 1802, and shall at the proper season cause to be plucked the summer hemp (or male hemp bearing no seed), and continue the winter hemp (or female hemp bearing seed) on the ground until the seed is ripe ;  the GOLD MEDAL, or FIFTY GUINEAS.

67*.   To the person who shall sow with Hemp (in drills at least eighteen inches asunder) the next greatest quantity of land in the same above-mentioned district, not less than twenty-five acres statute measure, in the year 1802, and shall at the proper season cause the same to be

plucked

plucked as above mentioned; the SILVER MEDAL, or TWENTY-FIVE GUINEAS.

CERTIFICATES of the number of acres, of the distance of the drills, of the plucking of the hemp, with a general ACCOUNT of the soil, cultivation, and produce, to be delivered to the Society, along with fourteen pounds of the hemp, and two quarts of the seed, on or before the second Tuesday in January, 1803.

*Premiums for Discoveries and Improvements*
*in Chemistry, Dying, and Mineralogy.*

68. PRESERVING SEEDS OF VEGETABLES.
For the best method of preserving the Seeds of Plants in
a state fit for vegetation a longer time than has hitherto
been practised, such method being superior to any known
to the Public, and verified by sufficient trial, to be communicated to the Society on or before the first Tuesday in
December, 1802; the GOLD MEDAL, or THIRTY GUI-
NEAS.

69. PREVENTING THE DRY-ROT IN TIMBER.
To the person who shall discover to the Society the cause
of the Dry-Rot in Timber, and disclose a certain method
of prevention superior to any hitherto known; the GOLD
MEDAL, or THIRTY GUINEAS.

The ACCOUNTS of the cause, and method of prevention,
confirmed by repeated experiments, to be produced to the
Society on or before the second Tuesday in December,
1802.

70. PRESERVING SALTED PROVISIONS FROM
BECOMING RANCID OR RUSTY. To the person
who shall discover to the Society the best, cheapest, and
most efficacious method of preserving salted Provisions
from growing rancid or rusty; the GOLD MEDAL, or
THIRTY GUINEAS.

                                        A full

A full description of the method, with proper CERTI-FICATES that it has been found, on repeated trials, to answer the purpose intended, to be produced to the Society on or before the first Tuesday in February, 1803.

71. CLEARING FEATHERS FROM THEIR ANIMAL OIL. To the person who shall discover to the Society the best and most expeditious method, superior to any hitherto practised, of clearing Goose-Feathers from their offensive Animal Oil, for the use of Upholders, in making beds, cushions, &c. the SILVER MEDAL, of TWENTY GUINEAS.

A quantity of such Feathers unstripped and so cleared, not less than forty pounds weight, with a full ACCOUNT of the process, to be produced to the Society on or before the first Tuesday in February, 1803.

72. REFINING WHALE OR SEAL OIL. For disclosing to the Society an effectual method of purifying Whale or Seal Oil from the glutinous matter that incrusts the wicks of lamps and extinguishes the light, though fully supplied with Oil; the GOLD MEDAL, or FIFTY GUINEAS.

It is required that the whole of the process be fully and fairly disclosed, in order that satisfactory experiments may be made by the Society, to determine the validity of the claim; and CERTIFICATES that not less than twenty gallons have been purified according to the process delivered in, together with two gallons of the Oil in its unpurified state, and two gallons so refined, be produced to the Society on or before the second Tuesday in February, 1803.

D 73.

73. MANUFACTURING TALLOW-CANDLES.
To the person who shall discover to the Society a method
of hardening or otherwise preparing Tallow, so that Candles may be made of it which will burn as clear and with
as small a wick as wax candles, without running, and may
be afforded at a less expense than any at present made with
spermaceti; the GOLD MEDAL, or THIRTY GUINEAS.

CERTIFICATES that 112 lb. of such Tallow has been
made into Candles, and 12 lb. of the Candles made thereof,
to be produced to the Society on or before the second
Tuesday in January, 1803.

74. CANDLES FROM RESIN OR OTHER SUB-
STANCES. To the person who shall discover to the
Society the best method of making Candles of Resin, or
any other substance, fit for common use, at a price much
inferior to those made of tallow only; the GOLD MEDAL,
or THIRTY GUINEAS.

Six pounds at least of the Candles so prepared, with an
ACCOUNT of the process, to be delivered to the Society
on or before the first Tuesday in December, 1802.

75. METHOD OF SEPARATING SUGAR IN A
SOLID FORM FROM TREACLE. To the person who
shall discover to the Society the best method of separating
Sugar from Treacle in a solid form, at such an expense
as will render it advantageous to the public; the GOLD
MEDAL, or FIFTY GUINEAS.

A quantity of the Sugar so prepared in a solid form,
not less than thirty pounds weight, with an ACCOUNT of
the process, and CERTIFICATES that not less than one
hundred

hundred weight has been prepared, to be produced to the Society on or before the first Tuesday in February, 1803.

76. PROOF-SPIRIT. To the distiller who, in the year 1802, shall make the greatest quantity, not less than one hundred gallons, of a clean marketable Spirit, from articles not the food of man or cattle, equal in strength or quality to the Proof-Spirit now in use, and at a rate not higher than the Spirit produced from corn or melasses; the GOLD MEDAL, or ONE HUNDRED GUINEAS.

Ten gallons of the Spirit, together with proper CERTIFICATES, and a full ACCOUNT of the expense and mode of making it, to be produced to the Society on or before the first Tuesday in January, 1803.

77. INCREASING STEAM. To the person who shall invent and discover to the Society a method, verified by actual experiments, of increasing the quantity or force of Steam, in Steam-Engines, with less fuel than has hitherto been employed, provided that in general the whole amount of the expenses in using Steam-Engines may be considerably lessened; the GOLD MEDAL, or THIRTY GUINEAS.

To be communicated to the Society on or before the first Tuesday in January, 1803.

78. SUBSTITUTE FOR TAR. To the person who shall invent and discover to the Society the best Substitute for Stockholm Tar, equal in all its properties to the best of that kind, and prepared from materials the produce of Great Britain; the GOLD MEDAL, or ONE HUNDRED GUINEAS.

A quantity of the Substitute, not less than one hundred weight, with CERTIFICATES that at least one ton has been manufactured, and that it can be afforded at a price not exceeding that of the best foreign Tar, together with an ACCOUNT of the process, to be delivered to the Society on or before the first Tuesday in March, 1803.

79. PREPARATION OF TAN. To the person who shall prepare in the most concentrated form, so as to be easily portable, and at a price applicable to the purposes of manufactures, the largest quantity, not less than one hundred weight, of the principle called by the French *Tannin*, which abounds in oak-bark and many other vegetable substances; the GOLD MEDAL, or FIFTY GUINEAS.

CERTIFICATES of the above quantity having been prepared, and a SAMPLE of not less than 28 lb. to be produced to the Society on or before the last Tuesday in January, 1803.

80. PREPARATION OF A RED STAIN FOR COTTON CLOTH. To the person who shall communicate to the Society the cheapest and most effectual method of printing or staining Cotton Cloths with a Red Colour, by an immediate application of the colouring-matter to the Cloth, equally beautiful and durable with the Red Colours now generally procured from decoctions of madder; the GOLD MEDAL, or THIRTY GUINEAS.

CERTIFICATES that the above process has been advantageously used on ten pieces of Calico, each twenty-one yards or upwards in length; one piece of the Calico so printed,

printed, a quart of the Colour in a liquid state, and a full Account of the preparation and application, to be produced to the Society on or before the second Tuesday in January, 1803.

## 81. PREPARATION OF A GREEN COLOUR FOR PRINTING COTTON CLOTH.

To the person who shall communicate to the Society the best and cheapest method of printing with a full Green Colour on Cotton Cloth, by an immediate application of the colouring-matter from a wooden block to the Cloth, equally beautiful and durable as the Colours now formed from the complicated process of the decoction of weld on alumine, and the solutions of indigo by earths or alkaline salts; the Gold Medal, or Thirty Guineas.

Certificates and conditions as for premium 80.

## 82. SUBSTITUTE FOR THE BASIS OF PAINT.

To the person who shall produce to the Society the best Substitute, superior to any hitherto known, for the Basis of Paint, equally proper for the purpose as the White Lead now employed; such Substitute not to be of a noxious quality, and to be afforded at a price not materially higher than that of White Lead; the Gold Medal, or One Hundred Guineas.

A quantity of the Substitute, not less than 50 lb. weight, with an Account of the process used in preparing it, and Certificates that at least one hundred weight has been manufactured, to be produced to the Society on or before the first Tuesday in January, 1803.

83. RED

**83.   RED PIGMENT.** To the person who shall discover to the Society a full and satisfactory process for preparing a Red Pigment, fit for use, in oil or water, equal in tone and brilliancy to the best carmines and lakes now known or in use, and perfectly durable; the GOLD MEDAL, or THIRTY GUINEAS.

One pound weight of such Colour, and a full disclosure of its preparation, to be produced to the Society on or before the first Tuesday in February, 1803.

*N. B.* It is not required that the Colour should resist the action of fire or chemical applications, but remain unaltered by the common exposure to strong light, damps, and noisome vapours.

**84.   ULTRAMARINE.** To the person who shall prepare an artificial Ultramarine, equal in colour, brilliancy, or durability, to the best prepared from Lapis Lazuli, and which may be afforded at a cheap rate; the GOLD MEDAL, or THIRTY GUINEAS.

The conditions are the same as in the preceding premium for the Red Pigment.

**85.   ANALYSIS OF BRITISH MINERALS.** To the person who shall communicate to the Society the most correct Analysis of any Mineral Production of Great Britain, hitherto either unexamined or not examined with accuracy; the GOLD MEDAL.

The ANALYSIS and sufficient SPECIMENS to be produced to the Society on or before the first Tuesday in January, 1803.

86.

86. PREPARATION OF SULPHURIC ACID FROM SULPHUR, WITHOUT THE USE OF ANY NITRIC SALT. To the person who shall prepare the largest quantity (not less than one ton) of Sulphuric Acid from Sulphur, without any Nitric Salt, of a specific gravity, not inferior to the best sulphuric acid of commerce; the GOLD MEDAL, or FIFTY GUINEAS.

CERTIFICATES that not less than the above quantity of such an acid has been prepared, together with a Sample, to be produced to the Society on or before the first Tuesday in January, 1803.

87. PREPARATION OF ANY ALKALINE OR EARTHY NITRATE. To the person who shall prepare, in Great-Britain, the largest quantity, not less than one hundred weight, of any Salt of Nitric Acid, with either earths or alkalis, by a method superior to those hitherto practised; the GOLD MEDAL, or ONE HUNDRED GUINEAS.

CERTIFICATES of the above quantity having been prepared, and a Sample of not less than 28lb. to be produced to the Society on or before the last Tuesday in January, 1803.

88. FINE BAR-IRON. To the person, in Great-Britain, who shall make the greatest quantity of Bar-iron, not less than ten tons, with coak, from coak-pigs, equal in quality to the best Iron imported from Sweden or Russia, and as fit for converting into steel; the GOLD MEDAL, or FIFTY GUINEAS.

SAMPLES, not less than one hundred weight, with CERTIFICATES that the whole quantity is of equal quality,

to

to be produced to the Society on or before the first Tuesday in January, 1803.

**89. PRESERVING IRON FROM RUST.** To the person who shall invent and discover to the Society a cheap composition, superior to any now in use, which shall effectually preserve Wrought Iron from Rust, tho GOLD MEDAL, or FIFTY GUINEAS.

A full description of the method of preparing the composition, with CERTIFICATES that it has stood at least two years unimpaired, being exposed to the atmosphere during the whole time, to be produced to the Society, with ten pounds weight of the composition, on or before the first Tuesday in January, 1803.

**90. REFINING BLOCK-TIN.** To the person who shall discover to the Society the best method of purifying or refining Block-Tin, so as to render it fit for the finest purposes to which grain-tin is now applied, and not higher in price; the GOLD MEDAL, or FIFTY GUINEAS.

CERTIFICATES that not less than three tons have been refined or purified, with a full detail of the process, and a quantity, not less than one hundred weight, of the Tin so refined, to be produced to the Society on or before the first Tuesday in January, 1803.

**91. GLAZING EARTHEN-WARE WITHOUT LEAD.** To the person who shall discover to the Society the cheapest, safest, most durable, and most easily fusible composition, for the purpose of glazing the ordinary kinds of Earthen-ware, without any preparation of Lead, and superior to any hitherto in use; the GOLD MEDAL, or THIRTY GUINEAS.

SPECIMENS

SPECIMENS of the Ware so glazed, with proper CER-TIFICATES of its having succeeded, and a Sample of the materials made use of, to be produced to the Society on or before the first Tuesday in February, 1803.

92. REFINING COPPER FROM THE ORE. To the person who shall discover to the Society the best method of separating, purifying, and refining Copper from the Ore, so as to render it fit for the finest purposes to which fine Copper is now applied, and by a process superior to any hitherto known or in use, and not higher in price; the GOLD MEDAL, or FIFTY GUINEAS..

CERTIFICATES that not less than three tons have been so prepared or refined, and a quantity not less than one hundred weight of the Copper so refined, to be produced to the Society on or before the first Tuesday in February, 1803.

93. MINERALOGICAL MAP OF ENGLAND AND WALES. To the person who shall complete and publish an accurate Mineralogical Map of England and Wales, on a scale of not less than ten miles to an inch, containing an account of the situation of the different Mines therein, and describing the kinds of Minerals thence produced; the GOLD MEDAL, or FIFTY GUINEAS.

CERTIFICATES of the accuracy of such Map, together with the Map, to be produced to the Society on or before the first Tuesday in February, 1804.

The Map to remain the property of the Society.

94. MINERALOGICAL MAP OF IRELAND. The same premium is offered for a Mineralogical Map of Ireland, on similar conditions.

95.

95. MINERALOGICAL MAP OF SCOTLAND. The same premium is offered for a Mineralogical Map of Scotland, on similar conditions.

96. NATURAL HISTORY. To the author who shall publish, in the year 1802, the Natural History of any County in England or Wales; the GOLD MEDAL, or FIFTY GUINEAS.

It is required that the several natural productions, whether animal, vegetable, or mineral, peculiar to the county, or found therein, be carefully and specifically arranged and described, in order that the Public may be enabled to judge what arts or manufactures are most likely to succeed in such county.

The Work to be delivered to the Society on or before the last Tuesday in January, 1803.

## Premiums in Polite Arts.

97. HONORARY PREMIUMS FOR DRAWING, BY NOBILITY. For the best Drawing, of any kind, made with Water-colours, Crayons, Chalk, Black Lead, Pen, Indian Ink, or Bister, by young Gentlemen under the age of twenty-one, sons or grandsons of Peers, or Peeresses in their own right, of Great Britain or Ireland, to be produced on or before the first Tuesday in March, 1803; the HONORARY MEDAL of the Society IN GOLD.

98. The same IN SILVER for the next in merit.

99, 100. The same premiums will be given, on the like conditions, to young Ladies, daughters or grand-daughters of Peers, or Peeresses in their own right, of Great Britain or Ireland,

101. HONORARY PREMIUMS FOR DRAWING, BY GENTLEMEN. For the best Drawing, of any kind, made with Water-colours, Crayons, Chalk, Black Lead, Pen, Indian Ink, or Bister, by young Gentlemen, under the age of twenty-one; to be produced on or before the first Tuesday in March, 1803; the GOLD MEDAL.

102. For the next in merit, the SILVER MEDAL.

103, 104. The same premiums will be given for Drawings by young Ladies.

N. B.

*N. B.* As the foregoing Honorary Premiums are intended only for such of the Nobility and Gentry as may hereafter become Patrons or Patronesses of the Arts; persons professing any branch of the Polite Arts, or any business dependent on the Arts of Design, or the sons or daughters of such persons, will not be admitted Candidates in these Classes.

105. DRAWINGS OF OUTLINES. For the best Outline, after an original group or cast, in plaster, of Human Figures, by persons of either sex, under the age of sixteen, the principal Figure not less than twelve inches; to be produced on or before the third Tuesday in February, 1803; the greater SILVER PALLET.

106. For the next in merit, the lesser SILVER PALLET.

*N. B.* These Drawings are to be made on Paper, and the original either to be produced to the Society, or to be referred to for their examination.

107. DRAWINGS OF LANDSCAPES. For the best Drawing of a Landscape after nature, by persons of either sex, under twenty-one years of age, to be produced on or before the third Tuesday in February, 1803; the greater SILVER PALLET.

108. For the next in merit, the lesser SILVER PALLET.

Each Candidate must mention, on the front of the Drawing, whence the view was taken; and the Drawings must be made with Chalk, Pen, Indian Ink, Water-colours, or Bister.

109. HISTORICAL DRAWINGS. For the best Historical Drawing, being an original composition, of five or more Human Figures; the height of the principal Figure not less than eight inches; to be made with Crayons, Chalk, Black Lead, Pen, Indian Ink, Water-colours, or Bister, and to be produced on or before the third Tuesday in February, 1803; the GOLD PALLET.

110. For the next in merit, the greater SILVER PALLET.

111. CHINTS PATTERNS FOR CALICO-PRINTERS. For the best original Pattern, in a new taste, of light or dark ground Chints for garment-work, fit for the purposes of Calico-Printers, by persons of either sex; the GOLD MEDAL.

To be produced to the Society on or before the second Tuesday in January, 1803.

The Pattern to which the premium is adjudged to remain the property of the Society.

112. For the next in merit, the SILVER MEDAL, on similar conditions.

113. COPPER-PLATE PATTERNS FOR CALICO-PRINTERS. For the best Pattern, in a new style, fit for the purposes of Calico-Printers, for garment-work; the SILVER MEDAL.

To be produced to the Society on or before the second Tuesday in January, 1803.

The Pattern to which the premium is adjudged to remain the property of the Society.

114.

**114. LINE ENGRAVINGS OF LANDSCAPES.** For the best Line Engraving of a Landscape, published in the year 1803, the size of the Engraving not less than eighteen inches by fourteen; the GOLD MEDAL.

To be produced to the Society on or before the last Tuesday in January, 1804; and the impression to which the premium is adjudged to remain the property of the Society.

115. For the next in merit, the SILVER MEDAL, on similar conditions.

**116. LINE ENGRAVINGS OF HISTORICAL SUBJECTS.** For the best Line Engraving published in the year 1802, of an Historical Subject, the size of the Engraving not less than eighteen inches by fourteen; the GOLD MEDAL.

117. For the next in merit, the SILVER MEDAL.

Conditions, &c. the same as in Classes 114 and 115.

**118. MODEL IN CLAY OR PLASTER.** For the best Model in Clay or Plaster of an Ornamental Design for the purpose of embellishing works of Architecture; the SILVER MEDAL, or TWENTY GUINEAS.

To be produced to the Society on or before the last Tuesday in January, 1803.

The Model not to be less than thirty inches by twelve.

*The*

*The following Premium (Class 119,) is offered in conformity to the Will of the late John Stock, of Hampstead, Esq.*

119. ORNAMENTAL DRAWINGS FOR ARCHITECTURAL DÉSIGNS. For the best Ornamental Drawing for the purpose of embellishing Architectural Designs, a SILVER MEDALLION, with the following engraved inscription: *The Premium given by the Society for the Encouragement of Arts, Manufactures, and Commerce, in conformity to the Will of John Stock, of Hampstead, Esq.* The Drawing to which the premium is adjudged to remain the property of the Society.

120. For the best Model in Clay or Plaster of a Design for the same purpose, the SILVER MEDAL.

The performances in these two Classes not to be less than thirty inches by twelve, to be made by persons under the age of twenty-one years.

To be produced to the Society on or before the last Tuesday in January, 1803.

121. PERSPECTIVE DRAWINGS OF MACHINES. For the best Perspective Drawing of Machines, by persons under eighteen years of age, the greater SILVER PALLET.

To be produced to the Society on or before the last Tuesday in January, 1803.

122. For the next in merit, the lesser SILVER PALLET, on similar conditions.

123. ENGRAVING ON WOOD, OR METAL BLOCKS. For the best Engraving on Wood, or Metal Blocks,

Blocks, of a subject or Allegorical Decoration for a volume of the Society's Transactions, proper to be prefixed
to the Premiums offered by the Society, and capable of
being worked with the letter-press; the GOLD MEDAL.

The engraved Wood or Metal Block, and two or more
impressions from it, to be produced to the Society on or
before the second Tuesday in February, 1803; and the
engraved Wood or Metal Block to which the premium is
adjudged, to remain the property of the Society.

The Engraving to be of a proper size to form an octavo
page in the volume.

124.   For the next in merit, the SILVER MEDAL, on
similar conditions.

125.   STATUARY MARBLE.   To the person who
shall discover, within Great Britain or Ireland, a Quarry
of White Marble fit for the purposes of Statuary, and
equal in all respects to those kinds now imported from
Italy; the GOLD MEDAL, or ONE HUNDRED POUNDS.

A Block of at least three feet in length, two in heighth,
and two in width, with an ACCOUNT of the situation of
the Quarry, and CERTIFICATES of its possessing considerable extent, to be produced to the Society on or before
the first Tuesday in February, 1803.

N. B.  In order to prevent useless expense or trouble to
the claimant in forwarding so large a Block, the Society
will be ready to examine any smaller specimen of the
Marble, and express their opinion of its value to the Candidate, before the Block required by the above premium is
produced.

126.

126. BRONZES. For the best Drapery-figure or Group cast in Bronze; if a single figure, not less than twelve inches high; and, if a group, not less than nine inches; and which will require the least additional labour to repair; the GOLD MEDAL, or the SILVER MEDAL and TWENTY GUINEAS.

The Cast to be exhibited to the Society before it is begun to be repaired, with the original figure or group, on or before the first Tuesday in February, 1802, together with a full Explanation of the whole process.

*Premiums*

## Premiums for encouraging and improving Manufactures.

127. MACHINE FOR CARDING SILK. For the best Machine, superior to any now in use, for Carding Waste Silk equally well as by hand; to be produced, together with a Specimen of the carding, on or before the first Tuesday in November, 1802; the SILVER MEDAL, or TWENTY GUINEAS.

128. CLOTH FROM HOP-STALKS, &c. To the person who shall produce to the Society the greatest quantity, not less than thirty yards, of Cloth at least twenty-seven inches wide, made in Great Britain, of Hop-Stalks or Bines, or other raw Vegetable Substances, the produce of Great Britain or Ireland, superior to any hitherto manufactured from such substances, and which can be generally afforded as cheap as Cloth of equal quality and appearance now made from hemp, flax, or cotton, and much finer in quality than any hitherto manufactured in England from Hop-Stalks, &c. the GOLD MEDAL, or THIRTY GUINEAS.

One pound of the Thread of which the Cloth is made, and thirty yards of the Cloth, together with proper CERTIFICATES that the whole is manufactured from Hop-Stalks or Bines, &c. to be produced to the Society on or before the first Tuesday in December, 1802.

N. B. The Society is already in the possession of Cloth made in England from Hop-Stalks or Bines, which may be inspected by application to the Housekeeper.

129.

129. WICKS FOR CANDLES OR LAMPS. To the person who shall discover to the Society a method of manufacturing Hop-Stalks or Bines, or any other cheap material, the growth of Great Britain, so as to render them equally fit for the purpose of supplying the place of Cotton, for Wicks of Candles or Lamps; TWENTY GUINEAS.

SAMPLES, not less than five pounds weight, of the Wicks so prepared, to be produced to the Society, with CERTIFICATES that the whole quantity is equal in quality to the Sample, on or before the second Tuesday in January, 1803.

130. PAPER FROM RAW VEGETABLE SUB-STANCES. To the person, in Great Britain, who shall, between the first of January, 1802, and the first of January, 1803, make the greatest quantity, and of the best quality (not less than ten reams), of good and useful Paper, from Raw Vegetable Substances, the produce of Great Britain or Ireland, of which one hundred weight has not been used in manufacturing Paper previous to January, 1801, superior to any hitherto manufactured from such Substances, and which can be generally afforded as cheap as Paper of equal quality and appearance now made from Rags; TWENTY GUINEAS.

N. B. The object of the Society being to add to the number and quantity of raw materials used in this manufacture, it is their wish to include every useful sort of Paper, and to introduce such natural products as can be easily and cheaply procured in great quantities.

The Society are in possession of two volumes containing a great variety of specimens of Paper made from Raw Ve-

getable

getable Substances, viz.—Nettles, Potatoe-hawlm, Poplar, Hop-bines, &c. which volumes may be inspected by any person, on application to the Housekeeper.

CERTIFICATES of the making such Paper, and one ream of the Paper, to be produced on or before the second Tuesday in January, 1803.

131. TRANSPARENT PAPER. To the person who shall discover to the Society a method of making Paper from the pulp that shall be perfectly transparent, and of a substance and body equal to foolscap, that shall take and bear common writing ink with the same facility and correctness as Writing-paper generally in use; the SILVER MEDAL, or TWENTY GUINEAS.

CERTIFICATES of the making such Paper, an ACCOUNT of the process, and one ream of the Paper, to be produced on or before the second Tuesday in January, 1803.

132. TAKING PORPOISES. To the people in any boat or vessel, who, in the year 1802, shall take the greatest number of Porpoises on the coast of Great Britain, by gun, harpoon, or any other method, not fewer than thirty, for the purpose of extracting oil from them; the GOLD MEDAL, or THIRTY POUNDS.

CERTIFICATES of the number, signed by the persons to whom they have been sold or delivered for the purpose of extracting the oil, to be produced to the Society on or before the last Tuesday in January, 1803.

133. OIL FROM PORPOISES. To the person who shall manufacture the greatest quantity of Oil from Porpoises taken on the coast of Great Britain, in the year 1802, not

less

less than twenty tons; the GOLD MEDAL, or THIRTY POUNDS,

CERTIFICATES of the Oil having been made from Porpoises actually caught on the coast of Great Britain, and two gallons of the Oil as a sample, to be produced to the Society on or before the last Tuesday in February, 1803.

## *Premiums in Mechanicks.*

134. GUNPOWDER-MILLS. To the person who, in the year 1802, shall invent and bring to perfection the most effectual method of so conducting the works of Gunpowder-Mills, in the business of making Gunpowder, as to prevent explosion; the GOLD MEDAL, or ONE HUNDRED GUINEAS.

CERTIFICATES and ACCOUNTS of the method having been put in practice in one or more Gunpowder-Mills in this Kingdom, and that it promises, in the opinion of the best judges concerned in such works, to answer the purpose intended, to be produced to the Society on or before the first Tuesday in February, 1803.

*N. B.* As an encouragement to persons to turn their thoughts to improvements of this nature, if any should be made on the present method of conducting the business of Gunpowder-making, which fall short of the total prevention of explosion, and they are sent to the Society for the sake of humanity, the papers so sent in will receive due consideration, and such bounty or reward will be bestowed thereon as they appear to merit.

135. TRANSIT-INSTRUMENT. To the person who shall invent and produce to the Society a cheap and portable Transit-Instrument, which may easily be converted into a zenith-sector, capable of being accurately and expeditiously adjusted, for the purpose of finding the latitudes and longitudes of places, and superior to any portable

Transit-

Transit-Instrument now in use; the GOLD MEDAL, or FORTY GUINEAS.

To be produced on or before the last Tuesday in January, 1803.

136. TAKING WHALES BY THE GUN-HARPOON. To the person who, in the year 1802, shall strike the greatest number of Whales, not fewer than three, with the Gun-harpoon; TEN GUINEAS.

Proper CERTIFICATES of the striking such Whales, and that they were actually taken in the year 1802, signed by the Master, or by the Mate when the claim is made by the Master, to be produced to the Society on or before the last Tuesday in December, 1802.

137. FAMILY-MILL. To the person who shall invent and produce to the Society the best-constructed Mill for grinding Corn for the use of Private Families, or Parish Poor; the construction to be such as to render the working of the Mill easy and expeditious, and superior to any hitherto in use; the GOLD MEDAL, or THIRTY GUINEAS.

The MILL, and CERTIFICATES of its having been used to good effect, to be produced to the Society on or before the first Tuesday in February, 1803.

N. B. Cheapness and simplicity will be considered as essential parts of its merit; and the Mill, or the Model, to remain with the Society.

138. MACHINE FOR RAISING COALS, ORE, &c. &c. To the person who shall invent a Machine for

E 4                                                              raising

raising Coals, Ore, &c. from mines, superior to any hitherto known or in use, and which shall produce the effect at a less expense than those already known or in use; the GOLD MEDAL, or FIFTY GUINEAS.

A MODEL of the Machine, made on a scale of not less than one inch to a foot, with a CERTIFICATE that a Machine at large on the same construction has been advantageously used, to be produced to the Society on or before the second Tuesday in February, 1803.

139.    MACHINE FOR RAISING WATER.    To the person who shall invent a Machine on a better, cheaper, and more simple construction than any hitherto known or in use, for raising Water out of wells, &c. from a depth of not less than fifty feet; the GOLD MEDAL, or FORTY GUINEAS.

CERTIFICATES of the performance of the Machine, and a MODEL of it, on a scale of not less than one inch to a foot, to be produced to the Society on or before the first Tuesday in February, 1803.

140.    MACHINE FOR MAKING BRICKS.    To the person who shall invent the best and cheapest Machine for making Bricks, superior to any hitherto known or in use, whereby the labour and expense of making Bricks in the usual mode, by hand, may be greatly diminished; FORTY GUINEAS.

A MODEL, with CERTIFICATES that a Machine at large, on the same construction, has been used to good effect for the purpose of making Bricks, and that at least one hundred thousand statute-bricks have been made therewith,

therewith, to be produced to the Society on or before the first Tuesday in March, 1803.

141. BORING AND BLASTING ROCKS. To the person who shall discover to the Society a more simple, cheap, and expeditious method than any hitherto known or in use, of Boring and Blasting Rocks in Mines, Shafts, Wells, etc.; the GOLD MEDAL, or THIRTY GUINEAS.

CERTIFICATES of the method having been practised with success, with a full description thereof, to be delivered to the Society on or before the first Tuesday in January, 1803.

142. HEATING ROOMS FOR THE PURPOSES OF MANUFACTURERS. To the person who shall invent and discover to the Society a method of heating Rooms, superior to any hitherto known or in use, and at a moderate expense, for the purposes of Painters, Japanners, and other Manufacturers, so as to avoid the necessity of iron or copper tunnels going through the Rooms to convey the smoke, whereby the danger from such tunnels may be prevented; the GOLD MEDAL, or FORTY GUINEAS.

A MODEL, or complete Drawing and Description of the method, with CERTIFICATES that it has been successfully practised, to be delivered to the Society on or before the last Tuesday in March, 1803.

143. IMPROVED VENTILATION. To the person who shall invent and produce to the Society a mode of permanently ventilating the apartments in Hospitals, Workhouses, and other crowded places, superior to any now known or used; the GOLD MEDAL, or FIFTY GUINEAS.

A.

A Model of the apparatus, and a full Account of the means by which the effect has been produced, with proper Certificates, to be delivered to the Society on or before the last Tuesday in February, 1803.

144. MILL-STONES. To the person who shall, between the first of February, 1802, and the first of February, 1803, prepare and bring into use the greatest number of Mill-Stones, taken from any Quarry in the United Kingdoms, equal in quality to the French Burrs, not less than thirty pairs; the Gold Medal, or Thirty Guineas.

Certificates that the said Mill-Stones were all taken from the same Quarry, with their prices and dimensions, that they are equal to the French Burr, not less than three feet eight inches diameter, and are actually in use, to be produced to the Society on or before the third Tuesday in February, 1803.

145. For the next greatest quantity, not less than twenty-five pairs; the Silver Medal, or Fifteen Guineas, on similar terms.

146. PREVENTING ACCIDENTS FROM HORSES FALLING WITH TWO-WHEELED CARRIAGES. To the person who shall invent and produce to the Society a method superior to any hitherto known or in use, to prevent Accidents from the falling of Horses with Two-wheel Carriages, especially on steep declivities; the Silver Medal, or Fifteen Guineas.

A Model of the apparatus, and a full Account of the means by which the effect has been produced, with
                                                    proper

proper CERTIFICATES that the same has been used with success, to be delivered to the Society on or before the second Tuesday in January, 1803.

147. CLEARING THE TURNPIKE AND OTHER ROADS IN WINTER FROM MUD, AND IN SUMMER FROM DUST. To the person who shall discover to the Society the most effectual and the cheapest method, verified by experiments, of clearing the Turnpike and other Roads of great resort, in Winter from Mud, and in Summer from Dust, or most effectully preventing the accumulation of either; the GOLD MEDAL, or FIFTY GUINEAS.

148. For the second best Account, the SILVER MEDAL, or TWENTY GUINEAS.

It is required that an accurate ACCOUNT of the method used, and every expense attending it, together with satisfactory CERTIFICATES of its being effectual, be delivered to the Society on or before the first Tuesday in March, 1808.

## Premiums offered for the Advantage of the British Colonies.

149. NUTMEGS. For the greatest quantity of merchantable Nutmegs, not less than ten pounds weight, being the growth of His Majesty's dominions in the West Indies, or any of the British Settlements on the coast of Africa, or the several islands adjacent thereto, and equal to those imported from the islands of the East Indies; the GOLD MEDAL, or ONE-HUNDRED GUINEAS.

Satisfactory CERTIFICATES, from the Governor, or Commander in Chief, of the place of growth, with an ACCOUNT of the number of trees, their age, nearly the quantity of fruit on each tree, and the manner of culture, to be produced to the Society on or before the first Tuesday in December, 1802.

150. CLOVES. For importing into the Port of London, in the year 1802, the greatest quantity of Cloves, not less than twenty pounds weight, being of the growth of some of the islands of the West Indies subject to the Crown of Great Britain, or any of the British Settlements on the coast of Africa, or the several islands adjacent thereto, and equal in goodness to the Cloves brought from the East Indies; the GOLD MEDAL, or FIFTY GUINEAS.

SAMPLES, not less than two pounds weight, with CERTIFICATES that the whole quantity is equal in goodness, together with satisfactory CERTIFICATES, signed by the Governor, or Commander in Chief, of the place of growth,

with

with an ACCOUNT of the number of trees growing on the spot, their age, and the manner of culture, to be produced to the Society on or before the first Tuesday in January, 1803.

151. PLANTATIONS OF BREAD-FRUIT TREES. To the person who shall have raised in any of the islands of the West Indies subject to the Crown of Great Britain, or in any of the British Settlements on the coast of Africa, or the several islands adjacent thereto, between the first of January, 1801, and the first of January, 1802, the greatest number of Bread-Fruit Trees, not fewer than one hundred, and properly fenced and secured the same; in order to supply the Fruit to the inhabitants; the GOLD MEDAL, or THIRTY GUINEAS.

Proper ACCOUNTS and CERTIFICATES, signed by the Governor, or Commander in Chief, of the methods made use of in cultivating the plants and securing the plantation, and that the trees are in a growing and thriving state at the time of signing such Certificates, to be produced to the Society, with SAMPLES of the Fruit, on or before the first Tuesday in January, 1803.

152. KALI FOR BARILLA. To the person who shall have cultivated, in the Bahama-Islands, or any other part of His Majesty's dominions in the West Indies, or any of the British Settlements on the coast of Africa, or the several islands adjacent thereto, in the year 1801, the greatest quantity of land, not less than two acres, with Spanish Kali, fit for the purpose of making Barilla; the GOLD MEDAL, or THIRTY GUINEAS.

153.

153.  For the next greatest quantity, not less than one acre; the SILVER MEDAL, or FIFTEEN GUINEAS.

CERTIFICATES, signed by the Governor, or Commander in Chief, for the time being, of the quantity of land so cultivated, and of the state of the plants, at the time of signing such Certificates, to be delivered to the Society, with SAMPLES of the Kali, on or before the second Tuesday in January, 1803.

154.  The same premium is extended one year farther.

CERTIFICATES to be produced on or before the second Tuesday in January, 1804.

155.  DESTROYING THE INSECT COMMONLY CALLED THE BORER.  To the person who shall discover to the Society an effectual method of destroying the Insect commonly called the Borer, which has, of late years, been so destructive to the Sugar-Canes in the West-India islands, the British settlements on the coast of Africa, and the several islands adjacent thereto; the GOLD MEDAL, or FIFTY GUINEAS.

The discovery to be ascertained by satisfactory CERTIFICATES, under the hand and seal of the Governor, or Commander in Chief, for the time being, and of some other respectable persons, inhabitants of the islands, or other place, in which the remedy has been successfully applied; such Certificates to be delivered to the Society on or before the first Tuesday in January, 1803.

156.  CULTIVATION OF HEMP IN UPPER AND LOWER CANADA.  To the person who shall sow with

Hemp

Hemp the greatest quantity of land in the province of Upper Canada, not less than six arpents (each four fifths of a statute acre), in the year 1802, and shall at the proper season cause to be plucked the Summer Hemp (or Male Hemp bearing no seed) and continue the Winter Hemp (or Female Hemp bearing seed) on the ground until the seed is ripe; the GOLD MEDAL, or ONE HUNDRED DOLLARS.

157. To the person who shall sow with Hemp the next greatest quantity of land in the same province of Upper Canada, not less than five arpents, in the year 1802, in the manner above mentioned; the SILVER MEDAL, or EIGHTY DOLLARS.

158. For the next greatest quantity of land, in the same province, and in a similar manner, not less than four arpents; SIXTY DOLLARS.

159. For the next greatest quantity of land, in the same province, and in a similar manner, not less than three arpents; FORTY DOLLARS.

160. For the next greatest quantity of land, in the same province, and in a similar manner, not less than one arpent; TWENTY DOLLARS.

CERTIFICATES of the number of arpents, the method of culture, of the plucking of the Hemp, with a general ACCOUNT whether sown broad-cast or in drills, the expense, soil, cultivation, and produce, to be transmitted to the Society, certified under the hand and seal of the Governor or Lieutenant-Governor, together with 28 lb. of the

the Hemp, and two quarts of the Seed, on or before the first Tuesday in November, 1803.

161, 162, 163, 164, 165.   The same premiums are extended one year farther.

CERTIFICATES, etc. as before mentioned, to be transmitted to the Society on or before the last Tuesday in February, 1804.

166 to 176.   Premiums exactly similar in all respects to those held out for the province of Upper Canada, are also offered for the province of Lower Canada, and are extended to the same period.

177.  IMPORTATION OF HEMP FROM CANADA. To the Master of that vessel which shall bring to this country the greatest quantity of marketable Hemp, not less than one hundred tons, in the year 1803, the produce of Upper or Lower Canada; the GOLD MEDAL.

178.  To the Master of that vessel which shall bring the next quantity, not less than fifty tons; the SILVER MEDAL.

CERTIFICATES satisfactory to the Society to be produced by the Master of the vessel on or before the first Tuesday in February, 1804, to testify that such Hemp was grown and prepared in Canada.

*Premiums*

## *Premiums offered for the Advantage of the British Settlements in the East Indies.*

179. BHAUGULPORE COTTON. To the person who shall import into the Port of London, in the year 1802, the greatest quantity, not less than one ton, of the Bhaugulpore Cotton, from which cloths are made in imitation of Nankeen, without dying; the GOLD MEDAL.

A quantity of the Cotton, not less than five pounds weight, in the pod, and five pounds carded, to be produced to the Society, with proper CERTIFICATES, signed by the Secretary to the Board of Trade of Bengal or Bombay, on or before the last Tuesday in February, 1803.

180. ANNATTO. To the person who, in the year 1802, shall import into the Port of London, from any part of the British Settlements in the East Indies, the greatest quantity of Annatto, not less than five hundred weight; the GOLD MEDAL.

A quantity of the Annatto, not less than ten pounds weight, to be produced to the Society, with proper CERTIFICATES, signed by the Secretary of the Board of Trade of the respective Settlement, that the Annatto is the produce of such Settlement, on or before the last Tuesday in February, 1803.

181. TRUE COCHINEAL. To the person who, in the year 1802, shall import into the Port of London,

F from

from any part of the British Settlements in the East Indies, the greatest quantity of the true Cochineal, not less than five hundred weight; the GOLD MEDAL.

A quantity of the Cochineal, not less than ten pounds weight, with proper CERTIFICATES, signed by the Secretary of the Board of Trade of the respective Settlement, that the Cochineal is the produce of such Settlement, to be produced to the Society on or before the first Tuesday in February, 1803.

CONDITIONS

# CONDITIONS FOR THE POLITE ARTS.

No person who has gained the first Premium in any Class shall be admitted a Candidate in a Class of an inferior age; and no Candidate shall receive more than one Premium in one year; nor shall they who for two successive years have gained the first Premium in one Class, be again admitted as Candidates in that Class.

No person shall be admitted a Candidate in any Class, who has three times obtained the first Premium in that Class.

No more than one performance in any Class shall be received from the same Candidate.

All performances (to which Premiums or Bounties are adjudged) shall remain with the Society till after the public distribution of Rewards in May, when they shall be re-delivered, unless mentioned in the Premiums to the contrary.

No Performance shall be admitted, that has obtained a Premium, Reward, or Gratification from any other Society, Academy, or School, or been offered for that purpose.

All Performances that obtain Premiums in the Polite Arts, must have been begun after the publication of such Premiums, except Line Engravings.

To encourage real merit, and prevent attempts to impose on the Society, by producing Drawings made or retouched by any other person than the Candidate, the Society require a Specimen of the abilities of each successful

F 2          Candidate

Candidate in Classes 97 to 122 inclusive, under the inspection of the Committee of Polite Arts, in every instance where such proof may appear necessary.

All Candidates in the Polite Arts are required to signify, on their Drawings, their age; and whether the Performances are Originals or Copies; and if Copies, whence they were taken.

Society's Office, Adelphi, *June* 1, 1802.

Ordered,

THAT THE SEVERAL CANDIDATES AND CLAIM-
ANTS TO WHOM THE SOCIETY SHALL ADJUDGE
PREMIUMS OR BOUNTIES, DO ATTEND AT THE SO-
CIETY'S OFFICE IN THE ADELPHI, ON THE LAST
TUESDAY IN MAY, 1803, AT TWELVE O'CLOCK AT
NOON PRECISELY, TO RECEIVE THE SAME; THAT
DAY BEING APPOINTED BY THE SOCIETY FOR THE
DISTRIBUTION OF THEIR REWARDS: AND BEFORE
THAT TIME NO PREMIUM OR BOUNTY WILL BE
DELIVERED, EXCEPTING TO THOSE WHO ARE ABOUT
TO LEAVE THE KINGDOM.

IN CASES WHERE THE SOCIETY MAY THINK FIT
TO ADMIT EXCUSES FOR NOT ATTENDING IN PER-
SON, DEPUTIES MAY BE SUBSTITUTED TO RECEIVE
THE REWARDS, PROVIDED SUCH DEPUTIES ARE
EITHER MEMBERS OF THE SOCIETY, OR THE SUPE-
RIOR OFFICERS THEREOF.

F 3 GENERAL

## GENERAL CONDITIONS.

As the great object of the Society in rewarding individuals, is to draw forth and give currency to those Inventions and Improvements which are likely to benefit the Public at large, Candidates are requested to observe, that if the *means*, by which the respective objects are effected, do require an expense or trouble too great for *general purposes*, the Society will not consider itself as bound to give the offered *Reward;* but, though it thus reserves the power of giving in all cases such part only of any Premium as the Performance shall be adjudged to deserve, or of withholding the whole if there be no merit, yet the Candidates may be assured the Society will always judge liberally of their several Claims.

It is required that the matters for which Premiums are offered, be delivered in without names or any intimation to whom they belong; that each particular thing be marked in what manner each Claimant thinks fit, such Claimant sending with it a paper sealed up, having on the outside a corresponding mark, and, on the inside, the Claimant's name and address; and all Candidates are to take notice, that no Claim for a Premium will be attended to, unless the conditions of the Advertisement are fully complied with.

No Papers shall be opened, but such as shall gain Premiums, unless where it appears to the Society absolutely necessary for the determination of the Claim; all the rest shall be returned unopened, with the matters *to* which they belong, if inquired after by the mark, within

**two**

two years; after which time, if not demanded, they shall be publicly burnt, unopened, at some meeting of the Society.

All Models of Machines, which obtain Premiums or Bounties, shall be the property of the Society; and, where a Premium or Bounty is given for any Machine, a perfect Model thereof shall be given to the Society.

All the Premiums of this Society are designed for Great Britain and Ireland, unless expressly mentioned to the contrary.

The Claims shall be determined as soon as possible after the delivery of the Specimens.

No person shall receive any Premium, Bounty, or Encouragement from the Society, for any matter for which he has obtained, or purposes to obtain, a patent.

A Candidate for a Premium, or a person applying for a Bounty, being detected in any disingenuous method to impose on the Society, shall forfeit such Bounty, and be deemed incapable of obtaining any for the future.

The Performances which each year obtain Premiums or Bounties are to remain with the Society until after the public distribution of Rewards.

No Member of this Society shall be a Candidate for, or entitled to receive, any Premium, Bounty, or Reward whatsoever, except the Honorary Medal of the Society. The Candidates are, in all cases, expected to furnish a particular Account of the subject of their Claims; and, where Certificates are required to be produced in claim of Premiums, they should be expressed, as nearly as possible, in the words of the respective Advertisements, and be signed by persons who have a positive knowledge of the facts stated.

Where

Where Premiums or Bounties are obtained in consequence of Specimens produced, the Society mean to retain
such part of those Specimens as they may judge necessary,
making a reasonable allowance for the same.

No Candidates shall be present at any meetings of the
Society or Committees, or admitted at the Society's
Rooms, after they have delivered in their Claims, until
such Claims are adjudged, unless summoned by the Committee.

*N. B.* The Society farther invite the Communications
of Scientific and Practical Men upon any of the subjects
for which Premiums are offered, although their experiments may have been conducted upon a smaller scale than
the terms of each require, as they may afford ground for
more extensive application, and thus materially forward
the views of the Society, and contribute to the advantage
of the Public. Such communications to be made by letter,
addressed to the Society, and directed to Mr. CHARLES
TAYLOR, the Secretary, at the Society's Office, in the
Adelphi, London.

The Models required by the Society should be upon the
scale of one inch to a foot. The Winchester Bushel is the
measure referred to for Grain; and as the Acres of different districts vary in extent, it is necessary to observe,
that the Society mean Statute Acres, of five and a half
yards to the rod or pole, when Acres are mentioned in
their list of Premiums; and they request that all communications to them may be made agreeably thereto.

*The Society desire that the Papers on different subjects sent
to them may be full, clear, explicit, fit for publication, and
rather in the form of Essays than of Letters.*

<sub>*</sub>* To

## *Additional Premiums in Mechanicks.*

182. CLEANSING CHIMNIES. To the person who shall invent and produce to the Society the most effectual mechanical or other means for Cleansing Chimnies from Soot, and obviating the necessity of Children being employed within the Flues, the GOLD MEDAL.

183. For the next in Merit, the SILVER MEDAL.

The mechanical, or other means, with CERTIFICATES of their having been used with proper effect, to be produced to the Society on or before the first Tuesday in May, 1803.

184, 185. The same premiums are extended one year further.

186. CHIMNIES CLEANSED. To the person who shall, during the year 1803, cleanse, or cause to be cleansed, the greatest number of Chimnies, at least two stories high, not fewer than three hundred, by any mechanical or other process which does not require the employment of Boys within the Flues, the GOLD MEDAL.

CERTIFICATES, signed by not less than two thirds of those housekeepers on whose premises the said means have been employed, and an account of the process, to be produced to the Society on or before the first Tuesday in February, 1804.

187. To the person who shall cleanse, or cause to be cleansed, the next greatest number of Chimnies, not fewer than one hundred and fifty, upon similar conditions to the above, the SILVER MEDAL.

———————

*₊* To persons inclined to leave a sum of money to this Society, by will, the following form is offered for that purpose :

*Item.* I give and bequeath to A. B. and C. D. the sum of             upon condition and to the intent that they, or one of them, do pay the same to the Collector for the time being of a Society in London, who now call themselves the Society for the Encouragement of Arts, Manufactures, and Commerce; which said sum of
I will and desire may be paid out of my personal estate, and applied towards the carrying on the laudable designs of the Society.

By Order of the Society,

CHARLES TAYLOR, Secretary.

PAPERS

# PAPERS

## IN

# AGRICULTURE.

# AGRICULTURE.

THE Gold Medal was this Session presented to John Hunter, Esq. of Gubbins, in Hertfordshire, for having planted 40,000 Oaks. The following Accounts and Certificates were received from him.

SIR,

I PASS so much of my time in the country, and allow myself so little of it for unavoidable occupations in London, that I seldom find leisure to attend at the Society for the Encouragement of Arts, &c. I shall therefore be obliged to you, if you will inform the Society, at any convenient opportunity, that, in the months of November and December last, I planted nearly forty thousand Oaks of the growth of three years, upon
a field

a field on my estate, not more than fifteen miles from town, after having made it a most capital fallow, and secured the plants with a mound of earth round each; and, in short, fenced and otherwise secured it from all depredations, in the most safe and secure manner, for the good of posterity. The field contains twenty-seven acres. If the Society should think a work of this sort worthy of any honorary gratuity, I shall be happy to receive it.

I am, Sir,

Your obedient Servant,

John Hunter.

*Gubbins, Herts,*
*11th Feb.* 1800.

To the Secretary.

THIS

THIS is to certify, that John Hunter, Esq. of Gubbins, in the parish of North Mims, in the county of Herts, did, in the autumn of the year 1799, set out and plant twenty-seven acres of land, part of his estate situated at Gubbins as aforesaid, with 40,000 Oak-Plants, all of which were of the growth of from two to three years previous to their being so planted; and that the method pursued in planting the same was by a good summer-fallow being given to the land; and the same is well fenced.

It is also further certified, that the said plantation was, and continues to be, well and sufficiently fenced and defended from the depredations of cattle, or any thing else that can tend to injure or destroy the same; and that the plants are at present in a healthy and thriving state.

G. STAINFORTH.

*Dec.* 1, 1801,

The

The Silver Medal of the Society was
this Session voted to the Reverend
Richard Yates, F. A. S. Chaplain
to His Majesty's Royal Hospital at
Chelsea, for the following Observations on the Cultivation and
Growth of Oak Timber.

SIR,

TO expatiate upon the vast importance of increasing the growth of
Oak-Timber, seems unnecessary.  The
national advantages resulting from this
source appear to be in general well understood; and yet the cultivation and
management of this most useful plant
has not hitherto obtained that degree of
attention which it most certainly merits.

Entirely to obviate, or even in some
measure to remove or lessen, the ob-
stacles that still continue to impede the
planting of Oaks, would therefore be
rendering an essential service to the nation.

tion. The desire of accomplishing so beneficial a purpose, has induced the judicious and public-spirited Conductors of the Society of Arts to propose a Premium for " ascertaining the best method " of raising Oaks ;"—in consequence of which, this Paper is submitted to their candid consideration. And as the statements here made are founded upon a sedulous and active experience of fifty years, it is presumed the *spirit* and *meaning* of the Society's proposal may have been observed, although it has not been possible (in this instance) *literally* to fulfil its terms ; at least, the very intention of promoting and forwarding the views of so enlightened and highly useful a Society, may, it is hoped, be accepted as an apology for calling their attention to these observations.

It forms no part of the present design to enter minutely into the various causes that continue to operate in obstructing the cultivation of Oak ; as there is one

G                                    of

of peculiar magnitude, the consequences of which are highly detrimental and injurious, and which it is therefore the principal object of this Paper to remove.

An opinion is generally prevalent, that the Oak is particularly slow in its growth, and requires a great number of years before it affords any advantage. This idea too often deters from planting, on account of the very great length of time it is supposed the land must be occupied before any return of valuable produce can be obtained from it, after a considerable expense may have been incurred in forming plantations.

This opinion I consider as entirely founded in error, and to have taken its rise in a great measure from the want of proper management that has hitherto commonly prevailed in the raising of Oaks: and in this Paper I shall endeavour strongly to state, that the Oak may be rendered very rapid in its growth, and that consequently land may be employed

ployed to great advantage in its cultivation, as a very considerable and profitable produce may, in a much shorter time than is generally supposed, be derived from proper parts of an estate thus employed.

Oak-Timber in this country, for the most part, appears in trees of a considerable extent of head, but seldom more than *twenty* or *thirty* feet in stem; and this, in many instances, the growth of a century. Now, by the course of management here proposed, it is conceived that trees, of at least *double this magnitude*, may be obtained in about half that time.

It is not my intention to attempt a proof of this proposition by theoretical deductions, but to appeal for its confirmation to the indubitable test of fact, which, from the event of repeated trials, impresses a conviction, that experience will be found to support and establish it in the most unequivocal manner.

It

It would be easy to enlarge much on the various qualities of soil, the nature and process of vegetation, and the peculiar properties of the Oak; but as these topics may be found amply and judiciously discussed in many other authors, who have expressly treated on these subjects, I shall decline all such speculations; and, with the hope of being more essentially useful, shall confine myself to a statement as simple and practical as possible.

The Oak, in the progress of its growth, spreads numerous roots near the surface of the ground, and in an horizontal direction: these assist in supporting and preserving the tree in its position, but seem to contribute very little to its increase and magnitude. The Oak appears to derive its chief nutriment and strength from a root that always descends at right angles to the horizon, and is called the tap-root. The first thing, therefore, to be observed is, that upon a judicious attention

attention to this peculiarity, the planter's success principally depends; and the neglect of this care is the constant source of error and disappointment. In all climates, and upon all soils, to preserve this tap-root from injury, and as much as possible to assist its growth, is a general, and indeed the most essential principle in the cultivation of Oak. With a due regard to this circumstance, the management of a plantation may be resolved into the three following practical directions :

*Previously* to planting the acorns, *loosen* the earth intended for their reception, by *deep trenching.*

*Never transplant*, or in any way disturb, the saplings intended for timber.

Keep the plant carefully *pruned*, till arrived at a proper height.

More fully to elucidate the subject, and to prevent the possibility of misapprehension, it may be proper to give a more detailed statement.

G 3 . In

In determining on a spot to form a plantation of Oaks for timber, it must always be recollected that the plants are to remain without removal in their first situation : the clearing and fencing may then be attended to as usual; and in the course of the winter, from September to March, the particular spots intended for the reception of acorns, may be prepared for that purpose, by digging a trench about three feet in width, and from three to six feet in depth, according to the closeness and tenacity of the soil. If grass-ground, the first spit should be placed at the bottom of the trench; and if more than one trench be necessary, they should be prepared in the same manner, preserving a distance of ten yards between each, if it be intended to employ the intermediate space in underwood, or for any other purpose.

Having made a careful selection of acorns that are perfectly sound, and in good preservation, they are to be planted
about

about the middle of March. Draw a drill in the centre of the trench; two inches in depth, if the soil be heavy and loamy; but three inches in a light and sandy earth. In this place the acorns two inches asunder, and cover them carefully with mould. When the plants appear, they must be weeded by hand in the rows, and the earth of the trench round them cleaned with a hoe, once a month during the summer. In October inspect the rows, and thin them by pulling up every other plant: attention will of course be paid to remove the weak and crooked plants, and leave those that are tallest and straitest. On the second year, the operation of thinning must be repeated, at the same time, and in the same manner; and, should any of the remaining plants have made side-shoots stronger than the general character, they must be smoothly cut off with a sharp knife, close to the leading stem. On the third year, the thinning is again to be

G 4 repeated,

repeated, and the general pruning commenced, by cutting off close to the leading stem all the side-shoots of the first
year; thus leaving the branches of two
years to form the head of the following
year. The removal of every alternate
plant must be continued yearly, till the
trees are about thirty feet apart, at which
distance they may remain for timber.
The pruning is to be continued, by removing every year, very smooth and close
to the main stem, one year's growth of
side branches, till the plants are arrived
at a stem of forty, fifty, or sixty feet,
and they may then be permitted to run
to head without further pruning.

The particular arrangement here recommended may be varied according to
any peculiarities of situation, regard being constantly had to the general and
most important principle of loosening
the ground *very deep* previously to planting the acorns. By this mode of culture,
Oaks may be raised in almost any soil;
but,

but, where it is possible, a loam or marl is always to be chosen. Oaks thrive much the best in such earth; and, when assisted by *deep trenching* and *judicious pruning*, attain in a few years to an immense size.

Those who have been accustomed to notice the slow growth and stunted appearance of Oak Trees, when denied the assistance of art, and left to themselves in the common way, would observe with astonishment the vigorous and rapid increase of plants under the management now pointed out.

The plants thinned out the first three or four years, though not fit to be depended upon for timber, as transplanting generally injures very materially the future growth, may be replanted in the intermediate spaces between the rows, for the purpose of being afterwards removed; or they may be usefully placed in hedges, or other spare and unoccupied spots of ground. They should be headed down at the time of transplanting, as this

this operation assists the process of nature, in reproducing or remedying any
injury the tap-root may have received
from the removal: and, if proper attention be given to loosening the soil for
their reception, and pruning them as
they advance, in most instances an adequate profit will be derived from the
labour bestowed upon them. After a
few years, the produce of the timber-
plantation will be found very advantageous. The young trees that are to
be removed yearly, will always find a
ready market for a variety of purposes,
unnecessary here to enumerate. In addition to these advantages, if by this
treatment of *deep trenching* previous to
planting, and *annual careful pruning*
during the growth, timber can be produced in about fifty years, of equal quality, and much superior in size, to that
which has been above one hundred years
growing under improper management,
or without the assistance of cultivation;

it

it will doubtless be allowed that a most beneficial, if not absolutely the best possible method of " raising Oaks," is here pointed out and ascertained.

This method of cultivation may perhaps be thought to occasion so much expense in manual labour as to prevent its being generally adopted: it might perhaps be sufficient to observe, that if the work be conducted with judgment and economy, the future produce would afford ample returns for all necessary expenditure: it should also be recollected, that the previous preparation of the ground, and the subsequent pruning of the plants, are both to be performed at that season of the year when a scarcity of work will enable the planter to obtain assistance upon easier terms; with this additional advantage also, of providing employment for the labourer at those times when the general state of agricultural business renders it difficult for him

to

to find maintenance for himself and family without charitable relief.

In 1750, at Ingestrie in Staffordshire, the seat of Lord Chetwynd, some plantations were formed and managed in a great measure according to the principles here stated, and the growth of the plants was so uncommonly rapid, and so extraordinary, that it could not but attract the notice of all concerned in the conduct of them. The attention to the subject, then excited, has been the occasion and ground of all the observations and experiments made from that time to the present, the result of which is given in this paper.

The extensive plantations of the late Lord Denbeigh, at Newnham Paddox, in Warwickshire, are well known and much admired. The whole has been conducted with great judgment. About a square acre has been employed in raising Oaks upon a plan nearly similar
to

to that now proposed, and affords the best and most convincing proof of the superior utility and efficacy of such management. Had the Noble Earl been now living, I should have been enabled to have laid before the Society some more detailed particulars: That, however, is now impossible; this Paper, therefore, in its present state may perhaps be thought not altogether unworthy of notice, as tending to forward the liberal designs of the Society, and contributing to the advantage of the Public, the author conceiving that the best method of raising Oaks is ascertained and stated in it.

Should the Society be in any degree inclined to join in this sentiment, it may perhaps induce them to make some alteration in the terms of their proposal; -as, according to the statements made in this Paper, and indeed from what may be seen in every part of the kingdom, in the character and appearance of Oaks growing without cultivation, it seems
ascertained,

ascertained, that " acorns set with the " spade or dibble, without digging or " tillage," can never be depended on to form good timber ; and even in the most favourable circumstances of this case, the growth will be exceedingly slow and precarious. The same may be said of " young plants, previously raised in " nurseries, and transplanted ;" for if the tap-root be cut, broken, or in any degree injured, which in transplanting it is almost impossible to avoid, that plant will seldom become a vigorous and flourishing tree. To form a course of experiments on such a plant as the Oak, is not a very easy matter. To fulfil explicitly the conditions of the Society would require a great length of time, and would be attended with considerable expense, from which future candidates may in a great measure be exonerated. The raising even one acre in the manner here ascertained might be productive of great pecuniary advantage, if the facts and

experience

experience detailed in this Paper are permitted to prove the inutility of the other two methods, and consequently to remove the necessity of employing so much ground upon them, at an expense they will never repay.

*Chelsea College, Nov. 4, 1801.*

To Mr. CHARLES TAYLOR.

The

The GOLD MEDAL, being the Premium
offered for planting LARCH-TREES,
was this Session adjudged to JOHN
CHRISTIAN CURWEN, Esq. of Work-
ington-Hall, in ·Cumberland; from
whom the following Account and Certificates were received, stating that he
had planted eighty-four thousand nine
hundred Larch-Trees.


DEAR SIR,

ENCLOSED you have Certificates,
with proper attestations, concerning
my plantations of Larch-Trees. I might
have called upon· my friend the Bishop
of Llandaff to answer for the progress
they already make. The growth of the
Larch is astonishing upon the highest
hills. I wish I could speak with any
satisfaction of my Oaks, for which I received the Gold Medal of the Society in
1787. I am again trying the planting
acorns, but am very dubious of success.
I am

I am inclined to suspect the rapid rise of the moss decays the stem of the Oaks, and is the means of their failure. I hope to plant two hundred thousand Larch, as many Oaks, and half the number of Ash, this season. Could I have procured Larch-seed, it was my intention to have made an effort to equal Mr. Johnes's claim, but that I must omit. Upon dry hills the Larch will answer a much better end than Oaks. Wherever there was moisture, the acorns however succeeded well, and are in a thriving state: but, upon the whole, I fear the dibbling of acorns in ground which cannot be previously cleaned, will be found to be very uncertain; when it is attempted, it would be wise to go over the ground, and put in fresh acorns for two or three years.

I have been engaged for some time past in feeding my work-horses, and those employed in my collieries, with

H                    potatoes

potatoes instead of hay. I boil them
with steam. I have for the last five
weeks consumed 150 stone per day, and
to each stone I put four pounds of cut
straw. I have reason to hope I shall
succeed; and when satisfied of it, the
whole process shall be submitted to the
public. An acre of hay produces 260
stone, and an acre of potatoes 1400 stone.
Supposing the seed to be equal, the gain
is immense, and would lead to very important consequences, by encouraging
the growth of wheat. The potatoe culture has been hitherto found too expensive to be carried to any very great extent. From the trials I have made, I
am inclined to believe the boiling of
potatoes would be found to be highly
advantageous in fattening cattle.

It requires 300 acres to furnish hay
for my work-horses; and, from precarious seasons, I am often subject to
great inconveniences; but should potatoes

toes be found to answer, thirty-five acres will be amply sufficient.

I am, with respect,

Your obedient Servant,

J. CURWEN.

*Keswick, Dec.* 1, 1801.

CHARLES TAYLOR, Esq.

THE following Certificates accompanied Mr. Curwen's claim, viz. From Thomas Hodgson, of Belle-Isle, stating, that at Belle Grange, in the parish of Hawkshead, he had planted for J. C. Curwen, Esq. between October, 1798, and April, 1799, six thousand Larches, and that the same are well secured by stone walls, and are in a most thriving state: From John Sander, of Keswick, stating, that at Belle Grange, near Windermere Lake, he had planted for J. C. Curwen, Esq. between October, 1798,

and

and April, 1799, sixty-eight thousand
Larch Firs, that they are well secured
by a stone fence, and are in a very
thriving state: From the Reverend Reg.
Brathwaite, Minister of Hawkshead,
dated 30th November, 1801, confirming
both the above statements, and stating,
that on a late view of the plantations
he has found them in a most thriving
condition: From William Unwin and
William Turnbull, stating, that at Brathwaite Edge, and Workington, they had
planted for J. C. Curwen, Esq. between
October, 1798, and April, 1799, ten
thousand nine hundred Larches, and
that the same are well secured by railed
fences, and in a very promising state:
And, lastly, from the Reverend Peter
How, Minister of Workington, dated
27th November, 1801, mentioning that
he has lately seen the above-named
planting, and that it appears to be in a
highly thriving condition.

The

The GOLD MEDAL, being the Premium offered for planting SILVER FIRS, was this Session adjudged to HENRY VERNON, Esq. of Hilton Park, near Wolverhampton; from whom the following Account and Certificates were received.

SIR,

I DO myself the honour of sending you the Certificates for my claim for planting Silver Firs. The plants now living are something more than six thousand two hundred and forty; and I have the pleasure to add, that the whole of my plantations are in a most flourishing condition.

I remain, with great respect,

Your most humble Servant,

HENRY VERNON.

No. 10, *Lower Wimpole-Street.*

Mr. CHARLES TAYLOR.

H 3 THIS

THIS is to certify, that, between the 24th of June, 1797, and the 24th of June, 1798, in a mixed plantation of Forest-trees, I planted ten thousand Silver Firs, which my master, Henry Vernon, Esq. had from Scotland, and which, under my care, have been twice transplanted before, in a plantation of many acres, on the left side of the great gates leading into the turnpike-road that passes from Wolverhampton to Cannock; of which number there are now growing 6,240, in a most healthful state, from four to upwards of six feet in height. The ground for these trees was trenched two spade-graft deep, and cast into five feet ridges, which I find, from long practice under my master, for whom I have planted many hundred acres of good land, to succeed for plants of all kinds in the most luxuriant manner.

All Mr. Vernon's plantations are uncommonly well protected by ditches five

feet

feet in width and three feet in depth, all cast on the sides of the plantations, with the additional security of posts and double rails of great strength, of oak, and double rows of quick, which being now six feet in height, are, as usual, about to be split, and laid down under the rails, when the plants fling out uncommonly strong new shoots, which, after growing two years, are headed, and then kept about two feet in height above the bank, and form an impenetrable thick hedge.

Given under my hand, this 11th day of December, 1801.

LAWRENCE GRAY,
Gardener to Henry Vernon, Esq.

The above Account was confirmed by the Reverend John Clare, Vicar of Bushbury.

The

The GOLD MEDAL, or THIRTY GUI-NEAS, at the option of the Candidate, being the Premium offered for planting OSIERS, Class 6, Vol. 19, was this Session adjudged to Mr. FREDERICK CLIFFORD CHERRY, of New Wood Farm, near Stoke D'Aubernon, in Surrey; from whom the following Accounts and Certificates were received, and who made choice of the pecuniary Reward.

SIR,

I BEG leave to present myself as a Candidate for the Premium offered by the Society for the Encouragement of Arts, etc. to the person who shall have planted the greatest quantity of land with Osiers, as I have planted sixty acres with the various kinds mentioned in the Society's advertisement, and which are in a very flourishing condition. I hope, at some future period, to have the

honour

honour of acquainting the Society with the progress of the various kinds, and every particular relative to the same,

I am, SIR,

Your most obedient Servant,

FREDERICK CLIFFORD CHERRY.

*Stoke D'Aubernon,*
*23d Nov.* 1801.

Mr. CHARLES TAYLOR.

SIR,

IN compliance with the desire of your laudable Society, I will give all the information in my power respecting the planting of Osiers at New Wood Farm; and happy shall I be, if any thing I can say may be thought to be in any degree interesting.

The soil is a strong clay, resting on a retentive clay subsoil of great depth. It

has

has long been in a state of tillage, and
is enclosed by flourishing woody hedges.
The soil is naturally of a weak nature,
has been much impoverished by bad
management, and, as arable land, is not
worth five shillings per acre.

The greater part of the plantation in
the year 1800 consisted of Oats, and received only one ploughing of a mean
depth, previous to planting. Nine acres
were wheat in 1800, after summer-fallow. Three acres in the same field, with
the nine, were sown with grass-seed in
the autumn of 1800, and were planted
at the same time with the rest, without
any preparation whatever, except that
of harrowing once in a place. Eight
acres, which were last planted, were in
various states of tillage; some were a
good fallow in 1800; some were sown
with grass-seeds in the autumn of that
year; and some were very grassy, and
had lain all the summer without ploughing. The grassy part, and the part sown
with

with grass-seeds, were ploughed once before planting; but the part which was summer-fallow was not ploughed.

The planting was begun on the 9th of February, 1801, and continued till the whole was finished, which was on the 23d of March.

The sets were large cuttings, of about eighteen inches in length, thrust into the ground by hand, leaving from four to six inches of their length above the surface.

They were all planted in rows from twenty-two to thirty inches asunder, and the sets from twelve to twenty-four inches asunder in the rows; but few were planted at the widest distances.

The plants made a more vigorous shoot in spring than they did afterwards; but they are allowed by judges to look uncommonly well. Very few sets have failed, perhaps not above a hundred on an acre, except in the field last planted, where the dead sets are more numerous. This

This. may be owing more to the treatment the sets received, than to the time
in which they were planted. : They were
brought round the North and South
Forelands, were put out of the ship into
a barge, and from thence into a waggon,
and then remained some time before
they were planted.

Those plants that succeeded wheat are
much the best Osiers ; and those planted
on the seeds, without ploughing, are
much the worst. They are invariably
the best where the ground is cleanest;
and from this circumstance I am led to
think, that summer-fallowing before
planting would be judicious management.

A neighbour of mine planted 350 sets
in his garden, 341 of which produced
Osiers; the rest died. The soil of the
garden is clay. They were planted the
latter end of March, in rows, thirty
inches by twenty-one inches asunder,
with beans between the rows. These

341

341 sets have produced a bundle of Osiers of about thirty-eight inches in circumference; and some of them are upwards of ten feet in length. This, I think, proves that the soil is congenial, and the tillage favourable to the growth of Osiers.

In the plantation already mentioned there are several sorts, but principally those known by the name of the New-kind. However, as I am not intimately acquainted with the varieties, I will not attempt to describe them.

Any farther information that the Society may require, and I have in my power to give, I shall be very happy to communicate.

I am, SIR,

Your obedient Servant,

F. C. CHERRY.

*New Wood Farm,*
*Stoke D'Aubernon, Feb. 16, 1802.*

CHARLES TAYLOR, Esq.

THIS

THIS is to certify, that Frederick Clifford Cherry, of the parish of Stoke D'Aubernon, in the county of Surrey, has, between the 1st of January and the 1st of April, 1801, planted sixty acres of Willows, commonly known by the names of Osiers, New-kind, and Red Willow, with not less than 17,000 on an acre; and that the same are now properly fenced, and in a thriving condition.

WM. ALLEN, Officiating Minister.
RICH. HARWOOD, Churchwarden.

The

The SILVER MEDAL, or TEN GUINEAS, at the option of the Candidate, being the Premium offered for planting OSIERS, Class 7, Vol. 19, was this Session adjudged to Mr. SETH BULL, of Ely, in Cambridgeshire; from whom the following Account and Certificates were received, and who made choice of the pecuniary Reward.

SIR,

ON reading over the list of Premiums offered by the Society for the Encouragement of Arts, etc. for the year 1801, I beg leave to claim the Premium for planting Osiers.

It may not be unnecessary to premise, that, in the year 1800, I purchased a piece of waste land that lies contiguous to the river Ouse, and is liable to be inundated by every flood. I mention this circumstance, because the value of such land is very little indeed for any other

other purpose than planting; and, on account of its situation for moisture, and the accumulation of fresh soil by the winter floods, is the most proper for that purpose. This land, which was more than eight acres, and was dry during the summer of that year, which was very favourable, I prepared by throwing it up into bars, or beds, each being about a pole in width, and raised them more than a foot higher than the natural soil, for the reception of the sets, or plants, in the Spring of 1801; and, in the months of March and April last, I planted each of them at the distance of exactly twenty-one inches, that is, 14,223 per acre. The season was fine for the purpose; and I have the satisfaction to add, that they have grown beyond my most sanguine expectation, the greater part being more than nine feet in height, and proportionably thick. I have spared neither expense nor care to keep them perfectly free from weeds,

and

ahd well fenced; and almost all of them will be, in the spring, fit to cut for the basket-maker's use, which is, I believe, an unexampled precedent for so large a quantity. The sorts consist of French, New-kind, West-country, Spaniards,. and a few Welch, and Osiers, all of the best quality. I have added the most respectable Certificates of the truth of the above statement. One of them is signed by Thomas Page, Esq. who received the Honorary Premium for planting Osiers in 1799; and the other by the Reverend Mr. Mules, Domestic Chaplain to the Bishop of Ely, and Mr. Lutt, junior, who authorise me to declare, that it is the finest piece of wood they ever saw for the first year of planting; and I think I may add, that it is universally allowed to be so by every person who has seen it.

I shall esteem myself very happy, should I be so fortunate as to receive the Society's Premium, the prospect of

I                         which,

which, I can assure you, acted as a stimulus to me in planting so large a quantity.

I am, SIR,

Your most obedient Servant,

SETH BULL.

*Ely, Cambridgeshire,*
16*th Nov.* 1801.

CHARLES TAYLOR, Esq.


Two Certificates, viz. one from Thomas Page, Esq. of Ely, and the other from the Reverend Charles Mules and Mr. Lutt, jun. accompanied this Letter, as above mentioned, and confirmed Mr. Bull's statement.

The

The SILVER MEDAL was this Session presented to CHARLES GIBSON, Esq. of Quermore Park, near Lancaster, for planting 6000 Elms; from whom the following Accounts and Certificates were received.

SIR,

I NOW enclose the statement of the plantations of Charles Gibson, Esq. on the subject of whose claim I troubled you early in November.

I am, SIR,

Your obedient Servant,

CHARLES ARNOLD.

*Bedford-Row,*
*8th Dec. 1801.*

CHARLES TAYLOR, Esq.

I 2 THIS

THIS is to certify, that the under-mentioned number of Trees have been planted on the estate of Charles Gibson, Esq. of Quermore Park, near Lancaster, from the 1st of December, 1798, to the 1st of April, 1799, viz. *Thirty-five thousand Forest-Trees*, two and a half feet in height, and at the distance of from three to four feet; consisting of nearly an equal quantity of Oak, Larch, Beech, Birch, Mountain Ash, Sycamore, Elms, and Firs, and a mixture of Ash, Hornbeams, and Chesnuts. The above are planted upon waste land, properly fenced, principally with a ditch and bank railed, and partly with stone walls, etc. Thirteen thousand five hundred are likewise upon arable land in tillage, and were well manured the year before planting. Twenty-seven thousand Thorn Quicksets were also planted in new fences made within the above-mentioned time, making four hundred and thirty
roods

roods of seven yards, at nine plants in one yard.

ADOLPHUS PERRIE, Superintendant.

*Quermore Park,*
 *April 7, 1799.*

CHARLES GIBSON.

$$N^o$$

$$\left.\begin{array}{r} 35,000 \\ 13,500 \end{array}\right\} \text{Trees.}$$

$$48,500$$

27,000 Quicks.

On

On inspecting the books, the number of Trees as above mentioned stand as follows :

| | |
|---|---:|
| Oak - - - - - - - - - | 7,500 |
| Larch - - - - - - - | 7,500 |
| Beech - - - - - - - | 6,500 |
| Sycamore - - - - - - -- | 7,000 |
| Elms - - - - - - - - | 6,000 |
| Scotch Firs - - - - - - | 2,000 |
| Spruce do. - - - - - - | 2,000 |
| Common Ash - - - - - - | 1,000 |
| Mountain do. - - - - - - | 2,000 |
| Birch - - - - - - - | 5,000 |
| Spanish Chesnuts - - - - - | 500 |
| Horse do. - - - - - - | 500 |
| Hornbeams - - - - - - | 1,000 |
| | 48,500 |

THE

THE Bishop of Landaff testifies, that he has seen, in January, the plantations of Charles Gibson, and that they are in a most flourishing and thriving state,

R. LANDAFF,

*March* 16, 1802.

SIR,

I WAS aware that the total number of Trees planted by me between the 1st December, 1798,. and the 1st of April, 1799, would fall short of other claimants; but I thought the Society would be glad to know that the desirable object of planting was pursued in this neighbourhood, though upon a small scale. On the receipt of yours of the 6th instant, I applied to the Gentlemen whose Certificate you have to this Letter, to inspect my plantations, in order to ascertain the state of the Elms, which they

I 4                      found

found to be in general in a healthy,
thriving condition.  It is hardly possible
to say what the distance is between each
Elm, as they are planted promiscuously
with seven or eight sorts of Trees, the
whole of which are three feet distant
from each other; but they were supposed to be about four or five yards
distant.  With respect to soil, about
three thousand, or one half that number,
were planted upon a stiffish soil, with a
clay bottom, pulverized by two crops of
corn previous to planting. The remainder
were planted on a light loam, rather
rocky, and which never had been, nor
ever could be, cultivated to advantage.
The holes for the plants were made two
feet in diameter, and much pains was
taken to break the sods in the uncultivated ground.  I gave from 1s. to 1s. 2d.
per hundred for making the holes.  The
plants were four years old when taken
out of my nursery, where they had been
two years, being purchased two-years-
old

old seedlings, and in general about two feet and a half in height. Those upon the clay succeed the best, probably from the ground being in better order. As they were planted for ornament as well as utility, great care has been taken to preserve the fences. I beg leave to observe, that it is my custom to plant thick (being near the sea), and to thin out about the third year, by transplanting; or, when the plants incommode each other, to make one plantation serve as a nursery for another, till they stand at proper distances to remain for timber. By this method, the removed plants carry up their thickness, and the roots of those which remain, being *in part* cut, put out into the filled-up holes the spring following innumerable fibres, and thrive better than before. I must however observe, that when the Trees become large, they must not be transplanted into very exposed situations. This is all the information in my power to give, and

and I fear you will find it very unimportant.

I have only to add, that, exclusive of the Elms planted between the 1st December, 1798, and 1st April, 1799 (being 6,000), I have planted upon my estate, in other years, about 2,000 more; and have now between four and five thousand in the nursery to go out next season.

I am, Sir,

Your obedient humble Servant,

Charles Gibson.

Mr. Charles Taylor.

The above Accounts are certified by Edmund Rigby, one of His Majesty's Justices of the Peace for the county of Lancaster, and P. M. Procter, Clerk, M. A. Perpetual Curate of Eaton.

The

The SILVER MEDAL was this Session presented to Mr. ROBERT BROWN, of Markle, near Haddington, in Scotland, for his Culture of BEANS and WHEAT in. one year on the same Land; from whom the following Accounts and Certificates were received of his repeated Experiments on this Culture.

### SIR,

I TAKE the liberty of transmitting to you an account of eighty-eight and a half acres of land drilled with Beans in the months of February and March, 1798, amongst which a few Peas were mixed, in order to improve the straw as fodder for horses, and for making ropes to tie the crop. The whole of the said land was sown with Wheat in the month of October the same year. I shall shortly

state

state the mode of managing the Beans, being ready to give any further information that may be required.

The land was first cross-ploughed during the preceding winter, and about twenty acres were dunged previous to this furrowing being given, and ten acres more in the spring, when the Beans were drilled. The quantity of dung applied to the acre was about twelve cart-loads, each drawn by two horses, the weight of which might be about a ton. The land at seed-time was clean ploughed over, and the drill-barrow followed every third plough, which gave an interval between the rows of twenty-six or twenty-seven inches. The quantity of seed sown was from seventeen to nineteen pecks per acre, as those who managed the drill sometimes from inattention allowed it to sow a degree thicker at one time than another. The kind of Beans sown was the common Horse-bean,

bean, mixed, as I have already said, with a trifling quantity of Peas; and the average produce per acre of the whole fields sown was nearly thirty-six bushels per acre, the produce being altogether 3,258 bushels, Winchester measure. They were reaped from the first to the middle of September, and the straw was used for supporting the working-horses during the winter months.

It is now proper I should explain my method of cleaning or ploughing the land, when the crop was on the ground, which was effected by a one-horse plough, without any hand-hoe being used. I first harrowed it completely before the Beans appeared above ground, and water-furrowed and griped it. As soon as the Beans would stand the plough, a gentle furrow was given, and women were employed to turn any of the earth from the plants which might have been thrown

thrown upon them. Every succeeding furrow was taken deeper, and the last was used for laying the earth up close to the plants, which I consider as of great importance. They were ploughed four times ; and I estimated the whole expense of cleaning them at four shillings per acre, and that of drilling and harrowing at one shilling and fourpence. In no other way can the ground be cleaned at a less expense.

The soil upon which they were sown was a loam of different varieties. I have for many years practised this mode of husbandry for raising Beans, which have uniformly been succeeded by Wheat, and shall be happy to give you any information in my power respecting the culture of them. This year I have 110 acres, all managed in the way described. I inclose two Certificates, one of the measurement, and the other from two farmers of character, that I had such

fields

fields in Beans and Wheat; and am,
respectfully,

Your obedient Servant,

ROBERT BROWN.

*Markle, near Haddington, Scotland,*
     *28th October, 1799.*

## Mr. CHARLES TAYLOR.

I, WILLIAM DICKINSON, sworn mea-
surer and land-surveyor at Linton,
in the parish of Preston, and county of
Haddington, North Britain, do hereby
certify, that I have measured the after-
mentioned fields, which were last year
drilled with Beans, and sown the same
year with Wheat, being part of the farms
of Markle and West-Fortune, possessed
by Robert Brown, Esq. and find the
contents of each, in English statute acres,
to be as under, viz.

*Upon*

*Upon Markle Farm.*

|   |   | A. |
|---|---|---|
| 1. Long Side - - - - - - | | 11.86 |
| 2. Wester Park - - - - - | | 7.70 |
| 3. Foreshot - - - - - - | | 24.82 |
| 4. Long Inless - - - - - | | 11.18 |
| | | 55.56 |

*Upon West-Fortune Farm.*

|   | A. |   |
|---|---|---|
| 5. North Crofts - - | 24.40 | |
| 6. Dingleton - - - | 8.54 | |
| | | 32.94 |
| | A. | 88.50 |

Amounting in all to eighty-eight and a half acres, English statute measure.

WILLIAM DICKINSON.

SIR,

SIR,

HAVING sown, according to the drill husbandry, four fields, consisting of eighty-nine acres, three roods, and six poles, English statute measure, with Beans, in the months of February and March, 1800, which were succeeded by Wheat sown in the month of October following, I beg leave to claim the Premium offered by the Society of Arts for these branches of husbandry.

The soil upon which these crops were raised was chiefly of that variety generally characterised as heavy loam, though part of it approached to a soft loam; and nearly the whole was incumbent upon a bottom retentive of moisture. Owing to the uncommon wetness of the autumn and winter months,. I was prevented from giving the ground more than one ploughing, except one field, consisting of nineteen acres nearly, which was first cross-ploughed, and afterwards

K        ploughed

ploughed in length. The remainder was sown with Beans, the intervals between the drills being twenty-seven inches, in the months of February and March, 1800, after one ploughing; and the whole eighty-nine acres were managed afterwards in the following manner:

The ground was completely harrowed before the plants appeared above ground, and ploughed with one horse as early as the Beans were able to stand the operation. This ploughing was repeated about two months afterwards, and so on as often as necessary. The whole was ploughed four times during the summer months, and a part had five ploughings; and a picking of annual weeds by the hand was given to one of the fields. The total expense of drilling, horse-hoeing, and hand-picking, amounted to about five shillings per acre, upon an average.

The kind of Beans sown was the common Horse-bean, mixed with a few Peas, which were the best part of the crop.

crop. The season during the whole of 1800 was remarkably dry, which stunted the crop on the outset. The plants were therefore very short, and the produce when thrashed was only eighteen Winchester bushels per acre; though I am convinced, if a greater portion of Peas had been mixed with the Beans, the return would have been much superior.

The ground, after carrying Beans, was in excellent order; and, without any dung, yielded me a fine crop of Wheat in 1801. The Wheat was sown after one ploughing, in the month of October, 1800,

I am, SIR,

Your obedient Servant,

ROBERT BROWN,

December 1, 1801.

MR. CHARLES TAYLOR.

SIR,

SIR,

ENCLOSED are Certificates of the crop of my Bean-fields of 1800, which were sown with Wheat in the October of that year. The Bean-crop was the worst I ever reaped, though, from being attentively cleaned, the ground was in good order for carrying a crop of Wheat the following year. The advantage of this mode of husbandry consists in this, that in the most unfavourable season the ground may be preserved in good order.

I have a fine crop of Beans this year, and I think the produce will be full thirty-six bushels per acre. I had about one hundred and ten acres under that grain, an account of which I shall probably send you next year.

I had only about thirty acres Spring Wheat this crop, last winter being so favourable as to admit a full sowing in October. With this small quantity I

did

did not think it necessary to offer myself as a claimant.

I am, SIR,

Your most obedient,

ROBERT BROWN.

The Certificates alluded to in the above Letter are from Mr. William Dickinson, land-surveyor at Linton, in the parish of Preston, and county of Haddington ; Mr. Alexander Dodds, farmer at Newmains; and Mr. Andrew Somerville, farmer at Atholstoneford; and confirm Mr. Brown's statement.

The

The THANKS of the Society were this
Session voted to T. S. DYOT BUCK-
NALL, Esq. M. P. for the following
Communication relative to the HAMP-
TON-COURT VINE.


SIR,

THE famous Hampton-Court Vine,
which I introduced into the 17th
Volume of the Transactions of the Society,
has this year received much splendour
from a new house graciously ordered to
be erected by his Majesty; this house
being three feet wider, and two feet
higher, than the old one. In order, likewise, that the Vine might sustain no
injury from the external air, during the
time of placing the new covering over
it, at my request the old building was
not removed until the other was fully
completed; which new building was
finished, and the glazing is going on,

and

and will be placed in its proper station in the spring of 1802.

At present the glass, from the increased width and beighth of the house, is 72 feet by 21 feet; and, by the enlargement of a perpendicular light of 72 feet by 3 feet, makes together 1,728 superficial square feet of glass, placed over one Vine, and filling the whole house.

From the best information I could collect, this Vine was planted in the year 1770; and, from the fortunate station it has acquired, with the attention which is given to all the valuable fruits raised within the royal gardens, Mr. Padley and I entertain no doubt but it may continue in health and full bearing for a great length of time. I have been more minute than otherwise I should, from the wish, that whenever any curious production is observed in the vegetable kingdom, some intelligent person would record it for posterity, in any popular publication of the time. Such attention

K 4 would

would be of very material service in Horticulture, and the habit would gradually remove many doubts which obstruct the progress of improvements.

This Vine was at first selected rather accidentally, for I remember five different Vines within the same building. As it displayed a vigour, and a disposition to fruitfulness beyond the rest, it induced the chief manager to order the others to be cut away as this advanced; and it has occupied the whole space of the building for about twelve years. This is without doubt the most complete fruit-bearing plant that ever came within my observation.

In the former memorial I mentioned that no other plants were placed to grow under this Vine; but it would have been more correct in me to have said, " No " other plant will thrive under the shade " of these Vine-leaves; for every pane " of glass is nearly covered on the under-" side, so that a clear uninterrupted " light

" light cannot extend to the ground, and
" that is found to be very necessary for
" the support of a healthy vegetation."

It is well worthy of remark, that this
Vine, from being excluded from the
external air, little heated by fire, kept
perfectly clean, and regularly attended
through all its progress, IS NOT SUBJECT
TO BLIGHT ; neither is it liable to many
other casual evils, to which fruit-bearing
trees are much disposed : and other
fruit-trees would be as clear from blight
as this Vine, were they as well guarded
from injuries.

In the Papers forming a Treatise on
Blight, which the Society have honoured
by publishing in their Transactions, I
remarked, " We cannot afford to place
" our plantations within hot-houses for
" their protection; yet the principles of
" blight being established, and known,
" that under shelter it may be prevented,
" will be found of very essential service
" in

" in general practice, by leading man-
" kind to advert to the natural causes
" of blight, and from those sources to
" establish a system of proper precau-
" tions; or, having happened, in part to
" remove the ill effects arising therefrom,
" as are expressed in Classes 80 to 83
" for the Premiums offered." This I
have much enlarged upon in former
Papers, to good purpose, for practice,
and here repeat: Prune, wash, manure,
and perform any operations rationally
tending to keep the *trees in health*; but
by all means scrape off the rotten bark,
and smear the trees over with oil, and
any cheap drug to offend the insects, as
recommended in the 18th volume.

When the area of glass was only 1,300
square feet, the Vine was permitted to
carry each year 1,800 bunches of grapes.
As the area is now enlarged to 1,730
feet, it is presumed the plant will well
support 2,400 bunches.

To

To such as are but little acquainted with subjects of this kind, it may seem singular that it should be possible to predict the number of bunches the Vine is to produce in each year. Such persons should be informed, that the plant is not permitted to follow its own natural propensities, either in growth or bearing, but is kept perfectly under the controul of the gardener. Were the plant left to itself, the individual grape or bunches would not be so large, neither would they ripen so well, or produce the beautiful bunches which are seen there at present.

This is a very proper place for me to request of those who are entrusted with the management of valuable fruits, to be attentive to thin them sufficiently in due time; to foresee how the crop is likely to fill up, by reflecting on the natural size of the fruit; and never to suffer any part of the tree to be overloaded, or the fruit much cluttered together.

gether. Such neglect not only injures
the present crop, but prevents the plant
from continuing in sufficient strength to
throw out the blossoms, and have them
duly impregnated for the next summer's
production. In the first Paper which I
presented to the public upon Orcharding, I took care to place this subject in
its proper light, observing, that it is the
fine fruit which sells the orchard, and
invariably produces the most credit,
pleasure, and profit to the grower.

I think, in some of the former Papers,
I have mentioned, that in the fruit-
bearing trees, the fruit improves as the
tree advances in strength, and after that
time as gradually declines. The Cherry
will go on some time longer.

The public should be attentive to
names and discriminations of the different fruits, as of consequence in the
improvement of the art. This Vine is
called the Black Hamburgh; but I
should suspect, from the freedom of
                              growth,

growth, health, and regular good bearing, that it is a new variety. This term,
with regard to fruits, is fully explained
in the 17th volume of the Transactions
of the Society, and in the second volume
of the Orchardist.

Where the stem enters the house, it
now girts sixteen inches; and, to give
some appearance of proof for what I
advanced with regard to the probable
duration, Speechley, on the Culture of
the Vine, mentions, that Strabo . observed that flooring-boards were cut out
of the stems of Vines; consequently
they must have grown to a large size
in those climates, and lived to a great
age : and very slight reflexion will convince the practitioners, that an extensive
forcing-house is the finest station in the
world for the grape, under such culture
as it will probably meet with in the royal
gardens; because a forcing-house may
be accommodated to any climate.

It.

It has been before remarked, that some branches of this Vine run more than a hundred feet, and that the grapes growing on the extreme ends are the finest fruit: and, to ascertain some experiments, Mr. Padley obligingly intends, when the time of training arrives, to attempt to lead one of the longest and clearest branches directly horizontal on the wall, under the highest range of glass. This idea will require some years to accomplish, but when effected will add 70 feet to the present 100, and will make a run of 170 feet round the three sides of the house. Thus, for instance, stem 8 feet $+ 72 + 21 = 101$; add the returned run of 70 feet from north to south, and the total will be 171 feet in length. I do not apprehend that any tree in Britain has run to such an extent.

I have been the more induced to attend to the culture and growth of this Vine, from a desire of improving the mode of forcing grapes, both as to the

manner

manner of applying the fire and construction of the buildings, so as to produce a great quantity of fine perfectly ripe forced grapes at a small expense. I wrote an Essay on this subject three years ago. Should any further material circumstance affect this Vine during my time, I shall take care to present the same to the Society.

I am, SIR,

Your most obedient Servant,

THOMAS SKIP DYOT BUCKNALL,

*Hampton-Court,*
*8th October,* 1801.

CHARLES TAYLOR, Esq. Secretary,

The

The THANKS of the Society were this
Session presented to THOMAS SKIP
DYOT BUCKNALL, Esq. for the fol-
lowing Communication on the NATURE
of the VARIETIES of ENGRAFTED
FRUIT-TREES, and his Plan for in-
creasing the Number of new valuable
Fruits.

  SIR,

SOME friends have requested that I
would introduce another Paper on
the Nature of the valuable Varieties of
engrafted Fruits, as they are of opinion
that the Essay in the 17th Volume of the
Transactions of the Society is not sufficiently extended for a subject so important to the Fruit-growers, and those
interested in the productions of Fruits.
As a proof of my willingness to make the
Orchardist as perfect as I can, I beg you
to present my compliments to the Society, with the following elucidations.

This

This is a subject in rural economy which ought to be much better understood than it is, in order to enable the planters to judge of the sorts proper to be planted, either as an article of pleasure, profit, or recreation; as much of the credit of the plantation must arise from judiciously choosing Trees of the best, new, or middle-aged sorts, and not of the old worn-out varieties, which latter cannot, in the planting of Orchards in common situations, ever form *valuable Trees*, and must end in the disappointment of the planter.

Engrafted Fruits, I have before said, and I now repeat, are not permanent. Every one of the least reflexion must see that there is an essential difference between the power and energy of a seedling plant, and the tree which is to be raised from cuttings or elongations. The seedling is endued with the energies of nature, while the graft, or scion, is nothing more than a regular elongation,

L                    carried

carried perhaps through the several re-peatings of the same variety; whereas the seed, from having been placed in the earth, germinates and becomes a new plant, wherever nature permits like to produce liké in vegetation; as in the oak, beech, and other mast-bearing trees. These latter trees, from each passing through the state of seedlings, are per-fectly continued, and endued with the functions of forming perfect seeds for raising other plants by evolution, to the continuance of the like species.

This is not the case with engrafted Fruits. They are doomed by nature to continue for a time, and then gradually decline, till at last the variety is totally lost, and soon forgotten, unless recorded by tradition, or in old publications.

Reason, with which Providence has most bountifully blessed some of our species, has enabled us, when we find a superior variety, to engraft it on a wild-ing stock, or to raise plants from layers

and

and cuttings, or even to raise up the roots, and thus to multiply our sources of comfort and pleasure. This, however, does not imply that the multiplication of the same variety, for it is no more, should last for ever, unless the species will naturally arise from seed.

Nature, in her teaching, speaks in very intelligible language, which language is conveyed by experience and observation. Thus we see that among promiscuous seeds of fruits of the same sort, one or more may arise, whose fruits shall be found to possess a value far superior to the rest in many distinguishable properties. From experience, also, we have obtained the power, by engrafting, of increasing the number of this newly-acquired tree, can change its country, give it to a friend, send it beyond the seas, or fill a kingdom with that fruit, if the natives are disposed so to do. Thus we seem to have a kind of creative power in our own hands.

L 2                    From

From the attention lately paid to the culture of engrafted Fruits, I hope we are now enabled to continue a supposed happily acquired tree, when we can find it, for a much longer duration than if such variety had been left in the state of unassisted nature; perhaps I may say for a duration as long again, or something more. After these sanguine expectations, I may reasonably be asked, to what does all this amount? for here there is no direct permanency—and why? The *why* is very obvious—because the kernels within the fruit, which are the seed of the plants for forming the next generation ⋅ of trees, will not produce their like. I allow they may do so accidentally; but nothing more can be depended on.

For example, suppose we take ten kernels or pips of any apple raised on an engrafted stock ː sow them, and they will produce ten different varieties, no two of which will be alike; nor will either

of

of them closely resemble the fruit from whence the seeds were collected. The leaves also of those trees raised from the same primogenious or parent stock, will not *actually* be a copy of the leaves of any one of the varieties or family, to which each is connected by a vegetable consanguinity. I intentionally used the word *actually*, because a resemblance may be found, though not much of that is to be expected.

I beg that what has been last mentioned may not be taken as a discouragement to attempts for raising new varieties. I was obliged to speak very strongly, in order to place the culture upon its true foundation. I think it need not be observed, that there is no acquiring a new variety, but through the means of a seedling plant; and therefore whoever wishes to succeed must attempt it that way, or wait till others in their plantations may more fortunately produce it.

L 3

In

·In choosing the seeds, that apple is most likely to produce the clearest and finest plants, whose kernels are firm, large, and well ripened. The size of the fruit is not to be regarded; for large apples do not always ripen their fruit well, or rather for cider the small fruits are generally preferred for making the strongest, highest-flavoured liquor. And from what I have been able to collect in the cider-countries, it is there the opinion, that an apple something above the improved crab promises the best success. This advantage also attends the practice: if there are no valuable apples raised from that attempt, these wildings will make excellent stocks to engraft upon.

Gentlemen who actually employ themselves in attempting to acquire new varieties, should remember that they ought to select all the sets, from the bed of apple-quick, whose appearance is in the least degree promising, and plant them together, at such a distance as to allow

each

each to produce its fruit, which will happen in about twelve, fifteen, or eighteen years. My friend Mr. Knight, who undoubtedly is the first in actual exertions for procuring these happily acquired new varieties, has had two plants bear fruit at six years old, and one at five. The cider-countries have offered several premiums for procuring new varieties, and some with good effect. Premiums have been given both to Mr. Knight and Mr. Alban.

When the new variety is to be raised from a valuable *admired* apple, I should recommend the placing these seeds in a garden-pot, filled with mould from an old melon-bed; carrying the pot into a retired situation near the water, and giving attention to run the plants to as large a size as is convenient within eighteen months. With this view, the pot should be placed in the green-house the first winter; and when the plants are afterwards to be set out in the spots,

L 4 they

they should not be placed under the drip of trees, or much exposed to the winds.

Two instances have been mentioned, the improved crab, and most admired apple; but prudence says, try all sorts, and something probably will arise; and the process is attended with little trouble or expense to a person who constantly resides in the country: yet, after all this scientific care, the apple may want flavour, and be in other respects nothing better than a common wilding.

It is an undoubted fact, and worthy of observation, that all the different trees of the same variety have a wonderful tendency to similarity of appearance among themselves; and that the parent stock, and all engrafted from it, have a far greater resemblance to each other, than can be found in any part of the animal creation; and this habit does not vary to any extent of age.

As

As an encouragement in attempting to increase the number of new valuable fruits, we can prove that the golden pippin is native English. The red-streak, a seedling of Herefordshire, if not raised, yet was first brought into notice by Lord Scudamore, and was for a long time called Scudamore's Crab, The Stire Apple was accidentally raised in the Forest of Dean, in Glocestershire, and took the name of *Forest Stire*. The cider made from this apple was the strongest the country ever produced, according to any living record. The Haglo-crab, the best cider fruit now remaining, was discovered in the parish of Ecloe, on the banks of the Severn; and, about sixty or seventy years ago, many scions were taken from this tree by Mr. Bellamy, and engrafted on seedling stocks about Ross. These are now grown old; and, to ascertain the age of the variety, I went with Charles Edwin, Esq. to Ecloes, in hopes of seeing the primogenious of this family. The

The proprietor of the estate acquainted Mr. Edwin that it had ceased to bear years ago, and was cut down. Those at Ross are but poor bearers now, and I should suppose the variety must be 140 years old, though Marshal, who wrote in the year 1786, mentions these trees were prolific, and he supposes the sort to be about eighty years old; but, from present experience, it must be much more. The Tinton Squash-pear is of Glocestershire; the Barland and Old-field were near Ledbury, Herefordshire. The two last pears clearly bear the names of the two fields where they were raised. The Barland fell about six years ago, visibly from weight and longevity, which was supposed to have been about 200 years. There have been many other names of estimation handed down to us, though the realities are now totally worn out, and have ceased to exist. Can any better proof be desired, that engrafted fruits are not permanent, than the regret

we

we feel for the loss of these old valuable fruits.

To make my Paper as short as convenient, I have dwelt only on the Apple and Pear; yet all the engrafted fruits are under the same predicament of the seed not producing its like, and the offspring in time falling into a nothingness of growth and bearing, though that space of time must certainly depend on the natural longevity and hardiness of the sort, soil, position, care, etc. All these are more fully expressed in the papers published in the different volumes of the Transactions of this Society, and the two volumes of the Orchardist, wherein the whole system is extended, to form a rational culture for the management of Standard Fruits.

It should be remembered, that as I am now alluding to the state of actual permanency, fifty years are to be accounted as nothing; and as often as we come to that point, we are compelled to resort

resort to our first assertion, " That en-
" grafted fruits are not permanent, they
" being continued from elongations, and
" not raised as a repetition of seeds."
This is the only rational way as yet introduced of accounting for the loss of the
valuable old varieties of fruits.   Should
a better system be introduced, I shall
readily adopt it ;  but this · sufficiently
answers the purposes of the planter.

Some years ago, from due investigation and thorough conviction, I propagated this principle; and it was published
in the 17th volume of the Society's
Transactions, in the following words :
" All the grafts taken from this first tree,
" or parent stock, or any of the descend-
" ants, will for some generations thrive ;
" but when this first stock shall, by mere.
" dint of old-age, fall into actual decay,
" a nihility of vegetation—the descend-
" ants, however young, or in whatever
" situation they may be, will gradually
" decline; and, from that time, it would
                                    " be

" be imprudent, in point of profit, to
" attempt propagating that variety from
" any of them. This is the dogma which
" must be received.  I do not expect a
" direct assent, neither do I wish it, for
" it should be taken with much reserve;
" but it is undoubtedly true." These
considerations should stimulate us in
searching after new varieties, equal, or
perhaps superior, to those of which we
regret the loss.

Observe that, from the time the kernel
germinates for apple-quick, should the
plant be disposed to form a valuable
variety, there will appear a regular progressive change, or improvement, in the
organization of the leaves, until that
variety has stood, and grown sufficient
to blossom and come into full bearing;
that is, from the state of infancy to
maturity; and it is this and other
circumstances, by which the inquisitive
eye is enabled to form the selection
among those appearing likely to become
valuable

valuable fruits.   But from that time the
new variety, or selected plant, compared
with all the engraftments which may be
taken from it, or any of them, these
shall shew a most undeviating sameness
among themselves.

It is readily allowed, that the different
varieties of fruits are easily distinguished
from each other by many particulars,
not only respecting their general fertility,
and the form, size, shape, and flavour
of the fruit, but also the manner of the
growth of the tree, the thickness and
proportion of the twigs, their shooting
from their parent stem, the form, colour,
and consistence of the leaf, and many
other circumstances, by which the variety
can be identified; and were it possible
to engraft each variety upon the same
stock, they would still retain their discriminating qualities, with the most undeviating certainty.

The proper conclusion to be drawn
from the statement in the last paragraph,

is

is this—that were any one to put the thought in practice on a full-grown hardy or crab stock, it would produce an excellent proof that engrafted fruits are not permanent. For if twenty different varieties were placed together, so that each might receive its nurture from the same stem, they would gradually die off in actual succession, according to the age or state of health of the respective variety, at the time the scions were placed in the stock; and a discriminating eye, used to this business, would nearly be able to foretell the order in which each scion would actually decline. Should it also happen that two or three suckers from the wilding stock had been permitted to grow among the *twenty grafts*, such suckers or wilding shoots will continue, and make a tree after all the rest are gone. A further consequence would result from the experiment: among such a number of varieties, each of the free growers would starve the delicate, and

and drive them out of existence only so much the sooner. It must be observed, that this supposed stem is the foster-parent to the twenty scions, and real parent to the suckers; and those the least conversant with engrafted fruits know the advantage acquired from this circumstance. And here it is worth while remarking, that a Gascoyne, or wild cherry, will grow to twice the size that ever an engrafted cherry did.

By an experiment we have had in hand for five years, it will appear that the roots and stem of a large tree, after the first set of scions are exhausted or worn out, may carry another set for many years; and we suspect a third set, provided the engrafting is properly done, and the engrafter chooses a new variety. Now the Ripston Pippin, of Yorkshire, is the favourite, as being a free grower and good bearer, with fine fruit. This how-ever may be certainly depended on, that when a new apple is raised from seed,

if

if a scion were placed in a retired situation, and constantly cut down, as a stool
in a copse-wood, and the apple never
suffered to fulfil the intentions of nature
in bearing fruit, the practitioners of the
following ages may secure scions from
that stool, to continue the variety much
longer. Hence, though I have written
as much as is in my power against permanency, yet I have taken some pains
to assure the planters, that forecast, selection, pruning, cleanliness, and care,
will make the orchards turn to more
profit for the rising generations, than
what they have done for the last hundred
years.

To place the nature of varieties in its
true light, for the information of the
public, I must maintain, that the different varieties of the apple will, after a
certain time, decline, and actually die
away, and each variety, or all of the
same stem or family, will lose their
existence in vegetation; and yet it is a

M                    known

known fact, and mentioned in the 17th
volume of the Transactions, that after
the debility of age has actually taken
possession of any variety, it will yet
thrive by being placed against a southern
wall, and treated as wall-fruit. Who,
however, can afford to raise cider at
that expense, except as matter of curio-
sity, to prove, that when the vital principle in vegetation is nearly exhausted,
a superior care and warmth will still
keep the variety in existence some time
longer?

It should be understood, that the external air of Britain is rather too cold
for the delicate fruits, which is the reason
why, in the Orchardist, I lay such a
stress on procuring *warmth* for the trees,
by *draining*, *shelter*, and *manure*. It
would be now lost time to attempt to
recover the old varieties as an article of
profit.

If I have not expressed myself, in this
Essay on the Nature of Varieties, with

so much clearness and conviction as
might have been expected, it should be
considered that it is an abstruse subject,
very little understood, and requiring at
first some degree of *faith, observation,*
and *perseverance.* The prejudices of
mankind revolt against it. They are
not disposed to allow the distinction of
nature; and they imagine, that in the
act of engrafting or multiplying they
give new life, whereas it is only continuing the existence of the same tree,
stick, or bud. Observe what I said
before:—the seed of the apple, when
placed in the earth, germinates, and
unfolds itself into a new plant, which
successively passes through the stages of
infancy, maturity, and decay, like its
predecessors. I might say, all created
nature is similar in this respect; though,
from the circumstance that varieties are
much longer-lived than man, the plants
have appeared to be possessed of eternal

M 2                                    powers

powers of duration: nothing sublunary, however, which possesses either animal or vegetable life, is exempt from age and death.

Within the last twenty years I have travelled many hundred miles, and conversed with the most intelligent men in each country; and I now want to convince mankind, for no other reason than because it is their interest so to believe, that there is in creation an order of beings (engrafted fruits) so formed, that we have the power of multiplying a single variety, to whatever number of trees we please;—that the first set arises from a small seed;—that the next and descendant sets are propagated by engraftings, or from cuttings, layers, etc.; —and that although these trees may amount to millions, yet, on the death of the primogenious or parent stock, merely from old-age, or nihility of growth, each individual shall decline,

in

in whatever country they may be, or however endued with youth and health. I say they shall gradually begin to decline; and in the course of time, or of centuries, to those who would prefer that expression, the *whole variety* will scarcely have a single tree remaining to show what the fruit was. Let those who are not disposed to assent to this statement, ask themselves what is become of the old lost varieties? did they die, or did wicked men maliciously cut them up?

I, who am firmly convinced of the truth of what I have advanced on this subject, have no doubt but that the same would happen by engrafting on the Oak or Beech, if the mast raised from the engrafted tree did not produce the like; for there the question turns.

Is it not known, that the woodman, in setting out his sapling oaks, always selects new seedling plants, and never

M 3                continues

continues one upon an old stool; and
that if he should so blunder, that tree,
from the stool, will neither have the
freedom of growth, nor the size or firmness of timber, equal to a new-raised
plant.

I wish I could persuade my friends,
that, with the same attention with which
the woodman acts, the planter is to raise
his orchard from the young fruits which
thrive in the neighbourhood, or are in
health and full bearing in the country
whence they are to be brought.

The fruit-grower should look to selection, cleanliness, and care. To me
it is a circumstance perfectly indifferent,
whether he is to use Mr. Forsyth's composition, Mr. Bulingham's boiled linseed
oil, or my medication. I only maintain
that the wounded parts of trees want
something to destroy the insects and
vermin, and heal the wood, from which
the trees are kept in health.

Let

Let those who are blessed with fruit-plantations attend to their preservation, and not leave them to the state of un-assisted nature.

I am, SIR,

Your most obedient Servant,

THO. SKIP DYOT BUCKNALL.

*Hampton-Court,*
*12th Oct.* 1801.

Mr. CHARLES TAYLOR,
Secretary, Adelphi.

The

The SILVER MEDAL was this Session presented to WILLIAM FAIRMAN, Esq. of Millers-House, near Sittingbourn, in Kent, for his Experiments on Extreme-Branch Grafting of FRUIT-TREES, from whom the following Account and Certificates were received, and to which an Engraving and Description are annexed.

SIR,

FROM much conversation with Mr. Bucknall on the idea of improving standard Fruit-trees, we could not but remark that in Apple Orchards, even in such as are most valuable, some were to be seen that were stinted and barren, which not only occasioned a loss in the production, but made a break in the rows, and spoiled the beauty and uniformity of the plantation.

To bring these trees into an equal state of bearing, size, and appearance, in
a short

a short time, is an object of the greatest importance in the system of Orcharding, and also for the recovery of old barren trees, which are fallen into decay, not so much from age, as from the sorts of their fruits being of the worn-out and deemed nearly lost varieties.

Having long entertained these thoughts, and been by no means inattentive to the accomplishment of the design, I attempted to change their fruits by a new mode of engrafting, and am bold enough to assert that I have most fortunately succeeded in my experiments; working, if I am to be allowed to say it, from the errors of other practitioners, as also from those of my own habits.

My name having several times appeared in the transactions of the Society for the Encouragement of Arts, etc. and having the honour of being a member of that Society, I thought no pains or expense would be too much, for the completion of so desirable an improvement,

ment. Under these impressions, and having many trees of this description, I made an experiment on three of them in March, 1798, each being nearly a hundred years old. They were not decayed in their bodies, and but little in their branches. Two of these were golden pippins, and the other was a golden rennet. Each likewise had been past a bearing state for several years. I also followed up the practice on many more the succeeding spring, and that of the last year, to the number of forty at least, in my different plantations. *

The attempt has gone so far beyond my most sanguine expectation, that I beg of you, Sir, to introduce the system to the Society, for their approbation; and I hope it will deserve the honour of a place in their valuable Transactions.

I directed the process to be conducted as follows: Cut out all the spray wood, and make the tree a perfect skeleton, leaving

---

* The average expense I calculated at 2s. 6d. each tree.

leaving all the healthy limbs; then clean the branches, and cut the top of each branch off where it would measure in circumference from the size of a shilling to about that of a crown piece. Some of the branches must of course be taken off where it is a little larger, and some smaller, to preserve the canopy or head of the tree; and it will be necessary to take out the branches which cross others, and observe the arms are left to fork off, so that no considerable opening is to be perceived when you stand under the tree, but that they may represent an uniform head. I must here remark to the practitioner, when he is preparing the tree as I directed, that he should leave the branches sufficiently long to allow of two or three inches to be taken off by the saw, that all the splintered parts may be removed.

The trees being thus prepared, put in one or two grafts at the extremity of each branch; and from this circumstance
I wish

I wish to have the method called *Extreme Branch Grafting.*

A cement, hereafter described, must be used instead of clay, and the grafts tied with bass or soft strings. As there was a considerable quantity of moss on the bodies and branches of the trees, I ordered my gardener to scrape it off, which is effectually done when they are in a wet state by a stubbed birch broom. I then ordered him to brush them over with coarse oil, which invigorated the growth of the tree, acted as a manure to the bark, and made it expand very evidently; the old cracks were soon, by this operation, rendered invisible.

All wounds should be perfectly cleaned out, and the medication applied as described in the Orchardist, p. 14. By the beginning of July the bandages were cut, and the shoots from the grafts shortened, to prevent them from blowing out. I must here, too, observe that all the shoots or suckers from the tree must

enjoy

enjoy the full liberty of growth, till the succeeding spring, when the greater part must be taken out, and few but the grafts suffered to remain, except on a branch where the grafts have not taken : in that case, leave one or more of the suckers, which will take a graft the second year, and make good the deficiency. This was the whole of the process. *

By observing what is here stated, it will appear that the tree remains nearly as large when the operation is finished, as it was before the business was under-taken; and this is a most essential cir-cumstance, as no part of the former vegetation is lost, which is in health fit to continue for forming the new tree.

It is worthy of notice, that when the vivifying rays of the sun have caused the sap to flow, these grafts inducing the

* The system succeeds equally well on pear, as also on cherry trees, provided the medication is used to pre-vent the cherry tree from gumming.

the fluid through the pores to every part
of the tree, will occasion innumerable
suckers or scions to start through the
bark, which, together with the grafts,
give such energy to vegetation, that in
the course of the summer the tree will
be actually covered over by a thick foliage, which enforces and quickens the
due circulation of sap. These, when
combined, fully compel the roots to
work for the general benefit of the tree.

In these experiments I judged it proper to make choice of grafts from the
sorts of fruits which were the most luxuriant in their growth, or any new variety, as described in the 17th and 18th
volumes of the Society's Transactions,
by which means a greater vigour was
excited; and if this observation is attended to, the practitioner will clearly
perceive, from the first year's growth, that
the grafts would soon starve the suckers
which shoot forth below them, if they
were

were suffered to remain *. With a view to accomplish this grand object of improvement, I gave much attention, as I have before observed, to the general practice of invigorating old trees; and I happily discovered the error of the common mode of engrafting but a short distance from the trunk or body, as in *Fig.* 1. There the circumference of the wounds is as large as to require several grafts which cannot firmly unite and clasp over the stumps, and consequently these wounds lay a foundation for after-decay. If that were not the case, yet it so reduces the size of the tree, that it could not recover its former state in many years, and it is dubious if it ever would; whereas, by the method of extreme grafting, as *Fig.* 3, the tree will be larger in three or four years, than before the operation

---

* This thought should be kept in suspense, as ten years hence it may appear otherwise. However, they will be valuable trees, and highly profitable, as will any other brought under the same system.

tion was performed. For all the large branches remaining, the tree has nothing to make but fruit-bearing wood; and from the beautiful verdure it soon acquires, and the symmetry of the tree, no argument is necessary to enforce the practice.

. *Fig.* 2 was my first experiment about eight years since. The error of No. 1 was there a little amended, and gave me the idea of engrafting at the extremity. Permit me to remark that those done in my Orchards, on the plan of *Fig.* 2, did not, neither were they able to bear so many apples last season, which was a bearing year, as those on the plan of . *Fig.* 3, which produced me about two bushels each tree of the finest fruit I had in my Orchards, from the third summer's wood only. Some engrafted with Ribston pippins were beautiful.

Mr. Bucknall visited me this summer for the express purpose of seeing my trees; and he says the manner of conducting

ducting the system is the happiest that ever was conceived. For when a tree has done its best, and has continued to extreme old-age, just disposed to fall into dissolution, as also when this is the case with trees in a stagnated and barren state, they are thus renovated, and may, with the greatest probability, continue valuable for fifty years to come. I need not say, do not make the attempt when the energy of growth is over; that will easily be seen by the body and arms, but more particularly from the size, figure, shape, and colour of the leaves, which give the proper indication of health or decay in vegetation.

Should the Society desire it, several gentlemen resident here, will gladly send up certificates to confirm the statements.

I remain, SIR,

Your most obedient Servant,

WM. FAIRMAN.

*Millers-House, near Sittingbourn, Kent,*
*Feb. 9, 1802.*

CHARLES TAYLOR, Esq.

N

#### CEMENT FOR ENGRAFTING.

| | |
|---|---|
| One pound of pitch | |
| One do. . . . rosin | To be boiled up to- |
| Half do. . . . beeswax | gether, but not to |
| Qtr. do. . . . hogslard | be used till you can bear your finger in it. |
| Qtr. do. . . . turpentine | |

### SIR,

THIS is to certify to the Society for the Encouragement of Arts, etc. that William Fairman, of Millers - House, Lynsted, Esq. has long been a steady and zealous promoter of the improvement of the standard fruits of the country; and that he planted one entire Orchard, of sixteen acres, ten years ago.

The system of extreme-branch grafting, now introduced to the public, he has had in contemplation full eight years, though not in its present style of

success

success and elegance; for he has been improving. In those operated upon within the last three or four years he has been wonderfully successful, and I am happy in an opportunity of adding my testimony to the advantages resulting from this method of renovating old fruit-trees.

An idea equal to the present system could not have fallen into better hands than those of Mr. Fairman. He is blessed with a good soil, cultivates the land well, and steadily attends to improvement. The gentlemen of the Committee, by looking at the three little sketches of drawings which represent the three trees, will see that *Fig.* 1 is so amputated, as not likely to continue in health, so as again to form a good tree; and that *Fig.* 2 will be many years before, if *ever* it does. But there are now many fine large trees in the state of *Fig.* 3, which have been engrafted but three or four years, and yet, as far

as

as structure goes, are complete already, and in two years much fine fruit may be expected.

The system is as follows: Make the trees perfectly clean, and keep them as uniformly large as is convenient.

In autumn, 1801, I spent some days at Lynsted, and several times walked over the Plantations with Mr. Fairman, and was very much pleased with their appearance.

I remain, Sir,

Your obedient Servant,

THOMAS SKIP DYOT BUCKNALL.

*February* 22, 1802.

CHARLES TAYLOR, Esq.
Secretary.

RE-

Mr Wm Sherman's Method of Extreme Branch Grafting.

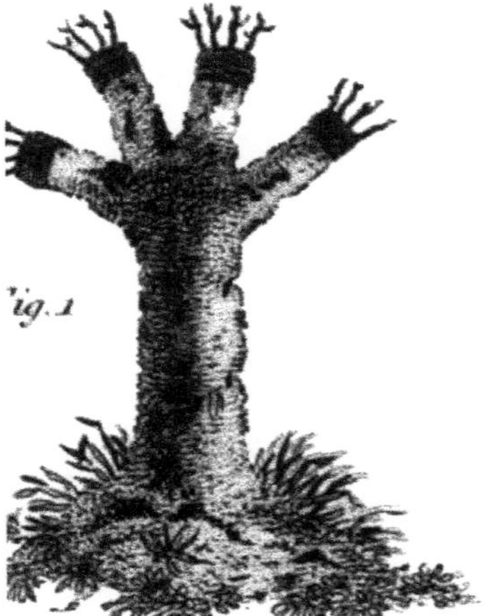

Fig. 1

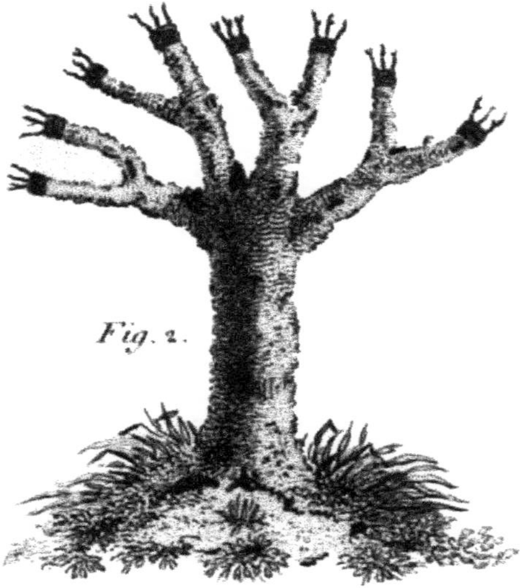

Fig. 2

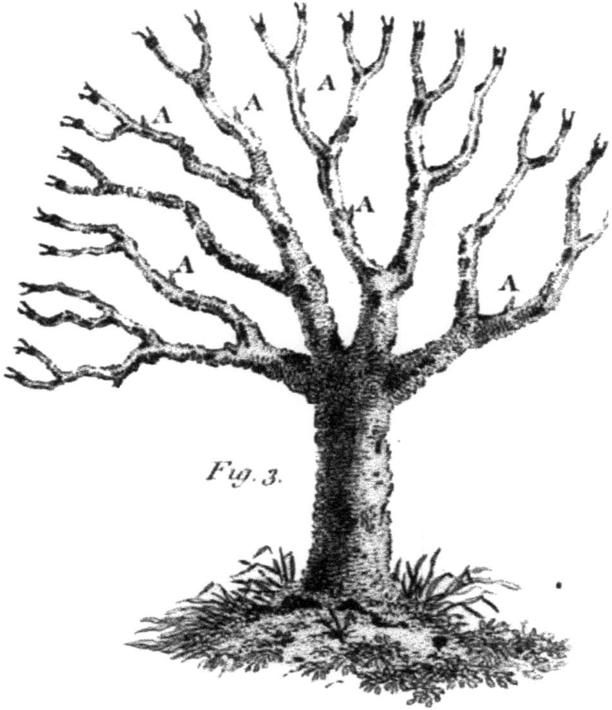

Fig. 3

REFERENCE *to the Engraving of* Mr. FAIRMAN's *method of Extreme-Branch Grafting*; Plate I. Fig. 1, 2, 3, 4.

*Figure* 1. displays the old practice, commonly called Cleft-Grafting.

*Fig.* 2. Improved experiment on *Fig.* 1, by engrafting higher up the tree.

*Fig.* 3. shows the method of Extreme-Branch Grafting, recommended from experience, by Mr. Fairman. Two grafts or cyons are there placed at the extremity of each branch; besides which, additional grafts are inserted in the sides of the branches; as, at AAAAAA, or where they are wanted to form the tree into a handsome shape.

*Fig.* 4. shows upon a larger scale than the former figures the method of applying the grafts at the extremity of the branches, and retaining them by the bass-mat bandage and cement.

N 3 THE

The GOLD MEDAL, being the Premium
offered for SOWING, PLANTING, and
ENCLOSING TIMBER-TREES, was this
Session adjudged to THOMAS JOHNES,
Esq. M. P. of Hafod in Cardiganshire;
from whom the following Accounts
and Certificates were received.

SIR,

I SHALL shortly forward to you the
particulars of the Timber-trees which
I have planted between the 1st of
October, 1797, and the 1st of May,
1799.

My plantations are generally made
on such land as I cannot plough, that
my best ground may be reserved for
grain and grass. I plant the sides of
mountains, which are almost universally composed of argillaceous shistus,
or slate-rock; the surface of which is
decomposed by exposure to the atmosphere,

sphere, and admits the roots of trees to penetrate therein, and to grow luxuriantly. The land betwixt the mountains consists of peat-earth, which, when well drained and limed, produces good grain, potatoes, yams, or grass. I am at present engaged in a course of experiments to ascertain what kind of cows will answer best in this country. A gentleman farmer, who was here last week, insisted that though the Guernsey cows gave but little milk, yet that it contained more butter and cheese than other cows milk. I therefore made a trial, and found the following result;

Devon cows .... gave of butter ....... 7 oz. $\frac{3}{4}$

Small Scotch cows        do.        ....... 6 oz.

Guernsey cows ...        do.        ........ 5$\frac{1}{2}$oz.

Devon cows .... gave of cheese ... 1 lb. 8 oz.

Small Scotch cows        do.        ....... 14$\frac{1}{2}$oz.

Guernsey cows ...        do.        ....... 13 oz.

I have sent my friend Dr. Anderson a sample of my Wheat grown here; and

N 4                    those

those to whom he has shown it said it was the finest they had seen.

My crop is supposed to be thirty bushels per acre; and yet there are persons, pretendedly knowing, who declared that Wheat could not be grown here.

This crop was on very high exposed ground.

I am, SIR,

Your obedient humble Servant,

T. JOHNES.

*Hafod,*
*September 25, 1801.*

To Mr. CHARLES TAYLOR.

*An*

*An* ACCOUNT *of* TREES *planted by* THOMAS JOHNES, *Esq. on Hafod Estate.*

PLANTED from October 1797, to October 1798, ten thousand Oaks, from one to two feet high; they were planted betwixt four and five feet asunder, according to the size of the plants: the ground was properly inclosed with a stone wall, five feet high.

Planted, betwixt the first of October, 1797, and the first of May, 1799, twenty-five thousand Ash-trees: they were from one to three feet high, and are planted on ground which could not be ploughed, or otherwise improved to advantage, being on the sides and lower parts of hills, as the upper parts of the hills are always planted with Larches. The trees look well, and make good shoots. From the nearest calculation I can make, I think there are not above five hundred

of

of them dead; the ground was previously well inclosed, and the Ashes are planted from six to eight feet asunder.

Planted, betwixt October 1797, and 1st May, 1799, four hundred thousand Larch-trees; all of them two years old seedlings, from twelve inches to two feet high: they are at this time looking very healthy, and make good shoots. They are planted upon the tops of the hills where there is a very·thin stratum of soil; they were planted about two feet asunder, and the ground inclosed previously with a stone wall. The Larches were all planted in the following manner:—A man with a spade, holding the edge of it towards him, makes a cut about six inches deep, if there is that depth of soil; he then turns the spade the right way, and makes a cut across the end of the other thus ⌐: he then works his spade backwards and forwards three or four times, to loosen the mold for the roots of the plants to grow therein.
A boy

A boy attends, with a bundle of trees, to assist every man: the boy puts one tree in each hole, and presses with his foot the turf hard about the roots, to make the tree stand firm.

Whilst the planter is making another hole, a person who attends the planting goes from one planter to another, to see that every man does his duty; he takes hold of the top of each tree, to see that they are properly planted and firm: they are generally put in so hard, that the top will break before they will pull up. If it be late in the spring season, and dry weather apprehended, I have found it of great service to drench the roots well in the following manner, viz: A hole is dug about two feet diameter, and the same in depth; it is then half-filled with water, and fine mold is added, to make it like thin mud; a man then takes as many trees in both his hands as he can conveniently hold and drench in the mud: having prepared

pared a heap of dry soil near the side of the hole, he alternately draws the roots of the plants through the above mud-hole and the dry soil, and thus the fibres of the roots are prevented from hardening or drying, as they would otherwise do.

Mr. Johnes has a plantation of Larches which were set in April 1796, which were treated in the above manner; and although they had no rain for almost two months after they were planted, I believe that out of eighty thousand thus planted on a very dry hill, not above two hundred of them died. The Larches were planted at two feet asunder, or about ten thousand to the acre. The soil where the Larch, Oak, and Ash-trees have been planted, is chiefly of a red loam, on a slaty rock.

The stone walls which surround the plantations are all kept in proper repair by a man who has a yearly allowance for that purpose. Mr. Johnes also em-

ploys

ploys a man to go daily round the plantations with a dog, to keep them free from trespass.

All the plantations are in a healthy and flourishing condition at this time.

JAMES TODD, *Gardener.*

*Hafod,*
*December* 31, 1801.

## Mr. CHARLES TAYLOR.

Certificates from the Reverend Lewis Evans, Minister of Eglwys Newydd, accompanied the above accounts, and confirmed the particulars. He stated that he had lately walked over the different plantations, and found them in a thriving condition. He added, that all the plantations made by Mr. Johnes. are on a soil that could not be otherwise cultivated at any moderate expence; that the kingdom in general will soon experience their beneficial effects,

effects, and reap incalculable advantages from them.

By an account received from Mr. Todd, in August, 1802, it is stated that he has measured a good number of Larches planted by Mr. Johnes, on a reddish loam, inclining to sand, in April, 1796, which when planted were from eighteen inches to two feet high; and he finds that they are now in general from ten to thirteen feet high. Some of the last year's shoots measured three feet, eight inches; and the greatest part of them are from two and a half to three feet. He observes that the medium growth of Larches in general, in Mr. Johnes's plantation, is from twenty inches to two feet each year; some years more, and some less.

[A further account of this Gentleman's improvements will be found in the Preface to the present Volume.]

The

The SILVER MEDAL was this Session presented to JAMES BEECH, Esq. of Shaw, near Cheadle, in Staffordshire, for his Plantations of TIMBER-TREES. The following Accounts and Certificates were received from him.

SIR,

HAVING made sundry improvements in planting and draining, I lay the account before the Society, in hopes of their approbation.

Betwixt June, 1798, and June, 1799, I planted 11,000 Oaks, 9,000 Sycamores, 9,000 Ashes, 17,000 Mountain Ashes, 3,000 Larches, 1,800 Elms, and 18,000 Beeches; making in the whole 52,600 trees. The trees are well fenced by banks, rails, and quickset hedges, and they are all in a healthy state.

I have drained 8,580 roods of land, at 69 roods per acre. The drains were generally made two grafts deep; fine

broken

broken stones were afterwards laid thereon, and over that turf-sod.

    I am, SIR,

       Your obedient Servant,

         JAMES BEECH.

*Cheadle, August* 13, 1799.

To the SECRETARY of the
    Society of Arts, etc.

    The above Account was confirmed by the Rev. William Eddowes, Minister, who testified, that the drained land, which was only worth five shillings per acre per annum, is now worth thirty shillings; and that he believes Mr. Beech has planted more Timber-trees than are stated in the account.

                      SIR,

SIR,

I RECEIVED your letter respecting my application to the Society; and, in answer thereto, inform you, that the Trees I have planted are as prosperous as possible, and well preserved with very nice quickset hedges growing round the different plantations. My land is very much upon the clay; it suits all kinds of Trees described in my letter exceedingly well, particularly Oak, which, in older plantations that I have made, shoots near four feet long in one year. Beech seems the least inclinable to answer on this soil. Part of the land was ploughed and thrown up into butts, and part planted in the turf. Those Trees planted on the ploughed ground flourish the most. The whole has been trenched with open drains, to let the wet off where necessary, which is a very material point. I sowed last spring about twelve

O strike

strike of Acorns, of which I will give you an account in a future letter.

    I am, SIR,

        Your obedient Servant,

           JAMES BEECH.

*Cheadle, October 22, 1800.*

    Mr. CHARLES TAYLOR.

    SIR,

I SOWED in the spring of 1799 about half an acre of land with Acorns. The quantity of Acorns sown were about twelve or thirteen strike. The land is taken from the common, and was previously well fallowed as the cleanest wheat fallow. I compute that at least one hundred and fifty Acorns were sown in a square yard, which makes about three hundred and sixty-three thousand in the whole. They are planted out as they come on in size, the youngest plants being left. I sowed, in the same spring, as many Ash Keys as produced at least fifty thousand plants, which have been

           thinned

thinned out, and distributed into plan-tations in the same manner. I also sowed, in the same spring, about fifteen strike of Mountain-Ash Berries. These cannot have produced less than four hun-dred thousand plants, which have been thinned out in the same manner when they began to injure the smaller plants.

The beds for the Ash and Mountain Ash were dug and made perfectly clean. The Mountain Ash seed did not spring so well as the others, as the birds will not suffer the Berries to ripen suffi-ciently.

This country is mostly of a stiff soil.

I am, Sir,

Your humble Servant,

James Beech.

*Cheadle, Dec.* 22, 1801.

Mr. Charles Taylor.

The above Accounts were certified by the Rev. William Eddowes to be a just statement.

O 2         The

The THANKS of the Society were this Session presented to Mr. SPENCER COCHRANE, of Muirfield, near Haddington, in North-Britain, for the following Communication on the CULTIVATION of SPRING WHEAT.

SIR,

IT is only a few months since I was informed that the Society of Arts, etc. were anxious to ascertain the advantages which may result from Spring-Wheat; that, in the case of an unfavourable autumn and wet winter, this mode may be practised, and be the happy means of counteractiug the bad effects of sowing as formerly, when the land was not in the wished-for state to receive the seed in autumn.

If you judge, Sir, the result of my experience for ten years can be of any use, I beg you will lay the following statement before the Society.

Since

Since the year 1790, I have been accustomed to sow a certain part of my farm with Wheat in the months of February and March, and have always succeeded both in the quantity and quality of the Grain produced; the same kind of Wheat being used by me for both the winter and spring sowings.

I ventured, in the year 1800, to sow forty-one acres of land, Scotch measure, with thirty-eight bolls of Wheat. The whole produce of good Grain was two-hundred and ninety-seven bolls, or seven and a quarter bolls per acre. The time of sowing was from the 24th of February to the 17th of March: the wet autumn and winter prevented me from getting the seed into the ground at the usual time. The whole crop was cut betwixt the 14th and 27th of September.

I remark that Wheat sown in the spring is about ten days later than that which is sown in October.

On

On a reclaimed marsh of five acres I sowed Wheat, the 17th of February, 1798, and reaped therefrom, the 8th of September the same year, sixty bolls, or thirty quarters, Winchester measure.

I flatter myself the Society will believe that my only motive for furnishing them with this account, is the desire of being useful to my country.

I am, SIR,

Your very obedient Servant,

SPENCER COCHRANE.

*Muirfield, near Haddington,*
*February 25, 1802.*

To Mr. CHARLES TAYLOR.

The

# PAPERS

## IN

# CHEMISTRY.

———————

CHEMISTRY

# CHEMISTRY.

The SILVER MEDAL was this Session voted to Mr. THOMAS WILLIS, of Lime-Street, London, for his Preparation of the BULBS of the HYACINTHUS NON SCRIPTUS, or COMMON BLUE-BELL, as a substitute for Gum-Arabic; the following Account of which was transmitted by him, with some of the prepared Powder.

SIR,

HAVING received a letter from Mr. Thomas Willis, relative to his discovery of the use of the Hyacinthus non scriptus, as a substitute for Gum Arabic; I request, at his desire, that you

you will lay the same before the Society
of Arts, etc.

     I am, SIR,

        Your humble Servant,

          JOHN BAKER.

*Grosvenor-Street,*
*March,* 1802.

   Mr. CHARLES TAYLOR.

   SIR,

I HAVE observed in the Appendix of
the last Monthly Review, in their
Report of the Chemical Annals, No. 115,
that mention is made of a letter from
Mr. Deyeux, to the authors of the
Annales de Chymie; in which an account is given that a gummy substance
had been discovered, by Mons. Leroux,
to be contained in the Bulb of the
plant called Hyacinthus non scriptus;

               and

and that the Reviewers only say, " This " article does not at present require any further notice than annunciation." As I know, Sir, your benevolent disposition in promoting and encouraging the Arts, the Sciences, and Manufactures of this Kingdom, I beg leave to offer the following observations on the above-mentioned article, which I think a subject proper to lay before your most excellent Society, and which I have no doubt may become of national utility.

In the year 1794, whilst collecting plants in a wood for botanical specimens, I observed that the root of the Hyacinthus non scriptus, the plant commonly called Blue-Bells, or Hare-Bells, was extremely mucilaginous; and on tasting it, I discovered only a very slight pungency. I collected a pound of the Bulbs, and, after slicing and drying them before a fire, they yielded about four ounces of powder. I thought that by keeping the powder some time, the little

little acridness might go off, as it does in the arum-root powder. I tasted it about six months after, and found it perfectly insipid. I concluded it might be rendered useful for food or nourishment, but at that time pursued the matter no further.

- In the spring of 1800, gum-arabic having been a long time very dear, and likely to continue so, I thought this mucilaginous root might answer some of its purposes, for external use. I therefore procured seven pounds and a half of the Bulbs, which, when sliced and dried, produced two pounds of powder. Being soon afterwards in company with Mr. Charles Taylor, Secretary to the Society of Arts, etc. I mentioned to him that I had discovered a root which grew in great plenty in this kingdom, yielded a very strong mucilage, and which I imagined would answer the purposes of gum arabic, in some of the manufactories. He said, if I pleased,

he

he would send some of it down to Manchester, to be tried by the calico-printers.

Three or four ounces of the powder were given him, and sent down there; he was informed, upon trial, that it answered the purposes of fixing the calico-printers colours, equally as well as gum-arabic; and in the same proportion, of an ounce and a half of the powder, to four ounces of the mordant. Mr. Taylor received the samples of the printed cottons on which it had been used.

On the 15th of January, 1801, I furnished Mr. Taylor with eight ounces more of the powder; but have not since heard the result.

As this root can be easily procured, and used at a less price than gum-arabic has been sold for several years past, I think it may be rendered of great utility; and the Society of Arts, etc.

by

by patronizing it, may be the means of making it a public benefit.

Care should be taken, and advice given, that the woods should not be left destitute of the roots; and it would be adviseable to offer premiums for cultivating the roots and offsets, as they are very increasing. By such means a constant supply may be had, if the roots answer the intended purposes.

I do not presume to offer any thing respecting the mode in which the Society may think proper to divulge the discovery, and promote the use of these roots; but I imagine, that if the roots are bruised and used fresh, they would answer the purpose better than when dried and powdered; and as it is now a proper time of the year for taking them up, and will continue to be so for two months, I wish that the discovery may be made known as soon as possible.

I have

I have sent you specimens both of the dried roots and powder, that they may be seen at the Society's rooms, by the calico-printers. What I have done have been scorched a little in drying; but the colour would be much better, if proper care was taken in drying them.

I am, SIR,

Your most obedient Servant,

THOMAS WILLIS.

*Lime-Street,*
*March* 17, 1802,

To JOHN BAKER, Esq.
one of the Members
of the Society of Arts,
etc.

From the trials made before the Committee with this Powder, with hot and

and cold water, from samples. of the printed cotton produced which had been printed therewith instead of Gum Senegal, and from experiments made in Manchester, it appears that the Hyacinthus non scriptus may, in many cases, be found a useful substitute for Gum-Arabic.

The

The following Processes for the EDUL-
CORATION of FISH-OIL were communicated to the Society by ROBERT.
DOSSIE, Esq. in the Year 1761; and
a Bounty of ONE HUNDRED POUNDS
was then voted to him for the same.
They have lately been enquired after
by different Members of the Society,
and are, on this account, published
in the present Volume, in their original
form.

*Explanation of the Principles on which
the* PURIFICATION *of* FISH-OIL *may
be performed, and of the Uses to which
it is applicable.*

THAT the fetid smell of Fish-oil is
chiefly owing to putrefaction, it is
unnecessary to show; but though this
be the principal cause, there is another
likewise, which is, ustion or burning the
oil, occasioned by the strong heat em-

P                          ployed

ployed for the extracting it from the
blubber of the larger fish, and which
produces a strong empyreumatic scent
that is not always to be equally removed
by the same means as the putrid smell,
but remains sometimes very prevalent
after that is taken away.

In order to the perfect Edulcoration of
Oils, there are consequently two kinds
of fœtor or stink to be removed, viz.
the putrid, and the empyreumatic; and
the same means do not always equally
avail against both.

The putrid smell of Fish-oil is of two
kinds; the rancid, which is peculiar to
oils; and the common putrid smell, which
is the general effect of the putrefaction
of animal fluids, or of the vascular
solids, when commixed with aqueous
fluids.

Fish-oil has not only rancidity, or the
first kind of putrid smells peculiar to
oils, but also the second or general kinds;
as the oil, for the most part, is commixed
with

with the gelatinous humour common to all animals, and some kinds with a proportion of the bile likewise; and those humours putrifying combine their putrid scent with the rancidity of the oil, and, in cases where great heat has been used, with that and the empyreuma also.

The reason of the presence of the gelatinous fluid in Fish-oil is this: that the blubber, which consists partly of adipose vesicles, and partly of the membrana cellulosa, which contains the gelatinous fluid, is, for the most part, kept a considerable time before the oil is separated from it, either from the want of convenient opportunities to extract the oil, or in order to the obtaining a larger proportion; as the putrid effervescence which then comes on, rupturing the vesicles, makes the blubber yield à greater quantity of oil than could be extracted before such change was produced; and the vesicles of the tela cellulosa, containing the gelatinous matter,

P 2 being

being also burst from the same cause, such matter being then rendered saponaceous by the putrefaction, a part of it mixes intimately with the oil, and constitutes it a compound of the proper oleaginous parts and this heterogeneous fluid.

The presence of the bile in Fish-oil is occasioned by its being, in many cases, extracted from the liver of the fish; which is not to be so profitably done by other means as by putrefaction; and the bile being consequently discharged, together with the oil from the vessels of the liver containing them, combines with it, both from the original saponaceous property of bile, and from that which it acquires by putrefaction.

This holds good particularly of the cod-oil, or common train, brought from Newfoundland; which, from its high yellow colour, viscid consistence, and repugnance to burning well in lamps, manifests sensibly the presence of bile and

and the gelatinous fluid; which latter, by the saponaceous power of the bile, is commixed in a greater proportion in this than in any other kind of fish-oil.

A tendency to putrify, or at most but in an extremely slow manner, is not an absolute property of perfect oils in a simple or pure state; but it is a relative property dependant upon their accidental contact or commixture with the aqueous fluid. This is evident from the case of oils concreted into a sebaceous form; which being perfectly oleaginous and uncombined with any water, except such as enters into their component parts will not putrify unless water, or something containing it, is brought in contact with them. But the fluid animal, and most vegetable oils, being compounded of perfect oils with other mixed substances, either sub-oleaginous or gelatinous, have always a putrescence *per se,* or tendency to putrify, without further admixture of aqueous moisture.

P 3                                        This

This commixture of heterogeneous matter in Fish-oil, particularly of the gelatinous fluid and bile, gives rise to a further principle of purification than *simple Edulcoration*, or the removing the fœtor; for the presence of such humours in the oil renders it subject to a second putrescence *per se*, supposing the first corrected; makes it unfit for the purpose of the woollen manufacture, as the heat through which this is in some cases employed, causes this matter to contract a most disagreeable empyreuma. It also prevents its burning in lamps, as well from its viscidity as from the repugnance which the presence of water gives to all oleaginous matter. It is therefore necessary to free the oil from this heterogeneous matter; after which it can be subject only to the rancid putrescence, or that which is proper to oils as such.

The substances which have been or may be applied to the removing or preventing

venting the effects of putrescence, are, acids, alkalies, metallic calces, neutral salts, ethereal and essential oils, vinous spirits, water, and air. With respect to acids, though they may be applied with effect to the removal or prevention of putrefaction in mixed animal and vegetable substances, yet they have not the same efficacy when, employed in the. case of oils ; for in a small proportion, without the subsequent aid of alkalies, they rather increase than diminish the fœtor, and in a large proportion they coagulate the oils, and change their other properties as well as their consistence. Though they might therefore be employed with the assistance of alkalies, yet requiring a more expensive and complex process, and not being moreover necessary, as the same end may be obtained by the use of alkalies only, they may be deemed improper for the purification of animal oils for commercial purposes. Alkaline substances, both salts and earths, are

the

the most powerful instruments in the edulcoration of oils; but as their action on putrid oils, and the method of apply-ing them to this end, are not the same in both, it is proper to consider them di-stinctly.

Of alkaline salts it is the fixed kind only which are proper to be used for the edulcoration of oils. Fixed alkaline salts, in a dissolved state, being com-mixed with putrifying animal substances, appear to combine with the putrid mat-ter, and mixing with some of the prin-ciples, form instantly volatile alkaline salts. On the less putrid they seem to act, after their combination, by an ac-celeration of the putrescent action, till they attain the degree which produces volatile salts. This is evident by the sensible putrid ferment and smell which appear after their commixture; but which gradually abating, the oil is ren-dered sweeter, much lighter-coloured, and thinner.

Their

Their great use in the edulcoration of Fish-oil arises, therefore, from their converting such parts of the gelatinous fluid and bile as are highly putrified, instantly into volatile salts, and causing a rapid putrefaction of the other parts; by which means the oil is freed from them by their dissipation. They do not, however, equally act on the parts of the oil on which the empyreumatic scent depends, unless by the assistance of heat; for when they are commixed with the oils without heat, in proportion as the putrid smell diminishes, that becomes more sensibly prevalent. The ultimate action of lixiviate salts on animal oils, except with respect to the empyreuma, seems to be the same either with or without the medium of heat; for the same urinous and putrid smell, gradual diminution of the colour, and fetid scent, happens in one case as in the other, except with regard to the acceleration of the changes; and such salts,

salts, where the purification is required to be made in a great degree, are a necessary means, as they are more effectual than any other substance that can be employed.

The use of lixiviate salts alone is not, however, the most expedient method that can be pursued for the edulcoration of oils, for several reasons. If they be used alone, cold, in the requisite proportions, they coagulate a considerable part of the oil, which will not again separate from them under a very great length of time; and when they have destroyed the putrid scent, a strong bitter empyreumatic smell remains. The same inconvenience, with relation to the coagulation of part of the oil, results when they are used alone with heat. The super-addition of common salt, (which resolves the coagulum and counteracts the saponaceous power of the lixiviate salt, by which the oil and water are made to combine) is therefore

fore necessary; and the expence arising from the larger proportion of
lixiviate salt, requires it to be employed
if no other alkali be taken in aid, and
renders the junction of alkaline earths
with it extremely proper in the edulcoration of oils for commercial uses.
Lime has also an edulcorative power
on animal oils; but it has also so strong
a coagulative action, that the addition
of a large proportion of alkaline salts
becomes, when it is used, necessary to
reduce the concreted oil to a fluid state;
and therefore this substance alone is not
proper for that purpose. The combination of lixiviate salt with lime, or the
solution commonly called soap-lye, has
an effectual edulcorative action on fetid
oils; but it makes a troublesome coagulation of part of the oil, if no common
salt be employed, and must be used in
such large proportion, if no alkaline
earth be added, as renders the method
too expensive.

, Lime

Lime has a power of combining with and absorbing the putrid parts of the gelatinous fluid and bile, when commixed with oil; and effects, either with or without heat, a considerable edulcoration of fetid oils; but it combines so strongly with them, either cold or hot, that the separation is difficult to be effected, even with the addition of brine; and the oil, when a large proportion of it is used, can scarcely be at all brought from its concreted to a fluid state, but by an equivalent large proportion of lixiviate salt: the use of lime therefore, alone, is improper, or even in a great proportion with other ingredients. But when only a lesser degree of edulcoration is required, a moderate quantity, conjoined with an equal or greater weight of chalk, which assists its separation from the oil, may, on account of its great cheapness, be employed very advantageously: it will in this case admit of precipitation from

the

the oil by the addition of brine. It may be also expediently used, when lixiviate salt is employed with heat for the most] perfect purification of oils; for it will in that case give room for the diminishing of the quantity of lixiviate salt, though the proportion be nevertheless so restrained as not to exceed what the proportion of lixiviate salt (just requisite for the edulcoration) can separate from the oil.

Chalk has an absorbing power similar to lime, but in a less degree on the putrid substance of oil; it does not, however, combine so strongly with the oil as to resist separation in the same manner, and is therefore very proper to be conjoined either with lixiviate salts or lime, as it renders a less quantity of either sufficient, and indeed contributes to the separation of the oil from them.

Magnesia alba or the alkaline earth which is the basis of the sal catharticus, and the singular earth which is the basis

of

of alum, both have an edulcorating
power on fetid oils; but, like lime, have
too strong an attraction with them
to be separated so as to admit of the
reduction of the oil from the concreted
state to which they reduce it; and therefore, as they are not superior in efficacy
to lime and chalk, but much dearer or
more difficult to be obtained, they may
be rejected from the number of ingredients that are proper for the purifying
of oils, with a view to commercial advantages.

Sea-salt has an antiseptic power on
the mixed solid parts of animals; but
used alone, or dissolved in water, it does
not appear to lessen the putrid fœtor of
oils, but on the contrary rather increases it. If, after their commixture
with it, they are subjected to heat, it
rather depraves than improves the oils;
but though by its own immediate action
on them it conduces so little to the
edulcoration of oils, yet it is a medium
for

for the separation of water and the alkaline substances requisite to be employed to that end. It is of great utility in the edulcorative processes: for when alkaline salts or earths combine with the water necessary to their action on the oils, or themselves form coagulums or corrections with it, a solution of salt will loosen the bond and dissolve the close union; so that the oil being separated will. float on the aqueous fluid, while the earth, if any be in the mixture, will be precipitated and sink close together to the bottom of the containing vessel.

Sal catharticus, glauber salt, nitrum vitriolatum, tartar, and other neutral salts, though they counteract putrefaction in the mixed or solid parts of animals, seem to have little effect on oils with respect to their edulcoration, and cannot therefore be ranked amongst the substances proper to be used for that purpose.

Lead

Lead reduced to the state of a calx, either in the form of minium or litharge, has a strong edulcorative power on fetid oils, and is indeed applied to that end, with respect to one kind of vegetable oil, for a very bad purpose, considering its malignant qualities on the human body.

In the case of train-oil, which will scarcely ever be considered among the esculent kinds in this country, the same objection against its use would not lie; and employed either with or without heat, it is a powerful absorbent both of the putrid and empyreumatic parts that occasion the fœtor.

As however there may be some prejudice against its use, even in any way, and as it is not absolutely necessary, I have not given it a place among the ingredients of the processes I recommend.

The ochrous earth of iron, commonly called red ochre, has an absorbing power

on

on the putrid parts of oil, but combines so strongly, that the separation is tedious even with the addition of brine; if, nevertheless, it is added when chalk and lime have been some time commixed with the oil, as in process the first, it will promote the edulcorative intention, and will subside along with them; and, as it has some advantage without increasing the expence, unless in the most inconsiderable degree, its use may be expediently admitted in that process.

Essential and ethereal oils are applicable to the prevention of putrefaction in the mixed and solid parts of vegetables, but are not so to the edulcoration of fetid oils; and if they had the desired effect, they would not, on account of their price, answer the commercial end, unless the due effect was produced by adding them to the oils in a very small quantity.

The same holds good of spirits of wine as of essential and ethereal oils, both with respect to their efficacy and the expense.

Q        Water

Water has an edulcorative action on fetid oils, by carrying off the most putrid parts of the gelatinous fluid or bile, in which, as was above explained, the principal fœtor resides, if the quantity added be large, and an intimate commixture be made of them by stirring them together for a considerable time: this only partially removing those heterogeneous putrescent substances, the remaining part soon acquires the same state and the oil again grows fetid, though not to the same degree as before.

Water is, however, a necessary medium for the action of salts and the separation of alkaline earths and calces of metals, when they are employed for the edulcoration of oils, as will appear from a consideration of my processes.

Air edulcorates oil by carrying off the most putrid parts, which are necessarily extremely volatile. It may be made to act on them either by simple exposure of them to it with a large extent of surface, or by forcing it through them by

means

fneans of ventilators as has been practised by some dealers; but is now, I
believe, neglected on account of their
finding the improvement of oils by it not
adequate to the trouble, as the gelatinous matter and bile, not reduced to
a certain degree of putrefaction, being
left behind, putrify again to nearly the
same degree as before.

It appears from these several observations, that the cheapest ingredients
which can be used for the edulcoration
of Train-oils, are lime and chalk, which
may, with the addition of a proper
quantity of solution of sea-salt or brine,
be made to procure a separation of
them from the oils, according to process
the first, so as to answer for some purposes; that the lixiviate salt is the most
powerful purifier of oils, and, with the
assistance of chalk and brine, will, without heat, according to process the
second, effect a very considerable degree of edulcoration; and that lixiviate

salt

salt used with heat, with the addition of lime and chalk, to save a part of the quantity which would otherwise be necessary, and of brine to procure a quick separation, will perform an edulcoration sufficient for all commercial purposes, according to process the third ; but that calcined lead and the ochrous earth of iron may, perhaps, be applied in some cases with advantage, where the oil is not designed for esculent use.

## PROCESS THE FIRST.

*For purifying Fish-oil in a moderate degree,*
*and at a very little expense.*

TAKE an ounce of chalk in powder,
and half an ounce of lime slacked
by exposure to the air; put them into
a gallon of stinking oil, and, having
mixed them well together by stirring,
add half a pint of water, and mix that
also with them by the same means.
When they have stood an hour or two,
repeat the stirring, and continue the
same treatment at convenient intervals
for two or three days; after which,
superadd a pint and a half of water, in
which an ounce of salt is dissolved, and
mix them as the other ingredients, re-
peating the stirring, as before, for a day
or two. Let the whole then stand at
rest, and the water will sink below the
oil, and the chalk subside in it to the

Q 3                          bottom

bottom of the vessel. The oil will become clear, be of a lighter colour, and have considerably less smell, but will not be purified in a manner equal to what is effected by the other processes below given; though, as this is done with the expense of only one ounce of salt, it may be practised advantageously for many purposes, especially as a preparation for the next method, the operation of which will be thereby facilitated.

### PROCESS THE SECOND.

*To purify, to a great degree, Fish-oil without Heat.*

Take a gallon of crude stinking oil, or rather such as has been prepared as above mentioned, and add to it an ounce of powdered chalk; stir them well together several times, as in the preceding process; and after they have been mixed some hours or a whole day,

add

add an ounce of pearl-ashes, dissolved in four ounces of water, and repeat the stirring as before. After they have been so treated for some hours, put in a pint of water, in which two ounces of salt are dissolved, and proceed as before: the oil and brine will separate on stand-ing some days, and the oil will be greatly improved both in smell and colour. Where a greater purity is required, the quantity of pearl-ashes must be in-creased, and the time before the addi-tion of the salt and water prolonged.

If the same operation is repeated several times, diminishing each time the quantity of ingredients one half, the oil may be brought to a very light colour, and rendered equally sweet in smell with the common spermaceti oil.

By this process the cod-oil may be made to burn; and, when it is so putrid as not to be fit for any use, either alone or mixed, it may be so corrected by the first part of the process, as to be

Q 4                       equal

equal to that commonly sold : but where this process is practised in the case of such putrid oil, use half an ounce of chalk and half an ounce of lime.

## PROCESS THE THIRD.

*To purify Fish-oil with the assistance of Heat, where the greatest purity is required, and particularly for the Woollen Manufacture.*

Take a gallon of crude stinking oil, and mix with it a quarter of an ounce of powdered chalk, a quarter of an ounce of lime, slacked in the air, and half a pint of water; stir them together; and when they have stood some hours, add a pint of water and two ounces of pearl-ashes, and place them over a fire that will just keep them simmering, till the oil appears of a light amber colour, and has lost all smell except a hot, greasy, soap-like scent. Then superadd

half

half a pint of water in which an ounce of salt has been dissolved; and having boiled them half an hour, pour them into a proper vessel, and let them stand till the separation of the oil, water, and lime be made, as in the preceding process. Where this operation is performed to prepare oil for the Woollen Manufacture, the salt may be omitted; but the separation of the lime from the oil will be slower, and a longer boiling will be necessary.

If the oil be required yet more pure, treat it, after it is separated from the water, &c. according to the second process, with an ounce of chalk, a quarter of an ounce of pearl-ashes, and half an ounce of salt.

*Observations on Process the First.*

This process may be performed on any kind of fish or seal-oil that is putrid and stinking, and will improve it in smell, and generally render the colour lighter, tighter, if previously dark and brown: it will also conduce to render these oils fitter for burning, which are, in their crude state, faulty in that point; but it will not meliorate them to the full degree they admit of even without heat, and should therefore be practised when only a moderate improvement is required.

Secondly. When the oil is taken off from the dregs and brine, the dregs which swim on the brine should be taken off it also, and put into another vessel of a deep form; and on standing, particularly if fresh water be added and stirred with them, nearly the whole remaining part of the oil will separate from the foulness; or, to save this trouble, the dregs, when taken off, may be put to any future quantity of oil that is to be edulcorated by this method, which will answer the same purpose.

*Observations*

*Observations on Process the Third.*

First.—This is most advantageously performed on Train-oil, called vicious whale-oil; and the more putrid and foul it may be, the greater will be the proportionable improvement, especially if there be no mixture of the other kinds of Fish-oils, particularly the seal, which do not admit of being edulcorated perfectly by means of heat, but require other methods: but when the vicious oil is pure from admixture of others, however stinking it may be, the bad smell will be removed by this process duly executed, and the brown colour changed to a very light amber; and these qualities will be much more permanent in this than in any crude oil, as it will not, from the degree of purity to which it is brought, be subject to putrify again under a great length of time, whether it be kept open or in close vessels.

The

The oil in this state will burn away without leaving the least remains of foulness in the lamp; and, being rendered more fluid than before, will go further, when used in the Woollen Manufacture, than any other kind, and will be much more easily scoured from the wool.

If nevertheless there be any branches of the Woollen Manufacture which require the use of a more thick and unctuous oil, this may be rendered so by the addition of a proper quantity of tallow or fat, of which a certain proportion will perfectly incorporate with the oil, the fluidity and transparency being still preserved, as well as all the other qualities that render it suitable to the intended purpose. This may be most beneficially done by adding a proper quantity of the refuse grease of families, commonly called *kitchen-stuff*, which being put to the oil, when moderately heated, will immediately dissolve in it, and let fall also its impurities or foulness to the
bottom

bottom of the vessel, and render the purified admixture a considerable saving to the manufacturers.

Secondly. The different qualities and dispositions of different parcels of vicious oil with respect to edulcoration, render various proportions necessary of the ingredients to be used: The quantities stated in the above process are the least which will effect the end in general, and frequently greater will be required; but this may always be first tried; and if it be found, after six or eight hours simmering of the mixture, that no gradual improvement is making in the smell and colour, but that the oil continues the same in those particulars, and remains also mixed with the chalk and lime, and in a thick turbid state, a fourth or third part of the first quantity of pearl-ashes should be added, and the simmering continued till the oil be perfect. As the quantity of the water is lessened by the evaporation, it is necessary to make fresh additions

additions from time to time, that there may be always nearly the original proportion.

Thirdly. If it be inconvenient to give the whole time of boiling at once, the fire may be suffered to go out and be re-kindled at any distance of time; and if, in such case, a small proportion of pearl-ashes dissolved in water be added, and the mixture several times stirred betwixt the times of boiling, it will facilitate the operation. The time of boiling may be also much shortened, if the chalk, lime, and pearl-ashes, be added for some days before, and the mixture frequently stirred.

PROCESS

## PROCESS THE FOURTH,

*Which may be practised alone, instead of Process the First, as it will edulcorate and purify Fish-oil to a considerable degree, so as to answer most purposes, and for Process the Third, when the whole is performed.*

Take a gallon of crude stinking oil, and put to it a pint of water poured off from two ounces of lime slacked in the air; let them stand together, and stir them up several times for the first twenty-four hours; then let them stand a day, and the lime-water will sink below the oil, which must be carefully separated from them. Take this oil, if not sufficiently purified for your purpose, and treat it as directed in Process the Third, diminishing the quantity of pearl-ashes to one ounce, and omitting the lime and chalk.

ROBERT DOSSIE. *

* The Dregs, remaining after the sundry processes above mentioned, will form an excellent Manure; as has been since noticed in Dr. Hunter's Georgical Essays.

# PAPERS

## IN

# MECHANICKS.

R

# MECHANICKS.

The Sum of TWENTY GUINEAS was this Session voted as a Bounty to Mr. JOHN WEBB, of Dorrington-Street, London, for his Improvement of a Gun-Lock, which is likely to prove of considerable advantage to Society, by preventing the numerous accidents that arise from the unexpected discharge of Fire-Arms; a Plate and Description of which lock are annexed, and a complete Model reserved in the Society's Repository.

### SIR,

I HAVE taken the liberty of sending to the Society an invention of mine, to prevent the accidents which frequently attend the use of Fire-arms, and which may be applied to the Gun-locks now in common use. It is con-

R 2                              trived

trived on such a principle, that when it is on full cock, and the trigger pulled in the common manner, it returns to the half cock only, unless, at the same time that the trigger is pulled, the pressure of the thumb is applied on a spring placed upon the butt or stock of the gun; in which case it gives fire in the usual manner. The intent of this invention is to guard against the casualties which arise when Fire-arms are left loaded, or the misfortunes which frequently happen from twigs of trees or bushes catching the trigger when sportsmen are passing through hedges.

I hope it will meet the approbation and encouragement of the Society, and am,

SIR,

Your humble Servant,

JOHN WEBB.

To Mr. CHARLES TAYLOR.

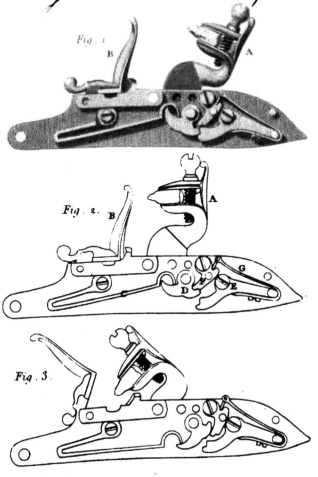

Fig. 1

B

A

Fig. 2. B

A

Fig. 3

Fig. 4.

K

*Description of Mr. John Webb's Gun-Lock, Plate II. Fig.* 1, 2, 3, 4, 5. *The Letters of the several Figures correspond together in the general Description.*

A is the cock—B, the hammer—C, the main spring—D, the tumbler—E, the large sear—F, the small sear—G, the sear spring—H, the shank or arm of the large sear—I, the shank or arm of the small sear—K, the thumb-piece —L, the trigger—M, the lever of the thumb-piece—N, the spring which holds the thumb-piece up, when not pressed upon by the thumb.

*Fig.* 1, is an interior view of the lock at full cock.

*Fig.* 2.—The same lock at half cock.

*Fig.* 3.—The lock when down.

*Fig.* 4.—The lock fixed in the gun-stock, in order to show the thumb-piece

R 3                              K and

K and the trigger L, with their mode of action. When the gun is held cocked in the usual manner, ready to fire, and the trigger L is pulled by the finger, the thumb, being pressed at the same time on the piece K, raises, by means of the lever M, moveable on a pin in its centre, the shank I of the small sear, and admits the cock to give fire as in the common way; whereas, if only the trigger L is pulled, the lock stops at the half-cock I; further motion being prevented by a notch in the small sear. A spring, N, screwed to the stock, returns the thumb-piece to its place, when the thumb is taken off.

*Fig.* 5 shows, on a larger scale, the construction of the tumbler, large and small sears, the sear-spring, and the manner in which they rise out of the bents of the tumbler.

The

The SILVER MEDAL was this Session presented to Mr. RICHARD KNIGHT, Ironmonger, of Foster-lane, Cheapside, for his method of BREAKING-UP LOGS of WOOD, for the purposes of Fuel, by blasting them with Gunpowder. The following Accounts and Certificates were received from him, a Drawing of the Apparatus is hereunto annexed, and the Implements are placed in the Society's Repository.

SIR,

I HAVE frequently observed the great difficulty, labour, and loss of time experienced in Breaking-up Logs of Wood, particularly for the purpose of fuel; such as the stumps and roots of large trees, which remain after the felling of timber, many of which, especially such as consist of the harder and

R 4 more

more knotty kind, as oaks, elms, yews, etc. are frequently left to rot in the ground, in order to avoid the necessary expense of breaking them to pieces in the common way, which is generally effected by the axe, and driving a succession of iron wedges with a sledge hammer; a laborious and tedious process. Sometimes gunpowder is used, by setting a blast in a similar way to that in mines or stone-quarries. This method, though less laborious than the former, is tedious, is attended with several difficulties, and requires considerable experience and dexterity, or the plug will be more frequently blown out than the block rent by the explosion. With a view, therefore, to obviate these difficulties, I have constructed an instrument, a sketch and description of which I now inclose for your approbation. The simplicity of its construction and application is such as almost to preclude an idea of its originality; but as it has hitherto

hitherto appeared entirely new to all my acquaintance, and as I do not know that any thing of the kind has ever before been presented to the Public, I am induced to think it may not be unacceptable; and should it appear to you an object worthy the attention of the Society of Arts, I shall be happy in making it public through a channel so highly respectable; and will, immediately on being favoured with your opinion, transmit to the Society a complete instrument with the necessary appendages, and a more minute description of its mode of application.

I am, SIR,

Your obedient humble Servant,

RICHARD KNIGHT,

*Foster-lane,*
*March 16, 1802,*

Mr. CHARLES TAYLOR,

The

...The inclosed Drawing represents the Instrument, which consists simply of a screw A, with a small hole drilled through its centre. The head of the screw is formed into two strong horns, for the more ready admission of the lever by which it is to be turned.

B represents a wire, for the purpose of occasionally clearing the touch-hole. When a block of wood is to be broken, a hole is to be bored with an auger of a proper depth, and a charge of gunpowder introduced. The screw is to be turned into the hole, till it nearly touches the powder; a quick-match is then to be put down the touch-hole till it reaches the charge. The piece of quick-match is about eighteen inches in length, which affords the operator an opportunity of retiring, after lighting it, to a place of safety.

The quick-match is made by steeping a roll of twine or linen thread in a solution of saltpetre.

DESCRIPTION

DESCRIPTION *of the Engraving of* Mr. RICHARD KNIGHT's *Method of Blasting Logs of Wood. Plate III.— Fig.* 1.

### SIR,

AS it may probably be a greater satisfaction to the Society to see the Instrument itself (a sketch of which I sent you last week, for the purpose of rending timber, logs of wood, etc, etc.) I now inclose a complete one, together with the necessary apparatus for its application, and of which I solicit the Society's acceptance.

*The following are the Articles inclosed.*

A, the rending or blowing screw, with a wire B, for the purpose of occasionally clearing the touch-hole, previous to the introduction of the quick-match.

C, an

C, an auger proper to bore holes, to receive the charge of the screw.

D, a gouge, to make an entrance for the augur.

E, a lever, to wind the screw into the wood, with a leather thong F attached to it, in order to fasten it occasionally to the screw, to prevent its being lost, in case it should be thrown out when the block is burst open; a circumstance which does not often occur: for in all my experiments, when the wood has been tolerably sound, I have always found the screw left fixed in one side of the divided mass.

A roll of twine is to be steeped in a solution of nitre, for the purpose of a quick-match, or train, to discharge the powder, by thrusting a piece thereof down the touch-hole, after taking out the wire B.

The first that was made was for J. Lloyd, Esq. of St. Asaph, the late

Member

Member for Flint, who, having a great quantity of timber on his estate, considers it a considerable acquisition; and at Overton-Hall, last summer, spoke so favourably of it, in my presence, to Sir Joseph Banks, that he immediately sent for his smith, and requested I would give him the necessary instructions for making one; but as I left that part of Derbyshire soon after, I had not an opportunity of seeing it finished. Since my return home, I have had several made, similar to that which I now present to the Society, which are better finished, and have sharper threads than smiths in general have an opportunity of giving them. Should the Society want farther explanation, I shall very readily wait upon them, if required, for that purpose, and remain,

Your very humble Servant,

RICHARD KNIGHT.

*Foster-lane,*
*March 24; 1802.*

Mr. CHARLES TAYLOR.

DEAR

DEAR SIR,

AFTER you left us last autumn, at Sir Joseph Banks's, his smith, who is a remarkably good workman, bestowed much needless time and trouble in making a blasting-screw; for he finished it in the highest style of polish, and, I think, made the thread of the worm too fine, or at least finer than was needful. However, it answered most completely, and very much to Sir Joseph's satisfaction, who lamented he had not seen such a contrivance many years ago, when a relation of his used to amuse himself with splitting the roots of trees, etc. in the common way. I have used the *Blasting-screw*, for so I shall call it, all the last and preceding winter, with the greatest success, and have gained many loads of fuel, which otherwise would have been suffered to rot, as the expense and labour in clearing the roots in the ordinary way renders the fuel

so

so procured too expensive; and since I have had the screw, I have observed some hundreds of roots in a rotting state in other places, from the want of knowing that there was such a contrivance as the screw. I think you would serve the public in no small degree, by devising some method of making its use known to the world.

When I was at Overton, some pieces of very tough, knotty, close-grained oak were picked from the timber-heap, for the use of the Gregory lead-mine, by Sir Joseph Banks's direction, and the screw severed some pieces four or five feet in length, and nine or ten in diameter, throwing them some feet asunder, to the surprise of the miners, who were assembled on the mine-bank. Sir Joseph took the screw with him to Revesby-Abby, in Lincolnshire, where, I understand, he had some large roots, that had lain by many years as useless; and I dare say he will give you a good account,

account, and bear testimony to the utility of the invention. We have used it without a single accident; but my neighbour, Lord Kirkwall, having procured one to be made by that which I had from you, one of his servants, in his Lordship's absence, I presume, put too much powder into the hole, and the screw was blown as high as a one-pair-of-stairs window, and passed through it into an apartment where a person then happened to be, but without any farther mischief than the loss of a pane of glass. Any one who uses the instrument will soon learn what depth of screw will be sufficient to split any root in proportion to its strength, taking care that the screw has sufficient hold to resist the force of the gunpowder, before the root is cleft. I think much powder may be saved by using a cotton match, impregnated by a solution of saltpetre, or any of the combustible matters generally made use of in fire-works; and by the

use

use of the cotton the hole through the screw may be lessened, which will add to the action of the confined powder; though a straw filled with powder, in the manner in which the miners use it, answers very well. Should any one be timid in using the screw, a chain or rope may easily be attached to the screw, and that fixed to any log, or fastened to a stake driven into the ground. If wood is rotten, the screw cannot act. I assure you, that when I go abroad, I constantly see great quantities of roots in a rotten state, about almost every farm-house, which would not be the case if the utility of the instrument were made public.

I am

Your much-obliged Friend

And humble Servant,

J. LLOYD.

*Wygfair,*
*March 26, 1802.*

To Mr. RICHARD KNIGHT.

S       A Bounty

A Bounty of TEN GUINEAS was this Session voted to Mr. JAMES WOART, of Fulham, for his Invention of a METHOD TO SECURE FROM DANGER TIMBERS or GIRDERS, injured by the Dry-rot, or by Time. Models on his plan are reserved in the Society's Repository for the inspection of the Public. Descriptions and two Plates of them are here annexed.

SIR,

THAT part of the Model I have sent herewith, which has moveable Iron Levers or Braces, *Plate III. Fig. 2,* represents the method I have employed, at the House of Hennege Legg, Esq. at Putney, in Surry, to support the Girders or Beams where their ends or bearings were entirely destroyed. Had the iron braces not been put in execution, new Girders must have been inevitably introduced, for reasons hereafter noticed. The bearing is not less than twenty-nine feet. The roof must have

been

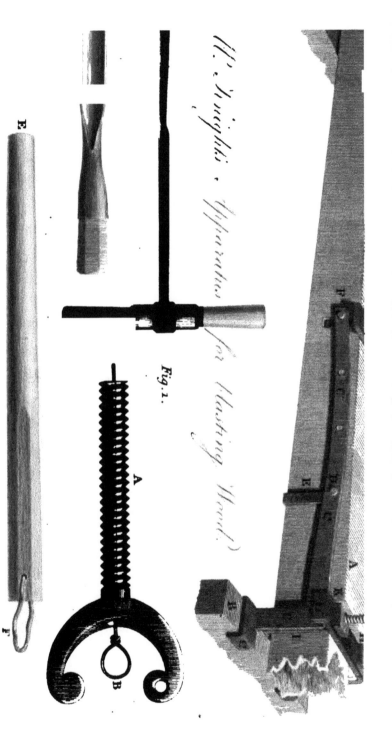

W. Knight's Apparatus for blasting Wood.

Fig. 1.

A

B

E

F

Lowry sculp.

been completely taken off, owing to the gutter-plate being placed across the girders, and the roof a double one.

The ceiling of the drawing-room, which is immediately under the Girders, must also have been destroyed.

This ceiling is highly ornamented, and supposed to be in value five hundred pounds, to which sum if the expense of taking off the roof, etc. is added, it would have cost eight hundred pounds to have reinstated the work; whereas, I believe, that the iron braces and workmanship in effecting this business, on my plan, did not amount to twenty pounds, for securing the four ends of the Girders, the ceiling, and the roof.

If my plan is approved of by the Society, I trust to their liberality for reward. I am, Sir,

Your humble Servant,

JAMES WOART.

*Fulham,*
*Nov. 25, 1801.*

Mr. CHARLES TAYLOR.

S 2

DESCRIPTION *of the Engravings of Mr. JAMES WOART's Inventions for securing Beams of Timber, decayed by time or injured by the dry rot.*

*Plate III. Fig. 2; and Plate IV. Fig. 1, 2, 3, 4. 5, 6, 7.*

Where the ends of the girder are decayed by time, or injured by the dry rot, they are often taken out, and new ones put in their place, at a great expense; and if the dry rot is in the walls, the ends of the new girder will be in danger of it again: such was the case at Eltham, in Kent, where in one house there were three new girders to one floor in the space of twenty years; whereas my method will be found infallible, executed at much less expense, and not subject to the dry rot, because the end of the girder may be cut off clear from the wall; and if an air grate is put on the outside, so as to admit air

to

to the end of the girder, it will remain
safe from injury.

*Plate III. Fig. 2.*—A, shews the end
of the decayed girder, with the braces
applied upon it.

BB, the templets or wall-plates on
which the Girder rests.

CCCC, one of the iron levers for raising and supporting the girder (there
being a similar one on the opposite
side). This lever is moveable on a pin
D, which comes through a hole in the
lever, distant about two feet from the
end of the girder. This pin forms part of
a coller E bedded in the girder. The lever
is six feet long, three inches wide, and
three fourths of an inch thick, and
extends from the wall-plate along the
side of the girder.

The extremity of the lever is moveable
on another pin F, projecting through it
from an upright iron G, bedded in the
side of the girder, and carrying a nut
and screw, which act on a cross plate H,
through which the upright iron passes.

S 3

At

At the other end of the lever, next the templet, is an iron collar I, bedded in the girder, which collar may be raised or lowered at pleasure, by means of the nut and screw K, forming part of it; and by aid of the cap-plate L, which presses upon the lever, and also clasps it to the girder by its bend at L.

As the *Plate III. Fig.* 2, shows only one side of the girder, and, as has been before observed, there being also a similar lever on the opposite side of the girder, their separate parts, method of connecting them, and their mode of action, are more fully explained in *Plate IV. Fig.* 1, 2, 3, where the same letters are made use of to point out the several parts.

*Fig.* 1.—E, shows the whole of the collar to be bedded in the side and bottom of the girder, and the pins DD, on which the two levers are moveable.

*Fig.* 2.—The cap-plate H, the two upright irons GG, with their nuts and screws,

screws, which act upon the extremities of the two levers by means of their pins F F.

*Fig.* 3.—The collar I, on which that end of the girder next the templet rests, the sides of which collar are bedded in the girder. C C are the claws or bended legs of the two levers which go into the templet. L is the cap-plate, KK are the nuts and screws.

At Mr. Legg's house, where the levers above mentioned were applied, the beams of the roof were so decayed that the roof was in imminent danger, the bearings were entirely rotten, and the beams were sunk three fourths of an inch, and pressing against the wall for support; if there had not been a large cornice underneath, supported by brackets, the whole roof must have fallen.

To put them in order, I first put shores or supports under each end of the two beams, on which the double roof lay, and then forced the four shores at once,

for

for the security of the roof, the work, and men. The iron levers, C, were then prepared, let into the templet, and fixed on each side of the beam, on the pins D, projecting from the collar E, bedded in the beam, about two feet from its end. When the whole apparatus was ready, on screwing the nuts on the upright irons G, at the extremity of the levers, the beam was raised to its proper height with great ease, although it was supposed there was above two tons weight on each beam, on account of the lead gutter, and gutter-beam betwixt the double roof, and the rich ornamented ceiling attached to the joice, which was not the least destroyed except where the iron-collar E was fixed, which was put up from the under side by cutting the ceiling the width of the collar. These beams were so decayed, and so hollow, that the common method of bolting plank on each side of the beam would not have been safe; and if it could have

been

been executed, the new planks would have been subject to the dry rot, and the roof still in danger, which is now prevented, as the iron is not affected by it. The beam-ends were cut clear from the walls, and the beams are suspended by means of the iron levers, whose feet rest on the templets of the walls. An air grate was made, on the outside of the wall, to admit a current of fresh air to the ends of the timbers. The roof is now much safer than when originally made, as the timber is secured from decay; and, owing to the collar E, the bearings are now two feet shorter at each end of the beam; the bearing on each beam being now, in the whole, four feet shorter than in its original state.

After the beams were brought to their proper height, and the levers and screws adjusted, screw-bolts were put into the timber, through holes purposely left in the lever, betwixt D and F, and the whole work thus perfectly secured.

*At*

*At the other end of the Girder M,*
*Plate III, is shown another method of*
*supporting Timbers, where the ends are*
*decayed.*

The particular irons used in this way
are shown in *Plate IV. Fig.* 4. N is a
collar for the girder; O, an iron frame
which rests on the templet; P P, two
nuts which raise the collar N. RR show
the clawed ends of the two bars of iron,
extending under the girder, bedded
therein, and screwed to it at their extremities, about five feet distant from
the templet.

*Fig.* 5, is one of the iron bars last
mentioned.

S is the claw or lap which projects
over the collar N.

T is the place where it is screwed into
the girder.

*Fig.*

*Fig.* 6 *and* 7. *Plate* IV. *explain a third method of securing decayed Timbers.*

*Fig.* 6, gives a side-view of a decayed girder: a, represents the templet; b, an iron lever, six feet long, nearly strait, being only cambered one inch, three inches wide, and three-quarters of an inch thick; this lever extends along the side of the girder c, and is secured fimly to it by the side-irons d d d d, which are two inches wide, and full half an inch thick, pointed at the ends. The higher ends of these side-irons are driven into the girder, and the lower points pass through holes in the lever, into the lower part of the girder, and are held close to the girder by staples e e e e: the side iron next the templet may be fixed slanting, in order that it may enter sounder wood. A claw, f, which is part of the lever, rests on the wall-plate a, and is bedded in it; an iron plate, g,

lying

lying under the girder and let into it, passes through the lever at h, connecting it with a similar lever on the opposite side, and which assists in the same way to support the girder: i, is a flooring joist, to show how deep the levers are inserted therein.

*Fig.* 7, shows the under part of the same girder; b b, are the bottoms of the two levers above mentioned, fixed to the girder by the side irons and staples before described; k k, the broad feet of the levers which lie flat upon the wall plate; ff, the two claws projecting from the feet, in order to bed in the wall plate; iiii are joists, partly cut through, to admit the iron levers to lie close to the girder: g shows the iron plate or collar on which the Girder bears; it is turned up an inch and a half at each end, to keep the levers close to the sides of the girder. This collar should be made out of inch-bar iron, with points projecting from it, in the same manner as the

collar

collar at D D, *Fig.* 1, to connect it with the levers, by passing through holes made through them for that purpose.

To fix the levers, put a shore two feet six inches from the wall, under the girder, to support it; then cut off the decayed end, and take out the templet, or part of the wall plate if decayed; and put in a stone templet for the irons to rest upon, with mortices in the stone to admit the claws of the lever: then fit the collar underneath the girder, two feet from the wall, to answer the holes in the lever; make an incision in the joists three-fourths of an inch wide, and three inches deep, to admit the levers; fix the levers on each side with the collar, so as to force up the levers together; then with slight shores force up the ends of both levers together, and fix the side-irons firm. The girder will thus be perfectly safe.

The templet or wall plates, on which the levers rest, are made of Portland stone,

stone, three feet long, nine inches wide, and five inches deep, with incisions or mortices made therein for the claws of the levers.

Certificates, confirming Mr. Woart's Improvements, were received from the Commissioners of the Navy, from Mr. Joseph Harris, smith, at Putney, and Mr. George Smith, surveyor, at Putney.

The

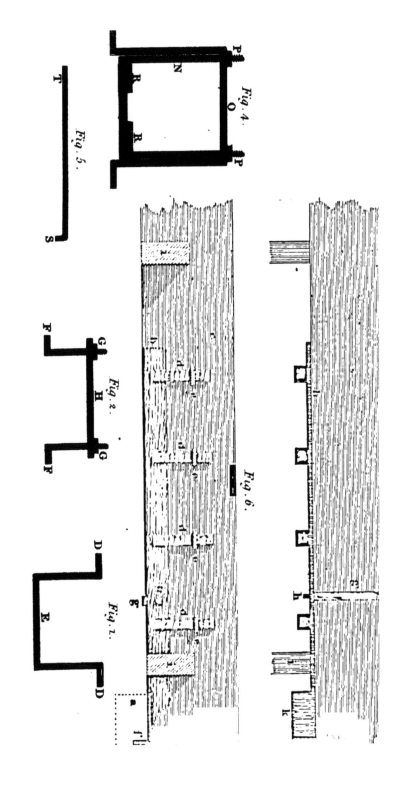

Fig. 4.

Fig. 5.

Fig. 2.

Fig. 6.

Fig. 1.

The GOLD MEDAL, or ONE HUNDRED POUNDS, at the option of the Candidate, being the Premium offered for the Discovery of a QUARRY OF MILL-STONES, equal to those known by the name of French Burrs, was this Session adjudged to Mr. JAMES BROWNHILL, of Alloa-Mills, near Stirling, in Scotland; who made choice of the Pecuniary Reward. The following Accounts and Certificates were received relative to these Mill-stones.

SIR,

AMONG the various premiums offered by the Society for the Encouragement of Arts, etc. I observe that there is one for the person who shall discover, in Great-Britain, a Quarry of Stone fit for the purposes of Mill-stones, for grinding Wheat, and equal in in all respects to that known by the name of French Burr. I have therefore taken the liberty of inclosing a particular account of the execution of a pair of those Mill-stones, which have been lately built at my Mills here, compared with the execution of the Burr-stones. The Mills are on a large scale; and the Alloa-mill Company, who carry on an extensive business, pay a high rent for them.

They have a very intelligent industrious man for their head miller, who, in consequence of the high price of French Burrs, and the very great difficulty of procuring any of them at present, was very anxious to try if any substitute could be found; and he flatters himself that he has been fortunate enough to find some Stones, in this neighbourhood, that will answer equally well as the French. Their performance has been such, that two other pair are bespoke; and in all probability many

more

more will be built before the time proposed for laying the discovery and claim before the Society. Should the discovery answer the present expectations, the Society will rejoice to find that the situation of the Quarry is so near this port, where any quantity of the rough stones, or in their more perfect state, can be easily transported to any place accessible by water-carriage.

I am, Sir,

Your most obedient humble Servant,

T. F. ERSKINE.

*Tower of Alloa, Clackmananshire,*
*June* 24, 1800.

Mr. CHARLES TAYLOR.

T  On

On the 20th of June, 1800, ground twelve Quarters of Wheat of three different qualities; six Quarters were ground on French-burr Mill-stone, and six Quarters on Mill-stones built of the Stone from Abbey's Craig, in Stirlingshire.

| Qrs. Bush. | | Sks. | Cwt. | Qrs. | lb. | lb. |
|---|---|---|---|---|---|---|
| 1 4 of Wheat 53½ lb. Avoid. per Bush. | | — | — | — | — | 645 |
| 2 .. Do. 57¼ ................ | | — | — | — | — | 924 |
| 2 4 Do. 56 ................ | | — | — | — | — | 1120 |
| 6 Qrs. | | .. | .. | .. | .. | 2689 |

*Produce of the above six Quarters, per French Burrs.*

| | Sks. | Cwt. | Qrs. | lb. | lb. |
|---|---|---|---|---|---|
| Of fine Flour........................... | 5 | — | 2 | 20 | 1476 |
| second do. ........................ | — | 2 | — | 3 | 227 |
| third do. ........................ | 1 | — | 2 | 9 | 345 |
| | 7 | — | 3 | 4 | 2048 |
| Bran ........................... | — | 4 | 3 | 17 | 549 |
| Waste ........................... | — | — | — | — | 92 |
| Weight as above.. | .. | .. | .. | .. | 2689 |

N. B. The Bran, measured with the Winchester bushel, and struck, turned out 26 bushels. Ground in three hours and forty minutes.

*Ditto per Abbey Craig Mill Stones.*

| | Sks. | Cwt. | Qrs. | lb. | lb. |
|---|---|---|---|---|---|
| Of fine Flour........................... | 5 | 1 | 2 | 27 | 1595 |
| second do........................... | — | 2 | — | 19 | 243 |
| third do........................... | — | 2 | — | 20 | 244 |
| | 7 | 1 | — | 10 | 2082 |
| Bran ........................... | — | 4 | 2 | 14 | 518 |
| Waste ........................... | — | — | — | — | 89 |
| Weight as above.. | .. | .. | .. | .. | 2689 |

The Bran measured 32 bushels, although 31 lb. lighter than that produced by the French Burrs. Ground in three hours and ten minutes.

**Each**

Each mill-stone is about twenty-five hundred weight, six pieces in the bed, and fourteen in the runner, four feet and a half diameter, eleven inches thick at the hem, and thirteen at the eye; each stone, divided into nine spaces, having ten circular roads in each space: they flag the bran, and do not heat the flour so much as French Burrs, being much evener in the face than the latter. I have ground four hundred quarters with them, and they have required but little dressing during the grinding of that quantity; but there is very little taken off them, as they are very hard.

A Certificate from James Brownhill, dated Alloa, January 16, 1801, declares that the Quarry, from which these stones are taken, is situated about a mile north-east from the Castle of Stirling, named Abbey Craig; and that it is a huge mass of whinn-rock of various texture, and strikes fire with steel; that the pair of stones sent to the Society are the first

that

that were made, and have ground about
a thousand quarters of wheat to the
satisfaction of the bakers.

It also states, that five quarters of
wheat were ground with them in a
hundred and eight minutes, the stone
making one hundred and thirty-one
revolutions per minute; heat of the flour
64° Fahrenheit's thermometer. The
stone being of a uniform hardness, executes its business better than the French
Burr-stones.

The produce of the above five quarters of wheat, 60lb. per Winchester
bushel, 2400lb.                                    lb.

Produced fine Flour . . . .     1464
        second do. . . . . .      222
        third   do. . . . . .      241
                                  ————
                                   1927

Broad bran 242 ⎫
Small   do. 200 ⎬ · · · · ·        442
                                  ————
                                   2369
                Waste. . .          31
                                  ————
                                   2400
                                These

These stones cost about twenty guineas
per pair, and, when first made, weighed
nearly twenty-five hundred weight each.
They require to be somewhat oftener
dressed than French Burr-stones; but
the time which is lost in dressing is
more than compensated in the after
execution. Taking in the time for dressing, these stones have, on an average,
ground thirty-six quarters in twenty-four
hours.

A letter from Mr. Erskine, dated
January 3, states, that many bakers,
from Glasgow and Paisley, have preferred the flour made from these stones,
to that ground by the French Burr. It
also states, that the place from whence
these stones were taken, is situated
near Stirling, close on the banks of the
Forth, called the Abbot's Craig. It is a
particular kind of that stone which is
known in this county by the name of
Whinn-stone, which resembles the stones
from Aberdeen, but is of a more open

T 3                          texture.

texture. There is reason to believe that stones of the same kind are to be found in various parts of Scotland; which Mr. Erskine flatters himself the Society will think enhances the discovery of James Brownhill.

A certificate from Andrew Lind, and G. Younger, bakers, dated January 16, 1801, certifies, that the flour ground by these mill-stones was equal in every respect to that ground by French Burr-stones.

A letter from John Burns, mill-stone builder, states, that he has been long employed as a builder of French Burr-stones, and that he has now been six months engaged in making mill-stones from Abbey Craig, which he has employed, and which make excellent work.

A letter from Mr. Erskine, dated January 17, 1801, confirms the above circumstances and signatures.

A letter from Mr. Erskine, dated April 7, 1801, informs the Society, that

he

he had forwarded for their inspection, samples of flour ground by the Alloa Mill-stones, and other samples ground by French Burr-stones, for comparative experiments. The Committee found those ground by the Abbey-Craig Stones to be the best.

A letter from William Glenn, dated Lithgow Mills, December 11, 1801, states that he was so well pleased with the mill-stones which he had procured from Abbey-Craig, that he had ordered another pair, and should leave off French Burrs entirely.

A letter from John Cowan, dated Hawk-head Mill, December 16, 1801, speaks highly in favour of the Abbey-craig Mill-stones, in comparision with the French Burr.

W. Crawford, in a letter, dated Bainsford Steam-engine, January 7, 1802, declares, that he has no hesitation in attesting that he considers the Abbey-craig Mill-stones to be superior to

T 4                     French

French Burr-stones for flour-manufacture; that, although they require to be oftener dressed than Burr Stones, they will grind considerably more wheat in a given time, upon an equal power; and that he considers them an invention highly beneficial to this Country.

A second memorial from James Brownhill, the claimant, dated Jan. 12, 1802, notices, that the first pair of mill-stones of the Abbey-craig kind, were set a-going at Alloa, in May, 1800; since which time thirty-six and a half pairs had been made; that all which had been used had given satisfaction; that they had been employed in various parts of Scotland; and that one pair had been sent to Prussia.

A letter from Alexander Bald, agent for the Alloa-Mill Company, dated January 13, 1802, greatly commends the Abbey-craig Stones, and observes, that flour ground with them gives great satisfaction; that when the power of the mill is able to grind three bolls per hour

with

with French Burrs (each boll being more than four Winchester bushels) the Abbey-craig Stones will grind three quarters of a boll more each hour; and from good wheat produce one eighth more of fine-flour per boll; that they are not under the necessity of running the Abbey-craig Stones so close set as Burrs, which enables them to feed faster without bringing an extra heat upon the flour.

A letter from Mr. Erskine, dated January 15, 1802, confirms the above Certificates, and states, that he is con-vinced, on any fair trial, the Abbey-craig Mill-stones will be found to excel all others yet made use of; that he will direct any further experiments to be made in that neighbourhood relative to them, which the Society may suggest, as the Alloa-Mill Company are convinced that the trial will prove how deserving poor James Brownhill is of having a good reward for his ingenuity.

He further adds, that mill-stones are now built at Alloa for sixteen guineas; which

which is very nearly about one fourth the price of French Burr.

A subsequent letter from Mr. Erskine, states, that Robert Redman, Esq. Corn-Exchange, London, has been lately at Alloa Mills, and, in consequence of seeing their effects, has ordered two pair to be sent to him in London, and is to send to the Alloa Mills some Essex-wheat, to be ground there, and the produce returned to him in London.

By accounts lately received from Alloa, the Society have been informed that the manufacture of these mill-stones is carried on with great success by Mr. James Brownhill, at Alloa Mills, in the county of Clackmanan, North Britain ; that he executes orders for them, addressed there, upon moderate terms; and that, from his experience as a miller, he takes care to build them of such a grain as will best suit the purposes for which they are ordered.

The

The GOLD MEDAL and FIFTY GUINEAS were this Sesson voted as a Bounty to Mr. HENRY GREATHEAD, of South Shields, for a BOAT of a peculiar construction, named a *Life-Boat*, in consequence of the lives of many persons shipwrecked having been preserved by it.

*Two Plates of this Boat are annexed to the following Communications on the Subject, and a Model of it is in the Repository of the Society.*

SIR,

A CONSIDERABLE time has elapsed since I had the honour to lay before the Society a Model of the Life-Boat of my invention.

I have now inclosed a particular account of its construction, in a letter from Mr. Hinderwell, explaining upon

what

what principle it is built, so as to render it superior to any other form of a Boat for the dangerous enterprises for which it was intended, and has been used.

I am, SIR,

Your humble Servant,

HENRY GREATHEAD,

South Shields, Jan. 1, 1802.

To Mr. CHARLES TAYLOR.

SIR,

IT is much to be lamented, that in an age enlightened by science, such a languid indifference should prevail on many important public occasions; and that the most excellent inventions should have to combat the force of inveterate prejudice.

How many valuable discoveries have languished in obscurity! How many useful projects have perished in embryo, deprived of the fostering aid of the public

public, and the patronage of influence and authority !—In the class of useful improvements for the diminution of the dangers incident to a maritime profession, the Life-Boat, invented by Mr. GREATHEAD, of SHIELDS, has a claim to a distinguished patronage.— An experimental conviction of its great utility in saving the lives of shipwrecked seamen, and of its perfect safety in the most agitated sea, has induced me to advocate the cause with a zeal proportioned to its importance; and it is a consolatory reflexion to my own mind, that my exertions have been successful in the introduction of a Life-Boat, in the port of Scarborough, and, I trust, not unprofitable towards promoting a similar establishment in other places.— The services which have been recently performed at this port, by means of the Life-Boat, in contributing to the preservation of the lives of the *crews* of *two vessels*, more than compensate for every labour.

labour.—I am far from the ambition of aspiring to any honorary testimony on this occasion. Actuated by the purest principle of philanthropy, my sole object is the benefit of the community, and to endeavour, by ardent recommendations, to excite a spirit of emulation, in order to introduce the Life-Boat, with its invaluable properties, into more general use. I am induced to submit, with the utmost deference and respect, to the consideration of the Society of Arts, &c. the following description of the Life-Boat, with some miscellaneous observations.—The construction of the Boat, agreeably to Mr. GREATHEAD's plan, is as follows:

The length is thirty feet; the breadth, ten feet; the depth, from the top of the gunwale to the lower part of the keel in midships, three feet three inches; from the gunwale to the platform *(within)*, two feet four inches; from the top of the stems (both ends being similar) to
the

the horizontal line of the bottom of the keel, five feet nine inches. The keel is a plank of three inches thick, of a proportionate breadth in midships, narrowing gradually toward the ends, to the breadth of the stems at the bottom, and forming a great convexity downwards. The stems are segments of a circle, with considerable *rakes.* The bottom section, to the floor-heads, is a curve fore and aft, with the sweep of the keel. The floor-timber has a small *rise* curving from the keel to the floor-heads. A bilge plank is wrought in on each side next the floor-heads with a double *rabbit* or groove, of a similar thickness with the keel; and, on the outside of this, are fixed two bilge-trees, corresponding nearly with the level of the keel. The ends of the bottom section form that fine kind of entrance observable in the lower part of the bow of the fishing-boat, called a *Coble,* much used in the North. From this part to the top of the

the stem, it is more elliptical, forming a considerable projection. The sides, from the floor-heads to the top of the gunwale, flaunch off on each side, in proportion to about half the breadth of the floor. The breadth is continued far forward towards the ends, leaving a sufficient length of strait side at the top. The sheer is regular along the strait side, and more elevated towards the ends. The gunwale, fixed on the outside, is three inches thick.—The sides, from the under part of the gunwale, along the whole length of the regular sheer, extending twenty-one feet six inches, are cased with *layers* of cork, to the depth of sixteen inches downward; and the thickness of this casing of cork being four inches, it projects at the top a little without the gunwale. The cork, on the outside, is secured with thin plates or slips of copper, and the boat is fastened with copper nails. The *thwarts*, or seats, are five in number, *double banked*,

*banked,* consequently the boat may be rowed with ten * oars. The *thwarts* are firmly stanchioned. The side oars are short, † with iron tholes and rope grommets, so that the rower can pull either way. The boat is steered with an oar at each end; and the steering-oar is one third longer than the rowing-oar. The platform placed at the bottom, within the boat, is horizontal, the length of the midships, and elevated at the ends, for the convenience of the steersman, to give him a greater power with the oar. The internal part of the boat next the sides, from the under part of the *thwarts* down to the platform, is cased with cork; the whole quantity of which, affixed to the Life-Boat, is nearly seven hundred weight. The cork indisputably

U contributes

---

* Five of the benches are only used, the Boat being generally rowed with ten oars.

† The short oar is more manageable in a high sea than the long oar, and its stroke is more certain.

contributes much to the buoyancy of the
boat, is a good defence in going along-
side a vessel, and is of principal use in
keeping the boat in an erect position in
the sea, or rather, of giving her a very
lively and quick disposition to recover
from any sudden *cant* or *lurch* which she
may receive from the stroke of a heavy
wave. But, exclusive of the cork, the
admirable construction of this boat
gives it a decided pre-eminence. The
ends being similar, the Boat can be
rowed either way; and this peculiarity
of form alleviates her in rising over the
waves. The curvature of the keel and
bottom facilitates her movement in turning, and contributes to the ease of the
steerage, as a single stroke of the steering-oar has an immediate effect, the boat
moving as it were upon a centre. The
fine entrance below is of use in dividing
the waves, when rowing against them;
and, combined with the convexity of
the bottom, and the elliptical form of
the

the stém, admits her to rise with wonderful buoyancy in high sea, and to
launch forward with rapidity, without
shipping any water, when a common
boat would be in danger of being filled.
The *flaunching*, or spreading form of the
boat, from the floor-heads to the gunwale, gives her a considerable bearing;
and the continuation of the breadth,
well forward, is a great support to her in
the sea; and it has been found by experience, that boats of this construction
are the best sea-boats for rowing against
turbulent waves. The internal shallow-
ness of the boat, from the gunwale
down to the platform, the convexity of
the form, and the bulk of cork within,
leave a very diminished space for the water
to occupy; so that the Life-Boat, when
filled with water, contains a considerably less quantity than the common boat,
and is in no danger either of sinking or
overturning. It may be presumed, by
some, that in cases of high wind, agi-

U 2                          tated

tated sea, and broken waves, that a boat of such a bulk could not prevail against them by the force of the oars; but the Life-Boat, from her peculiar form, may be rowed *a-head*, when the attempt in other boats would fail. Boats of the common form, adapted for speed, are of course put in motion with a small power; but, for want of buoyancy and bearing, are over-run by the waves and sunk, when impelled against them: and boats constructed for burthen, meet with too much resistance from the wind and sea, when opposed to them, and cannot in such cases be rowed from the shore to a ship in distress. An idea has been entertained, that the superior advantages of the Life-Boat are to be ascribed solely to the quantity of cork affixed. But this is a very erroneous opinion; and, I trust, has been amply refuted by the preceding observations on the supereminent construction of this boat. It must

be

be admitted, that the application of cork to common boats would add to their buoyancy and security; and it might be a useful expedient, if there were a quantity of cork on board of ships, to prepare the boats with, in cases of shipwreck, as it might be expeditiously done, in a temporary way, by means of *clamps*, or some other contrivance. The application of cork to some of the boats of his Majesty's ships* might be worthy of consideration; more particularly as an experiment might be made at a little expence, and without inconvenience to the boats; or may prevent pleasure-boats from upsetting or sinking.

The Life-Boat is kept in a boat-house, and placed upon four low wheels, ready to be moved at a moment's notice. These wheels are convenient in conveying the boat along the shore to the sea;

U 3 but

* The Launches.

but if she had to travel upon them on a rough road, her frame would be exceedingly shaken. Besides, it has been found difficult and troublesome to replace her upon these wheels, on her return from sea. Another plan has, therefore, been adopted. Two wheels, of nine feet diameter, with a moveable arched axis, and a pole fixed thereto for a lever, have been constructed. The boat is suspended near her center, between the wheels, under the *axis;* toward each extremity of *which* is an iron pin, with a chain attached. When the pole is elevated perpendicularly, the upper part of the axis becomes depressed, and the chains being hooked to *eye-bolts*, on the inside of the boat, she is raised with the utmost facility, by means of the pole, which is then fastened down to the stem of the boat.

The Scarborough Boat is under the direction of a Committee. Twenty-four fishermen,

fishermen, composing *two crews**, are alternately employed to navigate her. A reward, in cases of shipwreck, is paid by the Committee to each man actually engaged in the assistance; and it is expected that the vessel receiving assistance should contribute to defray this expence. None have hitherto refused.

It is of importance, that the command of the boat should be entrusted to some steady, experienced person, who is acquainted with the direction of the tides or currents, as much skill may be required in rising *them* to the most advantage, in going to a ship in distress. It should also be recommended, to keep the *head* of the boat to the *sea*, as much as circumstances will admit; and to give her an accelerated velocity to meet the wave. Much caution is necessary in approaching a wreck, on account of

U 4      the

---

* Two crews are appointed, that there may be a sufficient number ready in case of any absence.

the strong reflux of the waves, which is sometimes attended with great danger. In a general way, it is safest to go on the *lee* quarter; but this depends upon the position of the vessel; and the master of the boat should exercise his skill in placing her in the most convenient situation. The boatmen should practise themselves in the use of the boat, that they may be the better acquainted with her movements; and they should at all times be strictly obedient to the directions of the person who is appointed to the command.

The great ingenuity which has been displayed in the construction of the Life-Boat, leaves scarcely any room for improvement; but some have supposed, that a boat of twenty-five feet in length, with a proportionate breadth, would answer every purpose of a larger one. A boat of these dimensions would certainly be lighter, and less expensive; but whether she would be equally *safe* and

and *steady* in a high sea, I cannot take upon myself to determine.

Mr. Greathead, of South Shields, the inventor, undertakes to build these boats, and to convey them to any port in the kingdom. He is a worthy man, in whom a confidence may be reposed, and will build upon moderate terms of profit.

THOMAS HINDERWELL.

To Mr. CHARLES TAYLOR.

SIR,

I HAVE duly received your letter, and am greatly obliged to you for your polite attention towards me. Inclosed is a Certificate from the Gentlemen of South and North Shields, who are respectable men, and well versed in maritime affairs. Most of them are also known

known to Capt. Abel Chapman, an elder brother of the Trinity House, London. Capt. Reed, an elder brother of that House, whose benevolent views led him to try some experiments with one of these boats, may also be applied to.

Rowland Burdon, Esq. M. P. has authorised me to inform you, that he is in possession of certificates and documents respecting this boat, which may be referred to.

Having no regular journal of the transactions of these boats, I shall send you the principal events from some detached minutes.

They have been particularly patronised by his Grace the Duke of Northumberland. I built the Life-Boat for North Shields entirely at his expence, and he has endowed it with an annuity. I have since built another for him, which was sent to Oporto. As I am honoured with his correspondence, he also may be applied to. Besides the Life-Boats at the

the stations here, they have them now at Scarborough, Lowestoffe, Woodbridge; Montrose, and St. Andrew's, in Scotland. I am at present building one for Ramsgate; and am desired, by George Rose, Esq. M. P. to give him information respecting one for Christ Church, Hants. I am likewise applied to from Dublin, Liverpool, and other ports, concerning them.

I have been honoured with the Medallion from the Humane Society, on account of my Boat, and hope to merit the approbation of the Society of Arts.

I am, SIR,

· Yours, &c.

HENRY GREATHEAD.

*South Shields,*
*January* 12, 1802.

To Mr. CHARLES TAYLOR.

CERTI-

## CERTIFICATE FROM NORTH AND SOUTH SHIELDS.

WE, the under-signed resident Gentlemen and Ship Owners of South and North Shields, do certify, that the Life-Boat of South Shields, built in the year 1789, and the North Shields Boat, built in 1798, were invented and constructed by Mr. Henry Greathead, of South Shields; and have, during the last eleven years, been the means of saving between two and three hundred men, from ships wrecked in the course of that time, near the Mouth of Tynemouth Haven; and as the said Mr. Henry Greathead has made his models public, we recommend him to the Society instituted for the Encouragement of Arts, Manufactures, and Commerce; as deserving not only their countenance and support, but a reward suitable to the great good that has resulted to the community from this fortunate invention.

*South*

## South Shields.

WILLIAM MASTERMAN,
CUTHBERT MARSHALL,
HENRY HEATH,
JOSEPH WILLIAM ROXBY,
JOSEPH BULMER,
CUTHBERT HERON,
LOCKWOOD BRODRICK,
JOHN ROXBY,
ROBERT STEPHENSON,
JOHN MARSHALL.

## North Shields.

JOHN WALKER,
GEORGE FRENCH,
JOHN SCOTT,
SAMUEL HURRY,
WILLIAM CLARK,
STEPHEN WRIGHT, jun.
THOMAS HEARN,
HENRY TREWHITT,
WILLIAM CLARK, jun.
JOHN FENWICK, sen.

*January,* 1802.

*Particulars*

*Particulars relative to the Construction of, and Benefits received from, sundry Life-Boats, built by Mr. HENRY GREATHEAD, or under his directions, in and since the year 1789.*

———

ACCOUNT of the SOUTH-SHIELDS LIFE-BOAT.

FROM the declaration of Sir Cuthbert Heron, Bart. of South Shields, it appears, that when the Adventure was wrecked in 1789, on the Herd Sands, he offered a reward for any seamen to go off to save the men's lives, which was refused; and that the greatest part of the crew of the Adventure perished within 300 yards of the shore, and in sight of a multitude of spectators. The Gentlemen of South Shields immediately met, and offered a reward to any person who would give in a Plan of a Boat, which should be approved, for the preservation

servation of men's lives. Mr. Greathead gave in a plan, which met with approbation; a committee was formed, and a subscription raised, for the building of a boat upon that plan. After it was built, it was with some difficulty that the sailors were induced to go off in her; but, in consequence of a reward offered, they went off, and brought the crew of a stranded vessel on shore. Since which time the boat has been readily manned, and no lives have been lost (except in the instances of the crews trusting to their own boats); and, in his opinion, if Mr. Greathead's boat had existed at the time of the wreck of the Adventure, the crew would have been saved.

From other accounts it appears, that in the year 1791 the crew of a brig, belonging to Sunderland, and laden from the westward, were preserved by this Life-Boat, the vessel at the same time breaking to pieces by the force of the sea.

On

On January 1st, 1795, the ship Par-
thenius, of Newcastle, was driven on the
Herd Sand, and the Life-Boat went to
her assistance, when the sea breaking
over the ship as the boat was ranging
along-side, the boat was so violently
shaken that her bottom was actually
hanging loose; under these circumstances
she was three times off to the ship, without being affected by the water in her.

The ship Peggy being also on the
Herd Sand, the Life-Boat went off, and
brought the crew on shore, when the
plug in her bottom had been accidentally
left out; though she filled with water in
consequence, yet she effected the purpose in that situation.

In the latter part of the year 1796,
a sloop belonging to Mr. Brymer, from
Scotland, laden with bale goods, was
wrecked on the Herd Sand; the crew
and passengers were taken out by the
Life-Boat; the vessel went to pieces at
the time the boat was employed, the
goods

goods were scattered on the sand, and part of them lost.

In the same year, a vessel named the Countess of Errol, was driven on the Herd Sand, and the crew saved by the Life-Boat.

October 15th, 1797, the sloop called Fruit of Friends, from Leith, coming to South Shields, was driven on the Herd Sand. One part of the passengers, in attempting to come on shore in the ship's boat, was unfortunately drowned; the other part was brought on shore safe by the Life-Boat.

The account of Capt. William Carter, of Newcastle, states, that on the 28th November, 1797, the ship Planter, of London, was driven on shore near Tynemouth Bar, by the violence of a gale; the Life-Boat came out, and took fifteen persons from the ship, which the boat had scarcely quitted before the ship went to pieces; that, without the boat, they must all have inevitably perished, as the

X                    wreck

wreck came on shore soon after the
Life-Boat. He conceived that no boat,
of a common construction, could have
given relief at that time. The ships
Gateshead and Mary, of Newcastle, the
Beaver, of North Shields, and a sloop,
were in the same situation with the
Planter. The crew of the Gateshead,
nine in number, took to their own boat,
which sunk, and seven of them were
lost; the other two saved themselves, by
ropes thrown from the Mary. After
the Life-Boat had landed the crew
of the Planter, she went off successively to the other vessels, and brought
the whole of their crews safe to shore,
together with the two persons who had
escaped from the boat of the Gateshead.

Mr. Carter adds, that he has seen the
Life-Boat go to the assistance of other
vessels, at different times, and that she
ever succeeded in bringing the crews on
shore; that he had several times observed

served her to come on shore full of water, and always safe.

ACCOUNT OF THE NORTHUMBERLAND LIFE-BOAT.

THE Northumberland Life-Boat, so called from being built at the expence of his Grace the Duke of Northumberland, and presented by him to North Shields, was first employed in November, 1798, when she went off to the relief of the sloop Edinburgh, of Kincardine, which was seen to go upon the Herd Sands, about a mile and a half from the shore. Ralph Hillery, one of the seamen who went out in the Life-Boat to her assistance, relates, that she was brought to an anchor before the Life-Boat got to her; that the ship continued to strike the ground so heavily, that she would not have held together ten minutes longer, had not the Life-Boat arrived; they made her cut her cable, and then

X 2                    took

took seven men out of her, and brought them on shore; that the sea was at that time so monstrously high, that no other boat whatever could have lived in it. He stated, that, in the event of the Life-Boat filling with water, she would continue still upright, and would not founder, as boats of a common construction do; that he has seen her go off scores of times, and never saw her fail in bringing off such of the crews as staid by their ships.

It also saved (as appears from other accounts) the crew of the brig Clio, of Sunderland, when she struck upon the rocks, called the Black Middens, on the north side of the entrance of Tynemouth Haven.

October 25th, 1799, the ship Quintillian, from St. Petersburgh, drove on the Herd Sand, from the force of the sea-wind at N. E. knocked her rudder off, and was much damaged; but the crew were brought on shore by the Life-Boat.

Boat. The great utility of this Life-Boat is also confirmed by many other recent circumstances: one among which is that of the ship Sally, of Sunderland, which, in taking the harbour of Tyne-mouth, on December 25th, 1801, at night, struck on the bar: the crew were brought on shore by the Life-Boat, but the ship was driven among the rocks.

On the 22d of January, 1802, in a heavy gale of wind, from the N. N. W. the ship Thomas and Alice, in attempting the harbour of South Shields, was driven on the Herd Sand: the Nor-thumberland Life-Boat went to her assistance; took, as was supposed, all the people out, and pulled away from the ship to make the harbour, when they were waved to return by a man who had been below deck. On taking this man out they encountered a violent gust of wind, under the quarter of the ship; the ship at the same time drove among the breakers; and, entangling the boat

X 3 with

with her, broke most of the oars on that side of the boat next the ship, and filled the boat with water. By the shock, several of the oars were knocked out of the hands of the rowers, and that of the steersman. In this situation, the steersman quickly replaced his oar from one of those left in the boat, and swept the boat before the sea, filled with water inside as high as the midship gunwale: the boat was steered in this situation before the wind and sea, a distance far exceeding a mile, and landed twenty-one men, including the boat's crew, without any accident, but being wet.

.ACCOUNT OF THE SCARBOROUGH LIFE-BOAT.

Sir,

THE Life-Boat at Scarborough, which was built without the least deviation from the model and the plan. which you sent here at my request, has
even

even exceeded the most sanguine expectations; and I have now received experimental conviction of its great utility in cases of shipwreck, and of its perfect safety in the most agitated sea. Local prejudices will ever exist against novel inventions, however excellent may be the principles of their construction; and there were some, at this place, who disputed the performance of the Life-Boat, until a circumstance lately happened, which brought it to the test of experience, and removed every shadow of objection, even from the most prejudiced minds.

On Monday, the 2d of November we were visited with a most tremendous storm from the eastward, and I scarcely ever remember seeing a more mountainous sea. The Aurora, of Newcastle, in approaching the harbour, was driven ashore to the southward; and, as she was in the most imminent danger, the Life-Boat was immediately launched to

X 4
her

stone.
and f
morti
the le

Cer
Impro
Comn
Mr. ,i
and
Putne

land in safety. By means of the Life-Boat, built from your plan, and the exertions of the boatmen, seven men and boys were thus saved to their country and their friends, and preserved from the inevitable destruction which otherwise awaited them. The boat was not in the least affected by the water which broke into her when alongside the vessel; and, indeed, the boatmen thought it rendered her more steady in the sea. I must also add, that it was the general opinion that no other boat of the common construction could have possibly performed this service; and the fishermen, though very adventurous, declared they would not have made the attempt in their own boats.

We have appointed a crew of fishermen to manage the boat, under the direction of the Committee; and the men are so much satisfied with the performance of the boat, and so confident in her safety, that they are emboldened to adven-

adventure upon the most dangerous occasion. I have been thus circumstantial,
in order to show the great utility of the
Life-Boat; and, I should think, it
would be rendering an essential service
to the community, if any recommendation of mine should contribute to bring
this valuable invention into more general
use.

I remain, SIR,

Your most obedient Servant,

THOMAS HINDERWELL.

*Scarborough,*
*17th Nov.* 1801.

To Mr. HENRY GREATHEAD,
South Shields, the Inventor of the Life-Boat.

BY other accounts, furnished to the
Society, it appears that the Scarborough Life-Boat, on the 21st of November, 1801, was the means of saving
a sloop belonging to Sunderland, and
                                    her

her crew, consisting of three men and boys : also the Experiment, of London, her cargo, and crew consisting of eight men and boys, when in a distressed and perilous situation, on the 22d of January last, which facts are attested by eleven owners of ships resident in Scarborough.

In the course of the last twelve years, several ships and vessels, which have not been included in the above accounts, have been driven on shore in bad weather, and got off again afterwards: the crews have been saved by being taken out by the Life-Boats, whereas, if they had remained on board, they must have perished, the sea making a passage over them.

THE Duke of Northumberland presents his compliments to Mr. Taylor, and is extremely happy to hear that the subject of the Life-Boat is before the Society. Mr. Greathead has, un-doubtedly,

doubtedly, great merit ; and the Duke will be much pleased to hear that the Society considers him as deserving their notice. As the Duke cannot help feeling himself much interested on this subject, he shall be obliged to Mr. Taylor for any further communications he may please to make him relative to it.

It is with infinite satisfaction the Duke informs Mr. Taylor, that he has just received a letter from the North, to acquaint him that the Life-Boat had, on Christmas night, saved the crew of a vessel which was lost upon the rocks in óne of the most boisterous nights and violent wind that was ever known.

*Northumberland-House.*
  *Jan.* 18, 1802.

  To Mr. CHARLES TAYLOR.


THESE are to certify, that the Elder Brethren of the Trinity-House, having received repeated testimonies of

                          the

the utility of the Life-Boat, invented by Mr. Henry Greathead, of South Shields, in saving the lives of shipwrecked mariners, are of opinion, that the invention is of such national importance as to merit every possible encouragement.

By order of the Corporation,

(Signed)　JAMES COURT.

*Trinity-House,*
*4th February,* 1802.

S I R,

I AM sorry it was not in my power to pay more early attention to your favour of the 15th ultimo, having ever since been so much indisposed as to be confined entirely to my bed and chamber until within the last few days. I have now the pleasure to see by the papers, that the Society have already adjudged to Mr. Greathead a handsome gratuity

gratuity for his useful and ingenious invention; a reward, of all others, in my opinion, the most deservedly bestowed, as his Life-Boat has certainly preserved many brave seamen, both at Shields and Sunderland who must otherwise inevitably have perished.

It is truly astonishing to see with what zeal and magnanimity our watermen encounter the most tremendous seas, by means of this boat, which is found to answer every purpose for which it was designed, beyond the expectations of the most sanguine; and, were its use universally adopted, the general benefit would undoubtedly soon exceed calculation.

I am, SIR,

Your most obedient Servant,

WILLIAM ORTON.

*Sunderland,*
*April 30, 1802.*

To Mr. CHARLES TAYLOR.

SINCE

SINCE the award of the Society's bounty to Mr. Greathead, the sum of twelve hundred pounds has been voted to him by Parliament for his Life-Boat.

He has also received other rewards on the same account from the Trinity-House, and Members at Lloyd's, which have been noticed in the public newspapers.

*Description of the Engravings of Mr. H. GREATHEAD's Life-Boat.*

## PLATE V.

The fore part of the Engraving pre-sents a perspective view of the Life-Boat rising over a heavy surge, and going out to the assistance of a ship, which appears at the edge of the hori-zon, in distress.

In the Life-Boat are ten rowers pulling along to get to the ship.

At the lower end of the boat, a man is steering her with a long oar towards the ship, whilst another person is ready with an oar, at the higher end of the boat, to steer the boat on her return ; both ends of the boat being formed alike, in order to use either at will, in going to or coming from the ship.

The sheer or curve of the boat rising considerably from the centre to the stems, or ends, is clearly distinguished ; also

Drawn from a Model presented by Mr. Greathead to the Society ---

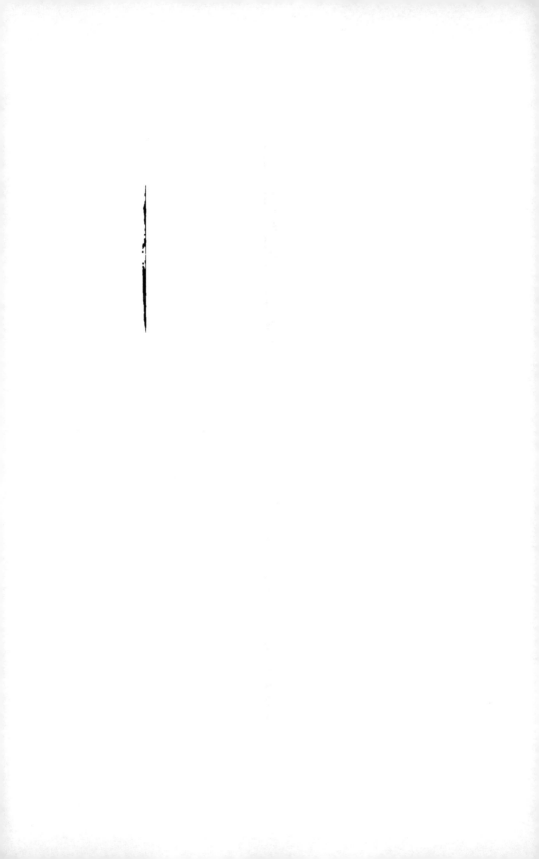

also the coating of cork, secured by slips of copper, along the outside of the boat, near the part where the rowers are seated.

N. B. It was first intended to have pointed out the particular parts of this Plate, by letters engraved upon it; but it being found that such insertions would be a disadvantage to the Engraving; and that, if any difficulties occurred, they would be clearly explained by letters in the following Plate of the sections; they have been here omitted.

*Plate VI. Fig.* 1.  *A longitudinal Section of the Life-Boat.*

| | |
|---|---|
| E E E | The sheer or curve of the boat. |
| I I | The two stems or ends. |
| K | The keel. |
| LL | The aprons, to strengthen the stems. |

MM

MM       The sheets, or places for passengers.

NN       Timber-heads, or boat-fastenings.

OOOOO   The tholes on which the oars are slung by grommets.

T         Flooring under the rowers feet.

*Fig. 2.*    *A cross Section of the Life-Boat.*

F F       The outside coatings of cork.

G G      The inside cork filling.

H H      The outside planks of the boat.

I         One of the stems of the boat.

K        The keel.

NN       The timber-heads.

P        The thwarts, or rowers seats.

R        One of the stanchions under the thwarts, each being thus firmly supported.

S        A section of the gang-board, which crosses the thwarts, and forms the passage from one end of the boat to the other.

                          T The

| | |
|---|---|
| T | The floor-heads, or platform for the rowers feet. |
| V V | The two bilge pieces, nearly level with the keel. |
| W W | The gunwales. |
| X | A ring-bolt for the head-fast, there being another also at the other end. |
| Y | Platform for the steersman. |

*Fig. 3: A Truck or Carriage with four Wheels, to convey the Boat to and from the Sea.*

| | |
|---|---|
| a | An oblong frame of wood, consisting of two long pieces, hollowed a little to admit the body of the boat, and secured by the cross pieces, b b. |
| cccc | Four low wheels, each sunk or hollowed in the middle, to run better upon a rail-way or timber-road. |

dd          . Two indents made in the side-
              · timbers, that the bottom of
                the boat may lie firm therein.
ee            Two small rollers, moveable,
              . in the cross timbers, for the
                keel of the boat to slide
                upon.
ff            Two long rollers one at each
              end of the frame, to assist in
              raising the boat upon or
              sliding it off the truck or·
              carriage.

*Management of the Life-Boat, from the
Boat-House to the Sea, and vice versâ, as
practised at Lowestoffe, in Suffolk.*

THE Life-Boat may be launched
    from any beach, when wanted, with
as much ease as any other boat, by proper assistance. The distance from the
boat-house, at Lowestoffe, to the shore,
is one hundred yards, and the boat's
crew can run her down in ten minutes.
                                When

When the sea does not tumble in upon the beach very much, the boat may be easily launched by laying the ways as far as possible in the water, and hauling the carriage from under her.

When there is a great sea on the beach, the boat must be launched from the carriage before she comes to the surf, on planks laid across, as other boats are launched; the people standing on the ends to prevent the sea moving them; then, with the assistance of the anchor and cable (which should be laid out at sea for the purpose), the boat's crew can draw her over the highest sea.

Upon the boat returning to the shore, two double blocks are provided; and, having a short strop fixed in the hole, in the end of the boat next the sea, the boat is easily drawn upon the carriage. The boat's crew can run her any distance upon a clear shore by the carriage of Mr. Greathead's contrivance.

*Account*

*Account of, and Instructions for, the Management of the Life-Boat.*

THE Boats in general of this description are painted white on the outside, this colour more immediately engaging the eye of the spectator at her rising from the hollow of the sea, than any other. The bottom of the boat is at first varnished (which will take paint afterwards), for the more minute inspection of purchasers. The oars she is equipped with are made of fir, of the best quality, having found by experience that a rove-ash oar that will dress clean and light, is too pliant among the breakers; and when made strong and heavy, from rowing double banked, the purchase being short, sooner exhausts the rower, which makes the fir oar, when made stiff, more preferable.

In the management of the boat, she requires twelve men to work her; that is, is, five men on each side, rowing double banked, with an oar slung over an iron thole, with a grommet (as provided) so as to enable the rower to pull either way; and one man, at each end, to steer her, and to be ready at the opposite end to take the steer oar, when wanted. As, from the construction of the boat, she is always in a position to be rowed either way, without turning the boat, when manned, the person who steers her should be well acquainted with the course of the tides, in order to take every possible advantage: the best method, if the direction will admit of it, is to head the sea. The steersman should keep his eye fixed upon the wave or breaker, and encourage the rowers to give way, as the boat rises to it; being then aided by the force of the oars, she launches over it with vast rapidity, without shipping any water. It is necessary to observe, that there is often a strong reflux of sea, occasioned by the stranded

wrecks,

wrecks, which requires both dispatch and care in the people employed, that the boat be not damaged. When the wreck is reached, if the wind blows to the land, the boat will come in shore without any other effort than steering.

I would strongly recommend practising the boat, by which means, with experience, the danger will appear less, from the confidence people will have in her from repeated trials.

HENRY GREATHEAD.

*South Shields,*
*October* 13, 1802.

SIR,

I SHALL have a complete model of my Life-Boat, on the scale of one inch to a foot, ready to send to the Society in a little time; and it having been much desired that the Life-Boat might be brought into general use, for ships, (in which case, it is a great object to have

her

her to sail), I have, in a model lately made, adopted the sliding keel (an improvement of the Dutch Lee-Board), with the addition of one of them at one end sliding angular, so as to correspond with the keel of the rudder, at any depth. This angular sliding keel is entirely new: I have shewn the improvement to several nautical men, who highly approve of it. I shall finish the model for the Society in the same manner.

The keels and rudder are attached in such a manner, that she can be easily divested of them, when necessary, and will then be the exact form of the original Life-Boat. I should have sent you the model before this time; but the orders for Life-Boats have been so numerous, and so generally pressing, that I have not yet had time to execute it.

The Life-Boats I lately sent to Whitby and Redcar, have recently been the means of saving the lives of many persons, from ships wrecked, who must otherwise

otherwise have perished; for the particulars of which, I refer you to the Newcastle Chronicle of the 11th instant, which I hope will be satisfactory to the Society, to whom I shall be very happy, on all occasions, to transmit my improvements.

I remain, Sir,

Your obliged and obedient Servant,

HENRY GREATHEAD.

*South Shields,*
*December* 17, 1802.

To Mr. CHARLES TAYLOR.

The

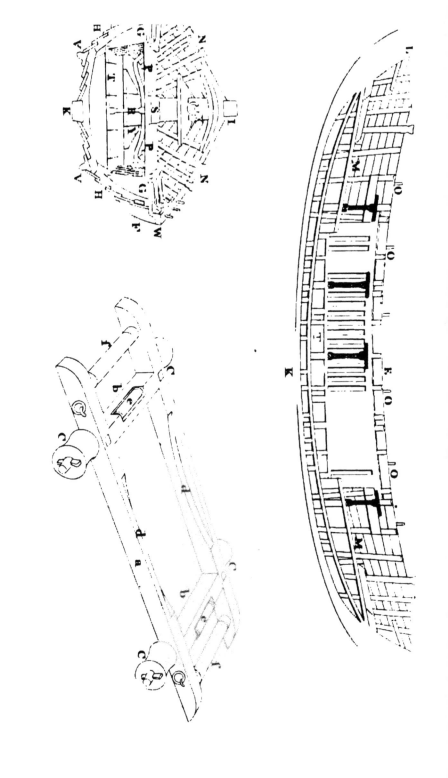

The GOLD MEDAL of the Society was
this Session voted to WILLIAM HALL
TIMBREL, Esq. of Streatly, in Berkshire, for an improved HERNIARY
TRUSS, and new-invented CALICO
CUSHION. The following Account
and Certificates were received from
him. A Model of part of the Human
Body, and the Trusses from which the
annexed Engravings are taken, were
presented by him to the Society, and
are placed in their Repository.

SIR,

I DESIRE you will present to the
Society of Arts, &c. a Model of part
of the Human Body, to which I have
applied the instrument called a Truss,
for the purpose of effectually keeping up
inguinal and scrotal ruptures; also, my
new invention, the Calico Cushion. You
will

will please to observe, that this subject
is not introduced to the Society, as arising from medical or surgical ideas; but
for the purpose, by mechanical means,
of causing relief to many afflicted persons, and assisting the cause of humanity. It is with this view I bring forward
the model and my inventions, and not
for the sake of any premium or bounty
from the Society.

     I am, Sir,

        Your humble Servant,

        WILLIAM HALL TIMBREL.
*May* 12, 1802.

    To Mr. CHARLES TAYLOR.


     S I R,

I BEG leave to explain the nature of
those improvements in the Truss and
Cushion, which I have had the honour of
presenting to the Society of Arts, &c.
Many of my suggestions are new, The
                         whole

whole system of immobility, and the combination of mechanical action, to produce sufficient pressure on the aperture, or ring of the abdomen, are decidedly so, as well as the formation of the Cushion of Calico.

The hoop or spring part of the Truss is formed in an exact circular line with the pad. The pad is broad, and nearly, though not entirely flat; its neck is short, to lie in the hollow of the groin; for, if the neck touched the thigh, the Truss would move and the rupture descend.

Not much edging of leather projects from the hoop, and but little stuffing is put on the inside, as it lessens the elasticity of the spring. A double truss should be united behind, by a strap and buckle, to let out or take in; and both the front and hind straps should be sewed nearly one inch backwarder than usual. These straps should also be lined and edged, to increase their power of action. I have substituted a buckle, and its

double

slip many others are folded, to the thickness of about three quarters of an inch; but the thickness must be regulated by the size of the patient. When the hollow in the groin is completely filled up, and the cushion quite immoveable, it is properly formed.

This Calico Cushion is to be worn under the pad or pads ᵢBB, of the Truss, as at CC and from time to time; an outer slip or two may be changed at pleasure, for the purposes of cleanliness, or restoring the cushion to a proper degree of thickness.

This cushion, when judiciously made, even with a bad Truss, if it is in a line with the aperture, will materially assist in keeping up a reducible rupture.

·The properties of the Calico Cushion are,

First, that it protects the spermatic cord from being injured by the hard pad of the Truss; which injury, in common trusses, often produces hydrocele, inflammation

inflammation of the spermatic vessels, hernia humoralis, &c. &c.

Secondly, by protecting the spermatic vessels from the injuries of pressure, it fulfils a *desideratum* never before obtained. It enables the patient to girt the Truss round the body with such an effective degree of tightness, that the rupture cannot descend.

Thirdly, by uniting the properties of softness and solidity, it yields to the form of the abdomen, and thus completely fills up the aperture, or ring, in the external oblique abdominal muscle, through which the rupture descends.

Fourthly, it affords an additional column of pressure; and the Truss being tightly fastened, keeps the omentum and intestines, all round and above the aperture, in a state of quietude, preventing any internal or partial descent of the bowels, &c.

It is necessary to repeat, that this Cushion, to obtain all its advantages,

Z                          must

must be formed of separate slips, folded over each other, and not of one piece of calico.

The method which I have used of placing the Truss, is in an exact circular line round the body, directly above the fissure of the posteriors; and the edge of the hoop part lodging on, over and above the great trochanter, and below the margin of the hip-bone, will keep the pad or pads of the Truss on the abdominal ring, producing ease, effect, and immobility.

The Truss, worn in the manner I describe, is not to be seen through the clothes, and it retains its elasticity a greater length of time than the old spiral trusses.

When the double Truss is put on, it should be pulled so very tight as to make the flesh between the two pads rise to the thickness of the fore finger; there will be no pain, for the pressure is

only

only where it ought to be, immediately under the pad or pads of the Truss.

The thigh-strap also must be sufficiently short, and pulled close to the flesh, to have its action on B.

A single Truss will have the same action for a single rupture, by using the same methods.

By minutely following the above instructions, the reducibly ruptured patient may be freed from pain or danger.

I have the honor to be, Sir,

Your most humble Servant,

WM. HALL TIMBREL.

*December 7, 1802.*

Certificates have been received from Mr. William Blair, Great Russel-street, Bloomsbury-square, and Mr. Thomas

Z 2 Payne,

Payne, Brook-street, Members of the
Royal College of Surgeons, in London,
confirming, by cases in their practice,
the utility of the improved Trusses and
Cushion, recommended by Mr. Timbrel.

Improved Trusses by Mr. Timbrel.

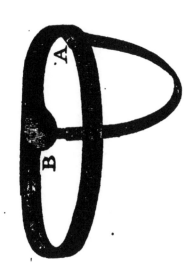

Single
Trusses.

Double
Trusses.

# PAPERS

## IN

# MANUFACTURES.

———————————

# MANUFACTURES.

A Bounty of Twenty-five Guineas was this Session voted to Mr. Thomas Clulow, No. 31, Old Cock-Lane, Shoreditch, for improving Looms in general, and for his invention of a Method of weaving Purses, Pockets, and Sacks.

*A Model of this improved Loom, and some Purses and Pockets wove upon this Plan, are reserved in the Society's Repository, for the inspection of the Public. An Engraving and Description of the Loom are annexed.*

SIR,

I HAVE made a small loom, agreeably to the orders of the Society, and hope it will answer their expectations. I have also brought models of sacks,

purses,

purses, pockets, and wallets, wove in the loom, to show what it is capable of doing.

The articles wove in this way will be less liable to lose their contents than those whose seams are sowed with the needle, and will wear longer, and be less liable to want repairs.

I have also made improvements in the manner of setting up looms in general, which I have explained in my present model; so that this loom not only shows a new invention in weaving, but also a method of setting up looms of all kinds, so as to do their work better than in the common way. Any reward which the Society may think proper to afford me, will be thankfully accepted, and gratefully acknowledged, by,

SIR,

Your obedient Servant,

THOMAS CLULOW.

*Shoreditch,*
*March 16, 1802.*

Mr. CHARLES TAYLOR.

AN

A N account of Mr. Clulow's plan for improving looms in general, particularly the Broad Silk Weavers Loom. (*See Plate* VII.)

An oblong frame A is laid down horizontally, and secured at the four corners with triangular braces, BBBB, to keep the frame properly square.

Four posts, CCCC, are fixed upright in mortice holes on the above frame. The front posts are supported both back and front with diagonal timbers, DDDD, to keep the breast roll E from giving way in the least by the heavy stroke of the batten FF on the quarter or work: the two hinder posts, GG, are held firm by two diagonal supports, HH, within the loom, to bear against the counter weights I I, and the great weight V, hanging on the work K, and the force of the batten F.

In a loom constructed on this plan, both strong and slight works may be made

made firm and good, without the loom having any shorings or supports; the advantages arising from which are the following, viz.

Poor indigent weavers being obliged to live in low-rented houses, the floors and party walls of the rooms where they weave are bad and weak, so that the common looms cannot be placed firm, and a man is perplexed to set up his loom in requisite order. If the loom is not set up firm, and secured from giving way in the working of it, no work can be made strong and good. One great disadvantage is done away by the bottom frame I use for fixing my loom upon, which can be placed by any common workman; whereas to set a loom up in the old method, requires great exactness and judgment, to prevent the work from being damaged.

If, in the common way, a loom is not properly put in the square, and firmly shored, which it is difficult to do, the

silk

silk chafes and cuts, the mind of the workman is harassed for want of knowing the real cause of it, or having sufficient knowledge to correct it; therefore the work is spoiled for want of a trifling alteration in the loom, and the blame frequently laid upon the silk when the error lies wholly in the loom.

If a common loom is put in its proper square, and has not a firm shoring or support, the work or cloth has not the firmness which it ought to have, and which it will have in my method. It frequently happens that the shorings or supports are too long and slender, or the places weak which they are fixed against, which causes a trembling motion in the loom; and if the loom shakes only the 100th part of an inch (which is not more on a moderate calculation than the breadth of each thread shot into the work), it will take out that stiffness there ought to be in the work; for if the loom does not stand firm against the

the stroke of the batten, the work will lie hollow, be flimsey, and, though it takes as much silk as good work, it does not look well, nor will sell for so much money: the poor weaver is therefore turned out of employment, not knowing where the error lies; and the employer suffers in his property.

If the shores to the common looms, after being placed, either fall by accident or through the continual shaking of the loom whilst working, which circumstances will sometimes happen in the middle of a piece of work being done, it is with great difficulty that the loom can then be put in square, or supported as it ought to be; therefore it occasions the work to be spoiled.

Besides these, other difficulties frequently occur to a weaver where the loom is not properly fixed, squared, and shored, which those persons conversant in weaving well know. I shall mention one material instance, where, if the loom is originally

ginally well set up in the common way, it may be liable to great disadvantage, viz. its situation in regard to light, which is a main point, as in that case it cannot be moved without great risk, if any work is in it; whereas, if the loom is made according *to my model*, the weaver may slide it to any exactness that is requisite, as a few inches moving will permit the light to fall on the work properly without injury to the work, as my loom is firm and squared, without requiring the aid of any shores.

What I have said relative to this matter, will, I hope, give a satisfactory elucidation of my plan.

THOMAS CLULOW.

WF

WE have examined this Model, and conceive it is a useful improvement.

Lea and Wilson, No. 26, Old Jewry.

Rennington, Wilson, and Co. Milk-street.

Gearing and Taylor, King-street, Cheapside.

Anthony Longuet, No. 23, Wood-street, Spital-fields.

Cotes, Titford, and Brookes, Union-street, Bishopsgate-street.

Hudswell, Thorp and Gardner, No. 30, Spital-square.

John Dubois and Sons, No. 20, Church-street, Spital-fields.

James Dickson and John Honyman, No. 7, Church-street, Spital-fields.

*March* 9, 1802.

*Description*

*Description of the Method of weaving Sacks, &c. in the Loom above mentioned. (See Plate VII.)*

L    The seat of the loom.

M    The treadles, six in number, to raise the harness.

N    The counter-meshes to raise the tumblers O, moveable on a pin a little beyond their centre, and which act on the harness P, by raising such parts thereof as they are attached to at their extremities.

Q    The work in the loom.

R    The reed which strikes the shoot or weft close up.

S    The back beam on which the warp or thread is wound.

T T    The rods to preserve the crossing of the threads.

V    The main weight suspended by a lever U, from a bar W near

its centre; the other end of
the lever is fastened by a cord
to the bottom frame of the
loom at X.

Y     The rack on the working beam.

Z     The catch to hold the teeth of
the rack.

To weave a sack, press down the second treadle on the right-hand side, and
throw one shoot with the shuttle; then
press down the second treadle on the
left-hand side, and throw another shoot;
then proceed in the same manner with
the third on the right, and the third on
the left, till a sufficient quantity is made;
then work the two outside treadles and
two shoots.

In weaving sacks, it is necessary between the finishing of one sack and the
commencement of another, to pass a
thin slip of wood through the threads,
in order to form a space between the
two sacks.

*improved Loom.*

# PAPERS

## IN

# COLONIES AND TRADE.

A a 2

## COLONIES AND TRADE.

The GOLD MEDAL, being the Premium offered for Plantations of BREAD-FRUIT TREES, was this Session adjudged to the Honourable JOSEPH ROBLEY, Esq. President and Commander in Chief, in and over the Island of Tobago, and its Dependencies, &c. &c. from whom the following Accounts and Certificates were received.

SIR,

IN consequence of the premium offered for the cultivation of Plantations of the Bread-Fruit Trees, in the British Colonies in the West-Indies, by the Society instituted at London, for the encouragement of Arts, Manufactures and Commerce, I have now the honour to transmit to you some papers on the

A a 3                           subject

subject of such a plantation on one of
my estates in this island, which I request
you to lay before the Society.

As the point of land on which the
trees are planted is somewhat singular,
both in soil and situation, I have judged
it necessary to subjoin a plan of the
land, the more clearly to convey to the
Society an idea of what I have described
to them in the paper which accompanies this letter, and to show the motives
which induced me to select this point
of land, rather than any other, for this
purpose; and also, from a conviction,
that if the utility of such land for Bread-
Fruit Trees was made public, many
pieces of similar land, in our West-India
Colonies, might be very profitably employed for this purpose, which at present
scarcely produce any provisions, or any
other product for the benefit of the
owners. I therefore hope the Society
will not think that my narration is tedious.

An

An awkward circumstance occurs on the present occasion, with respect to the certificate to be transmitted to the Society, from my being in command of the island; but as I judged it necessary to comply literally with the Society's advertisement, I have herewith transmitted a certificate, signed by me, in my official capacity: I have also annexed a certificate of my principal manager; and I will transmit a certificate, signed by some of the Members of Council, and the Speaker of the House of Assembly, whenever I can procure their attendance to inspect those plants.

A difficulty also occurs in sending samples of the fruit, in conformity to the advertisement of the Society, because the fruit will not keep more than two weeks after it is taken from the tree, and therefore cannot be sent to England in its natural state. I will however endeavour, by drying, pickling, or preserving in spirit, to send some fruit

for

for the inspection of the Society; but if
I succeed in this preservation, the sending them home must of necessity be
deferred, till the sailing of the ships in
April next, unless an opportunity offers
sooner.

As the Society are already in possession of a full and faithful description of
the amazing quantity of food which
the Bread-Fruit Trees produce, and of
the excellent quality of that food by
Dr. Anderson's letter to the Society,
dated St. Vincent, 24th December, 1797,
and published in the 16th Vol. of their
Transactions, perhaps it is not necessary for me to say any thing on a subject so well described to them already.
I will, however, so far corroborate what
Dr. Anderson says, that if I may judge
from the amazing quantity of fruit produced by the three trees which I have
here, and which have now been in bearing these six years, I am of opinion,
that when the whole of the point of land
is

is planted, it will contain about 1300 trees; and I think it will be equal to the support, in the Bread-Fruit kind of provision, of nearly a thousand negroes, which I have on this and two neighbouring estates,

I am, SIR,

Your most obedient humble Servant,

JOSEPH ROBLEY.

*Tobago Golden-Grove,*
  *25th Aug.* 1801.

Mr. CHARLES TAYLOR.

SIR,

HAVING written to you before on the subject of a plantation of Bread-Fruit Trees on one of my estates, called Golden Grove, in the parish of St. Patrick, in the island of Tobago, I shall now proceed to describe the point of land on which I have placed those trees,

i

in the manner described in the annexed plan.

This point of land is bounded on one side by a beautiful salt-water lagoon, and at the east end it is bounded by a steep bank of lime-stone rock, in some places mixed with a loose dry soil. The bank is about fourteen feet high, stretches from the lagoon to the sea, and completely fences in and secures the point of land to the eastward, from whence our trade winds generally blow. This point of land communicates with the estate, by means of a gate placed between the lagoon and the steep bank; so that it is wholly and completely fenced in by the lagoon, the sea, and this steep bank. It is likewise nearly perfectly level, and consists of a loose sandy soil; and when the tide is in, water is to be found in every part of it, at the depth of about two feet and a half from the surface; this water, though brackish, is drinkable. Having read all the late

voyages

voyages to the South-Sea Islands, I always observed in them, that the Bread-Fruit Trees were described as principally growing in low situations, near the sea, from which I first formed my opinion, that this point of land was well adapted for their culture; and in consequence of this idea, I had a very ardent desire to obtain some plants, in order to try the experiment.

In 1792, a vessel arrived at Martinique, from the Isle of France, with several plants, which were said to be of the true Otaheite Bread-Fruit; in consequence of which I sent to Martinique, and eagerly purchased some of them; but, to my very great disappointment, I found, when they came to bear, that all of them were of that sort only, which produces nuts: but my chagrin on this occasion was soon relieved, by the arrival of Capt. Bligh, at St. Vincent, in his Majesty's ship the Providence, in 1793, with many plants of the true Otaheite Bread-

Bread-Fruit, some of which were landed at St. Vincent, and placed under the care of Dr. Anderson, who has the charge of the Botanic Garden there, and who, with great kindness, sent me three of those plants in June 1793. These three plants I planted in a garden near my mansion-house, in a very deep, rich, black soil, where I paid every possible attention to them, in the hope of procuring an abundance of suckers for my favourite point of land: they flourished exceedingly, and produced fruit in 1795; and these three trees still continue to flourish and bear fruit in great abundance. Till last year, however, I could not obtain even one sucker from them; in consequence of which, I wrote to Dr. Anderson on the subject, who advised me to remove the earth from above the uppermost roots, and to wound and even cut some of them in half. I followed his advice, and laid bare many of the roots,

and

and bisected them in October 1800,
when they almost immediately began to
shoot suckers in abundance; insomuch,
that in December I had about 120 fine
plants, which I planted in small wicker
baskets, of about a gallon in size, first filling them with good rich loose soil: those
baskets I placed in the shade, and near
the water, with which I supplied them
whenever the weather required it; and
here I kept them during the dry season.
I preferred placing the plants in baskets,
to placing them in pots, because they
are lighter, and are more easily removed
from one place to another; and also because, when they are to be planted out
in the land in which they are to remain,
by planting the baskets with the plant
in it, the plant will not be at all checked
in its growth, as the baskets will soon
rot in the ground, so that the roots of
the plant easily extend themselves in the
adjacent soil, without impediment. From
this great and unexpected success in procuring

curing plants, I began very seriously to think of preparing the land at the Point for their reception; and as my visits to the Point were consequently very frequent, I perceived, that at very high tides the salt water flowed into some part of the land, on the lagoon side of it.  In order, therefore, to guard against any ill consequence from this circumstance, I immediately formed a bank all round the lagoon side, for about three quarters of a mile in length, ten feet in breadth, and three feet in height, towards the land side, and shelving gradually to the water.  This bank I formed of mud mixed with sand, and it is now perfectly solid, and water tight; and the influx of the sea has formed a very regular and easy sandy beach, all the way on the outside of the bank.

My next step was to plough one half of this point, in order to clear it of every noxious weed; for which purpose I ploughed it twice, and harrowed it

twice

twice over; I then divided it into beds of 27 feet in breadth across the point, from the sea to the lagoon, and planted

at the exact distance of 27 feet every way. I have already said, that brackish water was to be found all over this point at high water, at about $2\frac{1}{2}$ feet from the surface; and for some time, this circumstance made me uneasy, lest the brackish water should injure the trees, when their roots came to touch it; but accidentally reading a translation of Monsieur Labillardiere's voyage, in search of La Perouse, published by Stockdale in 1800, I met with the following remark, vol. 2, p. 105. " We walked some " time (says he) along the borders of " the shore, on which we saw a great " number of Bread-Fruit Trees in full " vigour, although their roots were " bathed with brackish water." Some time previous to reading this remark, I had tried the experiment, by taking a

part

part of this point into a garden and pinery, in which I also planted about ten of my most forward Bread-Fruit Plants, and where they flourish and grow faster than in any other place I have yet seen. The garden and pinery also flourish admirably, which I attribute to the loose sandy texture of the soil, which absorbs any water immediately, and of course prevents any damage from excessive rains. In the dryest season, too, the garden is equally flourishing, as in rainy weather, by the rays of the sun drawing the water through this loose soil, for the nourishment of vegetables; so that what I had dreaded as an evil, proves to be of the greatest advantage, and produces a spot of land, of about 45 acres, which is regularly watered twice in twenty-four hours, in all seasons, and without any expense. When I considered the lively interest which the Society have taken, in being the first to recommend the procuring the plants of

Bread

Bread Fruit, from the South-Sea Islands to those of the West Indies, for the benefit of their inhabitants; I determined to send those papers immediately to the Society, though my Bread-Fruit Plantation is but in its infancy, and only yet contains 153 plants; but which, when completed, will contain 1300, or thereabout. I cannot reckon on more than 20 plants per month from the roots of my three old trees; but when those I have now planted begin to sucker, any number may be obtained, so as to complete the point of land in a short time.

I hope the detailed account I have now given of the Bread-Fruit Plants, and of the situation in which I have placed them, will prove satisfactory: and as I observe that there has been only one claim for a plantation of Bread-Fruit Trees, and that from Jamaica, in 1798, if it shall appear to the Society that, from the numbers I have now planted, and which I am increasing every

B b                    month,

month, I am entitled to any premium, I shall esteem it an honour to receive it.

I am, Sir,

Your most obedient Servant,

JOSEPH ROBLEY.

*Tobago, Golden-Grove,*
  *25th Aug.* 1801.

To Mr. CHARLES TAYLOR.


Certificates from the Governor of the Island, from R. Robertson and Charles Wightman, Esqrs. Members of the Council, from Robert Paterson, Esq. Speaker of the Assembly, and from Mr. George Lyall, principal Manager of the Honourable President Robley's estates, accompanied these Papers, confirming the above statement, that 153 plants are now growing in a flourishing state, and are completely fenced in and protected.

The

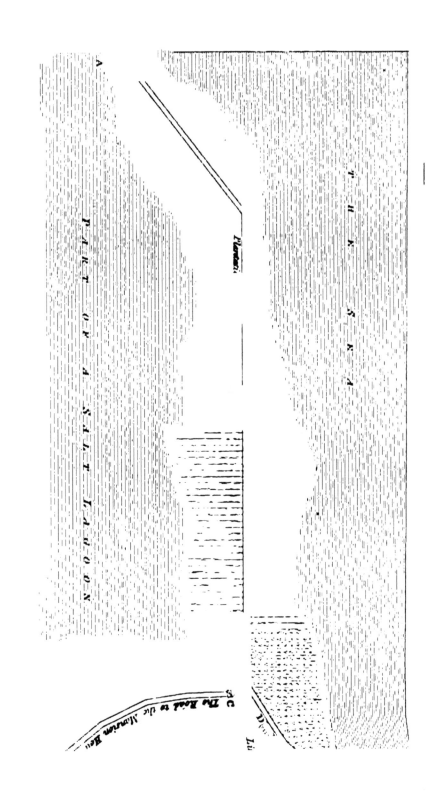

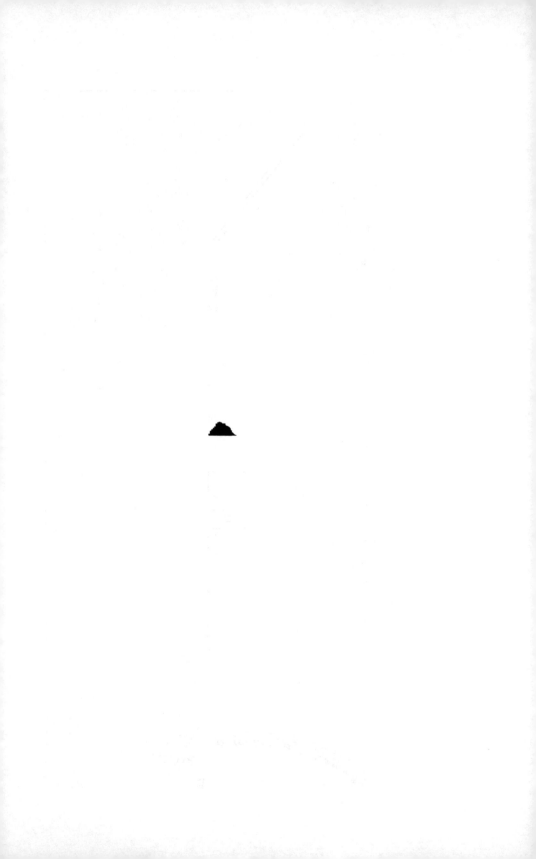

The GOLD MEDAL of the Society was this Session voted to Dr. ANDERSON, of St. Vincent, for the following Communications on CLOVES and CINNAMON produced in that Island. Specimens of the Articles sent are preserved in the Society's Repository, for the inspection of the Public; and a coloured Engraving of the Clove Plant is here annexed to its Description.

———

*Observations on the Clove Plant at St. Vincent, and the Cloves sent from thence to the Society.*

SIR,

IF you conceive the specimens of Cloves accompanying this letter (being the first produced in the garden), with some observations on the plant,

B b 2

merit

merit the attention of the Society, you will do me the honour to present them.

I am, Sir,

Your most obedient Servant,

ALEX. ANDERSON.

*Botanical Garden, St. Vincent,*
*April 23, 1800.*

To the Secretary of the
Society of Arts, &c.

THE Clove is an elegant little tree: that in the garden now bearing, is about eight feet in height, and the stem, near the ground, is about two inches in diameter. That so small a tree should bear fruit, I ascribe to its being from a layer. The nature of the plant is not yet well known in the West Indies; all the information I have heretofore received as to the culture of it, has
been

been for the most part from ignorance, or from ill intentions; and consequently has led me into errors on that subject, by which I have often lost the original plant: but I have always been so fortunate as to preserve an offspring by layers.

From the difficulty of preserving the plants, it naturally occurred to me, that I had adopted a soil not congenial to them, as I find that all other East-India plants thrive luxuriantly in the garden; and am by no means ignorant, that all plants, although originally from a barren soil, always prosper best in a rich one, when transplanted from their natural situation. I therefore tried them in the best soil I could select, adding thereto plenty of manure; at the same time, I also planted others of the same age and size in various other soils, without manure. The consequence has been, that those in the manured soil are thriving luxuriantly, of which that now bearin is one; while the others have failed, or are so sickly, that they never will arrive at maturity.

Since this, I have fortunately met with the *Herbarium Amboinense* of Rumphius, and find that he corroborates my idea.

It is a plant that loves the shelter of other trees to windward of it, but not so as to overshade it, as Rumphius observes. When fully exposed to the wind, it does not answer so well; but rich land, or manure in bad land, is what will answer best with it.

It is propagated by laying down the young branches in boxes, or in the ground, if they can be brought in contact with it. If the earth is kept moist, they will root in six months.

I suspect that the best mode in rearing it from seeds, is to put them in the earth where the plants are to remain; and if planted in the manner of a thicket, or from eight to ten feet apart, they

they will prosper better than when farther separated or scattered. This I find
to be the case with most plants of the
same species.

As all botanical descriptions of the
Clove appear to me to be imperfect,
at least agree not with the plant that has
flowered in the garden, I have ventured
to inclose an account of the fructifica-
tion as the parts appeared to me.
There are probably more than one species, as Rumphius's figures of it differ.

The specimens of the spice which I
have sent are dried by various modes,
some according to the directions of Rumphius; by some of the processes, they
are larger than by others. Whether that
may be the only advantage gained, or
which is the best mode of curing it, rests
with the Society to determine. It is to
be observed, that every part of the
plant, in an eminent degree, possesses
the same property as to taste. All these
specimens are gathered in the same

stag

stage, viz. when the flower-bud appears entirely red, which is when the corolla begins to rise previously to its falling off. This happens at sun-set. The morning of the same day is the proper time to collect them for drying. There is something very singular as to the formation of the flowers. In September, 1799, clusters of them were so far formed, that I looked for their expansion every day; none of them however opened till the March following, a period of six months. I began to imagine that, from the smallness of the plant, it had not sufficient vigour to bring them to maturity. However, I was agreeably disappointed; scarcely more than two flowers, and frequently only one, expands in the same day. To have the spice therefore in perfection, it is requisite to go over them every morning, collecting those that have the appearance of opening in the evening.

The leaves are a good substitute for the fruit, for culinary purposes.

*CARYO-*

## CARYOPHYLLUS AROMATICUS, CLOVE.

*Perianthium quadripartitum, laciniæ ovatæ, concavæ, persistentes.*

*Petala quatuor ovata, sessilia, conniventia, clausa, caduca.*

*Nectarium tetragonum integerrimum, concavum, apicem germinis ringens.*

*Filamenta numerosa subulata, in base calycis inserta, antheræ ovatæ, erectæ, bilocularios*

*Germen inferum, clavatum—Stylus subulatus, filamentis brevior. Stigma obtusum, drupa ovato-turbinata, calyce incrassato coronata.*

*Nux oblonga, glabra, unilocularis.*

REFERENCES TO THE ANNEXED COLOURED ENGRAVING.

No. 1. The natural size of the flower, and mode of its inflorescence.

2 T

2. The rudiment of the fruit in a longitudinal section, to show the insertion of the stamina.

3. The petals cohering; the stamina gradually raising them.

4. The petals ready to fall off.

5. The petals as they fall off adhering in a calyptra.

6. The natural size of one of the petals.

7. The fruit nearly ripe.

8. Longitudinal section through the middle.

*₊* From examination of the specimens of the Cloves sent, before a Committee appointed by the Society, it appeared that those dried in the smoke were damaged by it; that those dried in the sun were but of an indifferent quality; but that the Cloves dried in the shade were very little inferior to those produced in the East Indies, and well worth encouragement. •

*Observations*

## Observations on the Cinnamon from St. Vincent.

SIR,

AS the small quantity of Cinnamon I had the honour of sending to the Society last year, was insufficient to form a just idea as to its quality, I now send a large parcel in a box, dried at different times, and taken from branches of young trees of different ages; from which, it is hoped, the Society will be able to judge of the quality, and to decide which is the most proper period for taking it off, and the best mode of drying it. I am, with great respect,

SIR,

Your obedient humble Servant,

ALEXANDER ANDERSON.

*Botanical Garden, St. Vincent,*
*July 20, 1800.*

To the Secretary of the
Society of Arts, &c.

*₊* The quantity of Cinnamon sent from Dr. Anderson appears to have been originally more than twenty pounds in weight; but the package had been opened at the Custom-House, and the samples intermixed, so as not to permit the Society to recognize the particular distinctions noticed by Dr. Anderson: there was, however, an evident difference in some of the samples, in respect to appearance, taste, and smell; they were found generally to be inferior to East-India Cinnamon, but much superior to Cassia,

A further account of the varieties of the Cinnamon-plant, and some observations on the Clove-plant, relative to their state in the garden of St. Vincent, in the year 1798, from a communication by Dr. Anderson to the Society, may be found in the XVIth Volume of the Society's Transactions, p. 333.

# The Olive Tank

# REWARDS

## BESTOWED BY THE

# SOCIETY,

From October, 1801,

To June, 1802.

———————

*Society of Arts, Manufactures, and Commerce.*

ON Wednesday, the 2d of June, the Society held the last Meeting of that Session, and adjourned to the fourth Wednesday in October next.

On Tuesday, the 25th of May last, agreeably to the Resolutions of the Society, the Premiums and Bounties which had been then adjudged during the Session, were delivered to the Claimants from the Chair, by his Grace the Duke of Norfolk, the President, in the presence of a very numerous and respectable Assembly. The business was begun by an appropriate Speech from the Secretary, noticing the objects of the Society, from its institution in the year 1753, to the present time, and particularising the Rewards which had been then adjudged this Session.

The Rewards conferred are arranged under the following Classes:

## IN AGRICULTURE.

To JAMES HUNTER, Esq. of Gubbins, in Hertfordshire, for having planted 40,000 Oaks, the GOLD MEDAL, Class 11, Vol. XVIII. See page 77.

To the Rev. RICHARD YATES, of Chelsea, for his Essay on raising and promoting the Growth of OAKS, the SILVER MEDAL. See page 80.

To JOHN CHRISTIAN CURWEN, Esq. of Workington Hall, in Cumberland, for having planted 84,900 Larch Trees, the GOLD MEDAL, Class 35. Vol. XVIII. See page 96.

To HENRY VERNON, Esq. of Hilton Park, near Wolverhampton, for planting 10,000 Silver Firs, the GOLD MEDAL. Class 45. Vol. XVIII. See page 101.

To Mr. FREDERICK CLIFFORD CHERRY, of New Wood Farm, near Stoke D'Aubernon, in Surry, for plant-

ing

REWARDS. 365

ing 60 Acres with Osiers, the sum of
THIRTY GUINEAS. Class 6. See page
104.

To Mr. SETH BULL, of Ely, in Cambridgeshire, for planting eight Acres
with Osiers, the Sum of TEN GUINEAS.
Class 7. See page 111.

To CHARLES GIBSON, Esq. of Quermore Park, near Lancaster, for planting
6,000 Elms, the SILVER MEDAL. Class
27. Vol. XVIII. See page 115.

To ROBERT BROWN, Esq. of Markle,
near Hadington, in Scotland, for his culture of Beans and Wheat in one year on
the same Land, the SILVER MEDAL.
See page 123.

To WILLIAM FAIRMAN, Esq. of
Miller's House, near Sittingbourn, in
Kent, for his Experiments on Extreme
Branch Grafting of Fruit-trees, the
SILVER MEDAL. See page 168.

To THOMAS JOHNES, Esq. of Hafod,
in Cardiganshire, for having planted
400,000 Forest-trees, the GOLD MEDAL.
Class 63. Vol. XVIII. See page 182.

C c

To James Beech, Esq. of Shaw, near Cheadle, in Staffordshire, for his plantation of Timber-trees, the Silver Medal. See page 191.

## IN CHEMISTRY.

To Mr. Thomas Willis, of Lime-street, London, for his preparation of the Bulbs of the Hyacinthus non scriptus, or common Field Blue-Bells, as a substitute for Gum Arabic, the Silver Medal. See page 201.

## IN POLITE ARTS.

To George William Gent, Esq. of Upper Guildford-street, for a Drawing of Lewes Castle in Sussex, the Gold Medal. Class 89.

To Miss Elizabeth Mac Dowall, of Brook-street, Holborn, for a Chalk Drawing of the Virgin and Child, the Gold Medal. Class 91.

To Miss Winifred Barrett, of Stockwell, in Surry, for a Drawing of a

Land-

Landscape, the SILVER MEDAL. Class 91\*.

To Miss JACKSON, of Hanover-street, for a Drawing in Black Chalk, after an Engraving by BARTOLOZZI, the SILVER MEDAL.

To Miss BLACKBURNE, of Park-street, Westminster, for a Drawing of Demosthenes, from a Bust, the SILVER MEDAL.

To Miss MARY ANNE GILBERT, of Devonshire-street, Portland-place, for a Miniature Drawing of an Old Woman, after Nature, the SILVER MEDAL.

To Miss EMMA FARHILL, of Mortimer-street, Cavendish-square, for a Drawing of Peasants in a Storm, the SILVER MEDAL.

To WILLIAM STONE LEWIS, Esq. of High Holborn, for a Drawing of Outlines of the Laocoon, from a Cast, the larger SILVER PALLET. Class 92.

To GEORGE JONES, Esq. of Great Portland-street, Mary-le-bone, for a

C c 2      Drawing

Drawing of Outlines of Hercules and Antæus, from a Cast, the lesser SILVER PALLET. Class 93.

To RICHARD SPEARE, Esq. of Dean-street, Soho, for a Drawing, a View at Eltham in Kent, the greater SILVER PALLET. Class 94.

To Mr. RICHARD COOK, of Upper Charlotte-street, Fitzroy-square, for a Drawing of Mutius Scævola before Porsenna, the GOLD PALLET. Class 96.

To Mr. C. NESBIT, of Fetter-lane, for Engravings on Wood, the SILVER MEDAL. Class 103.

To Mr. RICHARD AUSTIN, of Paul's-alley, Barbican, for Engravings on Wood, the SILVER MEDAL. Class 103.

To Mrs. ELIZABETH COPPINS, of St. Stephen's, Norwich, for a Drawing in Crayons of Belisarius, copied from a Painting of Salvator Rosa, the greater SILVER PALLET.

To Miss FRANCES TALBOT, of Wymondham, Norfolk, for a Painting of a

Herb

Herb Girl, from Nature, the SILVER MEDAL.

To Miss BEAUCHAMP, of Langley Park, near Beccles, in Suffolk, for a Painting of a Landscape, copied from Both, the SILVER MEDAL.

To Dr. EVANS, for his Map of North Wales, FORTY-FIVE GUINEAS.

## IN MANUFACTURES.

To Mr. THOMAS CLULOW, of Shore-ditch, for his invention of weaving Purses, Pockets, and Sacks, in a Loom, and improving the construction of Looms in general, TWENTY-FIVE GUINEAS.

## IN MECHANICKS.

To Mr. HENRY GREATHEAD, of South Shields, in the Bishoprick of Durham, for his construction of a Cork Boat, by which the lives of many persons shipwrecked have been preserved,

the

the GOLD MEDAL and FIFTY GUI-
NEAS.

To Mr. RICHARD KNIGHT, of
Foster-Lane,. Cheapside, for his method
of clearing Land from Stumps of Trees,
and rendering them in a proper state for
Fuel, the SILVER MEDAL. See page
.247.

To Mr. JAMES BROWNHILL, of Alloa
Mills, near Stirling, in Scotland, for his
discovery of a Quarry of Stone, proper
for making Mill Stones, ONE HUNDRED
POUNDS. See page 271.

To Mr. JAMES WOART, of Fulham,
for securing Beams of Timber decayed
by the dry rot, or injured by accidents
in buildings, the sum of TEN GUINEAS,
See page 258.

To Mr. JOHN WEBB, of Dorrington
Street, London, for his improvement of
a Gun Lock, TWENTY GUINEAS. See
page 243.

IN

## IN COLONIES AND TRADE,

To Dr. ALEXANDER ANDERSON, of St. Vincent, for the culture of Cloves and Cinnamon, the GOLD MEDAL.

To the Honourable JOSEPH ROBLEY, of Tobago, for a plantation of Bread Fruit Trees, the GOLD MEDAL.

# P R E S E N T S

### RECEIVED BY THE

# S O C I E T Y,

### SINCE THE PUBLICATION OF THE NINETEENTH
### VOLUME OF THESE TRANSACTIONS.

## With the Names of the Donors.

-------------

### THE ROYAL SOCIETY.

THE sequel to the 90th Volume of the Philosophical Transactions. Quarto.

### THE SOCIETY OF ANTIQUARIANS.

An Account of the Durham Cathedral.

THE

THE ROYAL BRITISH INSTITUTION.

The Journals of the Royal Institution, from the 1st to the 12th inclusive. Octavo.

Lectures on Chemistry, by Mr. Davey.

Lectures in Natural and Experimental Philosophy, by Mr. Young.

THE DUBLIN SOCIETY.

The 1st, 2d and 3d Volumes of the Transactions of the Dublin Society. Octavo.

A Statistical Survey of the County of Wicklow.

A Statistical Survey of the County of Leitrim.

15 Copies of Essays on the Culture of Potatoes, from their Shoots, by Dr. Maunsell.

A Pamphlet on the Culture of Barilla.

THE LINNÆAN SOCIETY.

The Sixth Volume of their Transactions. Quarto.

THE

## THE BOARD OF AGRICULTURE.

Three Volumes, including Vol. 1 and 2, and Vol. 3, Part 1, of Communications to that Board. Quarto.

## AMERICAN PHILOSOPHICAL SOCIETY at PHILADELPHIA.

Vol. 2, 3, and 4, of their Transactions. Quarto.

## THE MANCHESTER LITERARY and PHILOSOPHICAL SOCIETY.

Six Volumes of their Memoirs, containing from Vol. 1 to Vol. 5, Part 2, inclusive. Octavo.

## THE MANCHESTER AGRICULTURAL SOCIETY.

Their Rules and Conditions for 1802.

## SOCIETY FOR BETTERING THE CONDITION OF THE POOR.

The 15th and 16th Reports of the Society, presented by Dr. Garthshore from the Committee. Octavo.

The

THE COMMITTEE OF WAREHOUSES OF THE HONOURABLE EAST-INDIA COMPANY, BY R. WISSETT, ESQ.

N⁰ˢ 2, 3, and 4, of the Plants of the Coast of Coromandel. Folio.

N° 2 of Descriptions of India Serpents. Folio.

Dr. JAMES ANDERSON.

The 6th Volume of Recreations in Agriculture. Octavo.

N. ATCHESON, Esq.

A Letter on the State of the carrying part of the Coal Trade.

Dr. DANCER, of Jamaica.

The Medical Assistant, or Jamaica Practice of Physic.

WILLIAM FORSYTH, Esq.

A Treatise on Fruit-Trees. Quarto.

JOHN

John Hinckley, Esq.

Link's Statistical Travels in Portugal.

Dr. Lettsom.

Hints to promote Beneficence, Temperance, and Medical Science. 3 Volumes, octavo.

Observations on the Cow Pock.

Sir Alexander Mackenzie.

Voyages from Montreal, on the River St. Lawrence, through the Continent of North America, to the Frozen and Pacific Oceans. Quarto.

Dr. Powell.

Observations on the Bile and its Diseases. Octavo.

Citoyen Pugh.

Observations sur le Pesanteur de l'Atmosphère.

### T. N. Parker, Esq.

A Practical Enquiry, concerning hanging and fastening Gates and Wickets. Octavo, with Models of Iron Work proper for the purpose.

### Monsieur J. C. L. Simonde.

Tableau de l'Agriculture Toscane. Octavo.

### Sir John Sinclair, Bart.

Ten Quarto Pamphlets, entitled, "Observations on the Manner of enabling Cottagers to keep a Cow."

### Colonel William Tatham.

A Bust of General Washington.

Communications concerning the Agriculture and Commerce of the United States of America. Octavo.

On the Labour of Oxen compared with Horses. Octavo.

On the Culture and Commerce of Tobacco. Octavo.

National

National Irrigation, or the various Methods of watering Meadows. Octavo.

On the Political Economy of Inland Navigation. Quarto.

WILLIAM HALL TIMBRELL, Esq.

New Inventions and Directions for Ruptured Persons.

Appendix to Ditto. Octavo.

ARTHUR YOUNG, Esq.

214 Numbers of the Annals of Agriculture. Octavo.

Letters from General Washington to Arthur Young, Esq. Octavo.

# A CATALOGUE

## OF THE

# MODELS AND MACHINES

Received since the Publication of the Nineteenth Volume of the Society's Transactions; with the Numbers as they are arranged, in the Class to which they belong.

---------

## AGRICULTURE. CLASS I.

No. XCII. **A** BRANCH of a Tree engrafted by William Fairman, Esq. See page 168.

MANU-

MANUFACTURES. CLASS III.

XXXIV.    A Model of an improved
Loom, and method of wea-
ving Sacks, by Mr. Thomas
Clulow. See page 353.

MECHANICKS. CLASS IV.

CXCIII.    A Gun, with a particular
Lock, to prevent the unexpected discharge of Fire-
arms, by Mr. John Webb.
See page 243.

CXCIV.    An Augre, Gauge, and
Blasting-Screw, by Mr. Richard Knight. See page 247.

CXCV.    A Model of a Method to
secure decayed Girders, by
Mr. James Woart. See
page 258.

CXCVI.    Ditto, by Ditto. See
page 267.

D d                        A Mode

CXCVII. A Model of a Life-Boat, by Mr. Henry Greathead. See page 283.

CXCVIII. A Model of a part of the Human Body, with a Truss and Cushion, by W. H. Timbrel. See page 331.

CXCIX. A Model of Iron-work for hanging Gates and Wickets, by T. N. Parker, Esq.

COLONIES and TRADE.

A dried Bread-Fruit, from Joseph Robley, Esq. See page 357.

Cloves and Cinnamon, from Dr. Anderson, of St. Vincent. See page 371.

# OFFICERS of the SOCIETY,

## AND

# C H A I R M E N

### OF THE SEVERAL

# C O M M I T T E E S,

Elected March 23, 1802.

———————

### PRESIDENT.

CHARLES Duke of Norfolk, F. R. and A. S.

### VICE-PRESIDENTS.

Charles Duke of Richmond, K. G. F. R. and A. S.

William Henry Duke of Portland, K. G. F. R. and A. S.

D d 2

Hu

Hugh Duke of Northumberland, K. G.
      F. R. and A. S.
Jacob Earl of Radnor, F. R. and A. S.
Charles Earl of Liverpool, LL. D.
Charles Earl of Romney, F. R. S.
Hon. Robert Clifford, F. R. and A. S.
Sir William Dolben, Bart.
Sir Watkin Lewes, Knt.
Thomas Pitt, Esq. F. A. S.
Caleb Whitefoord, Esq. F. R. and A. S.
Thomas Skip Dyot Bucknall, Esq.

### SECRETARY.

Mr. Charles Taylor.

### ASSISTANT-SECRETARY.

Mr. Thomas Taylor.

### HOUSEKEEPER.

Miss A. B. Cockings.

### COLLECTOR.

Mr. Stephen Theodore Borman.

CHAIR-

# CHAIRMEN OF THE SEVERAL COMMITTEES.

Elected March 23, 1802.

---

### ACCOMPTS,

James Hebert, Esq.
William Lumley, Esq.

### CORRESPONDENCE AND PAPERS,

Edward Bancroft, M. D. F. R. S,
Richard Powell, M. D,

### POLITE ARTS,

Matthew Michell, Esq.
George Meredith, Esq. F.A.S. P.R.I,

### AGRICULTURE.

John Middleton, Esq.
Matthias Deane, Esq.

Dd 3

MAN

### MANUFACTURES.

Mr. Joseph Champney
Mr. J. Pearsall

### MECHANICKS.

George Howe Browne, Esq.
Thomas Day, Esq.

### CHEMISTRY.

Edward Howard, Esq. F. R. S.
Henry Coxwell, Esq.

### COLONIES AND TRADE.

William Meredith, Esq.
Joseph Colen, Esq.

### MISCELLANEOUS MATTERS.

Joseph Jacob, Esq.
William Kirkby, Esq.

A LIST

# L I S T

OF

# CONTRIBUTING MEMBERS.

### NOVEMBER, 1802.

*N. B.* Thofe marked with ✱✱ pay Five Guineas annually; those marked with ✱, Three Guineas annually; those with P, are Perpetual Members; those with ✝✝ have served the office of Steward; and thosé marked with ✝ are Stewards eleƈt.

## A. .

✱   ARGYLL, John Duke of
     Athol, John Duke of, F. R. S.
  Anspach, Elizabeth Margravine of Brandenburgh
  Alvanley, Richard Lord, *Great George-street*
✝✝Anderson, Sir John William, Bart. M. P. *Adelphi Terrace*
  Aftley, Sir Jacob Henry, Bart. M. P. *Burgh Hall Norfolk*

D d 4

††P Abbot, Charles, Esq. *Pall-mall*, M.P. F. R. and
    A. S.

Abercromby, John, Esq. *Claygate, near Esher, Surrey*

Abdy, Rev. Thomas Abdy, *Cooper-sale, Essex*

Ablett, Joseph, Esq. *Manchester*

Adair, Alexander, Esq. *Pall-mall*

††Adam, William, Esq. *Albemarle-street*

Adam, William, Esq. *Lincoln's-inn-fields*

Adam, Joseph, M. D.

Adams, William, Esq. M. P. *Craven-street*

Adams, John, Esq. *Ely-place*

Adams, Dudley, Esq. *Fleet-street*

Adamson, Mr. David, *Oxford-street*

Affleck, Col. James, *Vere-street, Cavendish-square*

Agace, Daniel, Esq. *Gower-street*

Aickin, James, Esq. *Denmark-street, Soho*

Ainslie, Henry, M. D. *Dover-street*

Ainsworth, Mr. Richard, *Moss Bank, near Bolton*

Albin, William, Esq. *Tokenhouse-yard*

P Alexander, Claud, Esq.

††Alexander, Mr. Daniel, *Lawrence-Poultney-lane*

††Allen, Edward, Esq. *Clifford's-inn*

††Allen, John, Esq. F. R. S. *Clement's-inn*

††Allen, William, Esq. *Lewisham, Kent*

Allix, John Peter, Esq. *Swaffham-house, Cambridge-*
    *shire*

Anderson, David, Esq.

Anderson, James, LL. D. *Isleworth.*

P Andrew, Thomas Harrison, Esq. *Moss-hall, Finchley*

Andrews, Magnus, Esq. *Sackville-street, Piccadilly*

Andrews,

Andrews, Thomas, Esq. *Gray's-inn*

Angerstein, John Julius, Esq. *Pall-mall*

P Annesly, Honourable Richard, *Dublin*

P Antrobus, Edmund, Esq. *New-street, Spring-gar-*
    *dens*

Arbuthnot, George, Esq. *King-street, Golden-square*

Arkwright, Richard, Esq. *Cromford, Derbyshire*

Armstrong, Mr. John, *Pimlico*

Arnoldi, Mr. George, No. 3, *Church-yard-court,*
    *Temple*

P Ashby, Shuckbrugh, Esq. F. R. S. *Great Ormond-*
    *street*

Ashby, Henry, Esq. *St. Andrew's court, Holborn*

Ashton, Nicholas, Esq. *Woolton Hall, near Liverpool*

Ashton, Mr. Isaac, *Billiter-lane*

Aslet, Mr. Robert, *Bank, and Gracechurch-street*

††Atcheson, Nathaniel, Esq. F. S. A. P. R. I. *Ely-*
    *place*

††Atlee, Mr. John, *Wandsworth*

††Atlee, Mr. James, *Thames-street*

††P Aubert, Alexander, Esq. F. R. and A. S. *Austin-*
    *friars*

Aubyn, James St. Esq. *Plymouth-dock*


### B.

**Buccleugh, Henry Duke of

P Bute, John Earl of, F. A. S.

P Buchan, David Earl of, LL. D. F. R. and A. S.

. Bristol, Right Rev. Frederick Earl of, F. R. S.

Barrington,

Barrington, the Right Hon. Lord Viscount

P Beverley, Algernon Earl of

P Brownlow, Lord, F. R. and A. S.

Braybrooke, Richard Lord, *Lower Grosvenor-street*

Bolton, Thomas Lord, F. A. S.

P Balgonie, Lord

P Bouillon, Prince of, Philip D'Auvergne, Captain in the Royal Navy, F. R. and A. S.

Bruhl, his Excellency Count de, *Old Burlington-street*

Bruce, the Honourable Major-General, M. P.

Bowes, the Honourable George

Bowes, the Honourable Thomas, *Redbourn, near St. Alban's*

P Blacket, Sir Thomas, Bart.

Banks, the Right Honourable Sir Joseph, Bart. President of the Royal Society, K. B. and F. A. S. *Soho-square*

Baring, Sir Francis, Bart. M. P. *Devonshire-square*

Burgess, Sir James Bland, Bart. *Duke-street, Westminster*

Bruce, Governor James

††P Bacon, John, Esq. F. A. S. *Temple*

P Bacon, John, Esq. *Newman-street*

††Bacon, Anthony, Esq. *Newtown, near Newbury*

Bailey, Charles, Esq. *Swallowfield, Berks*

Bailey, James, Esq. *Lambeth*

††Baker, John, Esq. 12, *Grosvenor-street*

P Baker, William, Esq. *ditto*

Baldwin, Mr. Charles, *Union-street, Blackfriars*

Bancroft,

Bancroft, Edward, M. D. and F. R. S. *Francis-street, Tottenham-court-road*

Barber, John Thomas, Esq. *Southampton-street, Covent-garden*

P Barclay, David, Esq. *Walthamstow*

Barclay, Robert, Esq. F. L. S. *Terrace, Clapham*

✱ Barclay, Robert, Esq. *Lombard-street*

Baring, John, Esq. M. P. *Charles-street, Berkeley-square*

Barker, Richard, Esq. *Tavistock-street, Bedford-square*

Barker, Mr. Charles, *Chandos-street*

Barlow, Mr. J. *Great Surrey-street, Blackfriars*

P Barnard, William, Esq. *Deptford*

P Barnard, Edward, Esq. *ditto*

Barnard, Mr. Thomas, *Adelphi*

Barnard, Josiah, Esq. *Cornhill*

Barnard, Leonard, Esq. *Old Jewry*

††Barnardiston, Nathaniel, Esq. *Harpur-street*

Barnet, Edward, Esq. *Soho-square*

Barrett, Miss Eliza, *Stockwell*

Barrington, the Rev. George, *Durham*

Barry, Henry Alexander, Esq. *Eversley Lodge, Hants*

Barry, James, Esq. *Castle-street, Oxford-street*

Bartlett, Patrick, Esq.

P Bartolozzi, Francis, Esq. R. A. *North-end*

Barton, Rev. John, Chaplain to the House of Commons

Barwise, Mr. John, *St. Martin's-lane*

Bates, Mr. George Ferne, 73, *Hatton-garden*

Bate, John, Esq. *Bedford-row*

Batson, Edward David, Esq. *Lombard-street*
Baverstock, Mr. James, *Alton, Hants*
††Beale, Daniel, Esq. *Fitzroy-square*
P Bean, Mr. Nathaniel, *King's-road, Bedford-row*
P Bean, Mr. Isaac, *ditto*
Bearcroft, Philip, R. Esq. *Vere-street*
††Beard, John, Esq. F. A. S. *Doctors-commons*
Beatson, Robert, Esq. *Kilrick, Scotland*
Beaumont, Daniel, Esq. *Great Russel-street*
Beaumont, John, Esq. *Villiers-street, Strand*
Beazely, Charles, Esq. P. R. I. *Whitehall*
Beddall, Mr. John, *Jekyls, Fenchingfield, Essex*
Belches, Robert, Esq.
Belisario, Mr. John, *Gerard's Cross, Bucks*
Bell, William, Esq. *Norfolk-street, Strand*
Bell, Mr. Anthony, *Charlotte-street, Pimlico*
Belleew, Christopher K. Esq. *Inner Temple*
Bennett, James, Esq. *Bedford-square*
Bennett, Mr. William, *Mitre-court, Cheapside*
Bent, Mr. William, *St. Martin's lane*
Bentham, General Samuel, *Queen's-square, West-minster*
Bentley, Robert, Esq. *Bedford-street, Covent-garden*
††Benwell, Joseph, Esq. *Battersea*
Berkeley, John, Esq. *St. John's-square, Clerkenwell*
Berwick, Joseph, Esq. *Hollow-park, near Worcester*
Bevil, Robert, Esq. 24, *Chancery-lane*
Biddulph, Robert, Esq. M. P. *Arlington-street*
Bignell, William, Esq. *Seething-lane*
Bilsborow, Dewhurst, Esq. *Dalby-hall, Leicestershire*

†† Bingley,

††Bingley, Thomas, jun. Esq. *Coleman-street*

Bingley, Mr. John, *John-street, Tottenham-court-road*

Birch, Thomas James, Esq. Captain of the 1st Regiment of Life Guards

Birchill, Mr. Matthew, *Fulham*

Birkett, Dániel, Esq. *Trinity-square, Tower-hill*

††Birkhead, Charles, Esq. *Ryegate, Surrey*

Bish, Thomas, Esq. Stock Broker, *Cornhill*

Bishop, Nathaniel, Esq. *Yorkshire*

Bisset, Capt. Robert, Commissary-General, *Great Pulteney-street*

Biven, Edward, Esq. *Lambeth*

Blaauws, William, Esq. *Queen-Ann-street, West*

Black, Mr. George, *Princes-street, Bank*

Blackburne, John, Esq. M. P. F. R. S. *Park-street, Westminster*

††Blades, John, Esq. *Ludgate-hill*

Blair, Alexander, Esq. *Portland-place*

††Blake, William, Esq. *Aldersgate-street*

Blake, Robert, Esq. *Essex-street*

Blandy, John, Esq. *Reading*

Blandy, William, Esq. *ditto*

Blane, William, Esq. F. R. S.

Blicke, Charles Tufton, Esq. *Billiter-square*

Blizard, Mr. William, F. R. and A. S.

Blomefield, Colonel, *Shooter's-hill*

Boddington, Thomas, Esq. *Mark-lane*

Boddy, Mr. Francis, *Warwick-lane*

Boddy, John, Esq. *Thames-street*

P Boehm, Edmund, Esq. *Broad-street*

Bo

Bonar, Thompson, Esq. *Broad-street-buildings*

Booth, John, Esq. *Devonshire-street, Queen-square*

Borradaile, R. Esq. *Fenchurch-street*

Borradaile, William, Esq. *ditto*

Borron, Arthur Esq. *Warrington*

Bostock, the Rev. John, *Windsor*

Bostock, Samuel, Esq. *Borough*

P Bosville, William, Esq. F. R. S. *Gunthwaite Hall, Yorkshire*

Botfield, Thomas, jun. Esq. *Ditton, near Bewdley, Worcestershire*

Bovi, Mr. Mariano, *Piccadilly*

Boulton, Matthew, Esq. F. R. S. *Soho, near Birmingham*

Bousfield, George, Esq. *King's-bench Walk*

††Bowzer, Richard, Esq. 3, *Bedford-row*

††Boydell, John, Esq. and Alderman, *Cheapside*

Bracebridge, Walter, Esq. *Queen-square, Westminster*

Bracken, Rev. Thomas, *Upper John-street, Golden-square*

Braithwaite, Daniel, Esq. F. R. and A. S. *Post-Office, and Grenville-street, Brunswick-square*

Braithwaite, Mr. John, *Brook-street, Tottenham-court-road*

Bramah, Mr. Joseph, *Piccadilly*

Bree, Martin, Esq. *Arundel-street, Strand*

Breton, William, Esq. 52, *Upper Seymour-street, Portman-square*

Brettingham, Robert, Esq. *Grosvenor-place*

Brewer,

' Brewer, Mr. John, jun. *Ludgate-hill*

P Brickwood, John, Esq. *Billiter-square*

Brickwood, Mr. Nathaniel, *Thames-street*

Bridge, Mr. Thomas, *Southwark*

Bridgman, William, Esq. P. R. I. and F. L. S. ·76, *Old Broad-street*

‡†P Broadhead, Theodore Henry, Esq. F. A. S. *Portland-place*

Broadwood, James, Esq. *Charlotte-street, Portland-place*

Brockbank, Mr. Joseph, *Crescent, New Bridge-street, Blackfriars*

Brodie, Alexander, Esq. M. P.

‡†Brodie, Alexander, Esq. *Carey-street*

Brodie, Mr. John, *Clifford's-inn*

Brogden, James, Esq. M. P. *Park-street*

*P Brooke, Richard Brooke de Capell, Colonel, F.R.S. *Great Oakley, Northamptonshire*

Brounlie, John, M. D. *Carey-street, Lincoln's-inn*

Brown, Thomas, Esq. *Adelphi*

Brown, John, Esq. *John-street, Adelphi*

Browne, Isaac Hawkins, Esq. M. P. F. R. S. *South Audley-street*

'Browne, Francis John, Esq. M. P.

Browne, George Howe, Esq. *Bedford-street, Covent-garden*

Browne, Mr. Robert, *Kew*

Browne, Thomas, Esq. 34, *New Bridge-street*

Browning, Charles, Esq. *Horton Lodge, Epsom*

Bryan, Michael, Esq. *Pall-mall*

Bryer,

Bryer, Mr. Robert, 58, *Strand*

Buckle Lewes, Esq. 4, *Upper Seymour-street, Portman-square*

✱††Bucknall, Thomas Skip Dyot, Esq. *Baker-street, Portman-square*

Buckell, George, Esq. jun. *Chepstow, Monmouth-shire*

Buller, John, Esq. *Morval, Cornwall, and Gloucester-place, Portman-square*

Bunnell, Mr. Joſeph, 9, *Southampton-row*

Burdon, Mr. William, *St. Andrew's-court, Holborn*

Burdon, Rowland, Esq. M. P. *Grosvenor-square*

Burgess, John, Esq. *Brook Farm, Hants, or 107, Strand*

††Burgoyne, Montague, Esq. *Mark Hall, Harlow, Essex*

Burkitt, Mr. Alexander Sheafe, *Fleet-street*

Burnett, Robert, jun. Esq. *Vauxhall*

P Burney, Charles, M. D. *Greenwich*

Burton, Launcelot, Esq. *Newcastle-street, Strand*

Bury, Edward, Esq. *Walthamstow*

Butler, W. Esq. *Havant, Hants*

Butt, Mr. James Strode, *Paragon, Kent-road*

Butts, John, Esq. *Chatham-square*

Byerley, Mr. Thomas, *York-street, St. James'-square*

††Byfield, George, Esq. *Craven-street*

Byfield, Mr. George, *Craig's-court, Charing-cross*

C.

## C.

Carrington, Right Honourable Lord

Clermont, Earl

††Chetwynd, Richard Lord Viscount

Conyngham, Right Honourable William, F. A. S.

Cavendish, Hon. Henry, F. R. and A. S. *Gower-street, Bedford-row*

*††Clifford, the Honourable Robert, V. P. F. A. S. and P. R. I. *Edward-street, Portman-square*

Coghill, Sir John, Bart. *Coghill Hall, Yorkshire*

P Carnegie, Sir David, Bart. M. P.

Caldwell, Ralph, Esq. *Hilborough, Norfolk*

.††Caley, John, Esq. F. A. S. *Gray's-inn*

Callender, John, Esq. M. P. *Cumberland-place*

Caldecott, John, Esq. *Rugby, Warwickshire*

Calverley, Thomas, Esq. *Elm-court, Temple*

Campbell, Governor William

Campbell, Duncan, Esq. *Great Queen-street*

Carpenter, Charles, Esq. *Moditonham, Cornwall*

Cartwright, Charles, Esq. *India-house*

Cartwright, Rev. Edmund, *Marybone Park*

Cartwright, Rev. Edmund, jun. *Baliol College, Oxford*

††P Cater, Mr. Richard, *Bread-street, Cheapside*

Chalie, John, Esq. *Bedford-square*

Chamberlayne, John, Esq. *Bromley*

Champernoun, John, Esq. *Totness, Devon*

Champney, Joseph, Esq. *Cheapside*

E e                            Chapman,

Chapman, Mr. William, *King-street, Cheapside*
Charington, John, Esq. *Mile-end*
Cheek, J. M. G. Esq. *Evesham, Worcestershire*
Cheek, Mr. Henry, *Manchester*
Cherry, Benjamin, Esq. *Hertford*
Chippendale, Mr. Thomas, *St. Martin's lane*
Christie, Daniel Beat, Esq. *Fineden, near Welling-borough*
††Christian, John Giles, Esq. *Doctors-commons*
Christian, John, Esq. *Lincoln's-inn*
Claridge, John, Esq. *Upton-on-Severn, Worcestershire*
P Clark, Mr. James
††Clarke, Richard, Esq. Chamberlain, *Bridge-street, Blackfriars*
Clarke, Mr. Henry, *Gracechurch-street*
Clarke, Richard, Esq. *Worcester*
Clarke, John, Esq. *Edinburgh*
Clarke, William, Esq. *Tynemouth, Northumberland*
Clark, James, Esq. M. D. *Tavistock-street, Covent-garden*
Clark, George, Esq. *Brentford*
Clay, Rev. J. *Dorking, Surrey*
Clay, Henry, Esq. *Birmingham*
††Cleland, Walter, Esq. *Adelphi Terrace*
Cleveland, William, Esq. *Dowgate-hill*
Close, Rev. Henry John, *Ipswich*
Clough, Dr. *Berners-street*
Clough, Henry Gore, Esq. *of the Light Infantry Guards*
Cockett, Thomas, Esq. *Inner Temple Cloisters*

P Coggan,

P Coggan, Captain John, *East-India House*

Closs, Thomas, Esq. *Bermondsey-street*

Cole, Benjamin, Esq. *Battersea-rise, Surrey*

Cole, Thomas Comyns, Esq. *Woodstock-street, Bond-street*

Coles, William, Esq. *Scot's-yard, Bush-lane*

Coleman, Edward, Esq. Professor at the Veterinary College

†P Colen, Joseph, Esq. *New Inn*

Collier, Mr. Joshua, *Dartmouth-street, Westminster*

††Collins, Thomas, Esq. F. A. S. *Berners-street*

. Collins, Benjamin Charles, Esq. *Salisbury*

Collow, William, Esq. *Broad-street-buildings*

Colquhoun, Patrick, Esq.

†Combe, Harvey Christian, Esq. Alderman, M. P. *Great Russell-street, Bloomsbury*

Compton, Mr. Henry, *Charlotte-street, Pimlico*

††Conant, Nathaniel, Esq. *Great Marlborough-street*

P Coningham, James, Esq.

Constable, M. M. Esq. *Evringham, Yorkshire*

Cook, Charles Gomond, Esq. *Southampton-street, Covent-garden*

††Cooke, Mr. John Kenworthy, *Red-lion-square*

Cookney, Charles, Esq. *Staples Inn*

Cooper, Mr. Benjamin, *Earl-street, Blackfriars*

Cooper, Mr. Joseph, 9, *High Holborn*

Coore, John, Esq. *Winchester-street*

Cope, William, Esq. *Sanctuary, Westminster*

Copely, Thomas, Esq. *Netherall, near Doncaster Yorkshire*

P Coppe

P Coppens, B. M. D. *Ghent, Flanders*

Corbyn, Mr. John, *Holborn*

Cosser, Stephen, Esq. *Abingdon-street*

Cotton, Richard, Esq. *Duke-street, St. James's square*

Courtenay, Thomas Peregrine, Esq. 15, *Lower Grosvenor-sreeet*

† Coussmaker, Lannoy Richard, Esq. *Gower-street, Bedford-square*

Coussmaker, William Kops, Esq. *Brunswick-square*

Cowell, George, Esq. *America-square*

Cowper, William, Esq. *Featherstone-buildings, Holborn*

Cox, Robert Albion, Esq. *Little Britain*

Cox, Mr. William, *Beaufort-buildings*

P Coxe, Peter, Esq. *Surrey Road, Blackfriars*

††Coxwell, Henry, Esq. *Fleet-street*

Cradock, Joseph, Esq. M. A. and F. A. S. *Gumley, Leicestershire*

Craig, Charles Alexander, Esq. *Great Scotland-yard*

Crawford, John, Esq. *Newman-street*

††Crawshay, Richard, Esq. *George-yard, Thames-street*

††Crawshay, William, Esq. *ditto*

Crawley, Samuel, Esq. *Ragnall, Nottinghamshire*

Crichton, John, Esq. *Stephen-street, Rathbone-place*

Crillan, J. F. Esq. *of the Isle of Man*

Crippen, William, Esq. *Reduced Office, Bank*

††Criswell, William, Esq. *Bedford-row*

Crocker, Benjamin, Esq. Surveyor, *Bath*

Crocker, Mr. Abraham, *Froome, Somersetshire*

Crook, Thomas, Esq. *Tytherton, near Chippenham, Wilts*

Crook,

Crook, John, Esq.

Cross, William, Esq. *Thorngrove House, Worcester*

Crowder, William Henry, Esq. *Frederick's-place, Old Jewry*

††Crowther, Philip Wyatt, Esq. *Guildhall*

Cunningham, William, Esq.

Curwen, John Christian, Esq. M. P.


D.


**Devonshire, William Duke of

P Dartmouth, George Earl of, F. R. and A. S. and F. L. S.

Dundas, Thomas Lord, F. R. and A. S.

P Dolben, Sir William, Bart. V. P. M. P. *at Mr. Marten's, Poet's Corner*

Denham, Sir James Stewart, Bart. M. P.

Durno, Sir James

Douglass, Admiral John, *Chichester*

Dallison, Mr. Thomas, *Wapping*

Dalton, Mr. John, *Bread-street, Cheapside*

†Dampier, Edward, Esq. *Grove-place, Hackney, and Harpur-street*

Dancer, Mr. John, *Doncaster*

††P Daniel, John, Esq. *Mincing-lane*

Davis, Mr. Thomas

Davies, the Rev. J. D. D. F. R. and A. S. Provost, *Eaton*

Davies, Rees, Esq. *Swansea*

Davis,

[ 422 ]

Davis, Thomas, Esq. *Mark-lane*
Davison, Rev. Thomas Hartburn, *Northumberland*
Davison, Alexander, Esq: *Swarford, Northumberland, and St. James's square*
Dawes, John, Esq. *Pall-mall*
Dawson, Mr. Robert, *St. Paul's church-yard*
††Day, Thomas, Esq. *Leicester-place, Leicester-fields*
Deane, John, Esq. *Hartley Court, Reading*
††Deane, Matthias, Esq. 4, *Featherstone-buildings, Holborn*
Decort, Henry, Esq. *Hanover-street, Hanover-square*
Delafield, Joseph, Esq. *Castle-street, Long-acre*
Devaland, George, Esq. *Bloomsbury-place*
| De l'Hoste, Lieut. Colonel, *Weymouth-street, Portland-place*
††Dent, Robert, Esq. F. A. S. *Temple-bar*
Dent, John, Esq. M. P. F. A. S. *ditto*
P††Dent, William, Esq. *Battersea-rise*
Desanges, Mr. William, *Wheeler-street, Spitalfields*
Desanges, Mr. John Francis, *ditto*
Devall, Mr. John, *Buckingham-street, Portland-place*
Devenish, Mr. Thomas Courtney, *Villiers-street, Strand*
††Devis, Arthur William, Esq. Member of the Asiatic Society, Bengal, *Gerrard-street*
Dickinson, Henry, Esq. *Leadenhall-street*
P Dickinson, Charles, Esq. *Soho-square*
Dickson, Dr. William, 4, *Clipstone-street, Portland-road*
D'Israeli, Isaac, Esq. *King's-road, Bedford-row*

Ditcher,

Ditcher, Philip, Esq. *East Bergholt, Suffolk*

Dixon, John, Esq. *Phillimore-place, Kensington*

Dodd, Ralph, Esq. *Parliament-street*

Doe, Thomas, Esq. *Bygrave Park, Herts*

Dollond, Mr. Peter, *St. Paul's Church-yard*

Dollond, Mr. John, *ditto*

††Doratt, John, Esq. *Bruton-street*

Douce, Thomas Augustus, Esq. *Townmalling, Kent*

Doughty, John, Esq. *Aldermanbury*

P Douglass, William, Esq. *America-square*

Douglas, John, Esq. *Manchester*

Dowbiggin, Samuel, Esq. *Hatfield Regis, Herts*

Down, Richard, Esq. *Bartholomew-lane*

Downer, Henry, Esq. *Fleet-street*

Drake, Mr. Samuel, *Margaret-street, Westminster*

P Draper, Daniel, Esq. *St. James's street*

Draper, Mr. John, *Clayton-place, Kennington-road*

Driver, Mr. William, *Surrey-square, Kent-road*

Drury, Robert, Esq. *Covent-garden*

Duberley, James, Esq. *Soho-square*

Duckworth, George, Esq. *Manchester*

Dundas, Robert, Esq. M. P. *Somerset-place*

Dundass, David, Esq. *Richmond, Surrey*

Dunn, Samuel, Esq. *Adelphi*

Duppa, Baldwin Duppa, Esq. *Hollingbourn-place, near Maidstone, Kent*

P Dutton, John, Esq. *Catherine-court, Tower-hill*

††*Duval, the Rev. Philip, D. D. F. R. and A. S. *Newman-street*

Dyke, Thomas, Esq. *Doctors-commons*

## E.

P Exeter, the Most Noble the Marquis of, F, R. S, and S, A.

††P Egremont, George Wyndham Earl of

Eardley, Sampson Lord, M. P. F. R. and A. S,

P Egerton, Rev. Francis Henry, *Bridgewater-house, Pall-mall*

Einsiedel, his Excellency Count

Elphinstone, the Honourable William

Eden, Sir John, Bart. M. P.

Eden, Sir Frederick Morton, Bart. F, A. S.

Erskine, Sir William, Bart. M. P.

†† Eamer, Sir John, *Wood-street, Cheapside*

Erle, Henry, Esq. *Gower-street*

Eaton, Rev. Stephen, A. M. and F. A, S. *St. Ann's, Soho*

P Eaton, Peter, Esq. *Westford, Essex*

Echardt, Francis Fred. Esq. *Whiteland House, Chelsea*

P Eckersall, John, Esq. *Clareton, near Bath*

Eccles, the Rev. Allan Harrison, *Bow, Middlesex*

P Eccleston, Thomas, Esq. *Scaresbrick, Lancashire*

Edwards, John, Esq. *St. Paul's Church-yard*

Edwards, Samuel, Esq. *Stamford, Lincolnshire*

Edwards, Mr. John, *at Mr. Wood's*, No. 35, *Broad-street-buildings*

Edwards, Thomas, Esq. *Coleman-street*

Edwards, Hugh, Esq. 56, *Guildford-street*

Ellice, Alexander, Esq. *Great Pulteney-street, Bath*

Ellill,

Ellill, John, Esq. *Queen-street, Cheapside*
Elliot, John, Esq. *Pimlico*
Elliot, George, Esq. *South-street, Finsbury-square*
Elsley, Gregory, Esq. *Garden-court, Temple*
P Errington, John, Esq. *Stanhope-street, May-fair*
Esdaile, William, Esq. *Clapham*
Eustace, Major Henry, of the Engineers
Evans, Robert, Esq. *Great Surrey-street*
Evans, B. B. Esq. *Cheapside*
*††Ewer, Samuel, Esq. F. L. S. *Hackney*
P Ewbank, Andrew, Esq. *Upper Grosvenor-street*


F.

††Fife, James Earl of, F. R. and A. S.
††Falmouth, George Evelyn Lord Viscount
Finch, Honourable Captain William, *Albury, near Guildford*
P Fludyer, Sir Samuel, Bart. *Fludyer-street, Westminster*
P Fletcher, Sir Henry, Bart. M. P. *Southampton-row, Bloomsbury*
Farquhar, Sir Walter, Bart. *Conduit-street*
Fairman, William, Esq. *Lynsted, Kent*
Farmer, Richard, Esq. *Kennington*
Favenc, Abraham, Esq. *Size-lane*
Featherstone, Mr. William, *Adelphi*
P Felton, Samuel, Esq. F. R. and A. S. *Titchfield-street, Portland-place*
P Fermor, William, Esq.

††Ferris,

††Ferris, Samuel, M. D. F. R. and A. S. *Beacons-field*

Fidler, James, Esq. *Spa-fields*

Field, William, Esq. *Chatham-place*

Fielding, Jeremiah, Esq. *Bread-street, Cheapside*

Fincham, Francis, Mr. *Charing-cross*

Flamank, John, Esq. *Wallingford*

Fletcher, James, M. D.

Fletcher, John, Esq. 1, *Cecil-street*

Fludyer, George, Esq. M. P. *Fludyer-street*

Fonblanque, John, Esq. M. P. *Lincoln's-inn*

Forbes, David, Esq. 1, *Primrose-street*

Forrest, Digory, Esq. 28, *South Molton-street*

Forde, the Rev. Brownlow, D. D. *St. John's gate*

Forman, William, Esq. *Thames-street*

Forsyth, William, Esq. F. A. S. *Kensington*

Forster, William, Esq. *Hull*

Forster, John, Esq. *Bath*

Fothergill, Mr. John, 85, *Fenchurch-street*

Foulston, Mr. John, 100, *Pall-mall*

Fowler, Dr. William, *Cecil-street, Strand*

††Fowler, David Burton, Esq. *Fig-tree-court, Temple*

Fowler, Christ. Esq. Under-Secretary of the Tax Office

Fox, Mr. John, *Box Hill, Dorking, in Surrey*

P Franco, Jacob, Esq. *St. James's square*

Frankland, William, Esq. *Cavendish-square*

Franklin, Captain William

Franklin, James, Esq. *Dean's-place, Berks*

Fraser, Simon, Esq. *King's-arms-yard, Coleman-street*

Fraser,

Fraser, William, Esq. F. R. S. *Queen-square, Holborn*

Fraser, Mr. David, *Great Pulteney-street*

P Freeman, Stephen, Esq. *Coventry*

Fremantle, William Henry, Esq. *Stanhope-street, May-fair*

French, George, Esq. *Eastcheap*

Frizell, Capt. H. L. of the Prince of Wales's Own Fencibles

Fry, Edmund, Esq. *Type-street, Chiswell-street*

Fry, Mr. Joseph Storrs, *Bristol*

Fullarton, Colonel William, M. P. and F. R. S.

Fuller, Mr. John, *Pentonville*

Fulton, Henry, Esq. *Watling-street*

## G.

Gordon, Alexander Duke of, K. T. and F. R. S.

Glasgow, George Earl of, F. R. and A. S.

P Gallaway, Arundell Lord Viscount, M. P. and K. B.

P Greville, Right Hon. Charles, M. P. and F. R. S. *Paddington*

Greville, the Hon. Robert, F. R. and A. S. *Great Cumberland-street*

Grey, Sir Henry, Bart. *Howick, Northumberland*

††Gascoigne, Sir Thomas, Bart. F. A. S. *Partington, in the County of York*

Green, General Sir William, Bart. F. R. and A. S. *Chandos-street, Cavendish-square*

P Geary

P Geary, Sir William, Bart. M. P. *Oxen Heath, Kent*

Gwillim, Sir Henry, *Madras*

Galloway, James, Esq. *Gower-street*

Garden, Rev. Edmund, *New North-street, Red-lion-square*

Garnet, Robert, Esq. *Cripplegate*

Garthshore, Maxwell, M. D. F. R. and A. S. *St. Martin's lane*

Gee, John, Esq. *Wardour-street, Soho*

Gedge, Mr. William, *Leicester-square*

††Gellibrand, Thomas, Esq. *Bow*

Gent, Col. William, *Guildford-street*

Gibbes, George Smith, M. P. *Bath*

Gibbs, Harry Leeke, Esq. 1, *Clifford-street, New Bond-street*

Gilbert, Mr. Henry, *Holborn*

Giles, Peter, Esq. *Streatham Park, Surrey*

Gillet, Gabriel, Esq. *Guildford-street*

Gisborne, Thomas, M. D. *Clifford-street*

Gist, Samuel, Esq. *Gower-street*

Glanville, Mr. Edward, *Broad Sanctuary, Westminster*

P Godschall, William Man, Esq. F. R. and A. S.

Godwin, James, Esq. *Wingfield, Berks*

P Godwin, Richard, Esq. *Scot's-yard, Bush-lane*

Gold, Mr. John

Goldthwaite, Thomas, jun. Esq.

Goodwyn, Henry, jun. Esq. *East Smithfield*

Gooch, Captain George, *Clapham-road*

Goodhew, William, Esq. *Deptford*

Goodrich, Mr. Simon, *Admiralty, and Upper Eaton-street, Pimlico*

Gorsush,

Hendrie, Patrick, Esq. *Titchborne-street*

Henley, Henry Hoste, Esq. *Sandringham, Norfolk*

Hennell, David, Esq. *Foster-lane*

Henshaw, Benjamin, *Hoddesdon, Hertfordshire*

Hepworth, John, Esq. *York*

Heron, Patrick, Esq. M. P. *Blackheath*

Heriot, John, Esq. *Catherine-street, Strand*

Hewlet, Mr. William, *Strand*

Hewetson, John, Esq. *Tower-hill*

Hewett, William Nathan Wright, Esq. *of Belham House, near Doncaster, Yorkshire*

Hewitt, Mr. Henry Thomas, 3, *Dover-place, Kent-road*

Hicks, Mr. John, *Brighton*

Higgins, Matthew, Esq.

Hilton, John, Esq. *Ironmonger-lane, Cheapside*

Hill, Richard, Esq. *Plymouth, Glamorganshire*

Hill, Edward, Esq. *Albion-street, Blackfriars-road*

††Hinckley, John, Esq. F. A. S. *Inner Temple*

P Hoare, Charles, Esq. F. A. S. 37, *Fleet-street*

Hoare, Jonathan, Esq. *Stoke Newington*

Hobday, William, Esq. *Holles-street, Cavendish-square*

P Hobson, William, Esq.

Hobson, George, Esq.

Hodgson, Mr. George, *Lambeth-marsh*

Hodges, Mr. Richard, *Scotland-yard*

Hogard, Luke, Esq. *Frith-street, Soho*

P Holder, James, Esq. *Ash Park*

F f

P Holland,

P Holland, Henry, Esq. F. A. S. *Sloane-place, Knights-bridge*

Holland, Richard, Esq. *Half-moon-street, Piccadilly*

Holland, Mr. George, *High Holborn*

Hollis, Thomas Brand, Esq. F. R. and A. S. *Chesterfield-street*

Holcombe, Rev. William, *Canon of St. David's*

Holford, John Carteret, Esq. *Richmond*

Holmes, Mr. John, *Whitefriars*

Holme, Mr. William, *Bass-court, Thames-street*

Home, Patrick, Esq. M. P. *Gower-street*

Homfray, Samuel, Esq. *Mirthir Tidville, Glamorganshire*

Honeybourne, Mr. Robert, *Stourbridge*

Honyman, Captain Robert, M. P. *Royal Navy*

Hooper, Thomas, Esq. *Panty Goitre, Monmouthshire*

Horn, Nicholas, Esq. *St. Martin's lane, Cannon street*

Horner, Thomas, Esq. *Mell's Park, near Frome, Somersetshire*

Horridge, John, Esq. *Raikes, near Bolton*

Horrocks, John, Esq. M. P. *Preston, Lancashire, and Bridge-street*

Horton, Mr. William, *Newgate-street*

Hotham, John, Esq. *Middle Temple-lane*

P Houghton, William, Esq. *Conduit-street*

P Howard, Edward, Esq. F. R. S. *Nottingham-place*

Howard, Bernard, Esq. *Farnham, Suffolk*

† Howell, Richard, Esq. *Thames-street*

Howel

Howell, Mr. John, *Vine-street, Piccadilly*

Howell, James, Esq. *Somerset-place*

Howell, Edward, Esq. *Lindsey-row, Chelsea*

P Hudson, Vansittart, Esq. *Temple*

Hughes, Rev. Edward, Esq. *Kinmell Park, St. Asaph*

Hughes, Henry, Esq. *King's-road, Bedford-row*

Hulme, William, Esq. *Twydale, Kent*

Hunt, Rowland, Esq.

Hunter, John, Esq. M. P. *Bedford-square*

Hunter, John, Esq. *George-street*

P Hurst, Robert, Esq. M. P. *Horsham Park, Sussex*

Hart, Charles, Esq. *Wirksworth, Derbyshire*

Hussey, William, Esq. M. P. *Salisbury*

Hyde, John, Esq.


# I.

P Ilchester, Henry Thomas Earl of

Johnstone, the Honourable Lieutenant - Colonel Cochrane, M. P.

††Ingilby, Sir John, Bart. M. P. F. R. and A. S.

Johnston, Sir William, Bart. *Glocester-place, New-road*

Inglis, Sir Hugh, Bart. M. P. *Soho-square*

P Jackson, William, Esq. *Dowgate-wharf*

††Jacob, Joseph, Esq. *Greek-street, Soho*

P James, William, Esq. *Wellsbourne, Warwickshire*

Jamison, Mr. *Charing-cross*

P Idle, Christopher, Esq. P. R. I. *Strand*

Jeffery, George, Esq. *Throgmorton-street*

Jefferys,

Jefferys, Thomas, Esq. *Cockspur-street*

Jefferys, Mr. George

P Jenkins, Thomas, Esq. *Rome*

P Jenour, Joshua, Esq. *Chigwell-row, Essex*

Jenyns, Rev. George, *Bottisham Hall, Cambridge*

Jervoise, Jervoise Clark, Esq. M. P. *Hanover-square*

Jervoise, Thomas Clarke, Esq. *Vere-street, Cavendish-square*

Jessup, Mr. William, jun. *Farningham, Kent*

Jeudwine, Thomas, Esq. *Basinghall-street*

Ince, William, Esq. *Broad-street, Carnaby-market*

Innes, Hugh, Esq. *Tavistock-street, Bedford-square*

Johnes, Thomas, Esq. M. P. *Hafod, Cardiganshire*

††Johnson, John, Esq. *Mary-le-bone-street*

Johnson, John, jun. Esq. *Berners-street*

Johnson, James, Esq. *Lambeth-walk*

Johnson, Thomas, Esq. *Ely-place*

Johnson, Christopher, Esq. *Queen-square, Bloomsbury*

Johnston, Alexander, Esq. *Drury-lane*

Jones, Edward, Esq. *Wepre Hall, Flintshire*

Jones, John, Esq.

Jones, John, Esq. *Frankby, Wiltshire*

Jones, Mr. Francis, *Grosvenor-street*

Jones, Mr. John, *Charlotte-street, Mansion-house*

† Jones, Griffith, Esq. *Austin-friars*

Jones, Henry, Esq. *Old City Chambers*

Jones, Mr. David, 1, *Barton-street, Westminster*

Jones, Thomas, Esq. *Newcastle-street, Strand*.

Jones,

Lechmer, William, Esq. Captain in the Royal Navy, *Steeple Aston, Oxfordshire*

Lees, William, Esq. *Office of Ordnance, Tower*

Legh, George John, Esq. *High Legh, Cheshire*

††Legh, John, Esq. *Bedford-square*

Lenox, Colonel Alexander, *Charlotte-street, Portland-place*

Lester, Mr. William, *Northampton*

Lettsom, John Coakley, M. D. F. R. and A. S. *Basinghall-street*

P Levien, Solomon, Esq. 73, *Aldersgate-street*

Levy, Moses Isaac, Esq. F. A. S. *George-street, Hanover-square*

††Lewis, Percival, Esq. *Lincoln's-inn*

††Lewis, William, Esq. F. L. S *Holborn*

Lewis, Thomas, Esq. *Great James-street, Bedford-row*

. Leys, Thomas, Esq.

Lillingstone, A. Spoarre, Esq.

Linstow, Wilhelm Bernherd, Esq. *of Copenhagen*

Liptrap, John, Esq. F. A. and L. S. *Whitechapel-road*

Little, Mr. James, *Mortimer-street, Cavendish-square*

Llewellyn, John, Esq. *Penllargare, Glamorganshire*

Loat, Mr. Richard, *Long-acre*

Llewellin, Daniel, Esq. *Cowley-street, Westminster*

P Lloyd, William, Esq.

Lloyd, Thomas, Esq. *Buckingham-street, Strand*

Loyd, Lewis, Esq. *Lothbury*

* Lock, William, Esq.

Lockett,

· Lockett, George, Esq. *Southampton-place*

P Long, Samuel, Esq. M. P. *Hill-street, Berkeley-square*

Lovat, Samuel, Esq. *Loughton, Essex*

P Loveden, Edward Loveden, Esq. M. P. *Busket-Park*

Lowry, Mr. Wilson, *Titchfield-street*

Lowry, Mrs. Rebeckah, *ditto*

Lowten, Thomas, Esq. *Temple*

Lowth, Rev. Robert, *George-street, Hanover-square*

Loxdale, Thomas, Esq. *Braidley Lodge, near Bilson, Staffordshire*

††Lumley, William, Esq. *Lincoln's-inn-fields*

† Lynd, James, Esq. *Beaufort-buildings*

### M.

* .Macclesfield, George Earl of

* Morton, George Earl of, F. R. and A. S.

P Mount Norris, Earl of, *Stratford-place*

P Malmesbury, James Earl of, K. B. and LL. D.

· Milford, Richard Lord, M. P.

**Marsham, the Honourable Lord Viscount

*PMonckton, the Honourable Edward, M. P. *Portland-place*

Middleton, Sir Charles, Bart. M. P. *Hereford-street, May-fair*

Mac Pherson, Sir John, Bart. M. P. *Brompton*

Morshead, Sir John, Bart. *Hampton Court*

Monro,

Monro, Sir Hugh, Bart. *Gloucester-place, Portman-square*

P Mackreth, Sir Robert, M. P. *Cork-street*

Mac Cauley, Mr. Alexander, *Islington*

Macdonald, John, M. D.

M'Leod, John, Esq.

††Mac George, William, Esq. *New Bond-street*

Mackenzie, Alexander, Esq. 38, *Norfolk-street*

Macklin, John, Esq. 139, *Cheapside*

Macmurdo, Mr. Edward Longdon, *Bread-street*

P Macnamara, John, Esq. *Baker-street, Portman-square*

Mac Dougal, Mr. James, 418, *Oxford-street*

Mac Konochie, A. Lochart, Esq.

Magens, Dorrien, Esq. *Cavendish-square*

Maitland, Ebenezer, Esq. *Coleman-street*

Major, the Honourable John Henniker, M. P. F. R. S. and S. A. *Portman-square*

Malcolm, Mr. Jacob, *Stockwell*

Malton, James, Esq. *Norton-street, Portland-place*

Manley, John George, Esq. *Braziers, Oxon*

Mainwaring, Mr. Thomas, *Strand*

March, Mr. William, *Ludgate-hill*

Marks, Mr. John, Builder, *Princes-street, Hanover-square*

Marriott, John Martin, Esq. *Lamb's-conduit-street*

Marsland, Samuel, Esq. *Manchester*

Marsh, Mr. William, *South-street, Grosvenor-square*

Marshall, Andrew, M. D. *Bartlett's-buildings*

Marter, William, Esq. *Kensington*

Martin,

Martin, James, Esq. M. P. *Downing-street*

Martin, Matthew, Esq. *Parliament street*

Martin, James, Esq. 1, *Essex-court, Temple*

Martyn, the Reverend Thomas, B. D. F. R. S. F. L. S. *Professor of Botany, Cambridge*

Martin, Thomas, Esq.

††Maskall, Samuel, Esq. *Mitre-court, Milk-street*

Mason, John, Esq. *Cannon-street*

Masquerier, John James, Esq. 42, *Greek-street, Soho*

Matthews, Edward, Esq. *Sol's-row, Tottenham-court-road*

Maud, John, Esq. *Aldersgate-street*

Mawley, Edward, Esq. *Thornhaugh-street*

Mayhew, John, Esq. *Broad-street, Carnaby-market*

Mayhew, James, Esq. 35, *Great Pulteney-street*

† Mayniac, Francis, Esq. *St. John's square*

Meheux, John, Esq. *Hans Place, Sloane-street*

＊ Melville, General Robert, F. R. and A. S. *Brewer-street*

†† Meredith, William, Esq. *Harley-place*

††Meredith, George, Esq. F. A. S. P. R. I. *Notting-ham-place*

. Merry, William, Esq. *Gower-street*

Mestaer, Peter Everett, Esq. *New Broad-street*

. Metcalfe, Christopher Barton, Esq. *West Ham*

Meux, Richard, jun. Esq. *Liquor-pond-street*

Mellish, Samuel, Esq. *Gray's-inn*

Mellish, Thomas, Esq. *Kent-street, Borough*

††Meyrick, John, Esq. F. A. S. *Great George-street*

Meyrick,

Meyrick, Owen Patland, Esq. *Bodalgan, Anglesey*

Michele, Henry, Esq. *George-street, Adelphi*

†††Mitchell, Matthew, Esq. *Beaufort-buildings, Strand*

††Middleton, John, Esq. *Lambeth*

Medford, Rev. William, *Hurst, Berks*

Midgley, Mr. George Deakin, Chemist, *Strand*

P Midford, George, M. D. *Reading*

††Mildred, Daniel, Esq. *White-hart-court, Grace-church-street*

Miles, Mr. John, *Birmingham*

Millikin, Halley Benson, Esq. *Norfolk-street, Strand*

Millington, Langford, Esq. *Tooting, and Berners-street*

Millington, Mr. Thomas, *Golden-square*

P Mills, Abraham, Esq. *Fence House, Macclesfield*

Mills, Mr. George, *Old Swan-stairs*

Mills, Samuel, Esq. *Finsbury-place*

Milles, Thomas, Esq. 4, *New-square, Lincoln's-inn*

Miller, John, Esq. *Red-lion-square*

Miller, Mr. Samuel, 23, *Cleveland-street, Fitz-roy-square*

Milnes, Richard Slater, Esq. M. P. *Fciston, near Ferrybridge, Yorkshire*

Minchin, Thomas A. Esq. *Gosport*

Minier, Mr. William, *Strand*

Minier, Mr. Charles, *ditto*

Minish, Mr. William, *Whitechapel*

Minnitt, William, Esq. *Milbank, Westminster*

Mist, Mr. Henry, *Long-acre*

Mitchel,

Mitchel, Michael, Esq. *Walthamstow*
Mitchel, William, Esq. M. P.
Mitchell, Robert, Esq. *Newman-street*
Mitford, Robert, Esq. *Great Portland-street*
Montresor, John, Esq.
P Moore, Daniel, Esq. *Lincoln's-inn*
Morley, William, Esq. *New Broad-street*
Morse, Leonard, Esq. F. R. S. and A. S. *Great George-street, Westminster*
Morris, Mr. William, *Whitcombe-street*
Mortimer, Charles, Esq. *Greenhammerton, Yorkshire, and 42, Upper Grosvenor-street*
Morton, Thomas, Esq. *John-street, Adelphi*
††Moser, Mr. John, *Frith-street, Soho*
Munn, Daniel Rolfe, Esq. *Hammersmith*
Munnings, J. S. Esq. *Gray's-inn-square*
Murphy, John Barnwell, Esq.
Murrey, John, M. D. *Bury-street, St. James's*
Myers, Mr. William, *Aldersgate-street*
Myers, Thomas, Esq. *Park-place*

### N.

P Norfolk, Charles Duke of, President, F. R. and A. S.
**Northumberland, Hugh Duke of, V. P. K. G. F. R. and A. S.
††Northampton, Charles Earl of
Northesk, William Earl of
Nepean, Sir Evan, Bart. M. P. Secretary to the Admiralty

Nash,

Nash, Mr. Thomas, *Worcester*

Nash, John, Esq. *Dover-street*

Neill, Philip, Esq. *Temple*

Nethersole, William, Esq. *Essex-street, Strand*

Newbury, Jacob, Esq. *New Inn*

Newcombe, William, Esq. *Bank, and* 23, *Threadneedle-street*

† Newman, John, Esq. 80, *New Broad-street*

P Newton, Robert, Esq. *Norton-house, Berks*

P Newton, Andrew, Esq.

Newton, William Morris, Esq. *Wallington, Surrey*

Newton, Mr. John, *Lamb's-conduit-street*

De Neyva, Joseph da Cunha Para, Esq. *Artillery-place*

††Nichols, John, Esq. *Red-lion-passage, Fleet-street*

Nicholson, William, Esq. *Bartholomew Hospital*

Nichollson, Samuel, Esq. *Cateaton-street*

††Nicol, George, Esq. *Pall-mall*

Nixon, Rev. Robert, F. S. A. F. R. S. *Vale Mascal, Northbray, Kent,*

Noble, William, Esq. *Pall-mall*

Nollekens, Joseph, Esq. R. A. *Mortimer-street*

Nouaille, Peter, Esq. *Greatness, Kent*

Norman, Robert, Esq. *Cannon-street*

Northey, William, Esq. *Queen-street, May-fair*

Norton, Mr. John, *Tooley-street*

Nutting, Mr. Joseph, *King-street, Covent-garden*

O

[ 446 ]

## O.

P Ossory, John Earl of Upper, F. R. and A. S.
Ogilvie, Dr. *Doctors-commons*
Ogle, Mr. Thomas, *Abroad*
Oldham, John, Esq. *Grafton-street*
Oliver, the Rev. John, *Croombs-hill, Greenwich*
Ord, John, Esq. F. R. and A. S. *Lincoln's-inn-fields*
Orrell, Thomas, Esq. *Winsley-street, Oxford-street*
Osorio, Abraham, Esq. *Theobald's-road*
Ovey, Richard, Esq. *Tavistock-street*

## P.

\*\*Portland, William Henry Duke of, V. P. K. G.
F. R. and A. S.
\*\*Pitt, the Right Honourable William, M. P.
Pelham, the Right Honourable Thomas, M. P.
*Stratton-street*
† Peel, Sir Robert, Bart. M. P. *Bury, Lancashire*
\* Pusey, Honourable Philip, *Grosvenor-square*
Pulteney, Sir William, Bart. M. P. *Bath-house*
Paul, Sir George Onesiphorus, Bart. *Lower Grosvenor-street*
Prescott, Sir George, Bart. *Cheshunt*
Packer, Mr. William, *Charlotte-street, Bloomsbury*
Page, Francis, Esq. M. P. *Atsbon, Oxfordshire*
Page, Francis, Esq. *Newbury, Berks*
Page, Frederick, Esq. *ditto*

†† Page,

††Page, Mr. John, *High Holborn*

P Paice, Mr. Joseph, *Bread-street-hill*

Pakenham, Captain Edward, R. N.

Palmer, John Ahearn, Esq. *Uppingham, Rutlandshire*

Papworth, Mr. Thomas, 60, *Newman-street*

Parke, John, Esq. *Manchester*

††Parkes, Richard, Esq. *Broad-street, Bloomsbury*

Parker, David, Esq. *King's-mews*

Parker, Mr. William, *Fleet-street*

††Parker, Mr. Samuel, *Bridge-street, Blackfriars*

Parker, Mr. Thomas, *Fleet-street*

Parker, Samuel Walker, Esq. *White Lead Works, Newcastle-upon-Tyne*

Parkinson, Mr. Thomas, *Bury-place, Bloomsbury*

Parnell, Mr. Hugh, *Church-street, Spitalfields*

Parry, William, Esq. *Norton Hall, Wiltshire*

† Parson, S. P. LL. D. *Doctors-commons*

Paterson, William, Esq. *Devonshire-place*

Paxton, Mr. Christopher, *Aldersgate-street*

Patience, Mr. Joseph, *Wormwood-street, Bishopsgate-street*

Payn, James, Esq. *Maidenhead, Berks*

††Payne, Samuel, Esq. *Vauxhall*

Peachey, Col. M. P.

Peacock, Mr. Lewis, *Lincoln's-inn-fields*

Peale, Rembrandt, Esq. 12, *Fludyer-street, Westminster*

Pearce, William, Esq. *Craig's-court*

Pearsall, Mr. James, *Cheapside*

††Pearson, James, Esq. *Basinghall-street*

Peel,

Peel, Jonathan, Esq. *Lawrence-lane, Cheapside*

Peel, Joseph, Esq. *ditto*

Peirson, Peter, Esq. F. R. and A. S. *Inner Temple*

Pelerin, Henry Ferdinand, Esq. 12, *New North-street, Red-lion-street*

Pemberton, John, Esq. *Inner Temple*

Penruddock, Charles, Esq.

Penton, Mr. George, *New-street-square, Shoe-lane*

Pepys, W. H. jun. Esq. *Poultry*

P Perin, William Philip, Esq. F. R. and A. S.

Perrott, George, Esq. *Craycombe-house, Worcestershire*

Perry, John, Esq. *Blackwall*

Perry, James, Esq. *Strand*

Petrie, William, Esq. M. P. F. R. and A. S. *Hertford-street, May-fair*

Petrie, John, Esq. M. P. *Portland-place*

P Pettiward, Roger, Esq. *Baker-street, Portman square*

Phillips, John, Esq. *Ely*

Phillips, John, Esq. 13, *Southampton-street, Bloomsbury*

Phillips, Mr. Samuel, *St. George's-road, Blackfriars-bridge*

Phillips, Mr. Richard, *St. Paul's Church-yard*

Phillips, William, Esq. *Shinfield Park, Berks*

Phillips, Rev. William, *Mortimer, Berks*

Phillipson, Thomas, Esq. *Harpur-street*

Phipps, Jonathan W. Esq. *Pancras-lane*

Phipps, John Wathen, Esq. *Cork-street*

Pierrie, William, Esq. *Devonshire-street, Queen-square*

Pinney, Azariah, Esq. *Bride-court, Bridge-street*

Piper, Mr. Stephen, *Haverhill, Essex*

Pitman,

Pitman, Ambrose, Esq. *Green-street, Grosvenor-square*

Pitt, William Morton, Esq. M. P. and F. R. S. *Arlington-street*

P++Pitt, Thomas, Esq. V. P. F. A. S. *Wimpole-street*

Pix, George Banastre, Esq. *Alfred-place, Blackfriars-road*

Planta, Joseph, Esq. F. R. S. *British Museum*

Pocock, Charles, Esq. *Sowley, in the County of Southampton*

Pollen, George Augustus, Esq. *Hill House, Leatherhead*

Pollett, Mr. Robert, *North Weald, near Epping*

P Portman, Edward Berkeley, Esq. *Bryanston, near Blandford, Dorset*

Porter, William, Esq. *Copthall-court, Throgmorton-street*

Pote, Edward Ephraim, Esq. *East-Indies*

P Potter, Christopher, Esq. *Abroad*

Potter, George, Esq. *Charing-cross*

Powell, David, jun. Esq. *Little St. Helen's*

Powell; John Clark, Esq. *ditto*

++Powell, Arthur Annesly, Esq. *Devonshire-place*

+Powell, Richard, M. D. *Essex-street*

Powlett, William Powlett, Esq. *Sambourne, near Stockbridge*

Poynder, Thomas, jun. Esq. *Bishopsgate-street*

P Prado, Samuel, Esq. *Grafton-street*

Praed, William, Esq. M. P. *Tyringham, Bucks*

Pratt, Edward Roger, Esq. *Ryston House, Norfolk*

G g                                                    Pratt,

Pratt, John, Esq. *Lower Brook-street*
Preston, Mr. Thomas, *Strand*
Preston, Richard, Esq. *Temple*
Pricket, Thomas, Esq. *Wanstead, Essex*
Pringle, Mark, Esq.
Prinsep, John, Esq.
Pryce, Benjamin, Esq. *Bath*
Pugh, David Heron, Esq.
Purser, Mr. William, *Bennett-street, Blackfriars-road*

### Q.

\* Queensberry, William Duke of, K. T.

### R.

\*\*Richmond, Charles Duke of, V. P. K. G. F. R. and A. S.
\*\*Radnor, Jacob Earl of, V. P. F. R. and A. S.
Rosslyn, Earl of, *Russel-square*
\*\*Romney, Charles Earl of, V. P. and F. R. S.
\* Ryder, the Right Honourable Dudley, M. P.
P Rawlins, Sir William
††Ridley, Sir Matthew White, Bart. M. P. *Portland-place*
††Raby, Alexander, Esq. *Broad Sauctuary*
Radcliffe, John, Esq. No. 2, *New-inn*
Rae, John, Esq. *Broad-street-buildings*
Raggett, Richard, Esq. *Odiham, Southampton*
Raikes, Thomas, Esq. *New Broad-street*

P Ramey, John, Esq. *Ormesby, Norfolk*

††Ramsbottom, John, Esq. *Aldersgate-street*

††Ramsbottom, Richard, Esq. *ditto*

Randell, William, Esq. *Belmont-cottage, Vauxhall*

Rastrick, Mr. John, *Morpeth*

Rawlinson, Abraham, Esq. *Lancaster*

Rawlinson, Thomas, Esq. *ditto*

Reaston, Francis Bushell, Esq. *Queen Anne-street West*

Read, General Henry, *Ramsbury, Wiltshire*

Reeves, John, Esq. F. R. and A. S. *Cecil-street, Strand*

Reeves, Mr. William John, *Holborn-bridge*

Reeve, Joshua, Esq. *Dean-street, Canterbury-square*

Reeve, Mr. Richard, *Titchborne-street, Portland-place*

Reeve, Mr. Gilson, *Crutched-friars*

Reid, Mr. John, *Fan-street, Aldersgate-street*

††Reid, Andrew, Esq. *Cleveland-row, St. James's*

††Reid, John, Esq. *Bedford-square*

Reina, Mr. Peter Anthony, *Great Newport-street*

††Remington, John, Esq. *Milk-street, Cheapside, and Clapton*

Reynolds, Major Thomas Vincent

Ricard, the Rev. Francis, *Jersey*

Richardson, Mr. Charles, *Piazza, Covent-garden*

Riddell, Colonel John

P Ring, Thomas, Esq. *Reading, Berks*

Rivier, Philip, Esq. *Lawrence-Poultney-lane*

Roberts, Colonel Roger Elliott, 46, *Albemarle-street*

Roberts, Robert, Esq. *Paragon, Southwark*

P Roberts,

P Roberts, Thomas, Esq. *Charter-house-square*

Roberts, Rev. William Hancock, D. D. *Lough-borough House*

Robertson, William, M. D. *Golden-square*

Robertson, James, M. D. F. R. S. *Ibbetson's Hotel*

Robinson, Samuel Wakefield, Esq.

††Robinson, George, Esq.

P Robinson, Thomas, Esq. *Bentinck-street, Manches-ter-square*

Robinson, Mr. John, *Arundel-street, Strand*

Robinson, George, Esq. *Winchester-street*

Robinson, John, Esq. M. P. *Wyke House, Isle-worth*

Robins, Mr. John, *Warwick-street*

Robley, John, Esq. *Aldersgate-street*

††Robson, James, Esq. High Bailiff of the City of Westminster, *Conduit-street*

Rodes, Cornelius Heathcote, Esq. *Balborough, Derbyshire*

Rogers, Samuel, Esq. F. R. S. *Paper-buildings, Temple*

Rogers, Edward, Esq. 10, *Harcourt-buildings, Temple*

Rondeau, James, Esq. 3, *Shorter's-court, Throgmor-ton-street*

Roope, John, Esq. *Yarmouth*

Roper, Rev. Francis, *Wexham Parsonage, near Slough, Berks*

Roper, Mr. Robert, *Houndsditch*

Rose, George, Esq. M. P. *Old Palace-yard*

Rose,

Rose, George Henry, Esq. *St. James's square*

Rose, John, Esq. *Gray's-inn-square*

P Ross, General Patrick, F. R. and A. S. *Harley-street*

Rough, William, Esq. *Inner Temple*

Rowcroft, Thomas, Alderman, P. R. I. *Lawrence Poultney-lane*

Rowe, John, Esq. *Salisbury-court, Fleet-street*

Rowley, Owsley, Esq. *Hants*

Rowntree, Mr. Thomas, *Great Surrey-street, Black-friars-road*

Rucker, Daniel Henry, Esq. *Broad-street, City*

Ruggles, Thomas, Esq. F. A. and L. S. *Clare, Suffolk*

Runquest, Peter Andrew, Esq. *Bury-court, St. Mary Axe*

Rush, John, Esq. *Sackville-street*

P Russel, Jesse, Esq. *Goodman's-fields*

Russel, William, Esq. *Berwick, Northumberland*

## S.

\* Shrewsbury, Charles Earl of

P Suffolk, John Earl of

P Shaftesbury, Anthony Earl of, F. R. and A. S.

Scarborough, George Augustus Earl of

P Stanhope, Charles Earl of, F. R. S.

P St. Vincent, John Earl of

P Scarsdale, Nathaniel Lord

G g 3

Stuart,

Stuart, the Honourable Charles, M. P.

St. Aubyn, Sir John, Bart. F. R. and A. S. *Strat-ford-place*

Sheffield, Sir John, Bart. *Portland-place*

Smith, Sir John, Bart. F. R. and A. S. *Sydling, Dorsetshire*

††Sinclair, Sir John, Bart. M. P. F. R. and A. S.

Stephens, Sir Philip, Bart. M. P. F. R. and A. S.

††Smith, Sir William Sidney, K. S. M. P. R. N. *Cave, near Dover, Kent*

Stirling, Sir Walter, Bart. *Pall-mall*

Smith, General Edward, *Walmer House, Kent*

St. Barbe, John, Esq. *Seething-lane*

P††Salte, William, Esq. *Poultry*

Samuel, Mr. George, *Richmond-buildings, Soho*

Sanders, John, Esq. *Mortlake, Surrey*

Sandford, Rev. Thomas, *Isle of Man*

Sansom, Philip, Esq. *Fenchurch-street*

Sargeaunt, Mr. John, *Great Queen-street*

Sarel, Andrew Lovering, Esq. *Surrey-street*

Satterthwaite, Mr. John, *Mincing-lane*

Savage, Mr. James, *Great Queen-street*

Saunders, Thomas, Esq. *Haydon-square, Minories*

Saunders, George, Esq. F. A. S. *Oxford-street*

P Saunders, Edward Grey, Esq. *Harley-place*

Saxon, Mr. Samuel, *Parliament-street*

Sayer, Henry J. Esq. *Lincoln's-inn*

Scarbrow, Stephen, Esq. *Conway-street, Fitzroy-square*

Schaw, Lieutenant-Colonel John B.

Scholey,

Scholey, Mr. George, *Old Swan-stairs*

P Scott, David, Esq. *Devonshire-place*

P Scott, John, Esq. *Adelphi Terrace*

Scott, Robert, Esq. *Grosvenor-square*

Scott, Hugh, Esq.

Scott, John, Esq. *Tuffnel-place, Islington*

††Seale, Mr. David, *Peckham*

Seddon, Mr. Thomas, *Aldersgate-street*

P Selby, Henry Collingwood, Esq. 2, *Gray's-inn-square*

Serra, Isaac, Esq. *King's-road, Bedford-row*

Sewell, the Reverend George, *Byfleet, near Ripley, Surrey*

Sewell, Mr. George, *London-street, Fitzroy-square*

Shadwell, Henry, Esq. *Beverley, Yorkshire*

Shaw, John, Esq. *Great James-street, Bedford-row*

Sharp, Hercules, Esq. *Chester-place, Kennington*

Sharp, Cuthbert, Esq. *ditto*

††Sheldon, Thomas, Esq. F. R. S. *Tottenham-court-road*

Sheldrake, Mr. Timothy, *Strand*

††Sheplee, Richard, Esq. *Horslydown*

Sherwood, William, Esq. *Mark-lane*

Shiffner, Godin, Esq. *Weymouth-street, Portland-place*

P Shipley, Mr. William, Gent. *Maidstone, Kent*

P Shore, Samuel, Esq. *Norton-hall, Derbyshire*

P Shore, Samuel, jun. Esq.

Sibley, Joseph, Esq. *Market-street, Herts*

Sidney,

Sidney, John, Esq. *Court Lodge, Yalding, Kent*
Simeon, Edward, Esq. *of Salvadore-house*
Simonds, William B. Esq. *Reading*
Simpson, Mr. Thomas, *Chelsea Water-works*
Simpken, Mr. Charles, *Oxford-street*
Simpkin, Mr. Thomas, *Strand*
Skinner, Thomas, Esq. Alderman, *Aldersgate-street*
Skinner, William, Esq. *Finsbury-square*
Slack, Thomas Cartwright, Esq. *Bloomsbury-square*
Slade, John, Esq.
Slade, John Moore, Esq. *Chatham*
Smallwood, William, Esq. *Jerusalem Coffee-house*
Smart, Mr. George, *Camden Town*
Smirnove, Rev. James, *Upper Mary-le-bone-street*
• Smith, George, Esq.
P††Smith, John Spencer, Esq. M.P. *Dover, Kent*
††Smith, William, Esq. *Lombard-street*
Smith, William, Esq. M.P. *Park-street*
††Smith, Joshua, Esq. M.P. *Great George-street, Westminster*
Smith, Mr. Dedrick, *Gerard-street*
• Smith, Mr. Nathan, *Knightsbridge, Brighthelmstone*
. Smith, Captain William, of the Royal Navy
Smith, Henry, Esq. *Drapers-hall*
Smith, Mr. Richard, *Crown-court, Cheapside*
Smith, Mr. Edward, *Broad-street, City*
·††Smith, George, Esq. *Lombard-street*
Smith, Eaglesfield, Esq.
Smith, John Prince, Esq. *Serjeants-inn*

Smith,

Smith, Robert, Esq. F. R. S. and F. A. S. *Basing-hall-street*

Smith, Walthall Ridgway, Esq. 5, *New Inn*

Smith, Mr. Thomas, *Strand*

Soane, John, Esq. F. A. S. P. R. I. *Lincoln's-inn-fields*

Songa, Anthony, Esq.

Sowerby, John, Esq. *Watling-street*

††Sparks, Robert, Esq. *St. John's street*

††Sparks, Thomas, Esq. *Aldersgate-street*

Sparkes, Joseph, Esq. *Red-lion-square*

Sparkes, John, Esq. *Doughty-street*

Sparrow, Robert, Esq. *Portland-place, and Work-ingham-hall, Suffolk*

Spiller, James, Esq. *Guildford-street*

Spilsbury, Mr. William, *Snowhill*

Spilsbury, Mr. Charles, *ditto*

Splitgerber, Mr. John Christian, *Church-court, Walbrook*

Splitgerber, Mr. Frederick, *ditto*

Spottiswood, John, Esq. *Sackville-street*

P Spurrier, Mr. Isaac, *Greek-street, Soho*

Stackhouse, Thomas, Esq. *Featherstone-buildings, Holborn*

Stafford, Robert, Esq. Banker, *Huntingdon*

Standen, the Reverend J. H. Rector of Murston, *Kent*

Standish, Edward Townley, Esq. *Park-street, Westminster, and of Standish-hall, in Lancashire*

Stanhope, Walter Spencer, Esq. *Upper Grosvenor-street*

Stanley,

Stanley, George, Esq. *Ponsonby-hall, Cumberland*

· Stapleton, Mr. William, 1, *Water-lane, Whitefriars*

Steell, Robert, Esq. *Finsbury-square*

Steer, Charles, Esq. *Church-street, Spital-fields*

P††Steers, John William, Esq. F. A. S. 7, *Fig-tree-court, Inner Temple*

P Steers, James, Esq. *ditto*

*††Stephens, Francis, Esq. F. R. and A. S. Commissioner of the Victualling Office .

Stephens, James, Esq. *Camerlton-house, near Bath*

Stephens, John, Esq. *Reading* ·

Stevenson, Thomas, M. D.

Stevenson, James, M. D.

Stiff, Mr. Thomas, *New-street, Covent-garden*

Stirling, William, Esq. *Bread-street, Cheapside*

Still, Mr. Samuel Stanford, *Bankside, Southwark*

Stockwell, John, Esq. *Crutched-friars*

Stockdale, Mr. Jeremiah, *Holborn*

Stodart, William, Esq. *Golden-square*

Stone, Mr. Thomas

††Stone, William, Esq.

Stonard, Nathaniel, Esq. *Bow, Middlesex*

Storey, Robert, Esq. *Bedford-square*

Strachan, James, Esq. *Mincing-lane*

††Strange, James, Esq. M. P. *Bond-street*

Stratton, Mr. William, *Gutter-lane*

Street, Mr. James Wallis, *King-street, Bloomsbury*

Street, John, Esq. *Brunswick-square*

Stretton, William, Esq. *Broad-street, Soho*

Stutely, Mr. Joseph, jun. *Northumberland-street*

Suart,

Suart, Georgè, Esq. *Lancaster*

P Sulivan, Richard Joseph, Esq. M. P. F. R. and A. S. *Grafton-street*

Sulivan, John, Esq. M. P. *Chesterfield-street, Mayfair*

Sumner, George, Esq. *George-street, Westminster*

††P Sutton, Robert, Esq. *Finsbury-square*

Swaine, Edward, Esq. *Highbury Terrace*

Sykes, Mark Masterman, Esq. *Sledmere, Yorkshire*

Sykes, Richard, Esq. 3, *Walbrook*

Symmons, John, Esq. F. R. A. S. and L. S. *Paddington-house*

## T.

**Thanet, Sackville Earl of

Tabrum, Mr. Robert, *Gracechurch-street*

Tait, William, Esq. *Cardiff*

P Talbot, Thomas Mansel, Esq. *Penrie Castle, Glamorganshire*

Tapster, Mr. Richard, *Barnet, Herts*

††Tate, William, Esq. *Queen-street, Chelsea*

Tatham, Colonel William, *Staple's-inn-buildings*

Taubman, Major John, *Isle of Man*

Taylor, William, Esq. M. P. 32, *Pall-mall*

Taylor, William, Esq. *Charlotte-street, Bedford-square*

Taylor, John, Esq. *John-street, Adelphi*

Taylor,

Taylor, Mr. Josiah, *Holborn*

Taylor, Major Charles, *of 7th Light Dragoons*

Taylor, Thomas, Esq. *Friday-street, Cheapside*

P Teixiera, Abraham David, Esq. *Mincing-lane*

Tekell, John, Esq. *Lamb's-buildings, Temple*

Templer, James, Esq. *Stover-lodge, Devon*

Tennant, George, Esq. 21, *Southampton-row, Bloomsbury*

Test, Potter, Esq. *Great Portland-street*

Test, Thomas, Esq. 7, *Leicester-place*

Thomas, David, Esq. *Pay Office, Horse Guards*

Thomson, the Rev. Robert, D. D. *Kensington*

Thomson, Alexander, Esq. *Somerset-street*

P Thompson, William, Esq. *Leeds, Yorkshire*

Thompson, William, Esq. *Thames-street*

Thompson, Mr. John, *Duke-street, York-buildings*

P Thornton, Samuel, Esq. M. P. *Clapham*

Thornton, Major General William, *Grosvenor-gate*

Thornton, Dr. Robert

Tildesley, Thomas, Esq. *Hampton-court*

Tilloch, Alexander, Esq. *Carey-street*

Thoyts, William, Esq. *Southamstead, Berks*

Timbrell, William Hall, Esq. *Charlotte-street, Portland-place*

P Timson, William, Esq. *Moon Park, Surrey*

Tomkison, Thomas, Esq. *Dean-street, Soho*

Tomlins, Mr. Thomas, *Lambeth-marsh*

Tooke, William, Esq. *Gray's-inn*

Topham, Edward, Esq.

Totton,

Totton, Stephens Dinely, Esq. A. M. *Abroad*

Towne, Mr. Francis

Townsend, Francis, Esq. Windsor Herald, *Heralds College*

††Towry, George Philips, Esq. Commissioner of the Victualling Office

P Travers, Mr. Joseph, *Swithin's-lane*

Trelawny, John, Esq. *Everet-street, Russel-square*

Trenchard, John, Esq. *Welbeck-street*

Tresham, Henry, Esq. *George-street, Hanover-square*

Trevelyan, Walter, Esq. *Morpeth, Northumberland*

Trotter, John, Esq. *Soho-square*

Trotter, Captain John, *Wimpole-street*

P Tunstall, Marmaduke, Esq. F. R. and A. S. *Wycliffe, Yorkshire*

P Turnbull, John, Esq. F. R. and A. S. *New Broad-street*

Turner, Charles H. Esq. *Limehouse*

Turner, Thomas, Esq. *Caughley-place, near Sheffnall, Shropshire*

P Turner, John Frewen, Esq. *Cold Overton, Leicestershire*

P Tyers, James, Esq. *Little Eastcheap*

Tytler, Henry William, M. D. *Titchfield-street*

U.

## U.

P Uxbridge, Henry Earl of, F. A. S.

Upham, James George, Esq. *White-horse-street, Ratcliffe-highway*

Upton, Charles, Esq. *Derby*

## V.

P Valencia, Richard Lord Viscount, F. L. S.

Vernon, George Venables Lord, *Park-place*

P Villiers, Right Honourable J. C. M. P. *North-Audley-street*

Valangin, Francis, M. D. *Hermes-hill*

Valpy, the Reverend Richard, D. D. and F. A. S. *Reading, Berks*

Vandercomb, Joseph Fitzwilliam, Esq. *Bush-lane, Cannon-street*

Vaughan, Benjamin, Esq.

Vaughan, William, Esq. *Mincing-lane*

Venner, Corbyn Morris, Esq. *King's-bench-walk, Temple*

Vennor, Mr. Edward, Stationer, *Tower-hill*

††Vernon, John, Esq. *Bedford-square*

Vernon, Henry, Esq. *Hilton-park, Wolverhampton, or 10, Lower Wimpole-street*

Verrall, Richard, Esq. 10, *Harcourt-buildings, Temple*

Vidal, Emeric, Esq. *Brentford*

Vidler, Mr. John, *Milbank, Westminster*

Vidler,

Vigne, Stephen James, Esq. *Margaret-street, Westminster*

Vivian, John, Esq. *Gray's-inn*

Vivian, John, Esq. *Temple*

## W.

P Warwick, George Earl of, F. R. and A. S.

P Winchelsea, George Earl of, F. A. S.

Westmeath, Right Honourable Earl of

\* Williams, Sir Edward, Bart.

P Webb, Sir John, Bart. F. R. and A. S.

Wynn, Sir Watkin Williams, Bart. *St. James's square*

Willis, Sir Francis, Knt. *Charles-street, Berkley-square*

Wynne, the Right Hon. Sir William, LL. D. F. R. and A. S. *Doctors-commons*

Wadd, William, Esq. *Clifford-street*

††Wade, George, Esq. *Southampton-row, Bloomsbury*

Waistell, Mr. Charles, *High Holborn*

Wait, William, Esq. *Lawrence-Pountney-hill*

Wakefield, Mr. Edward, jun.

††Walcot, William, Esq. F. A. S. *Inner Temple*

P Wale, Gregory, Esq. *Shelford, near Cambridge*

Walker, John, Esq. F. R. and A. S. *Gower-street, Bedford-square*

Walker, John, Esq. *Argyll-street*

Walker, Thomas, Esq. *Woodstock, Oxon*

Walker, Mr. Daniel, *Great Pulteney-street*

Walker,

Walker, Mr. Thomas, *Epsom*

Walker, Thomas, Esq. *Russel-place, Fitzroy-square*

Walker, Thomas, Esq. *Croydon*

Walker, Joshua, Esq. *Rotherham*

Walker, Dean, Esq. *Conduit-street*

Waller, Charles, Esq. *West Wickham, Kent*

Waller, William, Esq.

Wallis, John, Esq. *Bodmin, Cornwall*

Walshman, Thomas, M. D. *Physician to the Surrey and Western Dispensaries*

Wansey, Mr. John, *Lothbury*

Wansey, Mr. George, *Warminster, Wilts*

Warburton, the Rev. W. P. *Lambeth-house*

P Ward, Mr. John, *Air-street, Piccadilly*

P Ward, Ralph, Esq. *Great Portland-street*

Ward, John, Esq. *Ludgate-street*

Warren, Peter, Esq. *Buckingham-street, Strand*

Watherstone, Dalhousie, Esq. *Duchess-street, Portland-place*

Watkins, George, Esq. *Featherstone-buildings*

Watkins, Jeremiah, Esq. *Charing-cross*

Watkins, Walter, Esq. *Groyney Works, near Abergavenny*

Watson, John, Esq. *Preston, Lancashire*

Watson, Lieutenant-General John, *Bryanstone-street*

P Watts, David Pike, Esq. 32, *Gower-street*

Watts, John, Esq. *Thames-street*

Weatherby, Edward, Esq. *Newmarket*

Webster, John, Esq. *Duke-street, Westminster*

P Wedgwood, John, Esq. F. L. S. *Charles-street, St. James's square*

Wedgwood,

Wedgwood, Josiah, Esq. *Etruria, Staffordshire*

Wedgwood, Thomas, Esq. *ditto*

Wenman, Charles, Esq. *Lambeth Walk*

P††West, Thomas Thompson, Esq. *Crown-court, Cheapside*

††West, Benjamin, Esq. President of the Royal Academy, and F. A. S. *Newman-street*

West, James, Esq. *Queen-Ann-street West*

Westcot, George, Esq. *Chelmsford*

Westmacott, Mr. Richard, *Mount-street, Grosvenor-square*

Weston, John Webbe, Esq. *Sutton-place, near Guildford*

Weymouth, Henry, Esq. *Battersea*

Whipham, Thomas, Esq. *Fleet-street*

White, Thomas, Esq. *Retford, Nottinghamshire*

††White, John, Esq. *Mary-le-bone*

White, John, jun. Esq. *ditto*

White, William Wood, Esq. *Walthamstow*

P White, Rev. Stephen, LL. D.

*††Whitefoord, Caleb, Esq. F. R. and A. S. V. P. *Adelphi*

Whitefoord, J. R. Esq. *Gloucester-place, Portman-square*

Whitfield, George, Esq. *Elm-court, Temple*

P Whitefield, Henry Fotherby, Esq. *Rickmansworth, Herts*

Whitehead, George, Esq. *Basinghall-street*

Whittingham, Mr. Charles, *Dean-street, Fetter-lane*

H h                    Whyte,

Whyte, John, Esq. *Brewer-street*

Whyte, Mr. William Peter, *Union-street, Bishops-gate-street*

Wiinholt, Claus Eduart, Esq. *of Copenhagen*

Wilberforce, William, Esq. M. P. *Palace-yard, Westminster*

Wilder, Lieutenant-Colonel Francis John

Wilkins, Jeffery, Esq. *Brecon*

††Wilkinson, John, Esq. *Brymbo, Denbighshire*

P Wilkinson, William, Esq. *Plasgrona, near Wrexham*

Wilkinson, Charles, Esq. *Soho-square*

Willet, John Willet, Esq. M. P. F. R. and A. S. *Grosvenor-square*

Williams, George Griffies, Esq. *Caermarthen*

Williams, Isaac Lloyd, Esq. *Southampton-street, Bloomsbury*

Williams, Mr. Nicholas

Williams, Mr. John, *Cornhill*

Williams, John Lloyd, Esq. *Somerset-street*

Williams, Joseph, Esq. *South-street, Finsbury-square*

Williamson, General Adam

Willich, Dr. A. F. M. *James-street, Covent-garden*

P††Willis, William, Esq. *Lombard-street*

P Willis, Robert, M. D. *Tenterden-street, Hanover-square*

††Willock, John, Esq. *Golden-square*

Wills, William, Esq. *Oxford-street*

Wilmot, John, Esq. *John-street, Bedford-row*

Wilson, Mr. Edward, *Strand*

Wilson,

Wilson, Thomas, Esq. *Navy Pay Office, Somerset-house*

Wilson, Rev. Mr. *Hall-place, Dartford, Kent*

Wilson, Thomas, Esq. F. L. S. *Gower-street*

Wilson, Matthew, Esq. *Red-lion-square*

Wilson, Joseph, Esq. *Milk-street*

Wilson, Mr. Thomas, *Fullwell Lodge, Twickenham*

Wilson, Mr. John, *Bedford-street, Covent-garden*

Wilson, Mr. Thomas, *St. John's College, Oxford, or Catherine-court, Trinity-square*

Wilson, Mr. Thomas, *Cheapside*

Wilsonne, Mr. William, *Basinghall-street*

Winder, Mr. John, *Shell Farm, Lenham, Kent*

Windus, William P. Esq. *Oxford-street*

Windus, Thomas, Esq. *Bishopsgate-street*

P Winne, Captain Isaac Lascelles

Winslow, Mr. Thomas, *Fullwell Lodge, Twickenham*

Winstanley, Mr. Charles, 38, *Newgate-street*

Winstanley, Henry, Esq. *Cheapside*

Winter, George, Esq. *Charlton, near Bristol*

Winter, James, Esq. *Inner Temple*

Winter, John, Esq. *St. James's street*

Wise, Matthew Blacket, Esq.

††Wisset, Robert, Esq. F. R. and A. S.

Wood, George, Esq. *New Broad-street-buildings*

Wood, John, Esq. *Cardiff*

Wood, William, Esq. *Cork-street*

Wood, John, Esq. *North-Cove, Yorkshire*

Wood, John, Esq. *St. Bartholemew's Hospital*

Woodburn, Mr. William, *St. Martin's lane*

Woodburn,

Woodburn, Mr. John, *St. Martin's lane*

Woodfall, Mr. George, *Paternoster-row*

P Woodhull, Michael, Esq.

Woodthorp, Mr. William, *Fetter-lane*

Worrall, Jonathan, Esq. *Micklam, near Dorking, Surrey, or at* Mr. John Bond's, *St. Mary-axe*

Worthington, Thomas G. Esq. *Jefferies-square, St. Mary-axe*

P Wotton, William Samuel, Esq.

Wrather, Mr. Rowcroft, *Charing-cross*

††Wright, Nathaniel, Esq. *Hatton-street*

P††Wright, Peter, Esq. *Lamb's-conduit-street*

Wright, J. Esq. *Market Drayton, Shropshire*

Wright, Mr. Robert, *Theobald's-road*

Wright, Mr. Joseph, *Surrey-place, Surrey-street, Strand*

Wrighte, Rev. Thomas William, A. M. F. A. S. *Somerset-place*

Wyatt, Samuel, Esq. *Albion Mills*

Wyatt, John, Esq. *Fleet-street*

Wyatt, James, Esq. R. R. *Queen-Ann-street East*

Wyatt, Jeffery, Esq. *Harley-street*

††Wynne, John, Esq. *Fig-tree-court, Temple*

††Wyndham, Thomas, Esq. M. P. *Dunraven, Glamorganshire*

Y.

## Y.

††Young, Sir William, Bart. M. P. F. R. and A. S.

P Young, Arthur, Esq. F. R. S. &c. *Bradfield-hall, Suffolk*

Young, Samuel, Esq. F. R. and A. S. *Gower-street*

Young, Mr. Thomas, *Little Britain*

## Z.

P Zenobio, Right Honourable Count Alvise

# INDEX.

## A.

Page

ACID, sulphuric, premium for the preparation
         of sulphur without nitric salt     39

ACORNS, set with the spade or dibble without
         digging or tillage, cannot be depended
         on to form good timber     94

AGRICULTURE, premiums in     7
               papers in     77

AIR, external, of Britain, too cold for delicate fruits     162
       edulcorates oil     226

ALLEN, Rev. William, certificate from, respecting
         Mr. Cherry's plantations     110

ANDERSON, Dr. the Gold Medal to     371

ANNATTO, premium for     65

APPLES, large, do not always ripen their fruit well     150

## B.

BAR-iron, fine, premium for making     39

BEANS, premiums for the cultivation of     13
      and WHEAT, premium for the cultivation of     13
      and WHEAT, a paper on the culture of     123

H h 4

BEANS, Method of ploughing the land when the
            crop of is in the ground            125
BEECH, James, Esq. the SILVER MEDAL to        191
BEETS, premiums for preserving        .        20
BHAUGULPORE, Cotton, premium for              65
BLIGHTS on Insects, premium for removing the
            ill effects of                     11
BLOCK-TIN, premium for refining               40
BLUE-BELL, common, bulbs from, a paper on the
            preparation of, as a substitute for
            gum arabic                        201
BORER, the insect, premium for destroying      62
BREAD-FRUIT trees, premiums for plantations of  61
            a paper on the plantations of     357
BRICKS, Machine for making, premium for        56
BRITISH Settlements in the East Indies, premiums
            for                                65
BROWNHILL, Mr. James, the Gold Medal to       271
BROWN, Mr. Robert, the Silver Medal to        123
BUCK-WHEAT, premium for the cultivation of     16
BUCKNALL, T. S. Dyot, Esq. thanks to      134, 144
BULL, Mr. Seth, Ten Guineas to                111

## C.

CABBAGES, premium for preserving        .     19
CANDLES, Tallow, premium for manufacturing     34
            premium for making from resin or
            other substances                  74
CARRIAGES, two-wheeled, premium for preventing
            accidents from horses falling with 58
CARROTS, premium for preserving               20

CEMENT,

CEMENT for engrafting trees 178
CHALK, the effect of, on the putrid substances of
　　　oil 221
CHEMISTRY, premiums in 32
　　　　　papers in 201
CHERRY, Mr. the Gold Medal to 104
　　　　Gascoyne, or wild, will grow to twice
　　　　　the size of one engrafted 160
CHETWYND, Lord, plantations of Oaks by 92
CHINTS, patterns for calico-printers, premium for 45
CINNAMON from St. Vincent, observations on the 379
CLOTH, Cotton, premiums for a preparation, of a
　　　　green colour, for printing 37
　　　　do. of a red stain for 80
　　　　from hop-stalks, premium for 50
CLOVE, a description of the 377
　　　　how propagated 374
　　　　the best mode of rearing from seeds 374
　　　　references to the coloured engravings of
　　　　the 377
CLOVES, premiums for 60
　　　　and Cinnamon, communications respec-
　　　　ting, from Dr. Anderson 371
CLULOW, Mr. Thomas, a bounty to, of twenty-five
　　　　guineas 345
COALS, machine for raising, premium for 55
COCHINEAL, true, premiums for 65
COCHRANE, Mr. Spencer, thanks to 196
COCKCHAFER, premium for destroying the grub of 25
COLONIES, British, premiums for the advantage
　　　　of the 60
　　　　and Trade, papers in 357

CONDITIONS,

CONDITIONS, general . . 70
COPPER, premium for refining from the ore 41
plate patterns for calico-printers, pre-
mium for 45
CORN, in wet weather, premium for harvesting 21
Machine for reaping or mowing, premium
for . . . 25
CROPS, rotation of, premium for 17
CURWEN, Christian John, Esq. the Gold Medal to 96

D.

DENBIGH, Lord, plantations of Oaks by 92
DICKINSON, Mr. William, certificate from, respec-
ting Mr. Brown's plantations 127
DOSSIE, Robert. See fish-oil
DRAWINGS, historical, premium for 45
ornamental, for architectural designs,
premiums for 47
DRY-ROT in Timber, premium for preventing 32

E.

EARTHEN-WARE, premium for glazing without lead 40
ELMS, a paper on planting 115
when large, must not be transplanted into
very exposed situations 121
ENGRAVING on wood, or metal blocks, premium
for 47
EXTREME Branch grafting, a paper on 168
process for, how to be conducted 170
FAIRMAN,

FAIRMAN, William, Esq. the Silver Medal to     168
FAMILY-MILL, premium for     55
FEATHERS, premium for clearing from their animal oil     33
FIRS, silver, a paper on the plantation of     101
FISH-OIL, a paper on the edulcoration of     209

    the putrid smell of, is of two kinds     210
    the reason of the presence of the gelatinous fluid in     211
    presence of the bile in, to what owing     212
    must be freed from the mixture of the heterogeneous matter     214
    what substances may be applied to the removing putrescence in     215
    processes for purifying     229, 230, 239, 232
FOREST-TREES, premiums offered for planting     7
FRUITS, valuable, ought to be sufficiently thinned in due time     139
    engrafted, not permanent     145
FRUIT-TREES, engrafted, a paper on the varieties of     144
    the size of not to be regarded in grafting     150

## G.

GIBSON, Charles, Esq. the Silver Medal to     115
GRASS, seeds, premium for raising     16
GRAY, Lawrence, certificate from, respecting Mr. Vernon's plantations     103

           GREATHEAD,

GREATHEAD, Mr. Henry, the Gold Medal to, and Fifty Guineas for his Life-Boat   283

GUERNSEY Cows milk, said to contain more butter and cheese than other cows milk   183

GUN-LOCK, a paper on the improvement of a   243
    description of a   245

GUNPOWDER-MILLS, premium for   54

## H.

HAGLO-CRAB, where discovered   153

HEATING-ROOMS, for the purposes of manufactures, premiums for   57

HEMP, premium for the cultivation of in Scotland   30
    ditto in Canada   62
    importation of Canada, premium for   64

HONORARY Premiums for drawing   43

HOPS, premium for destroying the fly in   26

HUNTER, John, Esq. the Gold Medal to   77

HYACINTHUS NON SCRIPTUS. See Blue-bell common

## I.

INSECTS, premium for preventing the blight of   10

JOHNES, Thomas, Esq. the Gold Medal to   182

IRON, premium for preserving from rust   40

IRRIGATION of Land, premium for raising water for the   29

## K.

# K.

KALI, for Barilla, premium for     61
KERNELS, what sort of to be chosen for sowing     150
KNIGHT, Mr. Richard, the Silver Medal to     247

# L.

LABILLARDIERE, Monsieur, extract from the
            Voyage of     367
LAND, arable, premium for ascertaining the com-
     ponent parts of     22
     lying waste, premium for improving     22
     premium for gaining from the sea     24
LANDAFF, the Bishop of, certificate from, respect-
        ing Mr. Gibson's plantations     116
LANDSCAPES, premium for drawing of     44
LARCH-TREES, a paper on the plantation of     96
LEAD, the effect of, on putrid oils     224
LIFE-BOAT, by Mr. Greathead, a description of the     283
     how to be used     295
     certificate respecting     300
     particulars relative to the construc-
        tion of, and benefits received from     302
     Description of the engravings of the     320
     Management of the, from the boat-
        house to the sea, and *vice versâ*     324
     Instructions for the management of the     326
LIME, the effects of, when commixed with oil     220
     and Chalk, the cheapest ingredients for the
     edulcoration of train-oils     227

LINE Engravings of Landscapes, premium for    46
      of Historical subjects    46
LLOYD, Mr. a paper from, on Mr. Knight's me-
     thod of breaking up logs    254
LOGS of Wood, a paper on the method of breaking up   247
     Description of the method of breaking up    251
LOOM, improved by Mr. Clulow    345

### M.

MAGNESIA ALBA, the effect of, on fetid oils    221
MANUFACTURES, premiums in    50
MANURES, premiums in    23
MAP, Mineralogical, of England and Wales, pre-
       mium for    41
        of Ireland    41
        of Scotland    42
MEADOW-HAY in wet weather, premium for making   21
MECHANICS, premiums in    54
      papers in    243
MILL-STONES, premium for    58
      a paper on    271
      Certificates respecting    275
MINERALS, British, premium for the analysis of    38
MODEL in clay or plaster, premium for    46
MODELS and Machines, catalogue of    400

### N.

NATURAL HISTORY, premium for    42
NITRATE, premium for the preparation of any
      alkaline or earthy    39
         NORTHUM-

NORTHUMBERLAND Life-Boat, account of the   307
        the Duke of, a letter from,
        on Mr. Greathead's Life-
        Boat   315
NUTMEGS, premium for   60


O.


OAK, principal obstruction to the cultivation of   82
      Observations on the growth of the   84
      Timber, a paper on the cultivation and
      growth of   80
OAKS, premiums for raising   8
      A paper on the plantation of   77
      of twice the present magnitude, may be
      obtained in fifty years   83
      Practical directions respecting the manage-
      ment of a plantation of   85
OCHROUS earth of iron, the effect of, on the pu-
      trid parts of oil   225
OFFICERS, List of   403
OIL, Whale or Seal, premium for refining   33
      Fish.   See Fish-Oil
OILS, essential and ethereal, not applicable to the
      edulcoration of fetid oils   225
ORE, machine for raising, premium for   55
ORTON, Mr. letter from, respecting Mr. Great-
      head's Life-Boat   318
OSIERS, a paper on planting   104
OUTLINES, premiums for drawings of   44

## P.

PAINT, premium for a substitute for the basis of    37

PAPER from raw vegetable substances, premium for    51

     transparent, premium for    52

PARSNIPS, premium for the cultivation of    15

     premium for preserving     .    20

PERRIE, Adolphus, certificate from, respecting

         Mr. Gibson's plantations     .    116

PIGMENT, red, premium for preparing    38

PIPPIN, Golden, is native English    153

PLANTING and Draining, a paper on    191

POLITE ARTS, premiums in        ˜    43·

         Conditions for the    67

POOR, labouring, premium for improving the con-

     dition of    28

PORPOISES, premium for taking    52

         Oil from, premium for    52

POTATOES, premium for preserving    20

         Observations on feeding with, instead

     of hay     .    98

PRESENTS received by the Society    492

PROVISIONS, salted, premium for preserving    32

## R.

RED-STREAK, the, a seedling of Herefordshire    153

REWARDS bestowed by the Society    383

ROBLEY, Joseph Esq. the Gold Medal to    357

ROCKS, premium for boring and blasting    57

ROADS, turnpike, premium for clearing from mud

     and dust    59

## S.

SACKS, description of the method of weaving, in
  Mr. Clulow's Loom       353
SCARBOROUGH Life-Boat, account of the    310
SALTS, neutral, have little effect in edulcorating oils 223
SCION of a new Apple, observation respecting   101
SALT-SEA, the effects of, on the putrid fœtor of oils 222
SALTS, Alkaline, the fixed, only to be used for the
  edulcoration of oils       216
SHEEP, premium for the cure of the rot in    26
  Premium for preventing the ill effects of
   flies on        27
  Premium for protecting      27
SILK, machine for carding, premium for    50
SPEECHLEY, Mr. observation of, respecting Vines 141
SPIRIT-PROOF, premium for making     35
SPRING WHEAT, a paper on the cultivation of   196
STAINFORTH, Mr. certificate by, to Mr. Hunter's
  plantations        79
STATUARY Marble, premium for the discovery of   48
STEAM, premium for increasing      35
STIRE Apple, where first raised      153
SUGAR, premium for separating, from treacle   34

## T.

TAN, premium for the preparation of     36
TAR, premium for substitute for      35
THRASHING Machine, premium for     25
TILLAGE, comparative, premium for     12

I i           TIMBER

TIMBER-TREES, premium for securing plantation of    ᵫ
      A paper on sowing, planting, and
         inclosing    182
TIMBERS, a paper on the method of securing
        from danger    258
      Description of the method of securing    260
TIMBRELL, W. H. Esq. the Gold Medal to    331
TRANSIT, instrument for    54
TREES, different, of the same variety, have a won-
      derful tendency to similarity of appear-
      ance    .   152
      planted by Thos. Johnes, Esq. an account of    185
TRINITY-HOUSE, certificate from the, respecting
        Mr. Greathead's Life-Boat    316
TRUSS, Herniary, an account of an improved    331
TURNIPS, premium for the comparative culture of    14
      for preserving    18

## V.

VARIETIES, different, of fruits, how distinguished    158
VEGETABLES, premium for preserving the seeds of    32
VENTILATION, improved, premium for    57
VERNON, Henry, Esq. the Gold Medal to    101
VINE, Hampton Court, communication relative to the    134
   not subject to blight    137
   probably a new variety    141

## U.

ULTRAMARINE, premium for preparing    38